ENGLISH PLACE-NAME SOCIETY. VOLUME XCIII
FOR 2016

GENERAL EDITOR

RICHARD COATES

PRODUCTION EDITOR

PAUL CAVILL

THE PLACE-NAMES OF LEICESTERSHIRE

PART VIII

THE SURVEY OF ENGLISH PLACE-NAMES
UNDERTAKEN WITH THE APPROVAL AND SUPPORT OF
THE ARTS AND HUMANITIES RESEARCH COUNCIL
AND
THE BRITISH ACADEMY

THE PLACE-NAMES OF

LEICESTERSHIRE

BY

BARRIE COX

PART EIGHT

RIVERS, ROADS, FOLK, ANALYSES, OVERVIEW, INDEX

NOTTINGHAM
ENGLISH PLACE-NAME SOCIETY
2019

Published by the English Place-Name Society,
School of English, University of Nottingham,
Nottingham NG7 2RD.

Registered Charity No. 257891

ISBN: 978-1-911640-01-1

Typeset by Paul Cavill
& Printed in Great Britain
by 4Word, Bristol.

CONTENTS

	page
Preface	vii
Corrigenda	ix
Abbreviations and Bibliography	xi
Leicestershire	1
Rivers and major streams	2
Minor streams	10
Early roads and ways	12
Place-names, field-names and river-names with pre-English elements	20
French place-names	20
Early personal names in Leicestershire place-names and field-names	20
Feudal and manorial names	32
Descriptive and other affixes	34
Place-names and field-names containing the names of identified persons or families	35
The names of identified persons in field-names with *headland* and *headley* in Glebe Terriers 1600–1745	50
Church dedications	54
Sacred springs and wells	57
Medieval and early modern parks	58
Inn and tavern names reflective of Leicestershire's social and industrial history and locales	60
Notes on the distribution and usage of elements	69
Phonetic symbols	83
Notes on the phonology of Leicestershire place-names	84
A Sense of Place: an Overview of the Place-Names of Leicestershire	93
Index to Part **8**	143
Combined index of the place-names of Leicestershire	151

PREFACE

My eighth volume of *The Place-Names of Leicestershire* completes the survey of this county's toponymy, publication of which, beginning in 1998, has taken over twenty years to present. From the outset, Dr Paul Cavill has meticulously prepared these volumes for publication. I owe him a huge debt of gratitude. The combined index of Volumes 1 to 7 which has been added to Volume 8 was compiled by Dr Kelly Kilpatrick.

Barrie Cox August 2019

Corrigenda

7 260 The first paragraph should be deleted.

7 330 Add: **lȳt** OE, adj. 'little'. *Lytbroc* (f.n. Staunton Harold).

7 333 Read: **mōt**, **(ge)mōt** OE, 'a moot, an assembly of people'. Swannymote Rock. Muttley Mead (f.n. Blackfordby), Muttons (f.n. Swannington).

Add: **mote** ME, 'a moat, a protective ditch filled with water around a building'. Moat Fm. *The Moate* (f.n. Garendon), Moats (f.n. Belton), *le Mote* (f.n. Woodhouse).

Abbreviations and Bibliography

Abbreviations printed in roman type refer to printed sources and those in italic to manuscript sources.

a.	*ante.*
Abbr	*Placitorum Abbrevatio* (RC), London 1811.
AD	*Catalogue of Ancient Deeds* (PRO), London 1890, in progress.
adj.	adjective.
Æthelweard	*The Chronicle of Æthelweard*, ed. A. Campbell, London 1962.
AN	Anglo-Norman.
Angl	Anglian dialect of Old English.
ASC	*The Anglo-Saxon Chronicle*, ed. B. Thorpe (RS), 1861.
Ass	Assize Rolls in PRO.
Banco	*Placita de Banco* (PRO Lists and Indexes), London 1909 and De Banco Rolls in Farnham.
BCS	*Cartularium Saxonicum*, ed. W. de G. Birch, London 1885–93.
Bede	Bede's Historia Ecclesiastica in *Venerabilis Baedae Opera Historica*, ed. C. Plummer, 1896.
Blore	Thomas Blore, *History and Antiquities of the County of Rutland*, Stamford 1811.
BM	*Index to the Charters and Rolls in the Department of Manuscripts, British Museum*, London 1900–12.
Brase	Brasenose College MSS (HMC).
BrCart	The Breedon Cartulary (Latin MS 222), Rylands Library, Manchester.
Brit	British.
Burton	William Burton, *The Description of Leicestershire*, London 1622.
c.	*circa*.
Camden	William Camden, *Britannia*, London 1590, translated by Philemon Holland, London 1610.
cent(s).	century, centuries.
cf.	compare.
ChancR	Chancellor's Rolls (as footnotes to *Pipe Rolls* (Pipe Roll Society)), in progress.
Charyte	Charyte's *Novum Rentale* of Leicester Abbey, incorporating Geryn's Rental (Bodleian Laud Misc 625), Bodleian Library, Oxford.
ChronPetr	*Chronicon Petroburgense* (Camden Society 47), London 1842.
Cl	*Calendar of Close Rolls* (PRO), in progress.
ClR	*Rotuli Litterarum Clausarum* (RC), London 1833–44.

Conant	Conant MSS, The Record Office for Leicestershire, Leicester and Rutland, Wigston Magna.
ContGerm	Continental Germanic.
Cor	Coroner's Rolls (various publications).
Crox	The Large Cartulary of Croxton Abbey (Add. MS 70), Duke of Rutland's Muniments Room, Belvoir Castle.
CroxR	Croxton Abbey Register (Add. MS 71), Duke of Rutland's Muniments Room, Belvoir Castle.
Ct	Court Rolls, The Record Office for Leicestershire, Leicester and Rutland, Wigston Magna; also in the Middleton MSS, Nottingham University Archives.
Curtis	J. Curtis, *A Topographical History of the County of Leicester*, Ashby de la Zouch, 1831.
Dane	F. M. Stenton, *Documents illustrative of the Social and Economic History of the Danelaw*, British Academy 1920.
dat.sg.	dative singular.
DB	Domesday Book; *Domesday Book, Leicestershire*, ed. P. Morgan, 1979.
Deed	Miscellaneous deeds in The Record Office for Leicestershire, Leicester and Rutland, Wigston Magna.
EETS	Early English Text Society.
el(s).	element(s).
EMBI	*Early Maps of the British Isles*, ed. G. R. Crone, Royal Geographical Society, 1961.
EnclA	Unpublished Enclosure Awards preserved in The Record Office for Leicestershire, Leicester and Rutland, Wigston Magna.
esp.	especially.
Farnham	G. F. Farnham, *Leicestershire Medieval Village Notes*, 6 vols., Leicester 1929–33.
Fees	*The Book of Fees* (PRO), 3 vols., London 1920–31.
fem.	feminine.
Ferrers	Ferrers MSS, The Record Office for Leicestershire, Leicester and Rutland, Wigston Magna.
FF	Leicestershire Feet of Fines (various publications).
Fine	*Calendar of Fine Rolls* (PRO), in progress.
Fisher	Fisher MSS, The Record Office for Leicestershire, Leicester and Rutland, Wigston Magna.
Flor	*Florence of Worcester's Chronicle* in MHB.
f.n.(s)	field-name(s).
For	Forest Proceedings in PRO.
freq.	frequent, frequently.
GarCart	Cartulary of Garendon Abbey (Lansdown 415), British Library, London.
Gret	Gretton MSS, The Record Office for Leicestershire, Leicester and Rutland, Wigston Magna.
Hastings	*The Manuscripts of the late Reginald Rawdon Hastings of the Manor House, Ashby de la Zouch*, vol. 1 (HMC) 1928.

HHunt	*Henrici Huntendonensis Historia Anglorum* (RS), London 1879.
HighwaysB	Keyham Highway Book, The Record Office for Leicestershire, Leicester and Rutland, Wigston Magna.
HMC	Historical Manuscripts Commission.
HP	*Henry of Pytchley's Book of Fees* (NRS vol. 2) 1927.
Hy1, Hy2 etc.	Regnal date, t. Henry I, Henry II etc.
ib, *ib*	*ibidem*.
Ipm	*Calendar of Inquisitions post mortem* (PRO), in progress.
ISLR	F. A. Greenhill, *The Incised Slabs of Leicestershire and Rutland*, Leicester 1958.
JEPNS	*Journal of the English Place-Name Society*.
KB	Cartulary of Kirby Bellars Priory, Rockingham Castle Library, Rockingham, Northants.
KCD	*Codex Diplomaticus Aevi Saxonici*, ed. J. M. Kemble, London 1839–48.
LAS	Publications of the Leicestershire Archaeological Society, later the Leicestershire Archaeological and Historical Society.
Laz	Cartulary of Burton Lazars (Cotton Nero C XII), British Library, London.
LCDeeds	Leicester Corporation Deeds, The Record Office for Leicestershire, Leicester and Rutland, Wigston Magna.
LCh	Leicestershire Charters, The Record Office for Leicestershire, Leicester and Rutland, Wigston Magna.
LeicSurv	*The Leicestershire Survey*, ed. C. F. Slade, 1956.
Leland	*The Itinerary of John Leland*, ed. L.T. Smith, 1906.
LinDoc	*Lincoln Diocese Documents 1450–1544* (EETS, Original Series 149) 1914.
LNPetr	*Liber Niger Monasterii S. Petri de Burgo* in Chron Petr.
Löfenberg	M. T. Löfenberg, *Studies in Middle English Local Surnames*. Lund 1942.
LRS	Publications of the Lincoln Record Society.
LTD	*Liber de terris Dominicalibus* of Leicester Abbey (Cotton Galba E iii), British Library, London.
Map	Various printed maps.
Map	Various unpublished maps in The Record Office for Leicestershire, Leicester and Rutland, Wigston Magna.
Margary	J. D. Margary, *Roman Roads in Britain*, revised edn. 1967.
ME	Middle English.
Merc	Mercian dialect of Old English.
Merton	MSS in the possession of Merton College, Oxford.
MHB	*Monumenta Historica Britannica*, ed. H. Petrie, London 1848.
MiD	Middleton MSS, University of Nottingham Archives, Nottingham.
Misc	*Calendar of Miscellaneous Inquisitions* (PRO), in progress.
ModE	Modern English.
Mon	Geoffrey of Monmouth's *Historia Regum Britanniae*, ed. A. Grinscombe, London 1929.

n.d.	no date.
Nichols	John Nichols, *The History and Antiquities of the County of Leicester*, 4 vols. in 8, 1795–1811.
nom.pl.	nominative plural.
NRS	Publications of the Northamptonshire Record Society.
O	First edition O.S. 1" maps.
OBret	Old Breton.
ODan	Old Danish.
OE	Old English.
OED	*A New English Dictionary*, ed. J. A. H. Murray *et al.*, 1844–1928; reissued with a supplement in 1933 as *The Oxford English Dictionary.*
OFr	Old French.
OIr	Old Irish.
ON	Old Norse.
Ord	Ordericus Vitalis, *Ecclesiasticae Historiae*, Paris 1840–45.
O.S.	The Ordnance Survey.
OScand	Old Scandinavian.
OSwed	Old Swedish.
P	*Pipe Rolls* (PRS), in progress.
p.	*post.*
Pap	*Calendar of Entries in the Papal Registers* (PRO), in progress.
Pat	*Calendar of Patent Rolls.*
Peake	Peake MSS (Nevill Holt), The Record Office for Leicestershire, Leicester and Rutland, Wigston Magna.
pers.n(s).	personal name(s).
PN -ing	E. Ekwall, *English Place-Names in -ing*, 2nd edn., Lund 1962.
p.n(s).	place-name(s).
Pochin	Pochin MSS, The Record Office for Leicestershire, Leicester and Rutland, Wigston Magna.
Polyolbion	M. Drayton, *Polyolbion*, London 1612, ed. J. W. Hebel, Oxford 1961.
poss.	possible, possibly.
ppl.adj.	participial adjective.
PRO	Records preserved in or published by the Public Record Office.
PRS	Publications of the Pipe Roll Society.
PrW	Primitive Welsh.
QuR	*Quorndon Records*, ed. G. F. Farnham, 1912 and 1922.
QW	*Placita de Quo Warrento* (RC), London 1818.
RC	Publications of the Record Commission.
Recov	Recovery Rolls in PRO.
RegAnt	*Registrum Antiquissimum of the Cathedral Church of Lincoln* (LRS 27–9, 51), 1931–58.
Rental	Various unpublished Rentals in local collections.
RGrav	*Rotuli Ricardi Gravesend Episcopi Lincolniensis* (LRS 20), 1925.
RH	*Rotuli Hundredorum* (RC), London 1812–18.

RN	E. Ekwall, *English River-Names*, 1928.
RS	Rolls Series.
RTemple	Rothley Temple Deeds, The Record Office for Leicestershire, Leicester and Rutland, Wigston Magna.
Rut	Duke of Rutland's MSS, Muniments Room, Belvoir Castle.
S	P. H. Sawyer, *Anglo-Saxon Charters*, 1968.
s.a.	*sub anno*.
Saints	*Die Heiligen Englands*, ed. F. Liebermann, Hanover 1889.
Sale	Particulars of sales in local and private collections.
Saxton	Christopher Saxton, *Atlas of England and Wales*, 1576.
sb.	substantive.
SelbyCa	*The Selby Abbey Cartulary* (YAA 10, 13), 1891–3.
Seld	Publications of the Selden Society.
ShR	Shangton Records, The Record Office for Leicestershire, Leicester and Rutland, Wigston Magna.
Speed	John Speed, *The Theatre of the Empire of Great Britain*, 1611.
surn(s).	surname(s).
Surv	Surveys in local and private collections.
TA	Tithe Awards, The Record Office for Leicestershire, Leicester and Rutland, Wigston Magna.
Terrier	Terriers in local and private collections.
v.	*vide*.
Val	*The Valuation of Norwich*, ed. W. E. Lunt, 1926.
Win	Winstanley MSS, The Record Office for Leicestershire, Leicester and Rutland, Wigston Magna.
WoCart	John de Woodford's Cartulary (Claudius A XIII), British Library, London.
Works	*Public Works in Medieval Law* (Seld 40), 1915.
Wright	J. Wright, *The History and Antiquities of the County of Rutland*, London 1684.
Wyg	Wyggeston Hospital MSS, The Record Office for Leicestershire, Leicester and Rutland, Wigston Magna.
YAA	Publications of the Yorkshire Archaeological Association: Record Series.
*	a postulated form.

Leicestershire

LEICESTERSHIRE

Ledecestrescire 1086 DB
Lægreceastrescira 1087 (c.1121) ASC (E)
Legrecestræscira s.a. 1081 (c.1131) Ord, *Legrecestrescira* 1130, 1155 P *et freq* to 1172 ib
Lerecestrescira 1101 × 09 Selby Ca, 1125 × 28 LNPetr
Leþecæstrescire, *Leðecæstrescire* 1124 (c.1124) ASC (E)
Leecestrasira 1126 RegAnt
Legercestescire 1171 P, 1173 ChancR, *Legercestrescire* 1184, 1187 P, *Legercestrescira* 1184 ib
Leircestr'scir' 1197, 1198, 1199, 1204 P, *Leircestr'schir'* 1205, 1206 ib
Laycestreschir' 1230 P, *Laycestrisir'* 1236 Fees
Leycestershire 1360, 1361 Cl *et freq* to 1456, 1457 ib, c.1545 Leland *et freq* to 1610 Speed
Leicetoureshire 1508 *Rut*
Leicestreshire 1529 LinDoc, *Leicestershyre* 1610 Camden

For the place-name Leicester, *v.* **1** 1; with OE **scīr** 'a shire, a county'.

Rivers and Major Streams

ANKER (rises south of Nuneaton in Warwickshire and flows 20 miles to the river Tame at Tamworth in Staffordshire).

Oncer c.1025, a.1085 (12) Saints
Anker 1240 Fine, 1247 *Ass*, 1343 Ipm, 1550 Pat *et freq*
Ancre 1262 *Ass*, 1332 Pat, c. 1540 Leland

A pre-English river-name which Ekwall RN 14–15 suggests is from a Brit ***ankro-** 'winding', from the Indo-European root ***ank**- 'bend', and thus descriptive of the stream's course. However, there is no independent evidence of a root ***ankro**-. Professor Kenneth Jackson points out that such an interpretation is at best 'speculative', *v.* K. Jackson, *Language and History in Early Britain*, 1953. The river is a county boundary marker.

AVON or UPPER AVON (rises near Naseby in Northamptonshire and flows past Stratford on Avon in Warwickshire to the river Severn at Tewksbury in Gloucestershire).

Afen 699 × 709 (11) BCS 123 (S 64)
Afene 780 (11) BCS 235 (S 118), 833 × 911 (11) BCS 537 (S 222)
Avene 1221, 1247 *Ass*
Avone 1428 AD

A PrW ***aβon** 'river' (Brit ***abonā**). The river is a county boundary marker.

CHATER (rises east of Halstead and flows 15 miles past Ketton in Rutland to the river Welland above Stamford in Lincolnshire).

Chatere 1263, 1286 *Ass*
Chater c.1540 Leland *et freq*

An unexplained river-name. Ekwall DEPN proposes a possible pre-English ***cēto-dubron** 'forest stream', from PrW ***cę̄d** 'a wood' and PrW ***dußr** 'water'. It runs through the former Leighfield Forest.

DEVON (rises south of Eaton and flows 18 miles to the river Trent at Newark in Nottinghamshire).

Dyuene e.Hy3, 1252, 1317, 1318, 1325 *Rut*, *Dyven*(*e*) 1252 Misc, 1326, 1351, 1433 Pat
Diuene 1253, Hy3, Edw1 *Rut*, *Diuine* Hy3 *ib*, *Diwin* Hy3 *ib*
Difune 1239 *Rut*, *Diffne* Hy3 *ib*
Deuen(*e*) Hy3, 1310 *Rut*, 1425 *Wyg*, *Deven* 1343 Pat, 1424 *Wyg*, 1474 Pat, *Devyn* 1447 *Rut*, *Deeven* 1495 *ib*, *Devon* 1582 *Ct*, 1641 *Recov et freq*
Dene 1576 Saxton, 1622 Burton, *Deane* 1610 Speed

Probably 'the black river', with reference to the deep ravine in which the Devon flows in its upper reaches; a Brit **Dubonā* from ***dubo**- 'black' (PrW ***duß**). Otherwise from a Brit ***dubno**- 'deep', again referring to the ravine of the upper Devon. An original **Dubnio*- might have undergone i-mutation and have given OE **Dyfene*.

EYE (rises near Saltby and flows to the river Wreake near Melton Mowbray).

Eye 1477 FF, c.1540 Leland, 1550 *Pochin*, *le Eye* 1555 Pat, 1561 (17) Surv
Eie 1477 FF, 1610 Speed, 1634 Fine

'The river', with OE **ēa**. The name Wreake appears to have replaced the name Eye in what were once the river Eye's lower reaches.

EYE BROOK (rises at Tilton and from above Allexton to its confluence with the river Welland at Caldecott in Rutland forms the boundary between Leicestershire and Rutland).

Litelhe 1218 *For*, 1227 ClR, 1227 *For*, *Litele* 1290 *ib*, 1300 Dane, *Litelye* 1276 RH, *Lytele* 1269 *For*, *Lytelee* 1376 *ib*
Litilhe 1218 Pat, *Lytylhe* 1414 *Conant*
Litle Eye c.1540 Leland, *Little Ey* 1610 Speed

'The little river', with OE **lȳtel**, **ēa**. A county boundary marker.

GWASH (rises near Owston and flows 20 miles through Rutland to the river Welland below Stamford, Lincolnshire).

Wasse 1198 FF, 1276 RH, c.1300 Blore, 137 AD
Wase 1266 *For*
Washe c.1540 Leland, *Wash* 1613 Polyolbion
Wæsch(*e*)) c.1540 Leland
Gwash 1607 Camden, *Guash* 1610 Speed, 1684 Wright, 1695 *Map*

The late form *Gwash* is a quasi-Welsh spelling, possibly introduced by the antiquarian Camden. Probably from OE ***wæsse** 'a wet place, a marsh', a term which became transferred to the stream as it flowed through wet terrain, rather than from OE **(ge)wæsce** 'a washing, a flood'. M. Gelling, *Place-Names in the Landscape* 59, suggests that ***wæsse** described land by a meandering river which flooded and drained quickly.

LIPPING (lost) (rises at Skeffington and flows past Stonton Wyville to the river Welland near Welham).

Lipping(*e*) 1218 *For*, 1227 ClR, 1228 *For*, 1276 RH, e.14 *ShR*
Lippingh 1284 *Ass*

The name no longer survives. Ekwall PN-ing 201 points out that the Leicestershire *Lipping* has a counterpart in the old district of Angel in Jutland – Lipping, originally no doubt the name of *Lipping Aa*, a stream. He suggests that Lipping in Jutland is an Anglian name that has lived on from before the Danish immigration there and that likewise the Leicestershire *Lipping* is an old Anglian river-name, perhaps derived from the Germanic root ***leib** 'to pour, to flow, to wet', *v.* Kristian Hald, 'Angles and Vandals', *Classica et Medievalia* **4**, Fasc.1, Copenhagen 1941, 66–7.

MEASE (rises near Ashby de la Zouch and flows to the river Trent at Croxall, Staffordshire).

Meys e.13 Nichols, 1247, 1272, 1330 *Ass*, 1347 Pat, *Meis* c.1235 Nichols
Mays 1330 *Ass*
Meeys 1467 × 84 *LTD*
Mese 1572 Map, 1610 Speed, *Messe* 1613 Polyolbion

The river-name is from OE **mēos** 'moss' which Ekwall RN 281–2 suggests was possibly extended like OE **mos** to mean 'a moss, a bog', hence perhaps 'the mossy, boggy river'. The river must have followed a swampy course. In the area of Measham, the boggy ground is still evident. Spellings with *-ei-*, *-ey-* and *-ay-* are probably due to AN influence.

ROTHLEY BROOK (rises at Stanton under Bardon and flows to the river Soar above Rothley).

Hathebroc m.13 *Fisher*, *Hathebrok(e)* 1276 RH, 1290 Banco, 1296 Hastings, 1344 Cl
Athebroc Hy3 Hastings
Hethebrok 1343 Ipm
Hadbrok(e) 1371 Ipm, 1445 LAS
Rothley Brooke c.1570 *Rental*

'The brook flowing through the heath', with OE **hǣð** and **brōc**. The stream has its source on the heathland which lies to the south and west of Charnwood Forest.

SAFFRON BROOK (rises at Oadby and flows to the river Soar at Aylestone).

Severne 1558 *Wyg*, *Seyverne* 1618 HP, *Sevne* 1622 ib
Syverne 1624 HP
Saffron 1638, 1708, 1745 *Terrier*, *Safforn* 1756 *EnclA*

An unexplained pre-English stream-name *Severne*, to be compared with the major river-name Severn in Gloucestershire. Ekwall RN 358 ff. derives the name from a Brit **Sabrinā*, from a root ***sab-**, ***sabar-**, perhaps meaning 'liquid', with the regular Brit suffix ***-inā**. The normal OE form would have been *Sæfern*, with a regular development to ME *Savern*. Note also the minor stream *Seuene*, Severn (**3** 213, 270) in East Goscote Hundred.

SENCE (1) (rises on Bardon Hill and flows 15 miles to the river Anker at Atherstone in Warwickshire).

Sheynch, *Schenych* 1307 Cl
Sence 1610 Speed, 1613 Polyolbion, 1622 Burton

The name is OE **scenc** 'a drink, a draught', here used in a laudatory way of a stream with a copious flow of good, clean drinking water; cf. the early spellings for Shenton (**6** 295). Shenton stands on Sence Brook, a tributary of the river Sence, which meets that river at Ratcliffe Culey.

SENCE (2) (rises near Billesdon and flows past Great Glen and Glen Parva to the river Soar above Narborough).

Glene 1402 Pap
Sence 1610 Speed, 1613 Polyolbion

The name of the river appears to have been originally *Glene*, which gave its name to the townships of Great Glen and Glen Parva (**4** 79 and **5** 103). This was probably in origin a river-name from Brit **Glaniā*, from ***glano-** (PrW ***glen**) 'clean, beautiful', hence 'the clean, pure one' alluding to a clear stream. The notion of the river as an earlier British name meaning 'the clean one' may be supported by its later name Sence (OE **scenc** 'a drink, a draught'). Was the meaning of this British name understood and adopted by the Anglo-Saxons? If so, at what period the OE version became dominant is uncertain. The *Papal Registers*, source of the 1402 form, suggests a late documentary survival of the earlier name. But with the lack of early forms, it cannot be decided whether the name Sence (2) arose independently or whether it is due to the transference of the name Sence (1) of the Shenton stream *supra*.

SMITE (rises near Old Dalby and flows 15 miles to the river Devon near Shelton in Nottinghamshire).

Smyte 1280 *Ass*, 1316, 1342, 1351 Pat
Smith(e) 1280 *Ass*, c.1540 Leland
Myte c.1540 Leland, *Mite brook* c.1540 ib
Snyte 1576 Saxton, 1613 Polyolbion, *Snite* 1622 Burton

The name is probably an OE **Smīte*, derived from OE *smītan* in its sense 'to strike'. Ekwall RN 373–4 proposes that *smītan* was used in the sense 'to glide, to slip', hence 'the gliding one' and not as Elements *s.v.* ***smīte** suggests, 'a dirty stream'. The Smite is not a muddy river.

SOAR (rises south of Sharnford and flows some 40 miles to the river Trent north of Ratcliffe on Soar in Nottinghamshire).

Sora 1147 (12) Mon, l.Hy2 Dane, l.12 *GarCart*, 1227 FF, 1271 Abbr, c.1292 *LCDeeds et passim* to 1378, 1399 *ib*
Sore 1211 × 25 (14), 1235 × 45 (14) *BrCart*, 1247 *Ass*, 1272 RGrav *et passim* to 1284 *Ass*, 1301 *Fisher et freq* to 1502 *LCDeeds et passim* to 1553 Pat
Soore 1344 *LCDeeds*, 1468 *Fisher*, 1548 Pat, 1550 ISLR, 1555 Pat, *Soor* 1397 Misc
Soure 1422 Fine, 1576 Saxton, 1579 EMBI, *Sowre* 1549 Pat
Soar 1613 *et freq*

An obscure pre-English name which may be identical with the rivers Saar and Serre on the Continent. Ekwall RN 374–5 suggests that the name may belong to the Indo-European root ***ser**-, ***sor**- 'to flow' in Latin *serum* and Sanskrit *saráti* 'flow', giving a PrW **Sār*, whence ME *Sōr* by retraction of OE *ā*.

SWIFT (rises north-east of Lutterworth and flows 12 miles to the river Avon at Rugby in Warwickshire).

Swift 1586 Camden, 1610 Speed, 1613 Polyolbion
the river of Swifte 1606 *Terrier*

An earlier name of the river was probably OE **Hlūtre*, derived from OE **hlūttor** 'clean, pure', hence 'the pure stream, the pure one', found in the early spellings of Lutterworth. Ekwall RN 387 interprets the present name as an OE **Swifte* meaning 'the winding stream'. He points out that the name cannot come from OE **swift** in its sense 'swift, rapid' since the river is slow-moving, dropping only 200 feet in 12 miles. He suggests OE **swift** in its sense 'moving in a sweeping manner', the adjective belonging to the verb *swīfan* 'to wend, to sweep' and that the earlier meaning 'sweeping' may have been preserved in some dialects and have been applied to a stream with a winding course. It should be noted, however, that surviving forms are late and may not represent an early name.

TRENT (rises 7 miles north of Stoke-on-Trent in Staffordshire and joins with the river Ouse to form the river Humber).

Trenta c.730 (8) Bede
Treonta c.1025, *Treante* a.1085 (12) Saints
(*andlang) Trenton* s.a. 679 (1121) ASC (E)

Trente 1086 DB, 1252 Cl, *Trent* 1310 Pat, c.1540 Leland *et freq*

A pre-English river-name of doubtful meaning, but perhaps formed from Brit ***tri**- 'through, across' and ***santōn** 'one who goes, travels', hence 'one who goes across, a trespasser', a name applicable to a river liable to flooding. A county boundary marker.

TWEED (rises south of Barwell and flows between Ambion Hill and Dadlington into Sence Brook, a tributary of the river Sence, at Shenton).

Tweed 1789 Map, 1831 Curtis, *Tweed River* 1927 Map

Unexplained. Lack of early forms makes it impossible to decide whether this is a surviving British or even pre-British river-name, to be compared with Northumberland's river Tweed. A transferred name, however, seems unlikely. No acceptable explanation of the name of the northern Tweed has yet been proposed. It is possible that the Sence Brook from Shenton to its meeting with the river Sence at Ratcliffe Culey was earlier known as the Tweed, a name which survived only in the stream's upper reaches.

WELLAND (rises near Sibbertoft in Northamptonshire and flows 70 miles to the Wash).

Weolud s.a. 921 (c.924) ASC (A)
Vueolod l.10 (e.11) Æthelweard
Welund s.a. 919 (a.1118) Flor
Weland(e) 1218, 1228 *For*, 1230 Cl, 1247 *Ass et passim* to 1610 Speed, *Welond*(*e*) 1227 Cl, 1247 *Ass*, 1275 RH, 1312 *Peake et passim* to 1411 Pat, 1445 Cl, *Welaund*(*e*) 1281 QW, 1286 *Ass*, l.13 *Peake*
Weiland 1199 (1330) Ch, *Weyland* 1200 Ch, 1263 *Ass*, 1365 Pat
Weylaund 1281 QW, 1285 Ipm, 1286 *Ass*, *Weyellaund* 1286 *ib*
Wylond 1351 *Peake*, *Wyland* 1422, 1466 *ib*, c.1540 Leland
Welland 1505, 1553 Pat *et freq*

This British river-name is discussed at length by Ekwall RN 445–6. He proposes that the first element may be Brit ***vesu**- 'good', the second a word for 'river' cognate with OIr *lúaid*- 'to move', OE *flēot* 'stream'. The change from the OE *Wēolud* to ME *Weland* may have been due to Scandinavian influence. Many Scandinavian river-names have a participial ending *-and*, a form unknown to OE examples. Alternatively, the base may be Brit ***u̯elu̯o** (PrW ***welwe**) 'winding, turning', descriptive of the river's extemely sinuous course.

Wreake (rises near Waltham on the Wolds and flows 18 miles to the river Soar near Rothley).

Werc Hy2 Dane, c.1235, 1237 AD
Wreþech 1224–30 Fees, *Wrethec* e.Hy3 Hastings, m.13 (1404), p.1250 (1404) *Laz*, l.13 (1449) *WoCart*, *Wrethek*(*e*) p.1250 (1404) *Laz*, 1276 RH, 1279 RGrav, 1284 *Ass et passim* to 1306 Pat *et freq* to 1370 *Peake et passim* to 1501 Pat, *Wretheck* 1284 *Ass*
Wrethic l.12 (1404) *Laz*, *Wrethyck* m.13 (1404), p.1250 (1404) *ib*, *Wrethyke* 1515 *LCh*
Wrethk 1319 Pat, 1321 Cl, 1323 Pat
Wreic 1243 Fees, *Wreik* 1496 *Ferrers*, *Wreyk*(*e*) 1299 Ipm, 1305 Ch, 1396 *Ferrers*, 1407, 1412 *RTemple et passim* to 1486 *Ferrers*
Wrek(*e*) 1254 Val, 1272 Cur, 1326, 1371 Pat, 1391, 1403 Cl *et passim* to 1433 *LCDeeds*, 1487, 1492 *Fisher et freq* to 1553 Pat *Wreek*(*e*) 1381 Fine, 1419 Cl, 1422 AD, 1601 *Terrier*, *Wreak* 1576 Saxton

The valley of the river Wreake is an area of strong Scandinavian settlement. Ekwall RN 472–3 proposes that the original form of the river-name was OScand **Wreiþk* (> *Wreþk* by shortening of *ei* > *e* before two consonants) from the Scandinavian adjective *vreiðr*, ON *reiðr*, OSwed *vrēþer* in the original sense of 'crooked, twisted'. Wreake is a very winding river. A suffix *-k* is common in Scandinavian river-names and is added directly to the stem. The common form *Wrethek* has svarabhaktic *e*. The early form *Werc* is to be explained by the metathesis of *Wrethk* > *Werthk* > *Werc*. This Scandinavian river-name may have replaced *Eye* in that OE-named river's lower reaches.

Minor Streams

burna

Auburn (**7** 188), *Bucksborn* (**7** 274), *Harbourn* (**7** 139), *Hawetburn* (**7** 39), *Holborne* (**3** 39), Medbourne (**4** 187), *Peseburne* (**5** 211), *Radbourn*, *Redburn* (**7** 110, 106), *Walesburne* (**7** 107).

brōc

Ashbrook (**6** 201), Ashby Brook (**5** 236), *Aylehambroke* (**7** 202), *Back Brook* (**1** 225), Baggrave Brook (**3** 73), Barkby Brook (**3** 21), *Basbrook* (**7** 190), Battling Brook (**6** 123), *Belton brook* (**7** 165), Billesdon Brook (**4** 4), *Bitteswell Brooke* (**5** 145), Black Brook (**4** 270, **7** 194), (*le*) *Blakebrok*(*e*) (**4** 123, **6** 171, **7** 56), Blower's Brook (**6** 197), *Bludbroke* (**4** 98), Boden Brook (**7** 255), *Bottesford browke* (**2** 27), *Bouden Brooke* (**4** 39), Bowbrook (**5** 14), Broomhill Brook (**6** 69), Burton Brook (**2** 63, 66), Burton Brook (**4** 21, 129), Bushby Brook (**4** 282), Campion Brook (**3** 37), *Charley Brook* (**7** 56), *Charnewodbrok* (**7** 56), *Clauson brooke* (**2** 48), Claybrook (**5** 57), Coplow Brook (**4** 5), *counsayle brooke* (**3** 133), *Cussington Brooke* (**3** 64), Dalby Brook (**2** 45, 50), Diseworth Brook (**7** 118), Dry Brook (**7** 57), Evington Brook (**4** 43), Feeding Brook (**5** 139, 300), Fishpool Brook (**3** 207), *flaxbroke* (**5** 88), *Fosbroke* (**1** 16), *Fosse brooke* (**6** 69), Fulbrook (**6** 94), Gaddesby Brook (**3** 103), *Galesbrok* (**7** 137), Gilwiskaw Brook (**7** 8, 264, 268), Grace Dieu Brook (**7** 261), *Hadbroke* (**6** 96), *Hallbrooke* (**3** 255), *Hathebroc* (**7** 6), *hea brooke* (**5** 215), *Hemington Brook* (**7** 108), *Hicklinge brooke* (**2** 48), Hobrook (**4** 51), *Holbroc* (**5** 169), Holbrook (**5** 190), *Holbrook* (**5** 127), Hooborough Brook (**7** 277, 283), *Horse Brook* (**1** 225), *Houghton Brook* (**4** 64, 112), *Hurst Brook* (**7** 200), King's Brook (**3** 131), *Kirkebrok* (**1** 211), Langton Brook (**4** 38, 55), *the Lea Brook* (**7** 240), *Littell brooke* (**5** 23), *littilbroc* (**7** 208), *Lockington Brook* (**7** 115), Lubbesthorpe Brook (**6** 41), *Lundesbroc* (**3** 224), *lusthornebroc* (**4** 35), *Lytbroc* (**7** 208), Medbourne Brook (**4** 88), Melton Brook (**3** 47), Moor Brook (**3** 234), *Neubold broke* (**2** 236), *the new brooke* (**2** 186), *Norbrooke* (**5** 177, 179), North Brook (**2** 242), *Old Broke* (**2** 186), Othorpe Brook (**4** 100), *Otter Brook* (**4** 100), Ox Brook (**3** 232), *pellebroke* (**6** 280), Polebrook (**6** 27), Queniborough Brook (**3** 183), Ramsley Brook (**7** 44), *Reed brook* (**4** 125), *Ricebrooke* (**6** 115), *Rolston brooke*, *Roluiston broc* (**4** 11, 72, **3** 225), Rothley Brook (**7** 186), Rushbrooke (**5** 113), *Saddington brooke* (**4** 92), Sandy Brook (**4** 100), Scalford Brook (**2** 181, 211), *Seavybroke* (**4** 104) Sence Brook (**6** 295), Shellbrook (**7** 17), Sherbrook (**2** 90), Shortcliffe Brook (**7** 141),

Sketchley Brook (**7** 104), *Skonte brooke* (**3** 110), Slate Brook (**6** 99, 223), *Smalebrok* (**6** 173), Smallbrook (**3** 187), *Small Brook* (**5** 197), Soar Brook (**6** 247), *Sough brook* (**3** 263), *Southbrook* (**4** 151), Sowbrook (**3** 76), Sower Brook (**6** 195), Spencer's Brook (**6** 314), Spinney Brook (**2** 183), *Stonton Brooke* (**4** 41), Stud Brook (**7** 49), *Sysonbe brooke* (**2** 193), *thurnborow brooke* (**2** 87), Thurnby Brook (**4** 279), *Walton Brooke* (**3** 207), Washbrook (**4** 22), Wash Brook (**5** 144, 166), *Westbrokys* (**4** 77), *Westfield brook* (**4** 101), West Meadow Brook (**7** 112), *Whebrooke* (**4** 127), *Whetstone brooke* (**5** 82), Willoughby Brook (**3** 280), Willow Brook (**1** 226), Willow Brook (**5** 114), Wisterbrook (**3** 209), *Wyothebroche* (**3** 226), *Wytewickebroc* (**7** 76), *Wythebroc* (**7** 217).

bekkr

Barkistonbec (**2** 205), *the Beck(e)* (**2** 34, 101, 130, **4** 287), *þe Beke* (**5** 108), *berres bek* (**6** 305), *Birtlebeck* (**2** 91), *Cawbecke* (**7** 81), *dalebeck* (**4** 64), *Eashbecks* (**2** 268), *Easte beckes* (**2** 268), *the Fulbeckes* (**2** 131), *Fulebekke* (**7** 172), *Fullbeck* (**3** 174), *grenemerebeck* (**2** 198), *Hengebeck* (**4** 236), *Hobeck* (**3** 13), *Holebec* (**3** 161), *Holebeck* (**3** 90), *Holebeck* (**3** 246), *Holbeck* (**2** 243), *Howbeck* (**3** 82), *Huntsbecke* (**4** 64), *Kirby Becks* (**6** 211), *Litelbek* (**2** 280), *litle beck* (**3** 83), *Litle Becke* (**2** 151), *Litle beckes* (**2** 115), *little beck* (**3** 109), Little Beck (**3** 13), *littlebeck* (**2** 198), *lyttelbeckes* (**2** 107), *mares becke* (**3** 13), *Mealebecke* (**4** 64), Middle Beck (**2** 37), *More Beck* (**2** 258), *Moorebecke* (**2** 210), Moore's Beck (**3** 116), Oback (**5** 142), *Osebec* (**3** 20), *Oxback* (**3** 119, 234), *Rudbeck* (**2** 183), Rundle Beck (**2** 205), Saltbeck (**2** 7), *Shepbekke* (**7** 138), *le Soughbek* (**2** 199), *Sowerbeck* (**2** 199), Stoney Beck (**2** 266), *stylbecke* (**3** 282), *Skyrbeck* (**2** 187), Tylers Beck (**2** 153), *Welbec* (**2** 238), *Westbeck* (**2** 82), *Westbeck* (**2** 217), *Willybek* (**6** 274), Winterbeck (**2** 23).

strēam

le Deuondestrem (**3** 117), *Dewell streame* (**3** 30), *Dewelstreme* (**3** 223), *Holbeck Streame* (**2** 243), *Newton Streame* (**3** 148), *Peyslond streme* (**3** 225), *Redmorestrem* (**3** 225), *Scrybestreme* (**3** 225), *Stockacre Streame* (**4** 249), *Whatley stream* (**5** 162).

Early Roads and Ways

Roman

Leicestershire was well served by surviving Roman roads in the Anglo-Saxon period. They radiated like the spokes of a wheel from Leicester at the hub. In the north, the great Fosse Way (Road I *infra*) from Lincoln to Exeter entered the county west of Old Dalby, ran almost due south to Leicester at the centre of the county and turned south-west to leave it near Claybrooke Magna. Gartree Road (Road II *infra*, in an earlier scholarly style *Via Devana* 'the road to Deva', i.e. Chester) ran south-east from Leicester to cross the county boundary (here the river Welland) south of Drayton. Salt Way (Road III *infra*), so called by Curtis in 1831, entered the county in the north-east, near Croxton Kerrial and ran west-south-west to cross Fosse Way at Six Hills and continued on the same bearing to Barrow upon Soar. After this, its precise route is lost, although it must have passed through Charnwood Forest and run on via the *vicus* at Ravenstone to Stretton en le Field and eventually to *Letocetum* (Wall in Staffordshire) on Watling Street. Road IV (now in part called Fenn Lanes) from *Manduessedum* (Mancetter) on Watling Street north-east to Leicester has not survived completely. Only short stretches of its length are still used. However, it was certainly intact and in use in the Anglo-Saxon period. Road V (unnamed) ran from the *vicus* on Gartree Road at Medbourne to *Durobrivae* (Water Newton) on Ermine Street. It is recorded in Leicestershire in 1547 as *Barnsdale strete* in Great Easton (*v.* Route F *infra*). The south-western boundary of the county is formed by Watling Street (Road VI), the main Roman artery from London to Chester. This road later marked the limit of the Danelaw.

The Roman road system was adopted by the Anglo-Saxons in the organization of local administration. The shire-reeve was based in Leicester. He would ride out along these Roman roads to various Hundred moots which gathered at convenient landmarks beside or no more than a mile from the road within a Hundred territory. For observations on these meeting places and their relationship with the

Roman road system, *v*. A Sense of Place: an Overview of the Place-Names of Leicestershire *infra*.

Road I (Fosse Way: Lincoln to Exeter; Margary 5e and 5f).

Foss 949 BM, 984 (12) KCD 643, n.d. (12) ib 1365, n.d. (12) ib 1359, *strata publica de Fosse* 965 (13) BCS 922, *Fosse* 1016 (12) KCD 723, 13 *MiD,* 1308 Pat, 1357 Works,1372 Cl, 1373 Pat, 1403, 1424 Cl, *Fossa* 1065 (14) KCD 817, c.1135 HHunt; with OE **foss** 'a ditch' and **weg** 'a road, a track'. The Fosse Way was so called because in the Roman fashion, it had a parallel ditch on one or both sides over its entire length.

Road II (Gartee Road, Leicester to Drayton and the south-east; Roman so-called *Via Devana*, Margary 57a).

The popular name Gartree Road is taken from the name of the hundred through which the road ran, *v*. Gartree Hundred (**4** 1). Earlier it is recorded as (*le*) *Stangate* m.13, l.13, 13, e.14 *ShR*, *Stanegate* e.14 *ib*, (*le*) *Stongate* e.13, 13 *ib*, *Stantgate* 1295 *ib*; with OE **stān** 'stone' and ON **gata** 'a road'. The form *Stantgate* is probably with OE **stǣniht** 'stony'. The name survives as Stoneygate in the Borough of Leicester. Gartree Road was used as a saltway in the medieval period, *v*. Route E *infra*.

Road III (Salt Way, Ermine Street near Grantham to Stretton en le Field and beyond; Margary 58a).

It is recorded as *the Street* 1605 *Terrier* in Eaton and Stathern, *the streete* 1601 *ib* in Scalford and Ab Kettleby (with OE **strǣt** 'a road') and in *Strethel* 1210 Nichols (with OE **hyll** 'a hill') in Old Dalby. This route is discussed further as Route A in Saltways *infra*.

Road IV (Fenn Lanes, Mancetter (*Manduessdum*) to Leicester; Margary 57b).

Early references to this road are only recorded in field-names. In Kirby Muxloe were *Strathawe* 1462 Cl, *Stratho*(*w*) 1506 Ipm, *Strathoe* 1403 Banco (with OE **strǣt** and **haga** 'an enclosure'). The road was used as a saltway, *v*. Route G in **Saltways** *infra*.

Road V (Medbourne to Water Newton (*Durobrivae*) on Ermine Street; Margary 571).

Recorded in Leicestershire as *Barnsdale strete* 1547 *Conant* in Great Easton (**4** 74). The road was used as a saltway; *v.* Route E in Saltways *infra*.

Road VI (Watling Street, London to Chester; Margary 1f and 1g in Leicestershire).

Referred to in Lutterworth as *the Streete* 1601 *Terrier*, the OE form was *Wæclingastræt*, the specific being the name of the Anglo-Saxon folk who gave their style to the fortified site at what became St Albans. The name meant originally 'the road of the Wæclingas' and was in all likelihood first applied to that part of the road between London and St Albans. For early forms and discussion, *v. The Place-Names of Hertfordshire* (EPNS 15), 7.

Road VII (Sewstern Lane; Margary 580).

In origin a prehistoric trackway, this road forms the county boundary with Lincolnshire for some ten miles in the north-east and was doubtlessly used as a major route in the Roman period.

It is recorded as *schirestreete* Edw1 *Crox* in Croxton Kerrial (with OE **scīr** 'a shire, a county'), *Lincolne Gate* 1601 *Terrier* in Harston (with ON **gata** 'a road') and in the late field-name *Straight Fold* 1850 *TA* in Muston (with OE **strǣt** and **fald** 'a fold, a small enclosure for animals').

Road VIII (King Street Lane, from the Roman *vicus* at Goadby Marwood to that at Thistleton).

A minor road recorded as *Westestrete* 1331 (c.1430) *KB* in Sewstern (with OE **west**), *the streete* 1578 *Terrier* in Coston and *Streetway* 1744 *Rental* in Waltham on the Wolds.

Anglo-Saxon

Ferdgate (Harby via Melton Mowbray to Gartree Road at Shangton).

le Ferdgate 13 AD, 'the army road, the military road', with OE **ferd** and ON **gata**.

Whether the road continued south beyond Shangton is uncertain, *v.* Route C in Saltways *infra*.

Medieval

Westmanway (Leicester towards Ashby de la Zouch).

> *Westermannesway* c1230 Farnham, *Westormaneweye* 1242 Fine, *Westirmanweye* 1336 *Ct*, *Westermanesweye* c.1350 *ib*, *Westermannesway* 15 *GarCart*, (*le*) *Westermannewey*(*e*) 15 *ib*, *Westermanwaye* 1520 *Terrier*, *Westman*(*e*)*way* 1520 *ib*

Literally 'the road of the western man', i.e. 'the road to the dwellers in the west', with OE **wester**, **mann**, **weg**. It is also recorded as *Westiring Weye* 1336 *Gret*, 'the road that leads in a westerly direction'. The participial adjective *westering* 'that goes to the west' is only cited from 1747 in OED.

Saltways
Salt was of great importance in the medieval period for the preservation of meat through winter. The numerous references to salt traffic in minor place-names is reflective of the importance of its distribution.

Route A. The Roman road (Margary 58a) from Ermine Street near Grantham via Croxton Kerrial and Six Hills to Barrow upon Soar was known as *Saltway* 1831 Curtis. In Croxton Kerrial it was *Saltegate* Hy3 *Crox*, *le Saltegate* Edw1 *CroxR*, *Saltgate* 1601 *Terrier* (with OE, ON **salt** and ON **gata** 'a road').

The road here crosses a stream at *Salteford* Edw1 *CroxR*, *Salterford* 1350 Nichols, *Salter's Ford* 1795 ib (with ME **saltere** 'a salt merchant'). Beside the ford was *Saltefordil* Edw1 *CroxR* (with **hyll** 'a hill'). At Six Hills the road crossed Fosse Way. Here near Wymeswold it was *Saltestrete* 1412 Cor.

The Roman road cannot be traced physically further west than Barrow upon Soar but the next parish westward is that of Quorndon where a saltway appears as *Saltgate* 1608 *Surv* and in neighbouring Woodthorpe *Saltegate* 1393 QuR. If the general line of the former road is continued to the west it arrives at Saltersford Bridge in Oakthorpe, the ford recorded as *Sawterford* 1467 × 84 *LTD*. Stretton (en le Field) 'the farmstead, village beside a Roman road' marks the further direction of this route.

Whether the saltway carried salt in the medieval period from salt-working at Saltby in the far north-east of the county is uncertain.

Route B. The early medieval bridges which crossed the river Trent at Hemington carried an important route from Leicester to Derby and beyond. That it was used as a saltway is indicated by *Salter Common* 1740 *Map* in Hemington, *Salter lane* 1605 *Terrier* in Hathern, *Salter way* 1695 *ib* in Diseworth, *Saltgate* 1605 *Surv* in Quorndon and *Saltegate* 1393 QuR in Woodthorpe. The last two instances mark the crossing of this route with that of the Roman road Margary 58a from Ermine Street to Stretton en le Field.

Route C. A stretch of saltway can be traced southwards from near Harby via Melton Mowbray where it is recorded as *Saltgate* 1445, 1449 Cl, *Saltergate* 1449 ib. Following the high ground south, it entered Burton Lazars where we find it as *Saltgate* m.13 (1404) *Laz*, 1288 (1404) *ib*, *Saltegate* 1300 (1449) *WoCart* and in *Saltgatte bryge* 1300 (1449) *ib*, *Saltgatebrigge* 1309 (1449) *ib* (with OE **brycg** 'a bridge'). It then followed the high ridge at Salter's Hill, here *Salters Gate* 1607 Brase. After this point, the route is uncertain. It probably continued through Twyford, across Streethill (*le Strete* 1396 Pat, *Streat hill* 1584 Ipm) in Lowesby parish and via Keyham where *the Salters Cloase* is recorded in 1778 *HighwaysB* and on to Leicester via *Saltersford Bridge* 1835 O in Humberstone.

It is probable that what became this saltway from Harby south was earlier called *le Ferdgate* 13 AD ('the military road', with OE **ferd** 'an army'), fording the river Wreake at Melton Mowbray, but whereas the salt route branched off to the south-west to enter Leicester, the *Ferdgate* continued south via Skeffington where *Staingate* 1290 Ch (with ON **steinn** 'stone') remembers it. As a saltway, it is recorded in Skeffington as *Salgate* 1601 *Terrier* and in neighbouring Goadby as *Salgate* 1467 × 84 *LTD*. It met Gartree Road at Shangton.

Route D. A saltway ran westward and south from Melton Mowbray where it is recorded as *Saltegate* 1334 *Pochin*, *Saltergate* 1449 Cl, through Asfordby where are found *Sawtrum Stones* 1580 Nichols (with **saltere**, **hamm** 'a meadow', **stān**) to Kirby Bellars where *Saltgate* p.1250 (1404) *Laz* is recorded, on to Hoby where there was a *Salterforde* 1322 Hastings and *Salterswong* 1703 *Terrier* (with ON **vangr** 'an in-field'), to Rearsby at the *Salters Close* 1648 *ib*, to Barkby as *Saltergate* 1464 × 87 *LTD* and *Saltersway* 1635 *Merton* and so to Thurmaston where the route as *Saltergate* 1320 × 40 *LTD* probably merged or was identified with Fosse Way.

Route E. The Roman *Via Devana* ('the road to *Deva'*, Margary 57a), later Gartree Road, was used in the medieval period as a saltway. Parishes lining its route record its saltway style at *Saltere gate* 1606 *Terrier* in Cranoe and *Salters Way* 1918 Sale in Slawston. *Saltersgate* 13 *Peake* in Nevill Holt and *Salteresgate* c.1200 *ib* in Drayton may rather refer to the Roman road Margary 571, a branch of Margary 57a from Medbourne to Water Newton, later also used as a saltway, *v*. Road V *supra*.

Route F. A stretch of saltway can be traced from Lutterworth parish where *Salter's Meare* 1629 Nichols (with **(ge)mǣre** 'a boundary road') is found, north-east into Misterton as *Salters Way* c.1680 *Terrier* and then into Kimcote where it is recorded as *Saltergateweye* e.14 *Wyg*, *Saltergate* 1318 *ib*.

The track followed an ancient ridgeway route here since it proceeded north as *Salt Riggeway* l.13 *ib* in Oadby where it met Gartree Road.

Route G. The Roman Fenn Lanes (Road IV *supra*) was used as a saltway in the medieval period. It is recorded as *Saustreet way* 1638 *Terrier* in Higham on the Hill, in *le Salters goore* 1552 *Ct* (with OE **gāra** 'a point of land') in Dadlington, as *Salter's Lane* 1784 *Surv* in Sutton Cheney and *Salter gayett* 1477 *Deed* in Thurlaston parish on its way to Leicester.

Route H. An ancient ridgeway route called *Salt Street* 1877 Sale entered the county at No Man's Heath near Appleby, crossed *Salt Hill* 1835 O on its way south-west through Wellsborough and onwards to cross the Roman Fenn Lanes (*v*. Road IV *supra*) near Sutton Cheney.

Ridgeways

Used of many routes in various parts of the county (*v*. **hrycg-weg** in vols **1** to **7**). In East Goscote Hundred, *The Ridgeway* in Barkby (**3** 22), *Long ridgway* and *Syston Ridge Way* in Queniborough (**3** 187), *Riggeweygate* in Skeffington (**3** 225); in Gartree Hundred, *Ridgwaye* in Great Glen (**4** 85), *Rigeweye* in Mowsley (**4** 199); in Guthlaxton Hundred, *Abouериggewey* in Bitteswell (**5** 31), *Ridgeway* in Claybrooke Parva (**5** 64), *Ridgway* in Gilmorton (**5** 100), *Ridgeway* in Glen Parva (**5** 106), *Riggeweye* in Kimcote (**5** 121), *Rygwey* in Knighton (**5** 128), *le Rigeweye* in Littlethorpe (**5** 73), *the Ridgeway* in North Kilworth (**5** 161), *Rugeweyus* in Oadby (**5** 170), *Ridgewaye* in Peatling Magna (**5** 177), *Ridgeway Greene* in Sutton in the Elms (**5** 47); in Sparkenhoe

Hundred, *Rugewey* in Appleby (**6** 20), *Rygeweys* in Bagworth (**6** 33), *ridge way* in Barwell (**6** 132), *Rigge waye* in Croft (**6** 70); in West Goscote Hundred, *Ridgeway* in Long Whatton (**7** 116), *Rigeweye* in Osgathorpe (**7** 167).

Portways and Portgates

Denoting a road leading to an important town, usually one with a market (with OE **port** 'a town with market rights, a market town, a market'). *le Portgate* in Burrough on the Hill (**2** 237) probably alludes to the old *Ferdgate* 'military road' to Melton Mowbray; *le Portweye* in Barkby (**3** 27) and *Port way* in Queniborough (**3** 187) refer to routes to Leicester from the north-east; from the east to Leicester are *Portgate* and *le Portwey* in Billesdon (**4** 5) and *le Portwey* in Humberstone (**3** 134); from the south-east into Leicester and alluding to the Roman Gartree Road are *Portgate* in Evington (**4** 49), *Portway* in Burton Overy (**3** 25), *le Portgate* in Stoughton (**4** 263), *Portgate* in Shangton (**4** 237) and *le portgat'*, *Le Porte waye* in Slawston (**4** 240); other major roads to Leicester from the south-east account for *Portwaye* in Great Glen (**4** 80) and *Portgate*, *Porteweye* in Wigston Magna (**5** 221); in the south-east *Portgate* in Gumley (**4** 90), *Portegate* in Great Bowden (**4** 183) and perhaps *Portgarth* (sic) in Husbands Bosworth (**4** 125) allude to roads to Market Harborough; in the south, *le Portwey* in Bitteswell (**5** 31), *Portway* in Claybrook Parva (**4** 63), *Port Way* in South Kilworth (**5** 197), *Portway* in Ullesthorpe (**5** 207) and *Portway* in Westrill and Starmore parish (**5** 21) may well refer to roads to Lutterworth; in the south-west of the county, *port way* in Leire (**5** 132), *le Porteweye* in Frolesworth (**5** 90), *Port Way* in Stoney Stanton (**5** 286) and *porte way* in Croft (**5** 70) no doubt refer to Fosse Way en route to Leicester; in the north-west, *Portweye* in Appleby (**6** 20), *Portway gatt* and *Portweye* in Swannington (**7** 217) and *Porteway* in Whitwick (**7** 76) allude to Ashby de la Zouch; in the north, *Porte Way* in Hemington (**7** 110) is presumably another style for the saltway Route B *supra*.

Colepit Ways, Colepit Gates, Colepit Lanes, Colecart Ways

OE **col-pytt** defined a place in which charcoal was made and such was largely the case through the medieval period. ModEng *coalpit* usually refers to a mineral coal mine. In Leicestershire, in the seventeenth century particularly, many road-names indicated the movement of various types of coals from their sites of manufacture or extraction. That such names maintained a longevity, especially where a *colepit way* was replaced by a *colecart way* or a *colepit high way*, suggests that many routes referred to the transport of pit-coal from The Coalfield in the west of the county, perhaps from early bell-pits and gin-pits, as well as from coal mines in the Bedworth area to the south-west beyond the county boundary in Warwickshire.

In Framland Hundred: *the Colepytgate* in Barlestone (**2** 202), *the Cole pit gate*, *the Coal pit way* in Bottesford (**2** 27), *Coal Pitt Lane* in Melton Mowbray (**2** 171), *the Colepytgate*, *the Coal Cart Road* in Redmile (**2** 197), *the Colepit way*, *Cole cart way* in Saxby (**2** 136), *the collpitt waie* in Scalford (**2** 214), *Coal pitt Lane* in Sysonby (**2** 192). In East Goscote Hundred: *the coale pitt way* in Belgrave (**3** 52), *Colepitte gate* in Hoby (**3** 117), *Coal-cart way* in Ratcliffe on the Wreake (**3** 196), *the Cole Cart way* in Rearsby (**3** 202), *the Coalcart Road* in Saxelby (**3** 109). In Gartree Hundred: *the Colepit way* in East Langton (**4** 40), *Colepitt Lane* in Kibworth Beauchamp (**4** 134), *Coal-Pit-lane* in Wistow (**4** 295). In Guthlaxton Hundred: *Colepitt Road* in Arnesby (**5** 7), *the Coal Pit Way* in Claybrooke Parva (**5** 63), *the Colepit highe waye* in Leire (**5** 134), *the Colepitt way* in Oadby (**5** 168) *Colepitwaye* in Peatling Magna (**5** 177), *colepit way* in Shawell (**5** 185), *Coale pitt way* in Wigston Magna (**5** 220). In Sparkenhoe Hundred: *the Cole Pitt Lane* in Barlestone (**6** 42), *Coal Pit Lane* in Braunstone (**6** 45), *Coalpit Lane* in Enderby (**6** 91), *Colepitt Way* in Kirby Muxloe (**6** 155). In West Goscote Hundred: *Coalcart Way* in Breedon on the Hill (**7** 38), *Coale Cart way* in Hathern (**7** 86), *the Coolepitt way* in Loughborough (**7** 137), *the Colecarte way* in Osgathorpe (**7** 166); *Coleway forth* (with OE **ford**) in Woodhouse (**7** 252) of 1477 (e.16) *Charyte* is the earliest reference to a coal route in the county.

Place-Names, Field-Names and River-Names with Pre-English Elements

Place-names: Breedon, Charley, Charnwood, Glen, Leicester, Leire.
Field-names: Barom Hill (**5** 98), Charnell Wood (**7** 28), Charnock Hill (**7** 47), Chitterman Hills (**7** 237), Creake Hill (**4** 256), *Finchit* (**3** 208), *Gricke* (**4** 134), Gun Hill (**7** 57), High Cademan (**7** 73), Mantles (**7** 214), Mindhill (**7** 44), *Panhill* (**7** 106), Pen Crag (**6** 88), Pen Hill (**6** 88), *Pennyston* (**6** 149), *Trunchit* (**3** 213).
River-names: Anker, Avon, Chater, Devon, *Lugge* (**5** 143), Mantle (**7** 214), Saffron, *Severn* (**3** 270), Soar, Trent, Welland and possibly Tweed.

French Place-Names

Beaumanor, Beaumont, Belgrave, Belvoir, *Grace Dieu* (**7** 25), *Fremantel* (**1** 155), Launde, Mountsorrel, *Normandy* (**1** 189), *St Marie de la Pré* (**1** 90).

French elements surviving in Leicestershire place-names and field-names include: *abbaie*, *bataille*, *beau*, *bel*, *burgeis*, *butt*, *calenge*, *castel(l)*, *copeis*, *de*, *dieu*, *en*, *ermitage*, *feire*, *forest*, *freide*, *frere*, *garite*, *goulet*, *grace*, *grange*, *gravele*, *la*, *launde*, *le*, *loge*, *maner*, *mantel*, *mirable*, *mont*, *park*, *pasture*, *pavement*, *place*, *plain*, *pré*, *sorel*, *torche*, *tour*, *val*, *vedeir*, *wareine*.

Early Personal Names in Leicestershire Place-Names and Field-Names

This list includes personal names used in place-names and field-names (the latter being dated). In some cases it is not certain that the examples contain the personal names cited but they may do so. Nor is it certain, especially in the case of field-names, that the place-name or field-name dates from the time of the personal name form cited; many Old English personal names continued in use and the place-names may therefore also have originated later than the Anglo-Saxon period. Old English names are given in their Anglian form while Scandinavian names are presented in Old Norse forms and where appropriate also in Old Danish forms. Names which are not independently attested are marked with an asterisk.

Old English

_Ab(b)a_ (Ab Kettleby, _Apecrosford_ Edw1, _Apewell_ 1467 × 84, _Ablondesaker_ 1336), *_Ailmar_ (< _Æðelmǣr_) (Elmesthorpe), *_Alflǣd_ fem. (_Alfleteþorn_ 13, _Alfletford_ 1292), _Alnōð_ (< _Ælfnōð_ and _Æðelnōð_) (_Alnotescroft_ 13 (1404), _Alnothesgraue_ 1477 (e.16), _Alistoe_ 1601), _Alwald_ (< _Ælfwald_ or _Æðelwald_) (_Alvestonmed_ 1242, _Alwoldecroft_ e.14), _Alwine_ (< _Ælfwine_ or _Æðelwine_) (_Alwinewong_ 13 (1404), _Alwiniscroft_ 13), _Andrew_ (_Anderchurch_), _Andrēas_ (_Andrislund_ 13), *_An(n)_ (_Anislo_ 1625, _Anniscoate greene_ c.1450, _Ansdoles_ 1606, _Ansloe_ 1638), _Anna_ (_Onneacre_ 13).

*_Ægel_ (Aylestone, _Ayleshou_ 14 (1467 × 84), _Hayleshou_ 14 (1467 × 84)), *_Ægil_ (_Ailiscarr_ e.17), *_Ægla_ (_Aylehambroke_ 1467 × 84, _Aylleham way_ 1467 × 84), *_Ælfa_ (_Alueton_ 1467 × 84), _Ælfhere_ (Illston on the Hill), _Ælfled_ (< _Ælflǣd_ fem. or _Æðelflǣd_ fem.) (_Alfledeweye_ 1477 (e.16)), _Ælfgār_ (_Algarmedewe_ 1336, _Algerystoft_ 1341), _Ælfhere_ (_Elverdale_ 1625), _Ælfnōð_ (_Alfnadgraue_ Hy3), _Ælfrēd_ (_Alueredwrofurlong_ Hy3), _Ælfrīc_ (_Alfricheston_ 13), _Ælfwald_ (_Alwoldecroft_ e.14, _Alwolmilnestede_ 1322, _Utteralwolton_ 1322), _Ælfweard_ (_Alwordissike_ 13, _Aylewartlount_ 1394, _Aylewurdland_ l.14), _Ælla_ (Alton Grange), _Ælle_ (_Aleshowe_ 1304, _alistoe_ 1601), _Æðelgār_ (_Algerystoft_ 1341), _Æðellāc_ (Allexton, _Adlokwell sike_ 1467 × 84), _Æðelmǣr_ (_Aythmesty_ p.1241), _Æðelnōð_ (_Aþelnodes gemære_ 962 (13)), _Æðelrǣd_ (Atterton, _Yolredemere_ Edw1), _Æðelðrȳð_ fem. (Atterton), _Æðelwald_ (_Alvestonmed_ 1242, _Alwelmilnestede_ 1322), _Æðelweard_ (_Alwordissike_ 13, _Aylwardesbroc_ Edw1, _Aylwartlount_ 1394, _Aylwurdland_ l.14), _Ætla_ (_Attelburo_ 1689).

Babba (Bablake, Baggrave, _Babbemor_ 1210, _Bapenhull_ 1423), *_Bacga_ (Bagworth), _Bad(d)a_ (_badfordale_ l.13, _badlowhyll_ 1467 × 84, _Badmore_ 1674), *_Bār_ (Husbands Bosworth, _Boarsgrove_ 1708), *_Bas(s)a_ (_Basbrook_ 1525, _baslandhill_ 1601), _Bēagmund_ (_begmans waye_ 1601), *_Beald_ (_Belteslowe_ 1310), _Bebbe_ (_Bebing_ 1292), _Bēda_ (_Bedehou_ e.14 (1467 × 84)), *_Bella_ (_Bellewellesik_ 1290, _Belloue_ a.1250 (1404)), *_Beorn_ (_Barnesdale_ 1505 (16), _Bermeswell_ 1262, _Berneswong_ 14 (1467 × 84)), _Beorhtstān_ (_Barsunlyge gate_ 1467 × 84), _Beornstān_

(*Barsunlyge gate* 1467 × 84), *Beornwulf* (Barlestone), *Bica* (*Bikethorn* 1385), **Bil*(*l*) (Billa Barrow, Billesdon), **Bil*(*l*)*a* (*Bilton* 1402), **Bisa* (*Bisgate* 1467 × 84), *Bisi* (*Bisgate* 1467 × 84), *Biscop* (*Bissopehul* c.1220), *Blæcmann* (*Blackmans ditch* 1648), **Blunt* (*Blunt Hurst* 1601), *Boia* (*Boycroft* 1663), *Bōsa* (Market Bosworth, *Bosseferthyng* 1395 × 1407, *Bossehowhyll* 1412, *Bosseland* 1407), **Brant* (Branston, Braunstone, *Branteslandis* 1290), *Branting* (Brentingby, Bruntingthorpe), *Brenting* (Brentingby, Bruntingthorpe, *Brentingeswong* l.13, *Brentyngsow* 1467 × 84), **Brōcheard* (Brascote), *Brōcwulf* (*Brokelesdale* p.1250), *Brūn* (*Brouneshull* 1467 × 84, *Brouneswong* 14 (1467 × 84), *Brounshow* l.13, *Brownsell* 1698, *bruniswong* l.13), **Brūncyng* (Bromkinsthorpe), *Brūning* (*Brounyngcroft* c.1180 (1449)), **Brynca* (*Bryngford* 1467 × 84), *Brȳni* (Bringhurst, *Brimston* 1601), *Bucca* (Buckminster), *Bucge* fem. (Great Bowden), *Budda* (Budewell 1789, Budmore 1786), *Bugga* fem. (Great Bowden), **Bula* (*Bulborow* 1620), *Byssa* (*Bussewelle* 1370).

Cada (*Long Caddoe* 1625), **Cagga* (Kegworth), **Canta* (*Kantelowe* 1210),**Catta* (*Catakeres* 1601), *Cǣgin* (Kensham 1779), **Ceagga* (Kegworth), *Cēna* (*Kenewelle schicke* 1262), *Cēolfrið* (*Chelverscroft* 1279), *Cidda* (*Chidmore* 1638), *Clac*(*c*) (*Clakshyll* 1467 × 84), *Cnapa* (*Knapcotes* Edw1 (1467 × 84)), **Cnoss*(*a*) (Knossington), **Cocc* (*Cochesdale* 13 (1404), *Cockislandis* 13), *Cola* (*Coleacker* 1703, *Collecroft* e.14 (1404)), **Cos*(*s*)*a* (Cosby, Cossington, Cosshill Mdw 1890), **Cott* (Cotesbach), *Cran* (*Cranesworth* 1439), *Crōc* (*Crokiswell* 1200 × 50), **Cropp* (Cropston), *Cudda* (*Cuddacre* 1607), *Cus*(*s*)*a* (Cossington, *Cusingedale* 1246), **Cwēna* fem. (*quenepittes* Edw1), *Cwēnild* fem. (*Quenildemilne* p.1250 (1404)), **Cybba* (Kibworth Beauchamp, ~ Harcourt), *Cyfel (North ~, South Kilworth), *Cyne* (*Kinypits* 1627), *Cynemund* (Kimcote, *Kilmundiscroft* Edw1), *Cynestān* (*Kynstoneswell* 1318), *Cynna* (*Kinwell*).

**Dagga* (*Dagnell* 1629), **Dædel*(*a*) (Dadlington), *Dealla* (*Dallewelle* 1199), *Dēor* (Desford), *Dēora* (*Derryngtonehawe* 1235 × 64), *Dēorwald* (*Deroldescroft* 13 (1404)), **Digoð* (Diseworth, Dishley, *Dixshaw* 15), *Dodd* (*Doddesdic* 1322, *Doddisholm* 1318, *Dodescroft* 1205, *Dodsicke* 1601, *dodspole* 1606), *Dodda* (*Doade Toft* l.12, *Dodyngton* 1467 × 85, *Dudgewell* 1625), **Dod*(*e*)*mǣr* (*Dodemeresdale* c.1230), **Dryhtburh* fem. (*Drihtburhlawe* Hy3), *Dudda* (*Dudwell* 1625, *Dutu'* 1200 × 50), *Dūfe* fem. (*douedale* l.13, *Dovedale* 1601, *Doveings* 1674, *Duuecroft* 1245 × 64 (14)), *Dunn*(*a*) (Castle Donington, Donington le Heath, *Dunesby* l.13, *Dunesho* 1205, *Dunncroft* 1221, *Dunnesdole* 1322).

Ēadberht (*Eberesmeeres* 1625), **Ē(a)din* (*Ensor* 1623), **Ēadlāc* (*Adlokwell syke* 1467 × 84), *Ēadmǣr* (Edmondthorpe), *Ēadmund* (*Eadmond Knowell* 1674), *Ēadrǣd* (*Edredeland* 1247), *Ēadrīc* (*Edricheslowebreche* 1328, *Edrichisthwong* 1467 × 84), *Ēadweard* (*Edwardes Lowe* 1606), *Eafa* (Evington), *Ealdstān* (*Alstertune* 1205), *Ealhrǣd* (*Yolredemere* Edw1), *Earna* (*Arnawes* Edw1 (1467 × 84)), *Ebba* (*Hebwell meere* 1612), *Ec(c)ga* (*eggeslades* 1200), *Eli* (*Elsteyn* 1467 × 84), **Ella* (*Elsteyn* 1467 × 84, *Elthornhurst* 1467 × 84).

Fin(n) (*Findale* 1606, *Finsdole* 1708 (18)), **Flecca* (Fleckney), *Folcbeorht* (*Fulbertdunstall* e.13), *Franca* (Frankley Mdw 1843), **Freoðuwulf* (> *Freoðulf*) (Frolesworth), *Fugel* (*Fulesdale* 1228), **Fulla* (*Fullworth* 1627).

Gārmund (*Garmundis croft* 1467 × 84), **Gǣrwald* (Garendon), **Gegn* (Gaynhurst 1846), **Gicel* (*kyglesberou* 1317), *Glappa* (*Glappewellegrif* 1210), *Glōr* (Glooston), *Gōd* (*Godushowhend* 1477 (e.16)), *Gōda* (*godd'pytte* Hy7, *Gothewode* 1467 × 84, *Gudwell* 1467 × 84), *Godel* (*Goldsburgh* 1395 × 1407, *golsworth* 1611), *Godgifu* fem. (*Godiuhauedlond* 13), *Godhild* fem. (*Gohildes*[ ] 13), *Gōdmund* (Gumley), *Gōdwine* (*Godewynwonge* e.14, *Godwinbarns* 1342, *Godwynhedland* 1341, *ubi Godwynesoxe moriebatur* 1343), **Golde* (*Goldsburgh* 1395 × 1407), *Goldgifu* fem. (*Goldiuethorn* 12), **Grīm* (*Grimeslade* 1601, *Grimmeswelle* 1298, *Grymyston* 1467 × 84, *Grymesacre* c.1456), **Grīma* (*Grimeslade* 1601, *Grimleys flatt* 1606), **Gūðhelm* (*Guttulmesholm* 1477 (e.16)), *Gūðlāc* (Guthlaxton Hundred, *Guddelokescroft* 1335 (1449), *Gudlokestoft* 13 (1449)), **Gydda* (*Gidhoubrigge* 1467 × 84), **Gyldi* (*Geldesmor* 1205), **Gylla* (*Gilwel* 1625).

**Hafoc* (*Hauechestoft* 1135 × 54 (1477), *haxelow* 1601), *Halda* (*holdewelle* 1373), **Hamela* (Hamilton), **Hana* (*Hanmulwell* 1467 × 84), **Hægel* (*Hayleshou* 14 (1467 × 84), *Healsey leas* 1625), *Hardulf* (< *Heardwulf*) (*Hardelueshaw* 1285 (1477)), *Hēahstān* (*Heckston* 1624, *Long Hexton* 1714), **Heddi* (*Heddesaker* 1195 × 1213 (14)), *Hefa* (Hevenborough 1842), **Helm* (*Helmesacre* 1467 × 84), *Hemma*, **Hemmi* (Hemington), *Hengest* (*Hengestland* 1410), *Here* (*heresaker* 1200), *Hereca* (*Harkewood* 1637), *Hereweard* (*Erewerde Wongge* 1330, *Herewardescroft* 13, *Herewardeswde* Hy2), *Herewine* (*le middelherwynhoue* e.13, *molendinum Harewyni* 1269), **Hica* (*Hickpoole* 1625), *Hilda* fem. (*Hildindam* 14 (1467 × 84)), *Hildebold* (*hyldbaldwell* c.1270 (1449)), **Hilding* (*Hildindam* 14 (1467 × 84)), **Hinca* (Hinckley), **Hlanca* (*Lankasick* 1705), **Hoccen* (*Hochynstun* 1467 × 84), **Hoda* (*Hodenhulle* e.13), **Hōla* (*holewolde* m.15),

**Holdbeorht* (*Holdberdesacre* e.14), **Hræfn* (*Rauenesty* 1467 × 84, *Rauenesthuett* c.1220, *le Rauenneshers* 1467 × 84, *Raunsdale* 1605, *Ravenaker* 1601, *Ravens Well* 1673, *Rawnseyth* 1467 × 84), **Hrencge* (*Rencheston* l.13), **Hring* (*Ringesdonland* 1336 (c.1430), *Rinksoe* 1638, *Ringsow* 1638), *Hringwulf* (*Ringlethorpe*), **Hroppa* (*Roppederne* 1227), **Hrōða* (Rothley), *Hrōðwulf* (Rolleston), **Hucel* (Hugglescote), *Hūda* (Hothorpe), *Hūdwine* (*Hudwynsty* 1467 × 84), *Hūn* (*Hunistonisholm* Hy3), *Hūna* (Huncote, *Hunwell* 1391), *Hūnbeorht* (Humberstone), **Hund* (*Houndsacre* 1652, *Howndusdall* 1467 × 84, *Hundeacre* e.14, *hundecliff* 1322, *hundewelle forlang* e.14, *Huntsbecke* 1638, *Ounderhounde croft* 1322), **Hūnrīc* (*Hunrikismor* p.1250), *Hunta* (*Huntethornhegge* 1434, *Huntewong* l.13), **Hut* (*Hutshoces* Edw1), *Hwīta* (Whitwick, Whittington Grange), **Hynkere* (*Inckerfield dale* 1577).

Ibba (Ibstock, *the Yvedyke* 1467 × 84), *Ifa* (Ives Head), *Ingeld* (*Inglesborowe* 1621), **Iola* (*yolwell* 1359), **Ippe* (Ipswell 1795), **Isa* (Isley Walton).

Kilvert (< ODan *Ketilfrith*) (Kilwardby).

**Lāca* (*lakynwell* 1475), **Lēoda* (*Leadenwell* 1601), **Lēof* (Leesthorpe), *Lēofa* (*Lenton Pit Croft* 1615), *Lēofgār* (*Leugereswellefurlong* p.1250 (15)), *Lēofing* (*leuinggesti* 1200 × 50 (e.15)), *Lēofrīc* (*Leverichesford* Hy3, *Leverychewell* 1529), *Lilla* (*Lillinge* 1086), *Loc*, **Loca* (Lockington), **Loda* (*Lodecroft* 1378), **Lub*(*b*) (Lubbesthorpe, Lubcloud, *Lubstock* 1688), *Lubba* (Lubenham), **Luca* (*Luq'stoa* 1190 × 1204), *Luda* (Loddington, *Ludecroft* 1467 × 84, *Ludewyk* m.13), *Luhhede* (Loughborough, *Ludewyk* m.13).

Mann (*Mawnsill* 1467 × 84, *molendinum de Man* 13 (1404)), **Mæg* (*Magsley* 1725), *Merewala*, *Merewald* (*St Morrills well* 1601), *Merewine* (*Mirnewelhill* 1467 × 84).

**Nægl* (Nailstone), *Nōðwulf* (Noseley).

Odda (*Odeney field* 1561, **Ordlac* (*Ordlachland* 1194 × 1213 (14)), *Ōsbern* (< ON *Ásbjǫrn*) (*Osbernesbrigge* Hy3, *Osberneswelle* p.1242, *Osbernmor* 1322, *Osbernwong* 1467 × 84), *Ōsgār* (*Osgar Well* 1601), *Ōsgod*, *Ōsgot* (< ODan *Āsgot*) (Osgathorpe, *Osgeberwe* 1477 (e.16), *Osgoteacre* 1324, *Osgotebreche* Edw1 (1467 × 84), *Osȝuthweyte* 1341, *Ossegodishaug* Hy3), *Ōsmund* (*Osemondeshoe* 1324, *Osmoundesdikys* 1467 × 84), *Ōswald* (*Oswoldacr'* l.13, *Oswoldiscroft* a.1290), *Ōsweard* (*Osewardiscroft* p.1250, *Oswardedole* e.13), *Ōswulf* (Owston, *Hosulweclif* 1467 × 84, *Oselueshagh* 1477 (e.16), *Ossulveshawe* c.1230, *Owsley leyes* 1625).

*_Pac(c)a_ (Packington), *_Pening_ (_Pennyston_ 1610), *_Peohtere_ (_Patrestonebrugge_ 1258), *_Peohtla_ (Peatling Magna, ~ Parva, Peckleton), *_Pīla_ (_Pylwelfurlonge_ 1495), *_Pinna_ (Pinwell), *_Pol_ (_Polwelthirne_ 1467 × 84), _Prim_ (Primethorpe), _Puda_ (_Pudwell_ 1720), _Pulta_ (Poultney).

*_Ranc_ (_Rankesberwe_ 1227), *_Ricel_ (Rickleburrow Hill), _Ricola_ (Rickleburrow Hill), *_Roppa_ (_Roppederne_ 1227), _Rūta_ (_Ruttewell_ e.13).

*_Sada_ (Saddington), *_Sædda_ (Saddington), _Sǣgēat_ (Saddington), *_Sǣhǣð_ (Saddington), _Sǣweard_ (_Sewardes wong_ 1550), _Sǣwīg_ (Sewstern, _Sewisthorpe_ 1534), _Sceaf_ (_Seueshouhille_ c.1230), *_Sceaft_ (Skeffington), _Scot_ (_Scotford slade_ 1601), _Secgge_ (_Segehishou_ Hy2), _Selewine_ (_Savincott_ 1695), _Sigebed_ (Sibson), _Sigebeorht_ (Sibson, _Siberdeslond_ 1456), _Sigefrið_ (Syston, _Sitheswong_ 1467 × 84, _Sythestones_ 1625), *_Sigehǣð_ (Syston, _Sitheswong_ 1467 × 84, _Sysom field_ 1670, _Sythestones_ 1625), _Sigehere_ (_Sirestonsty_ 1467 × 84, _Syreshamdikys_ 1320 × 40), _Sigerīc_ (_Sirichiswong_ l.13), _Sigeðryð_ (_Sythestones_ 1625), _Sigeweald_ (_Sywalholm_ 1331 (c.1430)), *_Sigeweard_ (Swadborough Spinney, _seuordebrigg_ 1309 (1449), _Sewardes wong_ 1550, _Siwardysakyr_ l.13, _Siwordlong_ 1467 × 84, _Sywordwong_ 1467 × 84), *_Snaroc_ (Snarestone), _Snell_ (_Snelistoft_ c.1230, _Snelleshou_ e.14 (1467 × 84)), _Snocca_ (Smockington), *_Soppa_ (Sope Well 1811), _Sprow_ (_Sproweslond_ 1467 × 84), *_Spyrling_ (_Spirlinghalfacre_ Hy3), *_Ster(r)_ (_Stereswod_ 1375), *_Stofn_ (Stonesby), *_Storm_ (Starmore), *_Strēon_ (_Strenscrosse_ 1627), _Stric_ (_Strykiswell_ 1550), *_Swan_ (Swannington, _Swanland_ 1750), *_Swǣf_ (Shearsby), *_Sweppi_ (Swepstone).

*_Tacca_ (_Tacwelle_ 1322), *_Tāda_ (_Tadberowe_ 1601, _Tadbogh_ 1380), _Tāta_ (_Tatmarsh_ 1749), *_Tǣcca_ (_Tacwelle_ 1322), *_Tǣsa_ (_Tasholm_ 1312), _Tēoða_ (Theddingworth), _Tila_ (Tilton), *_Tima_ (_timhull_ l.13, _Tymwell_ 1467 × 84), *_Tippa_ (_Typenhale_ 1421), _Tocga_ (_Togdoles_ 1467 × 84, _Toggwooe_ 1601), *_Tone_ (_Toniscote_ 1086 (Cotes de Val)), _Trump_ (_Trumpeshou_ l.13 (1404)), _Tubba_ (_Tubsford grounds_ 1598), *_Tucga_ (_Tugeland_ p.1250 (1404)), _Tutta_ (_Tuttebrugge_ 1212), _Tyrhtel_ (Tur Langton), *_Tyrli_ (Tur Langton).

Þēoda (Theddingworth), _Þēodbert_ (Tabbermear), *_Þorlāf_ (< ON _þorleifr_) (Thurlaston), _Þurstān_ (< ON _Þorsteinn_, ODan _Thorsten_) (_Thurstanestok_ c.1220, _Thurstoneswong_ m.13 (1404), _Thurston Werkhous_ 14 (1467 × 84)).

*_Waca_ (_Wakely furlong_ 1625), _Wada_ (_Wadlowhadland_ 1467 × 84), *_Walh_ (_Walsal leyes_ 1467 × 84), *_Wamba_ (_Wambeley_ 12, _Womburrowe_ 1611), *_Wælrǣd_ (_Walredestok_ m.13), *_Wændel_ (_Wandilberwdike_ 14

(1467 × 84)), **Wærcnōð* (Wartnaby), **Wærna* (Wornhill 1848), **Wēola* (Welham), **Weorð* (Worthington), **Wicg* (Wigston Parva), *Wi(c)ga* (*Wigenhoue* 13, *Wiggo* 1690, *Wiggin Well* 1638, *Wygacer* 1550, *Wygrydyng* 1337), *Wīcing* (Wigston Magna), **Wifel* (Willesley, Wilson, *Wifeles þorpe* 967 (14), *Hamirwyuelisbuskes* 1322, *Wylspole* 1467 × 84, *Wyvelswell* 1394), *Wīgmund* (Wymeswold, Wymondham, *Wymanstead* 1649, *Wymoundesforde* 1467 × 84, *Wymundesdisch* e.13), *Wīgstān* (Wistow), **Wīgðrȳð* fem. (Witherley), *Willa* (*Wilborough* 1723), *Wilheard* (*wileardes hyrste* 962 (13), *Willardesdik* 1332), **Wina* (*Wineworth* 1722), **Winegār* (*Wyngargore* 1467 × 84), *Wulf* (*Wolesberwe* 13, *Wolleswong* 1457 × 84, *Wolsterne* 1586, *Wolueswong* 1343), *Wulfa* (*Wlfewel* l.12, *Wolewell* 1467 × 84, *Wofawell* Edw2), *Wulfgār* (Wolvershill 1846), *Wulfgēat* (*Wolfetewong* 13, *Wulfitewell* 1320 × 40 (1467 × 84)), *Wulfhere* (*Wlferescote* 1208, *Wolesberwe* 13, *Wolscott* 1601, *Wolverakers* 1601, Wolvershill 1846, *Wulverstang* 1444), *Wulflāf* (*Wolesberwe* 13), *Wulfmǣr* (*Wulmereswell* Edw1 (1467 × 84)), *Wulfnōð* (*Wolnethebrigge* Edw1), *Wulfrīc* (*Wlrichegate* l.13, *Wolfrichwell* 13), *Wulfrūn* fem. (*wlruncroft* 1449, *Wulframhilheiland* 1200 × 50), *Wulfsige* (*Wulsipol* 1235), *Wulfstān* (*Wlstaneshil* e.13, *Wolstonwell* l.12), **Wuttoc* (*Ottokes Hawe* l.13), **Wynna* (Winston Bush 1845), **Winebald* (*Womble stone* 1625), *Wynnbald* (*Womble stone* 1625), **Wyrm* (*Wormhill* 1726, *wormwels hades* 1625), **Wyrma* (*Wormedale* 1606).

Scandinavian

Abbi ODan (Ab Kettleby), *Aki* ODan (Othorpe), *Alger* ODan (*Álfgeir* ON) (*Algersic* Edw1, *Algerystoft* 1341), *Ali* ODan (Welby, *Alby* 1612, *Alby poyl* 1364, *Alltoft* 1750), *Andor* ODan (*Arnþórr* ON) (*Andreslund* 13), *Api* ODan (Acresford, *Apedale* 1605, *Apethirne* 1467 × 84, *Apewell* 1467 × 84), *Ásbjǫrn* ON (*v.* *Ōsbern* OE *supra*) (Osbaston), *Ásfrøðr* ON (Asfordby), *Ásgeirr* ON (*Askar hyll* 1550), *Ásketill* ON (*Asketilthirn* 1331 (c.1430)), *Áslákr* ON (*Aslakaker* 14), *Asmund* ODan (*Osmoundesdikys* 1467 × 84), *Ásvaldr* ON (*v.* *Ōswald* OE *supra*) (*Oswoldacr'* l.13, *Oswoldiscroft* a.1290), *Auðgeirr* ON (*Aukersdale* 1601), *Azur* ODan (*Ǫzurr* ON) (*Longe Asserdam* 1694).

Bark ON (Barkby, Barkestone), *Barn* ON (Barsby), *Beli* ON (*Belloue* a.1250 (1404)), **Berg-Skáld* ON (Bescaby), *Berklingr* ON (Beckingthorpe), *Besi* ON (*Bestayft* 1520), *Bild* ODan (*Bíldr* ON) (Bilstone), *Bjǫrn* ON (*Berneswong* 14 (1467 × 84)), **Blað* ON (Blaston), *Blár* ON (Blaby), *Blesi* ON (*Blescop* 14 (1467 × 84),

Blesewelle 1265), *Bō* ODan (*Búi* ON) (Boothorpe), *Bondi* ODan (*Bóndi* ON) (*Bondehirne* 1389 (c.1430)), *Bothild* ODan fem. (*Bóthildr* ON) (*Botilde toft* e. Hy3), *Brandulfr* ON (*Brandolfis acre* 1322), *Brasi* ON (Prestop), *Brattr* ON (Prestop), *Breiðr* ON (*braso* 1467 × 84), *Broddi* ODan (*brodeby forde* 1601), *Brók* ON (Brooksby), *Brothir* ODan (*Bróðir* ON) (*brathorslade* c.1250), *Bruni* ODan (*Brúnn* ON) (*v. Brūn* OE *supra*) (*Brouneshull* 1467 × 84, *Brouneswong* 14 (1467 × 84), *Brounshow* l.13, *bruniswong* l.13), *Butr* ON (Blaby), *Butsi* ON (Blaby).

Drengr ON (*Drinchehul* 13), *Duve* ODan fem. (*Dúfa* ON) (*v. Dūfe* OE *supra*) (*douedale* l.13, *Douesing* 13, *Dovedale* 1601, *Doveings* 1674, *Duuecroft* 1245 × 64 (14)).

Egill ON (Aylestone, *Ailiscarr* e.17, *Ayleshou* 14 (1467 × 84), *Egulacres* Edw1 (1467 × 84), *Haylishou* 14 (1467 × 84)), *Eindriði* ON (Enderby, Enderdale 1820), **Erendi* ON (Arnesby).

Farmann ODan (*Farmanneshill* l.13), *Feggi* ON (*Feggakyr* 1352), *Fin* ODan (*Finnr* ON) (*Findale* 1606, *Fintesdale* 1212), *Fleinn* ON (*Flamston* c.1350), *Fótr* OScand (Foston), *Fræna* ON (Framland Hundred, *Franethorp* m.13), *Fræthi* ODan (Freeby), *Frethi* ODan (Freeby), **Friðgestr* ON (*Frethegestwong* Hy3), *Fugl* ON (*Fulesdale* 1228).

Gad ODan (*Gaddr* ON) (Gaddesby), *Gamal* ODan (*Gamall* ON) (*Gamelisholm* 1322, *Gamulpitte* 1544, *Gamulshadland* 1467 × 84), *Gøti* ODan (*Gauti* ON) (Goadby, Goadby Marwood), *Geilir* ON (Gelscoe Lane), *Germundr* ON (*Germundbrig* c.1230), **Gikel* ON (*kyglesberou* 1317), *Gilli* ON (*Gilhome Lane* 1709, *Gilleford* 1413, *Gillethorp* c.1130, *Gilleuro* 1322), *Grim* ODan (*Grímr* ON) (Grimston, *Grimesacr'* 1320 × 40 (1467 × 84), *Grimesgate* 13, *grimes hill* 1697, *Grimes holm* 1721, *Grimesholme* 1638, *Grimisholm* 1247, *Grimshul* c.1292, *Grimmeswelle* 1298, *Grimyston* 1467 × 84, *Grymesacre* 1456, *Grymeshill* 1477 (e.16), *Grymes holme* 1581, *Grymeswonge* 1605, *Grymiswode* m.13, *Grymyswong* 1507), *Gunild* ODan fem. (*Gunnhildr* ON) (*Gonnildesiche* 1261 × 93 (14), *Gunnildesty* l.13), *Gunni* ON (*Gon Wong* 1550, *Guneheng* l.13), *Gunnir* ON (*Gunirhale furlong* 1695), *Gunwor* ODan fem. (*Gunnvǫr* ON) (*Gunewarehil* 1269).

Hafgrímr ON (*haugrimhole* l.13), *Hagall* ON (*Hayleshou* 14 (1467 × 84)), *Hagleikr* ON (Hagglespit 1882), *Harald* ODan (*Haraldr* ON) (*Haraldespit* 1349), *Heggr* ON (*Heckston* 1624, *Long Hexton* 1714), **Hjarni* ON (*Herneshou* 14), *Hrafn* ON (Ravenstone, *Rauenesthuett* c.1220, *Rauenesty* 1467 × 84, *Rauenhishers* 1467 × 84, *Raunsdale* 1605, *Ravenesholm* 1330, *Ravensaker* 1601, *Ravens Well* 1673, *Rawnsacur* 1467 × 84, *Rawnseyth* 1467 × 84), *Hundi* ON

(*Ounderhounde croft* 1322, *Hundeacre* e.14, *Hundehoge* 1124, *Hundeholm* 1291, *Hundehou* l.13), *Hundr* ON (*Houndsacre* 1652, *Howndusdall* 1467 × 84, *Huntsbecke* 1638), **Húni* ON (Undale 1849), **Hunni* ON (Honey Wells 1850), *Hwelp* ODan (*Hvelpr* ON) (*Welpiswong* 13 (1404)).

Iarund ODan (*Iǫrundr* ON) (Arnesby), *Ingeld* ODan (*Ingjaldr* ON) (*Ingelemer* Hy3, *Ingle Sicke* 1605), *Ingi* ON (*Inge well* 1605, *Inggesickefeld* 1638), *Ingulf* ODan (*Ingulfr* ON) (*Ingle sicke* 1605), *Ingvar* ODan (*Yngvarr* ON) (Old Ingarsby, *Ingerfielde dale* 1577, *inkereshill* 1591), *Iólfr* ON (Illston on the Hill), *Iwar* ODan (*Ívarr* ON) (*Iuorscroft* 1244).

Kalfr ON (*Cawsome* 1606), *Kali* ON (*Cawthorpe felde* 1529), *Kani* (*Canby* 1745), *Kati* ODan (*Káti* ON) (Cadeby, Kates Hill, *Catehowe* 1347), *Kátr* ON (Coston, *Cayteston* m.13 (1404)), *Ketil* ODan (*Ketill* ON) (Ab Kettleby, Eye Kettleby, *Ketelesholme* 1245, *Ketilsschepine* 13 (1404), *Ketylsacur* 1467 × 84), *Keyia* ON (Keythorpe), *Klak* ODan (*Klakkr* ON) (Long Clawson, *Clakshyl* 1467 × 84), *Klippi* ODan (*Clipthorngate* 1290), *Klippr* ON (*Clippesclif* 14 (1467 × 84), *Clippesdal* 14 (1467 × 84), *Clipsthorne* 1477 (e.16), *Clipthorngate* 1290), **Kobbi* ON (*Cobdall'* 1467 × 84), *Kofsi* ON (Cosby), *Kol* ODan (*Kol(l)r* ON) (*Coleshenge* 13 (1404), *Coleston Greaves* c.1690, *Colisakyr* 1467 × 84, *Collesdeyle* e.Hy3), *Kol(l)* ODan, ON (*Coleacker* 1703, *Collecroft* e.14 (1404)), *Kollungr* ON (*Colinggrauehul* l.14), *Kopsi* ON (Cosby), *Krōk* ODan (*Krókr* ON) (Croxton Kerrial, South Croxton, *Crokislundeswong* Hy3, *Crokisthorn* 1467 × 84, *Crookesome* 1674), **Kroppr* ON (Cropston).

**Lauss* ON (Lowesby).

Manni ODan (*molendinum de Man* 13 (1404)).

Nafni ON (Naneby), *Nagli* ON (*Nevlebi* 1086), *Natfari* ODan (*Náttfari* ON) (*Nafferton* 1619).

Oddr ON (*Odstone* 12, *Oddestorp* 12), *Øthi* ODan (*Auði* ON) (Oadby).

Rafnhildr ON fem. (*Rauenyldecroft* 1317), *Ragnhildr* ON fem. (*Rayneswombe* 1601), *Rathi* ODan (*Hraði* ON) (*radiebidale* Edw1), *Rethar* ODan (*Hreiðarr* ON) (Rearsby, Rotherby), *Rolf* ODan (*Hrólfr* ON) (Rolleston, *Rollesdikes* 1381 (1467 × 84)).

Salt ON (Saltby), *Salti* ON (Saltby), *Sauðr* ON (*Sowsmer' syk* Hy7), *Saxi* ODan, ON (Saxby), *Saxulf* ODan (*Saxulfr* ON) (Saxelby), *Segrim* ODan (*Sǽgrímr* ON) (*Sigrimeswro* c.1200), *Sigsteinn* ON (Sysonby), *Sigulfr* ON (Sileby), *Sigvaldr* ON (Shoby, *Sywalholm* 1331 (c.1430)), *Sigwarth* ODan (*Sigvarðr* ON) (*seuordebrigg* 1309 (1449),

Sewardeswong 1550, *Siwardysakyr* l.13, *Siwordlong* 1467 × 84, *Sywordslade* c.1230, *Sywordwong* 1467 × 84), *Skarth* ODan (*Skarði* ON) (*Scarddesland* l.13), *Skeggr* ON (*Scechesholm* l.13, *Skegesmore* 1646), *Skeifr* ON (Shearsby), **Skjaldari* ON (*scalderdeyles* l.13 (1404)), **Skrápi* ON (Scraptoft, *Scrapholm* 1322), *Skrauti* ON (*Scroutesdeil* Edw3 (c.1430)), *Slagr* ON (Slawston), *Snípr* ON (Snibstone, *Snypwong* 1457 × 84), *Snjallr* ON (*Snelleshou* e.14 (1467 × 84)), *Sǫlsi* ON (*Sawsdall* 1601), *Spakr* ON (*Spakysdale* 1467 × 84), *Sprok* ON (Sproxton), *Stafn* ON (*Stoueneshil* e.14), *Steik* ON (*Stechesholm* l.13), *Sten* ODan (*Steinn* ON) (Stemborough Mill, Stainsby 1863, *stinesdale* m.13 (1404)), **Stofn* ON (Stonesby, *Stoueneshil* e.14), *Strákr* ON (*Stragdale* 1625), *Stríkr* ON (*Strykiswell* 1550), *Stúfr* ON (*Stouesdale* 1357 (c.1430)), *Styrkar* ODan (*Styrkárr* ON) (*Stirkerthorn* Hy3), *Styr* ODan (*Styrr* ON) (*Stereswod* 1375), *Sumarliði* ON (Somerby), **Svanhildr* ON fem. (*Swanildepol* Hy3), **Svartketill* ON (*Swartketilwong* 1253), *Sven* ODan (*Sveinn* ON) (*Sueynnisike* Edw1, *Swanland* 1750, *sweynwongsike* l.13), *Swart* ODan (*Svartr* ON) (*Swarsell* 1601).

Therir ODan (*Theyswong* 1467 × 84), *Thorger* ODan (*Þorgeirr* ON) (*Tocharsike* 13), *Thorir* ODan (*Þórir* ON) (*Thorsedale* 1611, *Thuersweye* m.13), *Þorketill* ON (Thurcaston), *Thormoth* ODan (*Þormóðr* ON) (Thurmaston, *Thurmodesthorpe* n.d.), *Thorir* ODan (*Þórir* ON) (*Thorscroppis* 1290), *Thorsten* ODan (*Þorsteinn* ON) (Thrussington), *Þorvarðr* ON (*Thuruerdesdole* p.11250 (1404)), **Þræingr* ON (Thringstone), *Þyrnir* ON (Thurnby), **Tōk* ODan (Toston Hill, *Thokeslandys* l.13), *Toki* ODan (*Tóki* ON) (Tugby, *Thokeslandys* l.13, *Tocharsike* 13).

Ulf ODan (*Ulfr* ON) (Ullesthorpe, Ulverscroft, *ulueswong* Hy3, *Wlfhull* 1357, *Wlfinges* 1322), *Ulfgeirr* ON (*Wilgercroft* e.14 (1467 × 84)), *Ulfketill* ON (*Ulketeleswod* 1244).

Vestmaðr ON (*Westmanmedwe* c.1275), *Vífill* ON (*Hamirwyuelisbuskes* 1322, *Wylspole* 1467 × 84, *Wyvelswell* 1394), *Vili* ON (*Wilborough* c.1723), *Víss* ON (*Wistoft* 13).

Wraghi ODan (*Weragland* m.13 (1404), Wragdale Cl 1844).

Anglo-Scandinavian

Cytel (*Chitilishill* e.14), *Halfdene* (*Haldeynisbroch* Hy3), *Ingold* (*hingoldysmer*1427, *yngoldiscroft* l.13 (1449)), *Riulf* (*Riolfhauedes* 1322), *Stark* (*Starkesmore* 1577, *Starkeswong* 1467 × 84), *Thōr*

(*Thorscroppis* 1290, *Thorsedale* 1611, *Thorslos* 1322, *Thorwong* 1424), *Thūr* (*Thurstokys* 1467 × 84), *Tōka* (*Tocharsike* 13).

Middle English and Continental

Abbe fem. (a pet form of OFr *Albrei* or *Aubree*) (Ab Kettleby), *Abel* (*Ablishmare* 1601), *Abraham* (*Abrahamwelle* Hy3), *Achard* AN (*Heuedland Achardi* 1331 (c.1430)), *Adenet* OFr (*Adeynetlond* 1407), *Agatha* OFr fem. (*crucem Agathe* Edw2), *Ailmer* (*Ailmeresbrigge* 13 (1404)), *Alain* OFr (*Allenwell* 1697), *Almus* fem. (*Almescroft* 1400), *Alred* (*Alredwro* 1337), *Anchier* OFr (*Anchire rode* 1477 (e.16)), *Anés* OFr fem. (*Anniscoate greene* c.1450), *Annot* fem. (*Annotesbuttes* 1320 × 40 (1467 × 84)), *Arkel* (*arkelgraue* 1295), *Arnold* ContGerm (*arnoldis ake* 1449, *Arnoldiswong* 1467 × 84), *Aunger* AN (*aungerleyes* a.1280 (1449)).

Bagot ContGerm (*Bagodeswong* 1467 × 84), *Baldwin* ContGerm (Bawdon Castle), *Bardolph* (*Bardolflane* 1332), *Bartil* (*Bartalcroft* 1418), *Basil* (*Basiltoftes* 1413), *Bernard* AN (*Barnard Pittes* 1300 (1449), *Bernardes Crosse* 1319, *Bernardhul* 13), *Bochard* OFr (Botcheston), *Bruno* (Bransford Bridge).

Cunmin OBret (*Cummaneswodesyke* 1247).

Dicun (*Dykonggreve* 1434), *Dobbe* (*Dobscroft* 1467 × 84), *Durand* ContGerm (Donisthorpe), *Duva* fem. (Dow Bridge).

Emelot fem. (*Emeloteslane* 1313), *Ernald* ContGerm (*Hernoldismor* p.1250), *Ernaut* OFr (*Ernotelandes* 1320 × 40 (1467 × 84)), *Emm* fem. (*Emmeslande* 1442).

Flambard OFr (*Flambuswong* 1467 × 84), *Flori*(*a*) fem. (*Floritoft* 1351), *Folcard* AN (*Folker Dale* 1550), *Fulbert* ContGerm (*Fulbertdunstall* e.13), *Fulco* OFr (*Fulkilfurlong* a.1250 (1404)).

Gawain (*Gahwenescroft* 13, *Gowyneyerdeland* 1477 (e.16), *Gueyne Well* 1374), *Gerard* ContGerm (*Gerardeswode* 1383, *Gerardisvro* 1260), *Germund* ContGerm (*Germundebrig* c.1230).

Hasteng (*Hastenglayes* 1335), *Heliot* OFr (*Helotecros* Hy2), *Herbert* OFr (*ad crucem Herberti* 13), *Herti* (*Herston* 1316), *Hobb* (*Hobbesyke* 1346, *Hobstacke foarde* 1601), *Hub* (a pet form of ContGerm *Hubald* or *Hubert*) (*Hubescot* 1220), *Hubert* ContGerm (*Huberetorp* c.1200), *Hue* OFr (*Huhehus* e.13).

Ingelberd ContGerm (*Inggulberdhille* 1392, *Ingleberdelye* 1391).

Johan OFr (*John* ME) (*Jonismere* Edw1), *Joseph* (*Lapidem Josep'* 1467 × 84).

Luke (*Luq'stoa* 1190 × 1204).

Mainard OFr (*Maynardesholm* c.1300), *Margaret* fem. (*ad crucem Margarete* 1467 × 84), *Martin* (*Martinhaw* a.1183 (14)), *Molot* fem. (*Molote Welle* 13 (1404)).

Nicol (*Nicholeswell* 1305), *Noe* (Knowlands 1782), *Noel* (Knowlands 1782).

Ogbert ContGerm (*Ogberdeswell* 1200 × 16), *Ogier* (*Ogerstone* 1410), *Oliver* (*Oliuercroft* 1284 (e.15)).

Paien OFr (*Paynisich* 1477 (e.16)), *Perre* OFr (*Peres Crosse* 1609), *Perkin* (*Perkynyerd* 1313), *Pippin* ContGerm (*pippineswell* 1625), *Popel* (*Poplestoft* l.12).

Randel (*Randles well* 1612), *Randulf* AN (*Randolfland* 1427, *Randulfwde* l.13), *Reiner* OFr (*Reynerwell* 14 (1467 × 84)), *Ricolf* ContGerm (*Ringlethorpe*, now Goldsmith Grange), *Robbe* (pet form of *Robert*) (*Robbe Wong* a.1183 (14)), *Robin* (*Robynholme* 1615, *Robynrig* 1601), *Robinet* (*Robynetisknolle* 1467 × 84), *Roger* OFr (*apud fontem Rogeri* 1467 × 84).

Samson (*Sampson Croft* 1320 × 40 (1467 × 84)), *Serlo* ContGerm (Shelthorpe), *Sott* (*Sottesbrugge* 1276, *Sottesmulne* 1247), *Spileman* (*Spilemaneswang* m.13 (1404), *Spilmandail* 1320).

Theobald OFr (*Thebeltoft* l.13), *Thomas* (*Thomysfurlong* 1467 × 84), *Tibald* OFr (*Tybbledecot* c.1290), *Tibaut* OFr (*Tybetoft* l.13).

Walchelin AN (*wacelinesholm* Hy3, *Warclingesslade* 1477 (e.16)), *Walter* ContGerm (*Walteresheye* 1285 × 93, *Walters hill* 1601, *Walterswerc* m.14), *Warin* ContGerm (*Warinhou* 1294, *Warinisholm* Hy3, *Warinwell* 1395), *William* OFr (*Williamwro* 1320 × 40 (1467 × 84)), *Wischard* OFr (*Wisheerdesty* 1344).

Feudal and Manorial Names

Suffixed family names of feudal and manorial holders are current in the following:
Ashby de la Zouch, Ashby Folville, Aston Flamville, Broughton Astley, Burton Overy, Carlton Curlieu, Cotes de Val, Croxton Kerrial, Dunton Basset, Goadby Marwood, Kibworth Beauchamp, Kibworth Harcourt, Kirby Bellars, Kirby Muxloe, Kirkby Mallory, Melton Mowbray, Newbold Verdon, Newton Burgoland, Newton Harcourt, Normanton Turville, Ratcliffe Culey, Staunton Harold, Stoke Golding, Stonton Wyville, Sutton Cheyney, Thorpe Arnold, Thorpe Satchville.

Manorial holders' names are prefixed in the following:
Catthorpe, Edmondthorpe, Nevill Holt, Shelthorpe.

Instances of the names of feudal and manorial holders which are found in early documents but which have not survived include:
Aston *Perer* (~ Flamville), Branston *Wandeville*, Burton *Burdet*, ~ *Lisley*, ~ *Pantouf* (~ Lazars), Cotes *Poutrell,* Croxton *Roos*, ~ *Sarazin* (~ Kerrial), Dalby *Chaucumbe* (Great ~), Dalby *Paynel*, ~ *Perer*, ~ *Tateshale* (Little ~), Eastwell *Arraby*, ~*Edenishouere*, Glen *Martel* (Great ~), Goadby *Quatremars* (~ Marwood), Higham *Basville* (~ on the Hill), Kettleby *Beler* (Eye ~), Kilworth *Rabaz* (North ~), ~ *Roger* (South ~), Kirby *Ayville*, ~ *de Sancto Amando*, ~ *Fouker*, ~ *Wasteneys* (~ Bellers), Marefield *Luterel* (Old ~), Newbold *Foleville*, ~ *la Saucey* (Newbold), Newton *Botiler* (~ Burgoland), Newton *Burdet*, ~ *Marmion* (Cold ~), Norton *Ricard* (East ~), Orton (~ *Quartremars*, ~ *le Saucey* (Coleorton), Ratcliffe *Burdet* (~ on the Wreake), Rearsby *Chaumberlain*, Saddington *Moeles*, Somerby *Quartremars*, ~ *Tateshale*, Sproxton *Boby*, ~ *Paynel*, Stanton *Ysabelle* (~ under Bardon), Stonton *Brudnell* (~ Wyville), Swannington *Arraby*, Sysonby *Perer*, Thorpe *Chauars*, ~ *Tybetoft* (Edmondthorpe), Thorpe *Montfort* (Woodthorpe), Tilton *Digby* (~ on the Hill), Walton *Malory* (~ on the Wolds).

From royalty, nobility and religious bodies:
king: King's Norton, King's Lane (**1** 46), King's Mills (**7** 48), King St (**2** 169), *le Kyngescroft* (**5** 167), *Kyngland* (**7** 53).
earl: Earl Shilton.
countess: Countesthorpe, Countess's Bridge, *Countasbrigge* (**6** 102), *Contescrosse* (**7** 75), *Countasfurlong* (**4** 262).

abbot: *þe abbotes byris* (**6** 279), Abbot's Close (**1** 182), *Abbot's Closse* (**3** 29), *le Abbotes feld* (**1** 214), *Abbotesherber* (**7** 231), *Abbottes Parke* (**1** 223), *Abbotispool* (**3** 51), Abbot's Spinney (**3** 29), *lez Abbotts Tippett* (**1** 194), *Abboteswode* (**7** 231), *Abbot's Wood* (**6** 102) (all alluding to the abbot of the Abbey of St Mary de Pratis, Leicester), *the abbottes hey* (**6** 18) (the abbot of the Abbey of St Modwen, Burton upon Trent, Staffordshire), *Abbotesmede* (**3** 15) (the abbot of the Abbey of St Mary, Garendon), *Holt Abbotes* (**4** 202) (the abbot of the Abbey of St Peter, Peterborough).
bishop: Bishop's Fee (**1** 12), Bishop's Water (**1** 225) (alluding to the bishop of Lincoln).
monk: *atte Monekes* (**3** 91) (Kirby Bellars Priory), *Monkesbroke*, *Monkesdam* (**3** 40), *monkyslong* (**6** 280) (Abbey of St Mary de Pratis, Leicester), *the Monkes Syche* (**7** 40) (Breedon Priory), *les Monkesleiges* (**7** 253) (Priory of St Mary, Ulverscroft), *Monkeswell* (**7** 216), *Monkkewode* (**3** 20), *Mounkeswod* (**7** 138) (Abbey of St Mary, Garendon), *the Monkes wonges* (**2** 115) (Abbey of St John, Croxton Kerrial).
nun: *Nuncraft*, *Nun Sicke* (**7** 122), *Nunnesti* (**7** 95), Nun Sick Cls (**7** 52) (Benedictine Priory of Langley), Nun's Cl, Nun's Lane (**2** 275), *Nunriges* (**2** 215) (Benedictine Nunnery of Nuneaton, Warwickshire).
prior: The Prior's Cl, *Priourscroft* (**2** 183) (either of Kirby Bellars Priory or Chalcombe Priory, Northamptonshire), *Le Pryours Close* (**3** 162) (of Launde Priory), Prior Fd (**7** 39) (of Breedon Priory), Prior Fd (**7** 251) (of St Mary's Priory, Ulverscroft), *le Priouresgores* (**2** 198) (of St Mary's Priory, Belvoir), *Priourslesu* (**6** 126) (of Hinckley Priory), *Pryor leyes*, *Prior Wonge* (**2** 74) (of Chalcombe Priory), *Priors slade* (**3** 225) (of the Abbey of St John, Croxton Kerrial), *the pryer wood* (**4** 150) (either of the Priory of St John the Baptist, Launde or of the Abbey of St Andrew the Apostle, Owston), *le Priorwode* (**6** 153) (of the Abbey of St Mary de Pratis, Leicester).

Holdings of the Knights Templars in Leicestershire included:
Rothley Temple (Rothley, **7** 185), The Temple (Wellsborough, **6** 265), *Minstreton Temple* (Misterton, **5** 154), *Temple clos*, *Templelands* (**3** 152), *le Templegore* (**2** 187), *Templeland* (**3** 97), *Templewong* (**2** 32).

The Knights Hospitallers of St John of Jerusalem held a Commandery at Old Dalby remembered in the style *Dalby Hospital*(*i*) 1254 Val, 1314 *GarCart* and earlier in (*Magister*) *Hospitalis Jerlm' de Daubi* 1206 P.

Descriptive and other Affixes

Albert Village, Appleby Magna, Appleby Parva, Ashby Magna, Ashby Parva, Ashby Woulds, Barton in the Beans, Breedon on the Hill, Husbands Bosworth, Market Bosworth, Great Bowden, Little Bowden, Nether Broughton, Burrough on the Hill, Burton Lazars, Burton on the Wolds, Long Clawson, Claybrooke Magna, Claybrooke Parva, South Croxton, Great Dalby, Little Dalby, Old Dalby, Castle Donington, Donington le Heath, Fenny Drayton, Great Easton, Frisby on the Wreake, Great Glen, Glen Parva, Market Harborough, Higham on the Hill, Houghton on the Hill, Illston on the Hill, Old Ingarsby, Ab Kettleby, Eye Kettleby, North Kilworth, South Kilworth, Church Langton, East Langton, West Langton, Old Marefield, Potters Marston, Cold Newton, Newtown Unthank, Normanton le Heath, East Norton, Orton on the Hill, Cold Overton, Peatling Magna, Peatling Parva, Ratcliffe on the Wreake, Sheepy Magna, Sheepy Parva, Stoney Stanton, Stretton en le Field, Great Stretton, Little Stretton, Sutton in the Elms, Thorpe Acre, Tilton on the Hill, Waltham on the Wolds, Walton on the Wolds, Long Whatton, Wigston Magna, Wigston Parva, Willoughby Waterless.

Nexus of two place-names occurs in Isley Walton, Newtown Linford, Norton juxta Twycross, Smeeton Westerby, Stanton under Bardon, Thorpe Langton.

Place-Names and Field-Names containing the Names of Identified Persons or Families

Not included here are: (1) the names of unindexed Leicester Borough houses, their owners, tenants and families of the years 1290–c.1850 listed in **1** 156–71; the names of unindexed unspecified Leicester Borough lands, their owners or tenants of the years 1200–1799 listed in **1** 206–9; (3) the names of unindexed Leicester Borough town yards, their owners or tenants of the year 1846 listed in **1** 172–5.

Abbots Cl (**5** 105), *Abbots close* (**5** 226), *Abrahams Pen* (**5** 167), Adcocks Garden (**2** 227), Adcocks Pen (**6** 223), Adderley's Mdw (**6** 111), Addison's (**5** 209), *William Adlingtons piece* (**3** 116), Thomas Aldridges Cottage Cl (**6** 12), *Agar's Lane* (**3** 135), *Airs Close* (**1** 182), *George Alcockes Wong* (**2** 276), Allens Cl (**6** 52), *Thomas Allens close* (**5** 214), *Alsops Lane* (**4** 44), *Allsop's Lane* (**3** 135), Allsopp's Lane (**7** 126), Almey's Lane (**6** 133), Almeys Mdw (**5** 131), *Alynforth* (**7** 202), *Wm. Andrews Eleven Acres* (**2** 299), *Andrews Far Close* (**1** 219), *Archers Close* (**1** 182), Archers First Cl (**6** 202), *Argills Farm* (**7** 15), *molendinum Jossine Argylle* (**6** 220), Arkwright Cottages (**5** 38), *Richard Armson his peece* (**2** 16), Armstead Cl (**6** 12), Armston's Mdws (**5** 68), Arnolds Croft Mdw (**7** 271), Arnold's Fm (**6** 232), *Robert Arnolds Farme* (**4** 97), *Robert Arnolds Homested Close* (**4** 103), *Tho. Asburys orchard* (**6** 329), *Joseph Ascouch his house* (**2** 247), *Ashers close* (**5** 180), Ashton's Fd (**5** 29), *Joseph Ashton House* (**2** 232), *John Astels Cottage* (**4** 45), *Jasper Astells Close* (**3** 202), *John Astie cloase* (**7** 100), *Attons Close* (**4** 101), Austins Cl (**3** 19), *Henry Austins yards end* (**3** 15), *Averys close* (**6** 179), Ayres Mdw (**5** 13), John Ayres Pasture (**7** 80).

Babington Rd (**7** 185), Bacchus Nook (**6** 12), Bess Bagley (**7** 58), Brett Bainbrigge's Folly (**7** 104), Bakers Croft (**6** 12), *Bakers Grave* (**7** 85), *John Baker his homestall* (**2** 276), *Thomas Bakers Closse* (**4** 226), *Thomas Bakers Ley* (**4** 114), Bakewell's Lane (**7** 78), Baldwin Lane (**1** 17), Bett Balls (**6** 59), John Ball Covert (**5** 123), Balls Croft (**6** 13), *George Balls Farm* (**6** 263), Ball Gap (**7** 172), John Ball Gap (**5** 188), *Robert Balls House* (**6** 171), Balls Wood (**6** 202), Ballards Fd (**7** 230), Ballards Nook (**6** 59), *William Balmes Cottage* (**6** 171), Bambrook (**6** 74), Banburys First Cl (**4** 247), Barbers Cl (**6** 111), *Barbereyslond* (**5** 93), *Baresbys farm* (**3** 97), *Barkers Wood* (**6** 115), Barlow's Lodge (**2** 94), *Richd. Barnes Close* (**2** 267), Barnes Hill Plantation (**3** 108), *Peter*

Barnetts House (**2** 228), Middle Barrs (**6** 237), Top Barrs Cl (**6** 59), Barrs Heath (**6** 202), Barrel's Nook (**2** 227), *Barry Bush* (**4** 84), *Mark Barsby's lays* (**3** 235), Barston St (**1** 17), *Robert Bartrams wong* (**2** 6), *Bases Close* (**2** 134), Basses Cl (**2** 79), *Basses Cottage* (**2** 141), *Basset hawe* (**7** 258), *Bassethey* (**6** 305), Bassett House (**6** 304), Bassett Lane (**6** 226), *Bassfords Close* (**1** 219), Bateman's Row (**1** 17), Bates Bridge (**6** 241), Bates Cl (**6** 129), Battes's Folly (**6** 114), Baxters Cl (**6** 296), *John Baxters Close* (**2** 66), *Baxter's Ct* (**1** 18), *Wm. Baxters house* (**3** 278), Baxter's Mdw (**6** 239), Baxters Plat (**2** 65), *William Bayleys Close* (**7** 165), Beadman's Bit (**4** 82), Beadmans Croft (**6** 309), Beales Cl (**5** 11), Beaumont Arms (P.H.) (**7** 78), *Sir William Beaumonts Close* (**7** 165), Becks Fm (**6** 211), *John Becks House* (**2** 288), *Becke tenement* (**5** 226), *John Beebys Farm* (**6** 298), Beeson's Barn (**3** 197), *John Beeson house* (**2** 232), Belcher's Bar (**6** 182), Belchers Cl (**6** 202), *John Bells House* (**2** 302), Bell's Plantation (**2** 133), *William Beltons Close* (**3** 56), *Will. Beltons Cottiers Closs* (**2** 153), Benfords Mdw (**6** 89), Benford St (**1** 19), Bennet Hill (**7** 172), Bennets Croft (**6** 216), Bennett's Close (**4** 260), Bennetts Leys (**5** 98), *Benningtons Close* (**1** 183), *Bennitts Close* (**3** 148), *Willm. Bennitts house* (**3** 248), Benskin's Barn (**3** 197), J. Benskin's farm (**7** 243), Bent's Cl (**6** 301), *Bents Close* (**1** 183), *Bent's corner* (**1** 19), Bent's Croft (**6** 80), *Bent's Farm* (**1** 180), *Josiah Bents hard Layes* (**4** 32), Bent's Hospital (**1** 96), Bents Mdw (**5** 105), *Bents peece* (**6** 229), *Bentlys penn* (**3** 139), Berner's Arms (P.H.) (**3** 5), Berridge Lane (**3** 47), Berridge's Mdw (**5** 84), *Berryes Close* (**6** 222), Berrys Cl (**2** 290), *Berrys close* (**2** 302), Berry's Lane (**6** 222), Roger Besk Lane (**2** 95), Beveridge St (**3** 34), Bevershams Close (**2** 56), Bickleys Cl (**6** 208), Biddles Heath (**6** 203), Biddles Mdw (**5** 73), Biggs Cl (**6** 224), Biggs Lodge (**3** 183), *Billars Close* (**1** 183), Billesdon's Hollow (**6** 161), Billington Rough (**6** 83), Bilson's Fd (**5** 232), *Birkley St* (**1** 19), Bishop's Croft (**7** 212), Tho. Bishops House (**2** 52), *Bishopps Leyes* (**3** 147), Blaise's Inn (**2** 59), Blands Hovel (**2** 298), *William Blastocks House* (**6** 171), *John Blees House* (**2** 288), Blick's Hollingree (**6** 74), *Blisses Close* (**1** 183), Blockley's Bogg (**5** 58), Bloomer's Mdw (**7** 64), *Edward Blowers Homestead* (**2** 82), Bloxam First Cl (**6** 46), Blunt's Lane (**5** 219), *William Blythes Cloase* (**2** 213), *Bodingtons Close* (**5** 93), *Bodycotts Close* (**5** 214), *John Bollards shopp* (**1** 118), *John Bolsors close* (**7** 141), *William Bolts Cottage* (**6** 148), *Bonds Close* (**3** 109), *Robert Bonner's Close* (**5** 21), Bonner's Lane (**1** 21), *Grace Bonsalls Close* (**7** 119), Bonser's Cl (**6** 129), Booth Wood (**7** 144), *Boothby Meadow* (**6** 135), Bootons Cl (**6** 60), Borsden's Mdw (**4** 15), Bostock's Cl (**7** 173), Botts Cl (**6** 145), Botts Lane (**6** 10), Polly Bott's

Lane (**7** 238), *John Boulbees old enclosure* (**7** 165), Bowles' Measom Cl (**7** 172), Bowleys Gorse Cl (**7** 113), Bowleys Lane (**6** 10), *Bowmar's Bleach Yard* (**1** 145), Bowmar's Lane (**1** 21), Bown's Yard (**6** 284), Boyer's Lodge (**6** 159), *John Boylstons close* (**6** 56), Brabazons (**4** 198), Bradburys Heath (**6** 203), Bradfield Bridge (**6** 295), Bradfords Cl (**6** 309), Bradley's Plantation (**7** 212), Top Bradshaw (**5** 166), Bradshaw's Fd (**6** 228), Brays Cl (**5** 91), Breedon Sq (**1** 22), Brewin's Bottom Cl (**6** 28), Brewins Collum (**5** 105), *Brickwoods Close* (**2** 242), Brier's Cl (**5** 236), *Thomas Briges his close* (**2** 235), *Brigg's Hospital* (**3** 81), Brigg's Lawn (**7** 51), *Robert Broadhirsts Close* (**7** 141), Broadhurst Hill (**7** 135), Bromes Wood (**3** 222), *Brookes's Main Plott* (**5** 106), Brooks Cl (**6** 89), Brooks Mdw (**7** 271), *Brookesbys great Close* (**1** 184), Broom's Cl (**3** 165), *Robt. Brownes Close* (**2** 48), Brown's Hill (**2** 163), *John Browns house* (**2** 152), *William Brownes house* (**3** 164), *Browns lane end* (**5** 214), *John Browns Open Pasture* (**2** 154), Brown St (**1** 22), Brown's Wood (**3** 221), *George Brownes yard end* (**2** 242), *Tho. Brudnels closse* (**4** 256), Bruin's Cl (**5** 33), *George Brushfields lane end* (**3** 166), Top Brunskill (**4** 298), Brutnall's Lodge (**3** 102), Bryans Cl (**6** 89), Buck's Cl (**7** 80), Buckley's Hollingree (**6** 74), Buckston Lane (**1** 23), *Buckstons Orchard* (**1** 176), *John Bulls pen* (**4** 84), *John Bullivant's Farm* (**2** 247), Bullocks Cl (**2** 227), Bulstroades road (**7** 257), Bunneys Cl (**6** 40), Bunny's Spinney (**2** 84), Burbages Barn Cl (**5** 41), *John Burbages Bastard Ley Close* (**3** 239), *Burbages Cottage* (**3** 55), *William Burbages House* (**2** 288), *John Burbages yard* (**7** 86), Burbidges Cunnery (**3** 165), *George Burbidges house* (**3** 164), *Burches Close* (**3** 123), *Richard Burchnalls Close* (**3** 77), Burchnall Spinney (**6** 176), *Burdets close* (**5** 176), Burdetts Cl (**5** 179), Burdetts Far Cottage Cl (**5** 42), Top Burdetts (**5** 236), *Burges Lane* (**1** 23), *Burges Pament* (**1** 79), Burgess St (**1** 23), Burleys Cl (**5** 80), *Thomas Burley's house* (**4** 45), *Burley's Lane* (**1** 24), *Burmans close* (**6** 314), Burnaby's Mdw (**4** 45), *Burnbyes little Close* (**2** 303), Burrows Cl (**4** 247), Burrows Farm (**5** 58), Bursnell's Paddock (**2** 290), Burton's Cl (**4** 75), Burtons Cl (**6** 292), *William Burtons House* (**2** 288), Burton Walk (**7** 127), *Edmund Burys House* (**2** 288), *Leonard Burys Close* (**2** 295), Buswells Mdw (**5** 158), Butcher's Cl (**3** 165), *John Butlers Close* (**5** 214), *Humfrie Buttons Rickstead* (**5** 119), Buxtons Cl (**5** 42).

gardinum Johannis Cagge (**1** 176), *John Calcrofts Bushes* (**2** 27), Calcroft's Close (**2** 7), *John Callams plott* (**2** 73), Camms Green Cl (**2** 300), Campion brook Common (**3** 37), *Campions house* (**2** 53), *Cants Close* (**2** 242), Cants Sand Cl (**2** 47), Cants Thorns (**2** 166), *Cants Woldes* (**2** 48), Carley St (**1** 25), Carington Arms (P.H.) (**3** 100), Carrs

Lane (**6** 127), *Carres Close* (**5** 214), *George Carricks Cottage* (**4** 45), *William Carts Close* (**5** 134), Cart's Lane (**1** 25), Carter's Mdw (**5** 232), *Carters Windmill* (**1** 148), *Cartwrightes close* (**5** 21), *John Cartwrights Close* (**5** 167), *Richard Cartwright's Farm* (**4** 414), *Cattesholme* (**1** 197), *John Caunts House* (**2** 288), Cave's Arms (P.H.) (**7** 279), Caves Cl (**4** 270), John Caves Close (**4** 165), Cave's Inn (**5** 182), Caves Leys (**5** 151), Chambers Cl (**5** 85), Top Chamberlain's Cl (**7** 64), *Chamberlain's Ct* (**1** 26), *Richard Chamberlaines farm* (**4** 299), *Chamberlains Homestead* (**3** 65), *Chamberlayne Arms* (P.H.) (**4** 14), *Mary Chamberlyns Lay* (**3** 139), *Chandlers Lodge* (**3** 86), Chandlers Mdw (**5** 42), Chapman's (**5** 175), Chapmans Big Fd (**5** 80), Chapmans Cl (**7** 89), Chapman's Mdws (**5** 6), Chapman's Spinney (**6** 261), William Charles's Cl (**3** 278), The Charltons (**5** 73), Charlton St (**1** 27), Chaveney Plantation (**7** 170), Chaveney's Lane (**7** 173), Cheatells Lane (**5** 151), Cheatle's Barn (**7** 12), Cheatle's Cl (**7** 64), Cheatles Cl (**6** 324), *Cheney Arms* (P.H.) (**3** 194), *Cheslyns Wonge* (**7** 119), Chester Cl (**5** 33), Chesters Mdw (**7** 199), Choyce's Upper Piece (**6** 259), Clare Fm (**6** 144), Clark's Barn (**1** 181), Clarks Cl (**5** 80), Clarkes Cl (**5** 42), *Tho. Clarkes farme* (**2** 57), Clarke's Fd (**6** 29), Clarke's Lodge (**5** 68), Clarkes Mdw (**5** 62), *Clarkes peece* (**5** 165), Clarke's Spinney (**5** 67), Clarksons road (**7** 257), *Robert Clays homestead* (**2** 242), *Claytons house and home close* (**2** 71), *Tho. Clements closse* (**2** 155), *Clerkes Barne* (**1** 181), *Clerkeson Lane End* (**2** 71), *Coatses Close* (**1** 184), Cobleys Lane (**4** 247), *Richard Cocks improved close* (**7** 204), Cockings Orchard (**6** 129), *tabernam Johannis Cok* (**1** 141), Coke Banke (**2** 71), *Coker's kitchen* (**1** 119), Samuel Coleman Allotment (**4** 160), Colemans Home (**5** 98), Coleman's Lane (**4** 160), *Coleuyldeyle* (**2** 43), *colleuelwylows* (**2** 28), Collier's Cl (**6** 100), *Lawrence Collings leyes* (**3** 166), *Jn. Collingtons caudhil* (**2** 303), Collingwood's Cl (**6** 53), *Collinsons Close* (**1** 184), Coltman's Sq (**1** 28), *Henry Colsons yard end* (**5** 168), Coltmans Five Acres (**5** 105), *Coltmans yard* (**5** 227), *Coluilewonge* (**2** 28), Coly's Cl (**6** 327), *Condy leys* (**7** 86), Cooke's Fm (**5** 96), *Cookes great Plott* (**2** 295), *John Cookes plott* (**2** 72), *Wm. Cookes shopp* (**1** 118), Cooks Cl (**6** 301), *John Cooks homestead* (**6** 62), Cooks Lane (**6** 227), *Tho. Cooks Pingle* (**2** 303), Cooper's Cl (**6** 13), Coopers Cl (**5** 62), Coopers Cl (**6** 64), Coopers Cl (**6** 89), Coopers Cl (**6** 202), *Coopers farme* (**5** 11), Cooper's Lane (**5** 83), *Copsons Farm* (**6** 291), *Copsons hedge* (**6** 69), Corah St (**1** 29), Corbetts Cl (**7** 257), Corbit Hall (**7** 63), Corners Piece (**4** 260), *Cort and Co's Foundry* (**1** 145), Cosbys Fd (**5** 80), *Cotons Maner* (**3** 203), Cotton Mill (**7** 199), *Cottons Close* (**4** 167), Cox's Cl (**6** 129), Cox's Cl (**6** 202), Cox's Lane (**7** 213),

Craddock St (**7** 127), Cradock Arms (P.H.) (**5** 126), *Joseph Cragg's little meadow* (**7** 232), Cramp's Cl (**6** 94), Cramps Cl (**6** 154), Cramps Croft (**6** 111), Gabriel Cramps Croft (**6** 224), Paul Crane's Cl (**5** 85), Crane's Lock (**4** 80), *Cranford medwe* (**1** 197), Cresswell Pl (**1** 30), Crick's Lodge (**4** 269), Crick's Retreat (**4** 80), *Croddins Garden* (**2** 185), *Henry Croslands House* (**2** 288), *Robert Croslands House* (**2** 288), *Thomas Crosons yards end* (**3** 139), Crosslands Cl (**2** 290), Crow Orchard Cl (**4** 217), Crowshaws Mdw (**6** 13), *Thomas Croxalls hedge* (**6** 314), *Cublyes gate* (**2** 106), Cullen Cl (**7** 67), Culyer's Cl (**6** 94), Curzon Arms (P.H.) (**7** 248), Curzon Arms Inn (**6** 307), Cuthbert Mdw (**6** 13), Cuthbert's Cl (**6** 41).

Big Daddy (**3** 37), *Josiah Dagleys Yard* (**6** 229), *John Daines House* (**2** 288), Dakins Bridge (**6** 241), Dakins Cl (**3** 61), Dalby Covert (**7** 48), Dan's Lane (**6** 206), *Danett Close* (**1** 185), Dannett's Hall (**1** 154), Darkers Cl (**4** 46), *Ann Davenports Close* (**5** 168), Dawkins Cl (**6** 53), Dawkins Croft (**6** 270), Dawkins Hill (**5** 92), Dawkins Lynch (**6** 224), Dawson's Lane (**6** 127), Dawsons road (**7** 257), Day's Plantation (**2** 287), Deacon Hill (**6** 29), Deakin's Bridge (**6** 166), Deakin's Cl (**6** 94), *Deakins Close* (**1** 185), *Deakins Farm* (**7** 15), Dennis St (**7** 66), *Dents meadow* (**1** 197), *Denton's Yard* (**7** 10), *Derkerweye* (**7** 51), *Francis Derrys House* (**2** 288), Dewell's Croft (**6** 212), Dewes Barn Fm (**7** 21), *Dewicks Cottage* (**2** 72), *Dewicks Vinehouse* (**2** 76), Dexters Cl (**7** 257), Dick's Cl (**5** 50), *Richard Dickens farme* (**2** 72), *Samuel Dickmans House* (**2** 288), *Wm. Dickmans Moor* (**2** 296), *Digby lane* (**3** 244), Dilks Cl (**6** 212), Dimmocks Hill (**6** 23), Dimmock's Mdw (**6** 14), *Disons peece* (**6** 315), Dixie Arms (P.H.) (**6** 166), Francis Dixon Lodge (**3** 134), Dixon's Square (**5** 139), *James Dixons Wong* (**2** 268), *George Dodsons Farme* (**4** 97), Dorman's Fd (**5** 158), Dormer's Hall Cl (**6** 14), Doubledays Cl (**2** 291), Doubledays Cl (**3** 19), Doubledays Red Earth (**2** 61), Dowell's Barn (**7** 97), Dowells Croft (**6** 111), *John Dowells yarde* (**6** 229), *Edward Drake his Farme* (**4** 97), Drakeleys Cl (**6** 168), *Ducketts Close* (**5** 16), *Ducketts farme* (**7** 203), Ducketts Hill (**5** 42), *Ralfe Dudleys house* (**3** 278), John Duffield's yard (**7** 153), *Dumbletons Spinney* (**5** 62), the Duns Croft (**6** 224), Duns Lane (**1** 32), *the Dunmore piece* (**2** 214), Dunmore's Hill (**4** 71), Durrance Cl (**2** 67), *Andrew Dyxons house* (**2** 202).

Eaglesfield Fm (**5** 130), Eales Fd (**5** 175), Earls Mdw (**5** 92), Earps Croft (**6** 81), Eaton St (**1** 33), Eboratts Cl (**6** 277), Ecobs Cl (**2** 300), Edens Cl (**7** 104), *Jn.^{n} Edgson Toft* (**2** 303), *William Edgsons House* (**2** 289), *Edgsons Pasture* (**2** 294), Edwin's Cl (**3** 145), *Stephen Edwins house & Cloase* (**3** 154), Ellaby's Spinney (**2** 63), Eller's Gorse (**3** 275),

Eliot's Lane (**6** 273), *Elliotts Cl* (**6** 301), Elton's Cl (**6** 14), *Matthew Eltons Closs* (**3** 211), Elton St (**1** 33), Everard's Cl (**6** 94), *Steven Everards orchard* (**6** 107), *Everarts willows* (**6** 315), *Everat yard* (**6** 293), *Hugh Exons Close* (**7** 120), *William Exons Flatt* (**7** 160), Exton's Barn (**6** 188), Extons Cl (**2** 273), *Thomas Exton Wong* (**2** 279).

Falconer's Nook (**7** 237), Fardells Barn Cl (**2** 291), Fardells Cl (**2** 300), *John Fardells House* (**2** 289), Fardell's Melton Hill (**2** 301), Farmer's Cl (**6** 295), *Farmers Close* (**1** 186), Farmer's Lane (**6** 29), Farmer's Mdw (**6** 14), *Richard Farmers Orchard* (**6** 326), *Farnamwode* (**7** 176), Faulkner's Cl (**4** 99), Felstead's Spinney (**2** 63), *Fenton St* (**1** 34), Ferneley's Cl (**3** 233), Ferrimans Cl (**3** 62), *Thomas Fewkes house* (**3** 278), *Fidelliswonge* (**4** 181), *Thomas Fipps house* (**4** 45), Fish's Plantation (**6** 10), Fishers Cl (**6** 284), *Fishers farme* (**2** 203), *Alderman Fisher's Mill* (**1** 148), *Fishers Moor* (**2** 296), *Fishers Pasture* (**2** 294), Fleming's Almshouses (**2** 24), Fleming's Bridge (**2** 24), Fletchers Spring (**6** 100), Flint's Fd (**5** 69), *Robt. Flowers closs* (**2** 152), Flude's Cl (**5** 85), Flude Lodge (**5** 235), Fludes Lunns (**5** 34), Flude Piece (**6** 154), *Robert Foremans close* (**5** 215), *Formans Close* (**2** 303), *Forman plat* (**2** 303), *Forsteres Mere* (**6** 320), *Fosters Close* (**2** 295), *Foulkes Plots* (**3** 52), Fowlers Cl (**2** 291), *Fowlers Pasture* (**2** 294), Fox Bridge (**6** 166), *John Fox's Farm* (**6** 298), Fox's Mdw (**6** 78), Fox's Monument (**6** 328), Fox's St (**1** 34), *John Franch Close* (**7** 252), Frank's Cl (**4** 82), *Freake's Ground* (**1** 148), Frearsons Cl (**6** 169), Frearsons lane (**7** 258), *Willm. Freckingham his wong* (**2** 198), Freeman Cl (**6** 100), Freeman's Cl (**5** 131), *Freemans Close* (**2** 64), Freemans House (**2** 67), Robert Freeman's Mill (**4** 25), *Freemans Orchard* (**2** 72), John Freer Allotment (**4** 160), Freer's Cl (**4** 160), *John Freestones Side land* (**5** 168), Frisbys Cl (**2** 233), *croftam Rog' Frisby* (**1** 186), *James Frisby House* (**2** 232), *Thomas Frisby House* (**2** 232), *Froanes farme* (**5** 11), *William Frostlins House* (**4** 45), Fulshaws Cl (**6** 208).

The Gadsby's (**7** 220), Gage's Cl (**2** 300), Gallard's Hill (**6** 45), *Gallards Warren* (**6** 49), Gallaway's Sq (**1** 36), *Gamballs hill* (**2** 295), Gambles Cl (**2** 300), *Gambles Close* (**1** 182), *Gambles Close* (**6** 91), *Gambles farme* (**5** 11), *John Gambles Homestead* (**3** 211), Martha Gambles House Cl (**4** 165), *Wm. Gamble his house and homestead* (**7** 252), Garners Barn Cl (**6** 14), Garners Cl (**6** 54), Garners Cl (**6** 111), Garner's Mdw (**5** 201), *Garnons Five Acres* (**2** 299), *John Garretts home close* (**7** 143), Gearys Cl (**6** 130), Geary's Flat (**6** 29), Gees Cl (**5** 42), Gee's Lock (**5** 104), Georges Cl (**2** 274), *Tho. Gerys Farm* (**6** 264), Gilberts Bit (**6** 54), *Gilbert Croft* (**7** 228), Gilbert's Fm (**6** 194), *Gilbertes Slade* (**4** 181), Gill's Slip (**2** 291), *Robert Gills Farm* (**2** 295),

Gilliams Butts (**5** 81), Gillings Piece (**6** 302), *John Gillyflowers Cottage* (**6** 148), *Gillyvers Close* (**6** 49), *William Gilsons Yard end* (**3** 105), Gimsons Cl (**6** 162), Gimsons Cl (**6** 208), Glover's Fd (**5** 29), *Richard Glovers House* (**6** 172), *Goadbys Close* (**1** 187), *Godbertes Rydyng* (**7** 216), Goddards Cl (**6** 54), *Goddins Hedge* (**5** 81), Godfreys Cl (**6** 14), Godfreys Cl (**6** 130), Godfrey's Fd (**5** 233), *John Goffs plot* (**3** 65), Goldsmith Grange (**2** 208), *Robert Gollins Meadow* (**2** 107), Good's Lane (**3** 228), Goodacre St (**1** 37), Goode's Cl (**5** 190), *Goodells Close* (**6** 91), Goodman's Fd (**5** 97), Goodmans Seeds (**4** 247), Goodwins Cl (**5** 225), Goodwin's Plantation (**7** 261), *Thomas Goodwins Wong* (**2** 276), *Joseph Goozes plott* (**5** 135), *Gores hedge* (**5** 145), Gore Lodge (**4** 164), *John Goude's Farm* (**3** 62), *Gounfreyholm* (**1** 201), *John Graves Sen*[r]*. House* (**2** 289), *William Grave's Close* (**7** 232), Gray St (**1** 38), Greens Cl (**6** 140), *Robert Greens Close* (**1** 187), *William Greens Close* (**3** 166), *Thomas Greens Farme* (**4** 97), Green's Lane (**1** 38), Green St (**1** 38), Greenwells Cl (**5** 86), *John Gregorie lea* (**3** 13), Gregory's Cl (**6** 47), Gregory's Cl (**6** 74), *Gregorys House & homested* (**2** 72), *croftis Margarete Grene et Agnetis sororis eius* (**1** 187), Gresley Fm (**6** 252), *Grews Farm* (**6** 298), *Grews Farm* (**7** 15), *John Grews Farm* (**6** 264), Top Grewcocks (**7** 221), Grey Cl (**7** 157), Grice's Cl (**2** 60), Grice's Hill (**2** 56), *pratum Henrici Grim* (**2** 297), Grimley Croft (**7** 65), Grove St (**1** 39), Groves Rice Nook Cl (**7** 113), *Thomas Grundleys house* (**3** 278), *Grymmeswode* (**7** 274).

Near Hacketts (**5** 92), Hackett's Cl (**6** 15), Halfords Cl (**4** 160), Halfords Cl (**5** 42), *Sir Richard Halfords Close* (**4** 162), Halford St (**1** 39), Halls Cl (**6** 302), Halls far Cl (**3** 62), *John Halls House* (**2** 289), Hallams Cl (**3** 186), *Hallam's Close* (**1** 187), Hallam's Fm (**7** 29), Hallam's Wood (**2** 103), Hames Cl (**3** 200), *Hamsterley place* (**2** 29), Hancock's Fm (**6** 206), *John Hancocks Orchard* (**2** 73), *Hancocks Platt* (**2** 73), *Harberts close* (**3** 241), *Harcourt St* (**1** 40), Hardingtons Croft (**7** 68), *Hardy's Cl* (**1** 40), *Tho. Hardys farm* (**3** 189), Hardy's Fd (**5** 6), Hardy's Gunsel (**3** 178), Harralds Mdw (**5** 59), *Hugh Harris's House* (**2** 141), *Richard Harris's Farm* (**2** 141), *harris wyllowes* (**3** 140), Harrison's Barn (**3** 255), Harrison's Cl (**6** 15), *Edw. Harrisons Farm* (**6** 298), *Thomas Harrisons Farm* (**6** 298), Harrison's Nursery (**1** 177), *William Harrolds Close* (**6** 285), *Hartopp Arms* (P.H.) (**4** 88), Hastings Arms (P.H.) (**7** 36), Hatchetts Croft (**7** 213), Hatton Lodge (**2** 46), *Robert Haucers House* (**2** 289), *Hawes's Lane* (**3** 135), *Jonathan Hawkins's homestall* (**3** 252), Hawkin's Pond (**7** 173), *Hawley's Lane* (**1** 41), Hawleys Styehedge Cl (**2** 91), *Barthol' Haycocks Farme* (**4** 97), *Tho. Haycocks Hags* (**4** 103), Haymes Allotment (**4** 82), R. Haymes

Homestead (**4** 248), *Haynes farme* (**2** 180), *Hayres Lane end* (**6** 20), Hazlerigg Fm (**3** 255), Heafield Lane Mdw (**6** 15), Heals Big Fd (**5** 206), Healy Cl (**6** 15), *John Heases Close* (**7** 121), Heathcote Arms (**6** 67), *Tho. Hebbs Close* (**7** 137), *Hebbes willowes* (**7** 177), *heines close* (**3** 16), *Hemmings Close* (**1** 187), Betty Henser's Lane (**7** 152), Henshaw St (**1** 41), *Hensoe bridge* (**2** 236), Hensons Red Hill (**7** 214), *Hericks hedge* (**5** 228), Herrick's Cl (**7** 173), Herrick Rd (**7** 248), Hexstalls Cl (**6** 203), Hextalls Cl (**6** 41), Hickleys Cl (**5** 43), Hicklings Spinney (**7** 185), Hickling's Sq (**1** 4), Hickmans (**6** 208), *Higinsons Hedge* (**6** 208), Higginsons Mdw (**5** 43), *William Hills close* (**4** 60), *Hills flat* (**6** 315), Hills's Barn Cl (**5** 158), Hincks Mdw (**6** 310), Hincks's Sq (**1** 42), Henry Hinds Slate House (**7** 228), Hipwells Cl (**5** 184), Hipwell Mdw (**5** 62), Hobill's Mdw (**5** 51), *Hodges farm* (**3** 98), Hodson's Ct (**1** 42), Hollands Mdw (**6** 130), Holland's Piece (**7** 213), Hollier's Walk (**6** 123), Hollis Hills (**6** 239), Holme St (**1** 42), Holmes's Croft (**6** 146), Holmes's Mill (**1** 149), Holt's Leys (**1** 204), Hook's Bridge (**6** 166), *Hookes Close* (**6** 297), Hookers Cl (**2** 301), Horns Cl (**4** 112), *John Horsepools House* (**2** 289), *Bartholomew Hortons pen* (**4** 227), Houghs Leys (**2** 196), *Houghton's Orchard* (**3** 212), *Thomas Houghtons Close* (**2** 141), Hubbards Cl (**5** 92), Hubbard's Fm (**5** 10), Hubbard's Fd (**5** 29), Hubbard Hill (**7** 174), Hubbards Orchard (**5** 81), *Christopher Huddlestones House* (**2** 289), Hudson's Cl (**7** 99), *Hudsons Hospital* (**2** 176), *the Hull acres* (**5** 94), Hull's Cl (**4** 59), Hulls Homestead (**4** 64), Hull St (**1** 44), Hulses Cl (**3** 62), *Hunfreisput* (**7** 223), Hunts Bondman Hayes ((**6** 224), Hunts Cl (**6** 140), Hunts Croft (**6** 327), Hunts Fd (**4** 261), *Hunts lane* (**4** 95), Hunts Leys (**7** 174), Hunts Lodge (**5** 235), Hunt's Road (**7** 24), Big Husses (**3** 209), *Hycksons house* (**2** 203).

Iliffe Bridge (**6** 63), *Iliffes farme* (**5** 11), *Edw. Illiffes ley* (**4** 136), *Ilyffes Yard end* (**5** 169), *Bartholomew Ilsons house* (**3** 164), *Imery Close* (**2** 296), *Rich. Ingleton his house* (**2** 248), Ireson's Nanhill (**4** 271), *Ironmongers Barne Closes* (**3** 57), Ivets Slip (**2** 183).

Jackson's Bridge (**6** 166), *Peter James's Farme* (**4** 97), *John James his House* (**3** 248), James's St (**1** 45), Jarrom St (**1** 45), Jarvis's Cl (**5** 175), Jayes Barn (**6** 161), Jayes Fd (**6** 89), Jebit's Cl (**6** 239), Jees Barn (**6** 112), *Jelleyes Closes* (**1** 188), Jelley's Mdw (**5** 206), *Tho. Jenkins meadow* (**4** 257), *Rich. Jenkinsons house* (**3** 164), *Jennens meadow* (**6** 332), *George Jermins Leye* (**3** 167), *Tho. Jervis House* (**2** 73), *Jervis Platt* (**2** 73), The Jessons (**3** 82), *Edward Jessons closs* (**2** 155), *Thomas Jessons Beck closs* (**2** 153), Jessons Mdw (**2** 153), Johnson's Cl (**6** 146), *Kett Johnsons Close* (**4** 157), *William Johnson's Farme* (**4** 45), *Richard Johnsons house* (**3** 166), *Thomas Johnsons house* (**2** 152), Johnsons

Piece (**2** 292), *Johnson's St* (**1** 45), *Johnsons Yard* (**7** 15), Harry Jones Mdw (**4** 76), Jordans Burroughs (**6** 224), Jordan's Fm (**6** 15), *Jordanes house* (**3** 175), *Judds Cottage* (**5** 11), *Daniel Judds Farme* (**4** 97), Judge Meadow Spinney (**4** 44).

Keck's Arms (P.H.) (**1** 130), Kelham's Cl (**5** 81), Thomas Kelhams Cl (**3** 107), *Stephen Kelhams piece* (**2** 274), *John Kellam his hows and homeyard* (**2** 73), *Kellys Factory* (**1** 146), Kendal's Mdw (**5** 69), *John Kendalls close* (**3** 132), *John Kendall Flatt* (**6** 316), Kendrick's Cl; (**6** 95), Kenney St (**1** 45), Kenny Cl (**5** 86), Kent St (**1** 46), *Daniell Keys Close* (**3** 248), Kibble Hill (**4** 112), *William Kiddiars close* (**7** 162), *Ann Kilby wid. her Farme* (**3** 149), *Kilbourne's Lawn* (**7** 51), Kimberlins Cl (**6** 61), King Cl (**7** 174), Kings Cl (**6** 310), Kings Fd (**5** 69), *John Kinges house* (**3** 154), Kings Mdw (**3** 151), Kings Orchard (**3** 159), King's Pasture (**7** 80), *Kings Windmill close* (**7** 142), Kinnes Mdw (**3** 50), Kinton's Cl (**5** 34), Kirk's Cl (**6** 95), *Daniel Kitchins Farm* (**2** 128), *Richard Knapp House* (**2** 232), *Knapps Close* (**2** 236), Knight's Cl (**5** 34), *Knights close* (**6** 191), Knight's Mdw (**6** 15), Knowles Spinney (**6** 182), *Kybbles closse* (**4** 266), *Kyghley yard* (**7** 87).

Lacyȝarte (**7** 106), *Charles Lakens Slade* (**6** 320), *Daniel Lambert* (P.H.) (**1** 126), Landers Cl (**7** 113), Langham's Bridge (**5** 223), Langley's School (**7** 12), *Langton close* (**4** 85), Larkin's Pasture (**6** 234), Latimer's House (**7** 230), Laundons (**4** 299), *Richard Laurences shop* (**1** 118), Lea's Burroughs (**6** 224), Leaders Fm (**5** 140), Lees Great Cl (**2** 153), Lee St (**1** 47), *Anthony Leesons House* (**2** 289), Leesons Pasture (**2** 292), Legates Cl (**5** 59), *Legats Close* (**5** 64), *Leighs close* (**2** 243), *Lentoncrofte* (**3** 39), Lett's Cl (**4** 192), *Levetts Turnopp close* (**3** 58), *Lewes Close* (**7** 177), Lewin St (**1** 47), *Lewis's Almshouses* (**1** 97), Lewis's Piece (**5** 105), Lillys Mdw (**6** 130), *Limbers House* (**5** 16), Richard Linneys Farm (**2** 257), *Linthwaite hedge* (**4** 85), *William Litherlands close* (**7** 167), *Richard Loasbies Meadow* (**3** 154), *Loes Cottage* (**3** 55), *Frances Lomleys farme* (**2** 83), *Thomas Lords Cloose* (**5** 82), Lords Croft (**6** 209), Lords Gorse (**2** 252), *George Lords House* (**2** 289), *Lord his yard* (**2** 254), Loseby Lane (**1** 48), *Loves Close* (**3** 212), James Loves Farm (**2** 257), Lowes Cl (**5** 176), Lowe's Mdw (**5** 6), Lowes Mdw (**5** 237), Lucas Cl (**5** 43), Lucas Cl (**6** 90), Lucks Mdw (**5** 184), *Ludlams Brewhouse* (**1** 141), *Lynes Yards End* (**2** 74).

Mabbses Orchard (**1** 177), *Magdaunce hous* (**2** 296), *Hither Magitts* (**6** 280), *Majors Close* (**1** 189), *Malsons Close* (**1** 189), Manns Cl (**3** 301), George Mans Fm (**2** 257), *Thomas Mans Close* (**2** 49), *Will. Mans close* (**2** 49), *Mansfield's Head* (P.H.) (**1** 132), Mansfield's Hollingree (**6** 74), Mansfield St (**1** 48), Markham Platt (**2** 292), Mariots Cl (**6** 169),

Marriott's Bridge (**2** 99), Marriott's Spinney (**2** 51), *Marshall Close* (**7** 123), Marshalls Cl (**6** 313), *James Marshall his closse* (**7** 167), Joe Marshall Fd (**3** 37), *Humphrey Marshalls house & close* (**3** 164), *Wm. Marshalls house* (**3** 278), Marsons Cl (**6** 61), Marston Bush (**3** 186), *Everard Marstons Leyes* (**3** 167), *Marstons Mill* (**1** 150), *Marstons Tan Yard* (**1** 146), *John Martins Close* (**5** 216), Martin's Mill Fd (**5** 207), Martinshaw Wood (**6** 222), Marvins Burroughs (**6** 224), Marvins Leys (**6** 30), *Miss Mason's Almshouses* (**1** 92), *William Masons Close* (**5** 216), Mason Fm (**4** 133), *Masseys House* (**6** 149), *Matlockes Cottage* (**3** 55), Mawby's Fds (**5** 7), *Thomas Mawstons Cottage* (**4** 45), May's Fm (**6** 283), Meadows's Cl (**2** 228), *William Mees Close* (**7** 122), *Melbornes Cottage* (**3** 55), Merrills Homestead (**2** 68), *Mervins medowe* (**6** 132), Messenger's Barn (**5** 40), Messenger's Barn (**6** 227), Messenger's Lodge (**3** 95), Metcalf St (**1** 49), Mettan's Spinney (**6** 128), *Michell pitt* (**7** 122), Miles Ford (**6** 295), Miles's Mdw (**6** 293), Millers Lash (**6** 54), John Miller's Orchard (**3** 83), *Millners close* (**3** 235), Mitchell's Spring Fm (**7** 112), Bottom Monks (**4** 56), *Rich. Monks Leys* (**5** 170), Moore's Arms (P.H.) (**6** 313), Moores Cl (**5** 81), Moores Cl (**6** 54), *Moore's Close* (**1** 189), *Arthur Moores Close* (**6** 107), *Geo. Moore's Close* (**6** 20), Moore's Covert (**6** 308), *Moors farme* (**2** 304), *Thomas Moor horsepool* (**6** 136), Joe Moore's Lane (**7** 249), Moore's Mdw (**5** 87), *Henrie Mores leas* (**4** 257), *Morris Closse* (**3** 17), Mortimers Cl (**6** 140), *Mortons close* (**1** 189), *Moselyes house* (**7** 274), Moseley's Plantation (**7** 9), *Motonlesowe* (**6** 141), *Motunsballok* (**6** 214), Moulds Croft (**5** 131), Mould's Mdw (**6** 16), *Moulds pen* (**5** 229), *Moulsoes close* (**2** 236), *Mugglestone's Nether Ground* (**7** 288), *Muglaston Pen* (**7** 15), *Murfin's yard* (**7** 130), Musson's Cl (**5** 176), *Mussons farme* (**5** 11), Edward Muxloes Farm (**2** 242).

Joseph Neal's Farme (**4** 45), Neale's Fm (**6** 124), Neale St (**1** 50), Needhams Cl (**3** 62), *Needham Halle* (**3** 5), Needhams Home Croft (**6** 106), Nevill Arms (P.H.) (**4** 188), *Newberrys Orchard* (**1** 178), Newcombe's Parlour (**2** 90), Nowell Spring Wood (**7** 238), Alderman Newton's School (**1** 112), *Nobles Close* (**2** 49), *Tho. Nobles close* (**2** 304), *Nobles Pasture* (**2** 294), *Noones Bridge* (**5** 170), *Jane Noon's Cottage* (**4** 45), Noon's Orchard (**1** 178), North's Lodge (**3** 192), Norton Fd (**6** 284), Norton St (**1** 52), Nutt's Bridge (**6** 124), *Oadhams middle Plott* (**2** 296), Joseph Oldershaw's Cl (**7** 52), *Olners Meadow* (**6** 320), Onebys Cl (**6** 131), Orams Cl (**5** 152), Orams Fd (**6** 163), Orgar Leys (**2** 183), *Orgerpark* (**2** 86), Orridges Town Cl (**7** 201), Next Ortons (**5** 35), Ortons Cl (**6** 16), Ortons Cl (**6** 209), Orton's Cl (**6** 254), Orton's Plantation (**6** 308), Orton St (**1** 53), *Ortons townes end* (**5** 199),

Osbourne St (**1** 53), Osbournes Mdw (**4** 287), Oswin's (**5** 190), *Oswins Bridge* (**3** 67).

Packwoods Mdw (**5** 159), *Paddies close* (**2** 244), Padge Hall (**5** 140), Page's Upper Cl (**5** 237), Paget Arms (P.H.) (**4** 164), Paget Fm (**6** 144), John Pagett's back yard (**7** 189), Pains Cl (**4** 193), Pains Cl (**6** 141), *Pakecroft* (**2** 92), *Pakemanswode* (**6** 156), *Pakyscroft* (**3** 20), *Will. Palins clos* (**2** 155), *William Palins house* (**2** 152), *Palletes house* (**5** 229), Palmer's Arms (P.H.) (**4** 215), Palmers Cl (**5** 43), *Anthony Palmers Close* (**1** 190), *Tho. Palmers Close* (**1** 190), *Palmers close* (**3** 57), *Palmers Cottage* (**3** 55), *Benjamin Palmers House* (**2** 232), Palmer's Lane (**4** 70), *Edward Palmers Leaes* (**7** 138), *Palmers peece* (**7** 191), *Palmers Pingles* (**6** 77), *Henry Palmers Spinay* (**4** 49), Palmers Trent Cl (**7** 105), *William Panes tonge* (**4** 195), Papillon Hall (**4** 164), Pare's Bridge (**6** 268), Pares St (**1** 54), Parkers Cl (**7** 22), *John Parkers Farme* (**7** 191), Parkers Mdw (**6** 16), Parkers Road (**7** 24), Parkers Yard (**7** 278), *Parnham Close* (**2** 98), *Thomas Parsons Close* (**7** 167), *Parsons Hey* (**7** 76), *Parsons Lane* (**3** 217), Parsonwood Hill (**7** 73), *Paskedenholm* (**2** 31), *Paskeden lane* (**2** 31), Passands Breach (**7** 67), *Passelewewong* (**1** 190), *Parchett's Farm* (**6** 113), Pawleys Mdw (**5** 105), Paynes Cl (**5** 207), Payne's Lane (**4** 188), *Paynes manor* (**4** 195), Peaches Cl (**3** 51), Peach's Cl (**4** 252), Peake's Covert (**2** 232), Peake's Flats (**2** 234), *John Peakes home close* (**7** 142), Peasons Cl (**6** 16), Peat's Barn (**7** 152), Pegs Cl (**6** 313), Peg Park (**6** 16), Pegg's Crow Tree Cl (**6** 310), Peggs Fm (**6** 318), Peggs Green (**6** 84), Peggs Lane Fd (**6** 213), Peggs Paddock (**4** 248), *Robert Pelsants Close* (**6** 173), *Pepper lane end* (**7** 148), Perkins' Arms (P.H.) (**6** 318), Perring's Well (**7** 13), Pettifors Fm (**6** 36), *Pexsall Corner* (**1** 55), Phillips Mdw (**5** 44), *Philpots House* (**2** 74), *Phipps's field* (**1** 190), *Wm. Phipps his house* (**3** 278), Pick's Lodge (**3** 86), Pickerings Cl (**6** 147), Pickering Grange (**6** 143), Pickering Wood (**7** 63), *Pickwells close* (**2** 304), Pike St (**1** 55), *Piners gate* (**4** 85), Plant's Cl (**6** 17), *Plantes milne* (**6** 243), Platts Cl (**7** 39), *Edward Plowrights house* (**3** 278), *Plumers Close* (**4** 280), *Peter Plummer's Farme* (**4** 45), *Thomas Plummer's Farme* (**4** 45), *Plummers lane* (**3** 75), Pochin's Bridge (**5** 223), Pochin St (**6** 68), Pocklington's Walk (**1** 143), Pollard's (**5** 7), Pollards (**5** 176), Pools Mdw (**6** 131), Porter's Barn (**5** 209), Porter's Bit (**5** 202), Porters Cl (**5** 15), *Joseph Porter his farme* (**2** 232), George Porters Fd (**7** 221), *Porters peece* (**5** 166), *Porters Townsend* (**2** 108), Poughers Cl (**5** 44), *Poultneys Close* (**1** 191), *Powers Woode* (**4** 78), Poynton's Barn, (**7** 277), Poynton's Cl (**6** 17), Prats Mdw (**6** 217), *John Pratts Tythe free piece* (**5** 216), *James Preston House* (**2** 232), Preston's Lane (**7** 79), Preston's Lodge (**4** 147),

Preston Stocking (**6** 141), Price's Top Cl (**6** 42), *Watson Prowdlove his cloase* (**2** 19), Puffer's Yard (**6** 228), Pullins Cl (**6** 112), *Purleyfurs* (**2** 290), *Pynders Close* (**1** 190).

Raggs Cottage (**3** 55), Raggs Pasture (**2** 154), Ralph's Bit (**5** 207), Ralphs Cl (**5** 44), Ralph's Cl (**5** 87), Ralph's Fd (**6** 84), Randles Mdw (**5** 92), *Rauenold pasture* (**3** 91), Ravens Cl (**4** 56), *Thomas Ravens Homestead* (**2** 304), Rawdon Arms (P.H.) (**7** 23), *Rawletts Close* (**1** 191), Rawson St (**1** 56), *Ray St* (**1** 18), *Raynors Oakes* (**6** 191), Raynors Orchard (**6** 189), *Raynors willows* (**6** 191), *Redys Close* (**1** 191), *Remington's Close* (**2** 108), Renals Fm (**7** 149), *Revell's Lane* (**1** 57), Reynolds Cl (**5** 176), Reynolds Cl (**6** 61), *George Rickards* (**7** 288), *Ridlingtons close* (**4** 157), Rileys Cl (**2** 154), Rileys Mdw (**6** 209), Rimington Mdw (**2** 127), *Ringroses Piece* (**1** 191), *James Rippins House* (**2** 289), *Thomas Rippins House* (**2** 289), Rippon's Plantation (**2** 144), Roberts Bit (**7** 222), Roberts Cl (**6** 131), Robinsons Barn Cl (**6** 129), *John Robinsons House* (**6** 122), Robinsons Mdw (**6** 125), Robinson's Orchard (**6** 55), *Willm. Robyns Closse* (**7** 167), Thomas Roe's Cl (**5** 87), *Rich. Roose his house* (**2** 248), Roses Home (**7** 105), *Ross Factory* (**1** 146), Rowells Croft (**6** 271), *John Rowses Close* (**2** 269), *Robert Rowse high leies* (**2** 153), Royce's Plantation (**2** 152), *royley close* (**3** 44), *John Rubbins closse* (**2** 155), *William Rubbins closse* (**2** 155), *John Rubbins house* (**2** 152), *Mary Rubbins house* (**2** 152), *Rubleys Close* (**1** 191), Ruding St (**1** 57), Russell St (**7** 129), *Robt. Rylys Bretlands* (**2** 153), *Ryngdoncroftes* (**2** 237).

Saddington Cl (**6** 311), *Sadmans forde* (**6** 249), *Salmon street* (**7** 131), Sander's Wood (**6** 79), *Tho. Sandersons piece* (**5** 216), Sansomes Cl (**6** 107), Sansomes Mdw (**6** 278), Sapcoat's Lodge (**2** 64), Sapcoat's Spinney (**2** 64), *George Sarsons barne* (**7** 138), Sarsons Homestead (**3** 75), *Brian Saterthwaite his myres* (**4** 72), Saunts Cl (**5** 70), Savages Cl (**7** 89), *Thomas Scarborrow House* (**2** 232), *John Scotts Farme* (**4** 97), *John Scotts Homestead Close* (**4** 103), Scotton's Mdw (**5** 30), Scrimshaw's Windmill (**2** 25), *Edward Seaman house* (**3** 164), Sedgleys Cl (**5** 184), Serjeant's Folly (**4** 292), *Shallcross Cottage* (**3** 55), Sharman's (**5** 7), Sharpes Cl (**2** 234), *Sharpes Close* (**2** 224), *John Sharps closs* (**2** 155), *John Sharpes close* (**2** 237), *Francis Sharp House* (**2** 232), *James Sharps house* (**2** 152), *Richard Sharpes house* (**3** 154), *Thomas Sharpes Leyes* (**3** 167), *Sharpe his Wonge* (**3** 84), John Willie Sharpless's (**3** 23), Shaw's Green (**7** 49), Shaw Highway Cl (**6** 101), Sheare Croft (**7** 13), Sheen Mdw (**5** 44), Sheldon Mdw (**6** 17), *Francis Shentons close* (**6** 132), Shenton's Mdw (**6** 90), Shepherds Cl (**6** 325), *Shepherds Cottage* (**6** 149), Shepherd's Hill (**7** 141), *Sheppards Lane*

(**2** 75), *Sheppards yard end* (**2** 75), Sherrards Cl (**6** 235), Sherrier's School and Almshouses (**5** 138), Shillacres Stiltons (**3** 166), *Shipley's Ct* (**1** 62), Shittlewood's Barn (**3** 269), *Joel Shuttlewoods piece* (**2** 183), Shuttleworth Lane (**5** 68), Simmond's Cl (**6** 75), Simon St (**1** 63), *Simons' Hospital* (**1** 97), Simpkin's Bridge (**5** 104), Simpkins Cl (**5** 111), Simpsons Caudhill (**2** 299), *John Simpsons House* (**2** 289), *Jasper Simpson's Pingle* (**3** 109), *Simpson St* (**1** 63), *John Simson House* (**2** 232), *Thomas Simson House* (**2** 232), Sissons Cl (**2** 293), *Joseph Sissons House* (**2** 289), Skerritts Home Spot (**2** 228), Skinners Cl (**5** 184), Slacks Fd (**6** 325), *Slaters close* (**5** 24), Slater St (**1** 63), Sleath Cl (**5** 44), Sleath's Lane (**5** 133), Joseph Slee's Farm (**7** 253), Smalley's Piece (**5** 167), *Smarts Close* (**1** 193), *Smithes Farme* (**2** 304), *Henry Smiths Close* (**2** 49), *Henry Smiths Close* (**4** 257), *John Smiths Close* (**2** 49), *Richard Smithes close* (**2** 244), *Robert Smiths Close* (**7** 2), *William Smiths Cottage* (**4** 45), *Smiths Free School* (**2** 201), *Thomas Smiths house* (**6** 173), Smith's Lodge (**2** 91), Smiths Mdw (**3** 97), Sneeps Mdw (**6** 213), Snells lane (**7** 145), Snell's Nook (**7** 147), *Snodon yarde* (**2** 75), Snow's Lodge (**4** 230), Edward Soar's Cl (**7** 252), Soars Lodge Fm (**5** 110), Great Southernwood Cl (**3** 63), *Sowters Close* (**7** 123), Sparke's Cl (**7** 175), Sparrow's Cottage (**5** 157), *Speechley's Close* (**1** 193), Spencefield Lane (**4** 44), Spencer's Brook (**6** 134), Spencers Cl (**5** 210), Spencers Cl (**6** 17), Spencers Cl (**6** 209), Spencer's Cl (**6** 101), Spencers Fm (**5** 59), *John Spencers Farme* (**4** 45), Spencers Pasture (**5** 63), Spencer St (**1** 65), *William Spreckleys cloase* (**2** 154), *Spreckley's Farm* (**2** 142), *William Sprecleys house* (**2** 152), *Spryggs gate* (**4** 41), *Mary Squires Copey* (**7** 253), *Edw. Squires hooke* (**7** 178), *Richard Stacy close* (**2** 237), *Michell Stacey House* (**2** 232), Stafford Leys (**6** 153), Henry Stamfords Leys (**4** 244), *Standleys Close* (**1** 193), *Stanleys house* (**1** 193), *Stanley's Meadow* (**1** 202), Stanley St (**1** 65), *Edward Stapleforths House* (**2** 289), *Thomas Stapleforths House* (**2** 289), Starbuck's (**6** 42), *James Starkes barne* (**7** 138), Statham Croft (**7** 81), Steel Cl (**2** 69), *Steeles close* (**2** 244), *Henry Steeles Seike* (**2** 83), *Steeles Yards end* (**2** 83), *Steevens hedge* (**5** 82), *Steeuensons Close* (**7** 178), Stevenson's Cl (**5** 30), Stevensons Mdw (**6** 271), Stimson's Cl (**7** 81), *Stockdale Terrace* (**1** 65), Henry Stokes Cl (**2** 101), Stokes Croft (**5** 84), *Storer's Almshouse* (**2** 176), *Storers House* (**2** 179), *James Storers Moult close* (**7** 142), *Alice Stringers close* (**2** 49), *Francis Stubbes his close* (**3** 149), *Sturgess' Sq* (**1** 65), Summerfields Burroughs (**6** 224), *Christofer Suttons Close* (**1** 193), Sutton's Flat (**7** 100), Sutton's Leys (**6** 24), Swainspark (**7** 20), Swains Pikes (**7** 273), *Swans Close* (**1** 193), *John Swan Sherrhoges close* (**3** 167), Swan St (**1** 65), *the Swann's Mill* (**1**

151), *William Swansons House* (**2** 289), Swingles Paddock (**4** 166), Swynfens Cl (**6** 278), Sykes Spinney (**3** 245), *Thomas Symson his Wonge* (**2** 19).

Taggs Yard (**7** 273), *Jone Taillours yard* (**1** 172), *Tailors way* (**5** 52), Talbot Lane (**7** 211), Talbot Place (**7** 280), *Tankett Sike* (**2** 124), *Tapps Close* (**6** 294), *Taskholme* (**1** 202), Taverner's Cottage Piece (**6** 13), *Tayllors Close* (**1** 194), *Tayllors farme* (**1** 181), *Taylors close* (**2** 304), *John Taylors close* (**6** 136), *Thomas Taylors close* (**3** 162), *Wm. Taylors house* (**2** 304), Taylor's Mdw (**5** 238), *Taylors penn* (**2** 49), Tealby's Fm (**5** 97), Tebbs Cl (**5** 81), *Tebbut's Square* (**1** 66), Temple Row (**1** 66), Thompson's Cl (**6** 42), *Thompson's Square* (**1** 66), *James Thomson's Farm* (**4** 45), Thornton's Cl (**5** 238), *Thornton Lane* (**1** 66), *Thomas Thorntons meadowe* (**6** 108), *William Thorps Farme* (**3** 190), *Joseph Thurlbys House* (**2** 289), Till's Cl (**6** 18), Top Tilley's (**5** 191), Tilleys Mdws (**7** 231), *Tillys Furze* (**4** 126), Timbrells Cl (**6** 325), Timson's Bit (**6** 55), Tipping's Gorse (**2** 104), Tomlins Cl (**2** 294), *Francis Tomlins House* (**2** 289), *Robert Tomlins House* (**2** 289), Tomlinsons Cl (**7** 52), Tomlinson's Park (**7** 81), Tompson's Cl (**7** 175), Tookey's Cl 38), Tookeys Garden (**3** 230), *Tookeys Orchrad* (**6** 138), Toon's Mdw (**2** 303), *Toones Farme* (**3** 154), Toones Fd (**6** 90), *James Toones House* (**2** 289), *Toones house* (**3** 55), Toone Nook (**6** 61), Toones Pasture (**7** 81), *Townsends Mill* (**1** 153), Trumans Cl (**6** 235), *Trygebarne* (**2** 19), Tryon Spinney (**3** 245), *tabernam Willhelmi Tubbe* (**1** 141), *Turners Close* (**2** 151), *Thomas Turviles house* (**6** 192), Turvilles Oaks (**6** 303), Twiggs Barn Cl (**5** 45), *Tylecoat House* (**6** 12), *Richard Typpin's Meadow* (**2** 109), *Charles Tyre House* (**2** 232).

Underwood's Cl (**7** 215), Underwood's Lodge (**3** 95).

Vann's Cl (**5** 238), Varnham's Croft (**6** 18), Varnhams Fd (**5** 70), Vendy's Old Plough (**4** 256), Verney Spinney (**5** 209), *Richard Vills Leyes* (**3** 167), *Sir George Villiers Cloase* (**2** 124), Vine St (**1** 68), Vowe's Gorse (**4** 96).

Wade Lodge (**4** 129), *Wage his close* (**3** 124), Wains Garden Cl (**6** 131), *Waites Nether Sick Leyes* (**2** 69), *John Waites Plott* (**2** 76), *Robert Wakelings Closs* (**3** 213), *Wakefields Close* (**5** 64), Wakefields Farm (**5** 60), Wale's Cl (**5** 26), Walkers Cl (**5** 233), Walkers Cl (**7** 42), *Adam Walker House* (**2** 232), *William Walkers piece* (**3** 121), *Thomas Walls Windmill* (**1** 153), *Wallets* (**2** 297), *Walsh Hall* (**1** 154), *Francis Walthoms Farm* (**2** 180), Waltons Cl (**5** 185), *John Waltons House & Vineyard* (**2** 76), *Adam Wands Beck close* (**2** 153), *Alice Wands house* (**2** 152), Wapples Six Acres (**5** 41), Ward's Cl (**4** 9), Ward's Cl (**5** 207), *William Wards Close* (**7** 89), Wards Fd (**5** 81), *Edward Wards House*

(**2** 289), *Thomas Wards house* (**6** 192), Wards Mdw (**7** 215), Wards Yard (**6** 107), Wardle's Paddock (**7** 81), *Tho. Warners Close end* (**3** 143), *Warner's Lane* (**3** 136), *Warner's lane* (**7** 131), *Warners Nursery* (**1** 179), Warrington St (**1** 68), *Wasteneyscroft* (**3** 93), *Wasteneyswod* (**7** 167), *Richard Wats close* (**2** 305), Waterman's Mdw (**3** 51), *Thomas Watkins house* (**2** 152), Watkin's Tofts (**2** 302), Watson's Fd (**5** 70), Watson's Gorse (**4** 34), *Watts's Causeway* (**1** 78), *John Waytes farme* (**2** 76), Webster's Cl (**5** 203), *Webster leys* (**5** 217), *Jo. Weightmans close* (**6** 136), *Weightmans Poole* (**5** 146), Wellengers Holt Cl (**6** 48), Wells Cl (**3** 51), Wells Cl (**5** 63), *Wenchlys ground* (**2** 57), First Whale (**5** 159), Whales Mdw (**5** 176), *Whateley meadow* (**6** 329), *Will' Whattons Farme* (**7** 190), Whatton Hill (**7** 175), *Wheat St* (**1** 69), *le Wheateley Bush close* (**2** 58), Wheatleys Magpie Spinney (**6** 324), *George Whiles Farm* (**6** 264), Whiles Wood (**6** 27), *Whites Cottage* (**3** 55), *Joseph Whites Cottage* (**4** 45), *Frances Whitels Farme* (**2** 270), Whitemans Cl (**5** 185), Whittle Hill (**7** 58), Near Whitwell (**4** 9), *Whitworth Terrace* (**1** 69), *Wigley's Arms* (P.H.) (**4** 230), Wigleys Yard (**4** 232), Hill Wignall's (**4** 206), Wigston St (**1** 69), *Wildes Close* (**7** 116), *Wilds farm* (**2** 76), Wild's Lodge (**2** 65), *Thomas Wildeges house* (**3** 278), *William Wiles House* (**2** 289), *Hannah Wilfords House* (**2** 289), *Wilkinses Close* (**1** 195), Wilkins Lane (**7** 67), Willey's Biggin (**5** 236), *Thomas Williams House* (**2** 289), *Henry Williamsons House* (**2** 289), *John Willowes close* (**2** 305), *Willowes Caudhill* (**2** 303), *Willowes Tofte* (**2** 305), *Wm. Willsforth close* (**2** 88), Wilson Arms (P.H.) (**3** 5), *Wilsons Lower Closes* (**4** 158), *Willsons meade* (**7** 241), *Thos. Wilmots Homestal* (**2** 151), Winfield's Lane (**3** 276), *Withers Farm* (**1** 181), Witseys (**5** 159), Wollertons Cl (**2** 61), Wood's Hill (**2** 51), Woodcock Fm (**7** 187), *Willyam Woodcockes yardes ende* (**4** 72), Joseph Woodford's Farm (**7** 252), Woodford's Mdw (**5** 203), *Wootons Wonge* (**7** 124), Worledge's Cl (**7** 81), *Robert Wormhills House* (**2** 289), Wormleightons Cl (**5** 101), Wormleighton's Fd (**5** 30), *Worrals Close* (**1** 195), *Thomas Worsdales Cloase* (**2** 20), *Thomas Worsdale his Wonge* (**2** 20), Wrask Fm (**6** 195), *Wrights close* (**2** 49), *John Wrights Close* (**6** 231), *Edward Wrights layes* (**2** 49), Wrights Mdw (**6** 126), Wyatt's Cl (**6** 18), *Wyattes Pen* (**5** 192), *Tho. Wyldes Cottage* (**3** 214), *Wylde Lease* (**1** 205), *Wylliam Wylfordes Closse* (**2** 88), *Wymbisshwong* (**2** 33), *Wyngerplace* (**1** 156).

York Castle (P.H.) (**1** 141).

The Names of Identified Persons in Field-Names with *headland* and *headley* in Glebe Terriers 1600–1745

The usual three great open-fields of a Leicestershire township were cultivated with the selions or strips in the furlongs having been allocated to villagers by lot to provide an equal spread of fertile ground. The headlands to these strips were principally used for turning the ploughs. Surviving headland names in Glebe Terriers present a range of the personal names of identified individuals given in the possessive case. Just how lasting such field-names were is uncertain since presumably the system of allocation by lot if annually carried out would have disrupted continuity of such a name in a particular location. Such instances as *Jane Bates's Headland* (**4** 189) and *William Paynes Headland* (**4** 193) repeated in the Medbourne terriers of 1697, 1700, 1703, c.1710, 1724 and 1762 are unique in Leicestershire archives and no doubt are the result of uncritical copying of terriers over some sixty-five years. The headlands of those folk of some social standing in their townships are generally styled as, for example, *Mr Hubberts Hadland* (**3** 203) or *Mr Law's Hadland* (**3** 141). Such individuals, together with widows as in *Widdowe Kirbyes hadland* (**3** 67) are rarely to be identified, as are those villagers only represented by their surnames, as in *Nuttalls hadland* (**3** 17) and *Walkers hadland* (**3** 143).

Similar names, but with *headley*, occur with far less frequency than those with *headland*. They appear to refer to headlands swarded over. Whether these were sometimes headlands of a great open-field which was left fallow for a particular year or whether they were occasionally grassed headlands in fields under cultivation is uncertain. In some instances, the terms *headland* and *headley* may have been used interchangeably. Such instances as *Thomas Gauthernes hadlaye* (**3** 140), *Tom Buggs Head Ley* (**2** 267), *Thomas Davenports grass hadley* (**5** 168), *John Perkins grasse hadland* (**5** 170), *Sumpters hadleae of grasse* (**4** 42) and *Ric. Niccolles ley-hadland* (**5** 20) are various alternative styles of their representation.

Villagers only identified in such ephemeral *headland* and *headley* names may otherwise be forgotten and for that reason the individuals recorded in these field-names are presented here.

Edward Allen (**5** 214), James Allen (**5** 214), Ralph Allen (**5** 214), John Andrews (**5** 167), George Ashby (**3** 147).

Richard Banbury (**5** 159), Sir Robert Banester (**3** 147), Thomas Barker (**5** 214), William Barnes (**3** 97), Jane Bates (**4** 189), John Bates

(**4** 84), Thomas Bates (**5** 167), John Bend (**2** 197), Thomas Bend (**2** 197), William Bend (**2** 197), George Bent (**6** 189), John Bent (**5** 214), Thomas Bent (**6** 189), Joseph Bentley (**3** 138), George Berrington (**7** 85), Thomas Berry (**4** 84), George Black (**2** 229), Valentine Blockley (**5** 119), George Bowley (**7** 85), Thomas Bowley (**7** 85), William Bowley (**7** 85), William Boyer (**5** 85), William Brabson (**5** 226), Robert Bradshaw (**6** 319), Thomas Brandard (**5** 167), Jane Bray (**6** 248), James Brett (**3** 117), Robert Brewin (**4** 161), John Brown (**5** 167), John Brown (**7** 245), Francis Brown(e) (**2** 42), Henry Brown(e) (**2** 48), John Brown(e) (**7** 166), Robert Brown(e) (**2** 48), William Brown(e) (**5** 119), Thomas Brudnell (**4** 256), John Buck (**3** 166), Tom Bugg (**2** 267), John Bull (**4** 84), Francis Burbage (**7** 176), John Burbage (**3** 97), John Burgess (**5** 214), William Burman (**6** 314), William Burnby (**2** 303), John Burney (**5** 211), William Buttery (**3** 139), Fulk Button (**5** 119), Thomas Buzzard (**4** 39).

John Calcroft (**2** 27), William Cant (**6** 135), Rafe Cart (**6** 319), John Cartwright (**5** 168), Sir Alexander Cave (**3** 123), Thomas Cave (**5** 151), John Chamberlin (**5** 108), Nan Chamberlin (**3** 147), Thomas Chamberlyn (**3** 139), Thomas Chawner (**7** 86), William Chawner (**7** 86), John Clark(e) (**3** 147), John Clark(e) (**5** 36), John Clark(e) (**5** 168), Richard Clark(e) (**5** 145), Thomas Clark(e) (**4** 40), William Clark(e) (**5** 168), Luke Coates (**2** 276), William Cobley (**4** 243), Leonard Coleman (**4** 40), John Cooper (**4** 40).

Thomas Davenport (**5** 168), Job Dexter (**4** 40), Sir Wolstan Dixie (**6** 173), William Dowell (**6** 326), James Dring (**2** 34), Francis Duckett (**5** 46).

Thomas Elkinton (**5** 185), Edward Ellis (**6** 179), Thomas Everard (**6** 315), John Exton (**7** 86).

Matthew Fielding (**3** 211), Thomas Findley (**5** 215), John Forrest (**2** 28), William Freckingham (**2** 198), George Freeman (**7** 86), William Freer (**5** 36), John French (**4** 68), Thomas Fulforth (**3** 16).

William Gadd (**7** 130), Thomas Gautherne (**3** 140), Edward George (**2** 113), William Gilbert (**6** 190), Francis Gollin(s) (**2** 107), James Goodman (**3** 83), John Gowerton (**2** 113), Leonard Green (**2** 229), William Green (**2** 229), John Gregory (**6** 190), William Gregory (**3** 13), Thomas Grin (**6** 315), Richard Gumley (**5** 81).

John Hackstall (**7** 120), Andrew Halford (**7** 120), Thomas Hall (**5** 120), William Hall (**5** 186), Edward Hands (**5** 186), Thomas Harley (**7** 167), Thomas Harman (**7** 87), Miles Harper (**4** 181), John Harriman (**7** 87), Thomas Hartopp (**2** 73), Edward Hartshorn (**7** 87), Hugh Hartshorn

(**7** 114), Peter Harvey (**7** 121), William Hawes (**3** 140), John Hayne (**3** 195), Robert Hayne (**3** 195), George Henton (**3** 118), William Henton (**3** 118), William Henton (Junior) (**3** 118), Thomas Hickling (**2** 114), William Hill (**6** 315), Thomas Horton (**4** 227), Nicholas Houghton (**3** 212), Roger House (**2** 18), Sir Scroop How (**2** 268), John Humberston (**3** 16), Edmond Hutchins (**4** 257).

Thomas Iliff(e) (**4** 136), Edward Iliff(e) (**4** 136), John Iliff(e) (**5** 169), Richard Iliff(e) (**4** 136), Robert Iliff(e) (**5** 169), Thomas Iliff(e) (**5** 120), William Iremonger (**7** 53).

Thomas Jackson (**5** 229), Thomas James (**3** 118), William James (**3** 118), John Johnson (**4** 227), Robert Jordain (**5** 169).

William Kellam (**3** 16), Henry Kemp (**3** 148), Jonathan Kerby (**5** 145), Thomas Kerby (**5** 145), Robert Kilby (**3** 195), Thomas Killpack (**5** 56), John King (**6** 326), Matthew King (**3** 119), Thomas King (**4** 241), George Knowles (**7** 121).

Charles Laken (**6** 320), Randle Laken (**6** 320), Robert Langdale (**7** 87), John Lea (**3** 195), Henry Lester (**7** 87), Job Lester (**4** 41), Robert Lilly (**7** 121), William Love (**3** 16), Henry Lowth (**4** 78).

John Martin (**5** 216), George Matthew (**2** 115), John Meadow(s) (**5** 170), William Mee (**7** 54), William Merriman (**7** 122), Jack Milner (**3** 16), John Morrice (**3** 17), William Morris (**2** 115), William Mouldsworth (**3** 204).

Robert Neal (**2** 115), Thomas Newton (**6** 286), Richard Nicoll (**5** 120), Thomas Noon (**5** 120).

Thomas Oram (**5** 46), William Orgill (**7** 122), George Orton (**3** 219), John Orton (**6** 320).

Richard Patchett (**2** 269), William Paybody (**5** 16), William Paine (**4** 193), Katherine Palmer (**7** 88), Nathaniel Palmer (**7** 88), William Palmer (**2** 115), Robert Parsons (**7** 88), Thomas Parsons (**7** 88), Francis Pawley (**5** 229), Robert Peale (**7** 88), John Perkin(s) (**5** 170), Sir Ambrose Phillips (**7** 88), James Pick (**3** 119), Sir Edward Pickering (**4** 41), Richard Plummer (**5** 170), John Pratt (**5** 216).

James Quick (**3** 84).

William Randon (**7** 122), John Raven (**2** 108), John Raynor (**6** 191), Christopher Read (**2** 116), Hugh Rest (**2** 199), Edward Rimmington (**2** 108), Bryan Robinson (**2** 116), Richard Rowse (**2** 269).

Thomas Sanderson (**5** 216), John Savage (**7** 89), Richard Sharp(e) (**3** 84), William Sharp(e) (**2** 116), Sir Robert Shirley (**3** 195), William Simpson (**2** 49), Richard Sketchley (**6** 320), Edward Smart (**6** 303), John Smith (**3** 213), Richard Smith (**5** 47), John Sowter (**7** 123), Ralph Sowter (**7** 123), Edward Spencer (**4** 244), William Spick (**2** 161),

Edward Squiers (**7** 178), William Squiers (**7** 178), Thomas Stableford (**3** 213), Adrian Stables (**7** 178), Richard Stables (**7** 178), William Stanley (**5** 217), Robert Steel (**2** 116), Robert Stokes (**2** 161), Francis Stubbs (**3** 149), John Sumner (**2** 116), John Sutton (**7** 123).

John Taylour (**3** 143), Matthew Taylour (**3** 149), John Thomas (**6** 326), John Throne (**7** 89), Thomas Throne (**7** 89), Thomas Titterton (**7** 89), Joseph Tomlinson (**7** 89), John Tooley (**5** 171), John Towers (**2** 117).

Thomas Veroe (**2** 117).

John Wakelin (**3** 213), Henry Walford (**6** 326), William Walker (**2** 244), William Wall (**7** 78), William Ward (**7** 89), Thomas Warner (**3** 143), John Webster (**5** 217), Anthony Weston (**3** 271), Elizabeth Whitmore (**5** 217), Richard Wight (**7** 116), William Wild (**7** 116), George Wilford (**2** 88), Richard Wilkin (**3** 69), William Wilson (**3** 143), Edward Winterton (**5** 121), William Wood (**5** 186), Austin Woodkeep (**2** 305), William Wooton (**7** 124), William Worsdale (**2** 20), Robert Wright (**5** 46), William Wright (**2** 255).

Church Dedications

All Saints: Asfordby, Beeby, Blaby, Cadeby, Cossington, Dunton Bassett, East Norton, Gilmorton, Hoby, Husbands Bosworth, Isley Walton, Keyham, Kimcote, Kirkby Mallory, Knipton, Leicester, Long Whatton, Loughborough, Lowesby, Lubenham, Nailstone, Narborough, Newtown Linford, Othorpe, Peatling Magna, Pickwell, Ragdale, Ratcliffe Culey, Rotherby, Sapcote, Scraptoft, Seagrave, Shawell, Sheepy Magna, Somerby, Swinford, Theddingworth, Thorpe Acre, Thurcaston, Thurlaston.
Christ Church: Coalville, Leicester, Smeeton Westerby.
Holy Rood: Bagworth, Packington.
Holy Trinity: Ashby de la Zouch, Barrow upon Soar, Buckminster, Hinckley, Leicester, Normanton le Heath, Norton iuxta Twycross, Staunton Harold, Thrussington.
St Andrew: Aylestone, Burton Overy, Carlton, Coston, Countesthorpe, Foxton, Great Easton, Kegworth, North Kilworth, Owston, Peatling Parva, Prestwold, Thringstone, Tur Langton, Twyford, Welham.
St Bartholomew: Kirby Muxloe, Quorndon, Snarestone, Sproxton, Welby.
St Botolph: Ratcliffe on the Wreake, Shepshed, Sibson.
St Catherine: Burbage, Houghton on the Hill.
St Cuthbert: Great Glen.
St Denys: Eaton, Evington, Goadby Marwood, Ibstock, Stonton Wyville.
St Dionysius: Market Harborough.
St Edith: Orton on the Hill.
St Edward King and Martyr: Castle Donington.
St Egelwin the Martyr: Scalford.
St George: Leicester, Swannington.
St Giles: Barlestone, Blaston, Medbourne, Stretton Magna.
St Guthlac: Branston, Stathern.
St Helen: Ashby de la Zouch, Gumley, Plungar, Saddington, Sharnford.
St Hilda: Moira.
St James: Ab Kettleby, Birstall, Burton Lazars, Charley, Coalville, Dadlington, Drayton, Huncote, Little Dalby, Newbold Verdon, Sutton Cheney, Twycross.
St John: Aldeby, Enderby, Goadby, Grimston, Rolleston.
St John the Baptist: Belton, Billesdon, Buckminster, Cold Newton, Croxton Kerrial, Enderby, Glooston, Heather, Hugglescote, Hungarton,

King's Norton, Little Stretton, Muston, Old Dalby, South Croxton, Whitwick.
St John the Evangelist: Shenton, Thurmaston.
St Leonard: Holwell, Horton, Leicester, Misterton, Swithland.
St Luke: Gaddesby, Laughton, Newton Harcourt, Thurnby.
St Maragaret: Blackfordby, Leicester, Stoke Golding.
St Martin: Desford, Leicester, Stapleford.
St Mary: Anstey, Ashby Folville, Ashby Magna, Barkby, Barwell, Bitteswell, Bottesford, Brentingby, Broughton Astley, Bruntingthorpe, Burrough on the Hill, Carlton Curlieu, Chadwell, Coleorton, Cotesbach, Elmesthorpe, Freeby, Garthorpe, Great Bowden, Harby, Hinckley, Humberstone, Leicester, Lutterworth, Melton Mowbray, Nether Broughton, Nevill Holt, Noseley, Osgathorpe, Potters Marston, Queniborough, Snibstone, Stoughton, Thorpe Arnold, Walton on the Wolds, Wigston Parva, Willoughby Waterleys, Wyfordby, Wymeswold.
St Mary and All Saints: Stanton under Bardon.
St Mary and St Hardulph: Breedon on the Hill.
St Mary and St Nicholas: Wanlip.
St Mary and St John the Baptist: Rothley.
St Mary Magdalene: Kilby, Knighton, Peckleton, Shearsby, Stapleford, Waltham on the Wolds.
St Mary the Virgin: Shackerstone, Sileby.
St Matthew: Overseal, Worthington.
St Michael: Appleby Magna, Brooksby, Cosby, Cranoe, Croft, Diseworth, Fenny Drayton, Hallaton, Harby, Illston on the Hill, Ravenstone, Rearsby, Stoney Stanton, Stretton en le Field, Thorpe Satchville, Thurmaston, Wartnaby.
St Michael and All Angels: Edmondthorpe, Harston, Loddington.
St Nicholas: Bringhurst, Fleckney, Frolesworth, Knaptoft, Leicester, Little Bowden, Lockington, Mowsley, Shangton, South Kilworth.
St Paul: Woodhouse.
St Peter: Allexton, Arnesby, Ashby Parva, Aston Flamville, Bardon, Belgrave, Braunstone, Church Langton, Claybrooke Parva, Galby, Glenfield, Hathern, Higham on the Hill, Horninghold, Kirby Bellars, Knossington, Leire, Market Bosworth, Markfield, Mountsorrel, Netherseal, Oadby, Saltby, Saxby, Saxelby, Shackerstone, Stockerston, Stonesby, Swepstone, Syston, Thornton, Tilton on the Hill, Whetstone, Witherley, Wymondham.
St Peter and St Paul: Barkestone.
St Philip and St James: Groby, Ratby.

St Remigius: Long Clawson.
St Simon and St Jude: Earl Shilton.
St Swithin: Great Dalby.
St Thomas: Catthorpe, Glen Parva, Willesley.
St Thomas à Becket: Frisby on the Wreake, Skeffington, Tugby.
St Wilfred: Kibworth Beauchamp.
St Wistan: Wigston Magna, Wistow.

Lost churches in the Borough of Leicester recorded in 1220 in the Matriculus of Hugh de Welles are those dedicated to **St Clement** (**1** 83) and **St Peter** (**1** 87). The parish church of Newbold Verdon now dedicated to **St James** is earlier recorded as *ecclesiam parochiali Sancte Marie* 1485 (**6** 195) while that of Stoney Stanton now dedicated to **St Michael** is earlier recorded as *ecclesie Sancti Petri* 1312 (**6** 83).

Sacred Springs and Wells

The grouped instances are presented by date in order of recording.

Annwell 1550 (**2** 65, Burton Lazars)
St An Hill (?) 1625 (**6** 171, Market Bosworth)
St Annes Well 1638 (**4** 37, East Langton)
Annie well c.1638 (**2** 143, Wyfordby)

Croswell 1467 × 84 (**3** 26, Barkby)
Cross-well m.18 (**6** 172, Market Bosworth)

*Haliwell*e l.12 (**7** 146, Nanpantan)
Haliwelle m.13 (1404) (**3** 90, Kirby Bellars)
Halywell 1279 (**5** 184, Shawell)
Halywell 1347 (**7** 17, Prestop)
Halywell 1467 × 84 (**3** 241, Thurmaston)
Halywell 1487 (**7** 90, Rothley)
le holywell 1477 (e.16) (**3** 146, Hungarton)
Holiewell 1606 (**4** 33, Cranoe)
Holywell 1615 (**7** 8, Ashby de la Zouch)
Holy Well 1811 (**6** 222, Ratby)

Ladywell 1605 (**3** 148, Hungarton)
Ladywell 1709 (**5** 216, Whetstone)
Lady Well 1776 (**4** 175, Market Harborough)
Our Lady's Well 1798 (**4** 204, Nevill Holt)
Lady Well 1840 (**6** 184, Nailstone)

St Morrills well 1601 (**4** 104, Hallaton)

Sevenewelles c.1280 (**6** 214, Kirkby Mallory)
Seuenewell 1343 (**4** 183, Great Bowden)
Schowell 1477 (e.16) (**7** 106, Lockington)
Showell 1601 (**5** 15, Ashby Parva)
Seaven well 1625 (**6** 318, Orton on the Hill)
Seaven Wells 1694 (**4** 167, Lubenham)
Senwells 1841 (**7** 81, Coleorton)

Medieval and Early Modern Parks

Medieval parks here are those initially recorded c.1140 to c.1485 and Early Modern parks those between 1525 and 1575.

Leicester Borough

Abbey 1553 (**1** 223)
Beaumont 1341 (e.16) (**1** 223)
Bird's Nest c.1545 (**1** 223)
Old Park 1517 (**3** 52)

Framland Hundred

Burton Lazars 1300 (**2** 64)
Croxton Kerrial 1189 (**2** 103)
Eye Kettleby 1541 (**2** 190)
New Park, Belvoir 1525 (**2** 9)
Old Park, Belvoir 1343 (**2** 8)
Orgerpark, Melton Mowbray 1400 (**2** 186)
Thorpe Arnold 1325 (1449) (**2** 280)
Wymondham 1462 (**2** 295)

East Goscote Hundred

Barrow upon Soar 1139 × 47 (**3** 37)
Gaddesby 1559 (**3** 96)
Launde 1375 (**3** 161)

Gartree Hundred

Cold Overton 1218 (**4** 152)
Evington 1335 (**4** 44)
Old Park, Noseley 1544 (**4** 20)
Powers Park, Great Easton 1486 (**4** 74)

Guthlaxton Hundred

Kimcote 1467 × 84 (**5** 121)

Sparkenhoe Hundred

Bagworth 1308 × 27 (**6** 25)
Bardon 1270 (**6** 35)
Barron Park, Newtown Unthank 1360 (**6** 79)
Burghpark, Ratby 1343 (**6** 225)
Kirby Muxloe 1525 (**6** 152)

Newhall Park, Thurlaston 1373 (**6** 299)
Tooley Park, Peckleton 1373 (**6** 206)

West Goscote Hundred

Beaumanor Park, Woodhouse 1477 (e.16) (**7** 248)
Bradgate Park, Newtown Linford 1292 (**7** 156)
Breedon on the Hill 1309 (**7** 39)
Burleigh Park, Nanpantan c.1545 (**7** 147)
Donington Park, Castle Donington 1229 (**7** 48)
Garendon 1282 (**7** 141)
Great Park, Ashby de la Zouch 1575 (**7** 13)
Great Park, Belton 1440 (**7** 27)
Isley Walton 1543 (**7** 95)
Rothley 1270 (**7** 191)
Whitwick 1327 (**7** 73)

Inn and Tavern Names reflective of Leicestershire's Social and Industrial History and Locales

Abbey Inn (Leicester): named from St Mary de Pratis Abbey, Leicester.

(Whitwick): named from Mount St Bernard Abbey in adjoining Charley parish.

Ashby Arms (Hungarton): Shuckbrugh Ashby (d.1792) rebuilt a large part of Hungarton village, while W. W. Ashby of Quenby Hall was Lord of the Manor of Hungarton in 1846.

Bakers' Arms (Thorpe Langton): Thomas Smith, mine host 1846–63, was also a baker; typical of a nineteenth-century tavern keeper's dual occupations.

Bath Inn (Shearsby); located at the former Shearsby Spa.

Beaumont Arms (Coleorton): Coleorton Hall was built 1804–08 for Sir George Beaumont, a friend of William Wordsworth.

(Whitwick): Sir George Beaumont of Coleorton Hall was a major landowner here in 1846.

Belvoir Castle (Leicester): named from the castle, the seat of the Duke of Rutland, the county's senior aristocrat.

Boot (Houghton on the Hill): Thomas Webster, mine host in 1846, was also a bootmaker; typical of a nineteenth-century tavern keeper's dual occupations.

Bowling Green (Measham): located beside the early bowling green of 1823.

Bradgate Arms (Cropston): alluding to Bradgate, the former home of Lady Jane Grey, queen of England in 1553.

(Newtown Linford): as above.

Bricklayers' Arms (Bagworth): William Dikes, mine host in 1863, was also a bricklayer; another example of a tavern keeper's dual occupations in this period.

(Donington le Heath): John Neal, mine host in 1877, was also a builder.

Butchers' Arms (Husbands Bosworth): Francis Groocock, husband of the tenant Lucy Groocock in 1846, was a butcher.

Cardigan Arms (Cranoe): the Earl of Cardigan was Lord of the Manor in 1863.

Carington Arms (Ashby Folville): Francis, Lord Carington, founded The Almshouse here in 1673 for seven poor men, while F.H. Carington Smith-Carington was Lord of the Manor in 1925.

Cave's Arms (Donisthorpe): Sir John Browne Cave owned a great part of the parish in 1835.
Cave's Inn (Shawell): named from Edward Cave, an eighteenth-century landlord.
Chamberlayne Arms (Blaston): Thomas Chamberlayne of Horninghold was a major landowner here in 1846.
Chandlers' Arms (Shearsby): Richard Bottrill, mine host in 1846, was also a chandler.
Cheney Arms (Ashby Folville): Edward Hawkins Cheney of Gaddesby Hall was a major landowner here in 1877.
(Gaddesby): Edward Hawkins Cheney was the principal landowner of the parish in 1877.
Cinquefoil (Leicester): the cinquefoil has been the centrepiece of Leicester's coat of arms since at least 1343.
Cradock Arms (Knighton): Sir Edmund Cradock Hartopp was Lord of the Manor in 1807, while the Reverend Edward H. Cradock of Brasenose College, Oxford, was Lord of the Manor in 1877.
Crispin's Arms (Leicester): Crispin was the patron saint of cobblers and shoemakers and Leicester a centre for footwear manufacture in the nineteenth century, with 200 such tradesmen recorded here in 1846.
Curzon Arms (Twycross): named from the Hon. Captain Frederick Curzon of Twycross, 1877.
(Woodhouse): W. M. Curzon-Herrick was Lord of the Manor and chief landowner of the parish in 1925.
Daniel Lambert (Leicester): Daniel Lambert (1770–1809) was a former keeper of Leicester town jail who eventually toured the country making money by exhibiting his huge bulk. At his death he weighed 53 stones.
De Lisle Arms (Shepshed): Ambrose de Lisle was Lord of the Manor in 1877.
Denbigh Arms (Lutterworth): the Earls of Denbigh were Lords of the Manor in the nineteenth century.
Dixie Arms (Market Bosworth): Sir Wolstan Dixie, Lord Mayor of London, bought the manor in 1567 and founded the Free Grammar School here in 1593. Sir Willoughby Dixie was Lord of the Manor in 1846.
Duke of Rutland (Hinckley): named from the county's senior aristocrat.
(Leicester): as above.
Dysart Arms (Buckminster): Buckminster Park was the seat of the Earls of Dysart.

Earl de Grey's Arms (Burbage): Countess de Grey founded the National School in the village in 1825.

Earl of Stamford's Arms (Leicester): named from the Parliamentarian general of the English Civil War. Leicester was held for Parliament against King Charles I during the war and the siege of 1645. The earl was 2nd Baron Grey of Groby in 1614 and then Earl of Stamford in 1628.

Engine (Ullesthorpe): relating to the adjacent former Midland Counties Railway.

Ferrers' Arms (Staunton Harold): the Rt. Hon. S. E. Shirley, 10th Earl Ferrers and Viscount Tamworth was Lord of the Manor in the nineteenth century.

Fish and Quart (Leicester): patronized by the porters of Leicester's fish market who traditionally drank their ale from quart pots.

Foundry Arms (Leicester): in Foundry Lane; cf. Iron Founders' Arms *infra*.

Fox and Hounds (Witherley): a traditional inn name, but established here in response to the stables and kennels built in Witherley c.1835 for the Atherstone Hunt.

Freeman's Arms (Leicester): named from the status of Freeman of Leicester, originating in the late twelfth century.

Granby Inn (Bottesford): named from the Marquis of Granby, heir of the Duke of Rutland, *v.* **Marquis of Granby** *infra*.

Granby's Head (Walton on the Wolds): as for the **Granby Inn** *supra*.

Graziers' Arms (Husbands Bosworth): nineteen graziers are listed for Husbands Bosworth in White's Directory of 1877.

Great Central (Loughborough): named from the former Great Central Railway which opened in 1899.

Harborough Arms (Melton Mowbray): named after the Earls of Harborough of Stapleford Hall.

Hartopp Arms (Gumley): Sir Edmund Cradock Hartopp was Lord of the Manor and principal landowner of Gumley in 1846.

Hastings Arms (Ashby de la Zouch): William, Lord Hastings, Edward IV's Lord Chamberlain, was granted the manor of Ashby in 1464, obtained licence to crenellate its castle in 1474 and was beheaded at the behest of Richard III in 1483.

(Breedon on the Hill): Sir Charles Hastings was a major landowner in Breedon in 1846.

(Coalville): the Marquis of Hastings was Lord of the Manor in 1846.

(Ibstock): the Marquis of Hastings was a major landowner here in 1846.

Heanor Boat (Leicester): named from the canal narrow boats which brought coal from Heanor and district in the Derbyshire coalfield to Leicester by way of the Soar Navigation, following the river's canalization.
Heathcote Arms (Croft): the Reverend R. B. Heathcote was a major landowner in the parish in 1863.
Hercules (Sutton Cheney): named from the Hercules monument in adjacent Bosworth Park.
Hermitage Inn (Whitwick): named from the famous ancient hermitage in nearby Shepshed parish.
Howe Arms (Twycross): Earl Howe was Lord of the Manor in 1846 and the occupier of neighbouring Gopsall Hall.
Iron Founders' Arms (Leicester): located near Court and Co.'s Foundry north of Belgrave Gate; cf. the **Foundry Arms** *supra*.
John o' Gaunt (Twyford): John of Gaunt (d. 1399) was a major landowner in Leicestershire. His second wife, Constance of Castile, was buried in the Collegiate Church of The Newarke, Leicester.
Keck's Arms (Leicester): Anthony James Keck was M.P. for Leicester in 1765, while George Anthony Leigh Keck was a Freeman of Leicester in 1800.
King Richard III (Leicester): the king was buried in Leicester in the chancel of church of the Grey Friars after his death at the Battle of Bosworth in 1485. His body was discovered in excavations at the friary site in 2012 and reinterred in St Martin's Cathedral, Leicester.
Lancaster Arms (Desford): King George V, in right of the Duchy of Lancaster, was Lord of the Manor of Desford.
Lord Bassett Arms (Sapcote): the Bassetts were Lords of the Manor of Sapcote; note William Bassett, lord of Sapcote and Sheriff of Leicestershire in 1163.
Loudoun Arms (Measham): named from Edith Rawdon-Hastings, Countess of Loudoun and wife of Lord Donington.
(Wilson): as above. The village school was erected by Lord Donington in 1877 in memory of his wife Edith.
Magazine (Leicester): named from the fifteenth-century gatehouse of The Newarke, Leicester, which was called the Magazine Gate; it was used to store the town's arms and ammunition during the siege of Leicester of 1645 in the Civil War.
Mansfield's Head (Leicester): John Mansfield was Mayor of Leicester in 1815 and M.P. for the town in 1818.
Marquis of Granby (Aylestone): the title of the heir of the Duke of Rutland. John Manners, Marquis of Granby 1721–70, was leader of the

victorious cavalry charge against the French at Warburg in 1760. He was Commander-in-Chief of the British Army in 1766. A national hero, many inns and taverns were named after him.

(Birstall): as above.

(Great Glen): as above.

(Hinckley): as above.

(Leicester): as above.

(Loughborough): as above.

(Melton Mowbray): as above.

(Whitwick): as above.

Note also **Granby Inn** and **Granby's Head** *supra*.

Maynard Arms (Bagworth): in 1761, Baron Maynard founded the building and endowment of a village school for Bagworth. In 1846, Viscount Maynard was patron of the Vicarage and owner of its revenues.

Mercers Arms (Hinckley): in 1666, mine host was John Cave, also a mercer.

Midland Railway (Syston): named from the former Midland Counties Railway.

Moira Arms (Moira): the Earl of Moira developed mining of local coal c.1800 and was chief promoter of the Ashby de la Zouch Canal which opened in 1804.

Moira Arms Inn (Castle Donington): as above.

Moore's Arms (Norton juxta Twycross): George Moore was a major landowner in Norton in 1846.

Munday Arms (Loughborough): Mrs Ann Munday of Bower Cottage, Loughborough, is listed among 'the gentry' in White's Directory of 1846.

Navigation (Kibworth Harcourt): named with reference to the Grand Union Canal, 1846.

(Leicester): located adjacent to the Leicester Navigation Canal, 1846.

Navigation Inn (Ashby de la Zouch): named with reference to the Ashby de la Zouch Canal.

(Kegworth): alluding to the canalization of the river Soar at Kegworth and beyond.

(Moira): named with reference to the Ashby de la Zouch Canal, as above.

Nevill Arms (Medbourne): Charles Nevill of Nevill Holt was Lord of the Manor of Medbourne in 1846.

Newarke Tavern (Leicester): adjacent to The Newarke, the fourteenth-century new 'work' or walled enclosure with towers and gatehouse.
Old Bowling Green (Leicester): named from the former bowling green on the Horse Fair site.
Old Three Cranes (Kegworth): Robert Crane, who was mine host in 1846, had altered the name of the tavern by 1863 from the Old Three Crowns to reflect his ownership.
Packe Arms (Hoton): C. W. Packe was Lord of the Manor of Hoton in 1846.
Paget Arms (Loughborough): named from the Paget family of Nanpantan Hall.
(Lubenham): Thomas Tertius Paget was Lord of the Manor of Lubenham in 1877.
Palmer's Arms (Owston): Frederick Palmer of Withcote Hall was Lord of the Manor in 1863.
Peacock (Croxton Kerrial): alluding to the peacock as part of the coat of arms of the Manners family, the Dukes of Rutland, of Belvoir Castle.
(Loughborough): as above.
(Lutterworth): as above.
(Market Harborough): as above.
(Melton Mowbray): as above.
(Syston): as above.
Peacock Inn (Belvoir): as above.
(Redmile): as above.
Porter's Lodge (Leicester): formerly the lodge at the entrance to the Earl of Huntingdon's house in the old Swinesmarket, Leicester.
Railway (Coalville): originally the ticket office of the former Leicester and Burton Branch Railway.
(Glenfield): named from the Leicester and Swannington Railway.
(Leicester): at the former railway station in Campbell St which preceded the London Road Station.
Railway Arms (Kibworth Beauchamp): named from the Leicester and Hitchin Branch Railway.
Railway Inn (Albert Village): named from the former Leicester and Burton Branch Railway.
(Barrow upon Soar): named from the former Midland Railway.
(Great Easton): named from the former Rugby and Stamford Railway; located at the disused Rockingham Station.
(Kirby Muxloe): named from the former Leicester and Swannington Railway.

(Leicester): at the terminus of the former Leicester and Swannington Railway near West Bridge.

(Mountsorrel): named from the former Mount Sorrel Railway, a mineral line connecting the quarries to the former Midland Counties Railway.

(Ratby): named from the former Leicester and Swannington Railway.

(Sileby): named from the former Midland Counties Railway.

(Swannington): named from the former Leicester and Burton Branch Railway.

Railway Tavern (Ashby de la Zouch): named from the former Leicester and Burton Branch Railway.

(Loughborough): named from the former Midland Counties Railway.

(Worthington): named from the former Midland Railway whose extension in 1874 passed through Worthington parish.

Rawdon (Castle Donington): from Francis Rawdon, Earl of Moira, who was Lord of the Manor of Ashby de la Zouch and a developer of the Ashby de la Zouch Canal and the Leicestershire coalfield.

Rawdon Arms (Moira): as above.

Reservoir Inn (Cropston): named from the large reservoir in the parish.

Roundheads Inn (Leicester): Leicester was held for Parliament against King Charles I during the Civil War and the siege of 1645; the forces of their supporters were popularly known as Roundheads and Cavaliers respectively.

Royal Red Gate Inn (Fenny Drayton): styled ‘royal’ because Queen Adelaide, widow of King William IV, stayed here on her occasional visits to Earl Howe of Gopsall Hall in Twycross. ‘Red Gate’ is of uncertain origin. Possible is an otherwise unrecorded alternative name for Fenn Lanes, alluding to the clays hereabouts, with ‘gate’ in its local sense ‘road’.

Rutland Arms (Bottesford): alluding to the Dukes of Rutland of Belvoir Castle.

(Hoby): as above.

(Knipton): as above.

(Leicester): as above.

(Loughborough): as above.

(Melton Mowbray): as above.

Spade Tree Inn (Swepstone): locally, a ‘spade-tree’ was the handle of a spade; a former landlord was a maker of these.

Square and Compass (Snarestone): Richard Roberts, mine host in 1846, was also a joiner.

Stamford and Warrington Arms (Breedon on the Hill): the Earl of Stamford and Warrington of Bradgate Hall, Groby, was Lord of the Manor in 1863.

(Coalville): also named from the Earl of Stamford and Warrington who was a major landowner in Coalville.

Stamford Arms (Groby): the Earl of Stamford and Warrington was Lord of the Manor in 1846.

Station (Broughton Astley): named from Broughton Station on the former Midland Counties Railway.

(Loughborough): named from the local halt on the former Midland Counties Railway.

Station Inn (Swannington): named from a halt on the former Leicester and Burton Branch Railway.

Tailors' Arms (Leicester): named from *the Company of the Taylers of the Burrough of Leicester* of 1689. There have been two instances of this hostelry name in the town.

Talbot Arms (Whitwick): a fourteenth-century effigy, supposedly of Sir John Talbot (1325–65) of Swannington, lies in the parish church.

Talbot Inn (Swannington): named from the Talbot family. William Talbot was lord of Swannington manor in 1278, the property remaining with the Talbots until the death of Sir John Talbot in 1365.

Union (Glen Parva): a bargeman's tavern on the former Union Canal, now the Grand Union Canal.

Vauxhall Wharf (Leicester): named from Leicester's own Vauxhall Gardens of the late eighteenth century, an imitation of London's well-known pleasure resort of the mid seventeenth century at Vauxhall.

Wentworth Arms (Elmesthorpe): Lady Noel Byron, Baroness Wentworth, financed the improvement of land here by drainage in 1863.

(Kirkby Mallory): Thomas Noel, Viscount Wentworth (d. 1815) was Lord of the Manor.

Wigley's Arms (Scraptoft): named from the Wigley family of Scraptoft Hall, as Sir Edward Wigley (d. 1710) and James Wigley (d. 1765).

Windmill Inn (Redmile): named from Redmile Windmill, recorded 1846.

Woodboy (Leicester): probably with a name via Woodboy Street from young gatherers of firewood or 'woodboys' in Abbey Park.

Woolcombers' Arms (Leicester): reflective of Leicester's wool-yarn industry of the nineteenth century. There have been two instances of this tavern name in the town.
Woolstaplers' Arms (Leicester): the source as **Woolcombers' Arms** above.
York Castle (Leicester): named from John York, the tavern's landlord in 1846.

Notes on the Distribution and Usage of Elements

Each of the volumes of the Leicestershire Place-Name Survey is provided with a list of elements relevant to its particular place-names. For fuller discussion of the significance and use of each element, reference should be made to *English Place-Name Elements* (EPNS vols. 25 and 26, amended in JEPNS 1), *The Vocabulary of English Place-Names* (EPNS, in progress), M. Gelling, *Place-Names in the Landscape*, 1984, M. Gelling and A. Cole, *The Landscape of Place-Names*, 2000.

āc is very common in the north-west, the west, the south-west and south, with another concentration south-east from Leicester along Gartree Road to the county boundary with Rutland. Instances are sparse in the north-east in Framland Hundred.

alor is common in the north-west, occurs occasionally in the south, but apart from one instance, is absent from the north-east.

askr occurs only twice, in Long Whatton and Wymeswold at the northern boundary of the county.

æcer is very common in f.ns. from the 12th and 13th cents., but is generally indistinguishable from ON **akr**. Compounded with numerals, descriptive words, early personal names and surnames.

æppel is used of the apple-tree, but very infrequently; only 5 instances, 3 of which are in the immediate Leicester area.

æppel-trēow, common in the north-west, the west and south-west of the county, but only a few examples are recorded in the east, these along the county boundary.

æsc is very common throughout the county.

æspe is rare; a group of such names occurs in the north-west in a line from Breedon on the Hill to Hemington.

bekkr. There are 58 recorded stream-names with this element, 8 as a simplex and 50 compounded with a substantive or adjective as the specific. Of these, 44 are to be found in the Hundreds of Framland and East Goscote in the north-east. For the rest of the county, only 14 instances are recorded, 5 for Gartree, 2 for Guthlaxton, 3 for Sparkenhoe and 5 for West Goscote and the Leicestershire parts of Repton and Gresley Hundred. Variations of *Holebeck* (with **hol** 'lying in a hollow, running in a deep hollow') are most common with 7 examples and *Litelbeck* (with **lȳtel, lítill** 'little') also with 7 instances. In East Goscote, spellings with *beck* are sometimes replaced by *back* in the later 17th cent., as in Asfordby, Cold Newton, Thrussington and Tilton on the Hill parishes.

berg is very common throughout the county. The OE Anglian and the ON forms cannot be distinguished one from the other but either may be presumed when combined with an OE or ON element. It is used of both hills and tumuli.

birce is rare, except in West Goscote Hundred where 6 instances are recorded.

bold is used occasionally, typically with the specific **nīwe** 'new'.

brōc is very common throughout, with a ratio of 2:1 against stream names with **bekkr**.

burh as a final el. is rare in major names; **burh-tūn** occurs 3 times as a major compound, **burh-stall** once only, while **burh-stede** is recorded 4 times in f.ns.; **burh** is used as a defining word with reference to Hinckley, Mountsorrel and Ratby. Burrough on the Hill and Ratby Burroughs are major pre-Saxon fortifications.

burna is recorded in a dozen instances, 8 in minor stream-names, 3 in compounded f.ns. Only in Medbourne has it given a major place-name. The 4 instances as minor stream-names lie close to the river Trent in the north-west. The element is largely absent from the east.

bȳ is common with 80 instances but the distribution and structure of the names are markedly regional. In Framland, there are 22 such names. Of these, 9 (plus 3 possible) are compounded with an ON pers.n., 2 (plus 1 poss.) with an OE pers.n., 3 (plus 4 poss.) have an ON el. as the specific, while 2 (plus 6 poss.) have an OE el. as specific. 2 instances of **bȳ** are added to an OE place-name. In East Goscote, there are 23 p.ns. with **bȳ**, of which 16 are compounded with ON pers.ns., 2 (plus 2 poss.) have ON els. as their specifics and 3 (plus 2 poss.) have OE els. There are no instances in the hundred of OE pers.ns. in compound with **bȳ**. In Gartree Hundred, only 8 instances of p.ns. with **bȳ** are recorded. Of these, 2 (plus 2 poss.) have ON pers.ns. in compound, 2 (plus 2 poss.) have ON els. as their specifics, while only 1 (plus 3 poss.) names in **bȳ** have an OE el. as specific. There are no instances in the hundred of an OE pers.n. in compound with **bȳ**. In Guthlaxton, 11 p.ns. with **bȳ** are recorded. Of these, 3 (plus 2 poss.) have ON pers.ns. in compound, 6 have OE els. as specifics. There are only 2 possible instances with OE pers.ns., but no names with ON els. as specifics. In Sparkenhoe, 13 p.ns. with **bȳ** are recorded. Of these, 3 have ON pers.ns. compounded, (4 plus 1 poss.) have ON els., while 3 (plus 2 poss.) have OE els. as the specifics. No p.ns. with **bȳ** in this hundred have OE pers.ns. in compound. In West Goscote Hundred, only 3 p.ns. with **bȳ** are known.

Only 1 has an ON pers.n. (this anglicized) in compound. There are no instances of OE pers.ns. with **bȳ**. There are no examples with ON els. as specifics, but 2 with OE els. (of which 1 has **bȳ** added to an OE p.n.).

Of the 80 p.ns. with **bȳ** in the county, 34 (plus 7 poss.) are compounded with ON pers.ns., only 2 (plus 3 poss.) are compounded with OE pers.ns., 11 (plus 9 poss.) are compounded with ON els. (these include 3 instances of **kirkju-bý(r)**), while there are 17 (plus 13 poss.) examples with **bȳ** compounded with OE els., of which 2 (plus 1 poss.) are instances of earlier OE p.ns. to which **bȳ** has been added.

Their distribution and type are significant. The notable high concentration of names in **bȳ** is located in the valley of the river Wreake and its immediate environs. Here there are 25 certain instances of ON pers.ns. in compound, with no examples whatsoever with OE pers.ns. While a scattering of names with **bȳ** lies along the Roman Fosse Way and Fenn Lanes, both running south-west from Leicester, such names are largely absent from the west of the county. Three later names with **bȳ** lie in Ashby de la Zouch parish (Ashby itself, Blackfordby and Kilwardby) but otherwise the north-west of the county is devoid of these names. There are none in the uplands of Charnwood Forest. The concentration of p.ns. with **bȳ** plus ON pers.ns. in the valley of the river Wreake is to be accounted for by appropriation of this land by Scandinavians after the break-up of the Great Army in 877 and colonization in years following.

castel(l) is used of 14 medieval fortifications: of major surviving stone-built castles, of slighted examples and of motte-and-bailey remains, as at Ashby de la Zouch (**7** 7), Bawdon (**7** 237), Belvoir (**2** 6), Castle Donington (**7** 47), Groby (**6** 98), Hallaton (**4** 95), Hinckley (**6** 123), Kirby Muxloe (**6** 152), Leicester (**1** 9), Mountsorrel (**7** 152), Quorndon (**7** 173), Sapcote (**6** 226), Sauvey (**2** 283) and Whitwick (**7** 72). Ten of these lie in the west of the county.

cat(t) is common, its principal use in f.ns. in the east (especially in Gartree Hundred), with a noticeable concentration also in the north-west.

ceastel is rare, with only 2 possible examples: in Croft (**6** 68) and in Desford (**6** 74). In Leicester (**1** 9), it is early confused with **ceaster**.

chesecake is fairly common in f.ns. in the eastern half of the county in the 17th and 18th cents. It is rare in the west and north-west.

clif is common, but especially present in the west and north-west. Used of abrupt features and steep slopes.

clos(e) is very common in later f.ns. It appears as early as 1253 (*le Croft clos*, **2** 28), 1349 (*Cleyclos*, **3** 65) and 1391 (*Williamesclos*, **7** 76).

clūd is rare, but used especially in West Goscote Hundred, as Breedon Cloud Wood (**7** 36), Cover Cloud (**7** 156), Lubcloud (**7** 196) and *Caloucloudelowes* (**7** 59).

cot is common. 15 townships have the element as the generic. It is freq. in f.ns., in which 18 instances of *lambcot* are recorded, a compound only absent from the north-west.

croft is rare in township names with only Ulverscroft and Croft (in Sparkenhoe) extant, but very common in medieval and modern f.ns., esp. combined with pers.ns., surns., words for crops, farm animals, shape and size, and various village structures. The el. is freq. in 14th- and 15th-cent. f.ns. The earliest instances are *middelcroft* l.12th (Plungar, **2** 206), *Wellecroft* 1212 (Leire, **5** 136) and *Dunncroft* 1221 (Fleckney, **4** 52).

cros is common and survives in 100 instances referring to standing crosses. Only Twycross represents a settlement name. 12 names with **cros** as a generic have a surn. or pers.n. as their specifics. 31 standing crosses have a locational el. or p.n. as their specifics, some of these presumably representing boundary markers between townships. 6 crosses are described as 'white' (as *le Wite Cros* m.13 (1404) in Burton Lazars, **2** 76), no doubt alluding to the colour of the stone used, 5 of these in the north-east. A *Rede Crosse* stood in Leicester in 1494, possibly of reddish granite from nearby Mountsorrel. Damaged crosses are characterized by *stump* 'the broken off stump of something' in 4 instances and *hēafodlēas* 'without a top' in 3 examples. Of particular interest are *Gegecros* (Oadby, **5** 168), a congregating place for beggars and the unique *the Wooden Crosse* (Coston, **2** 156), current in 1578. *Corn Cross*, *Sage Cross* and *Shepe Cross* in Melton Mowbray, Pedlars Cross in Lutterworth and *Saltecros* in Shepshed were locations for trade.

cumb is used regularly in the north-east and east, minimally in the south and west.

dalr is freq. but it is difficult in later spellings to distinguish from **deill**. Plural forms with *-dales* are sometimes indicators of the latter.

dæl appears infrequently and is difficult to distinguish from **dalr**.

deill is common but is difficult to distinguish from **dalr** except where plural forms with *-dales* indicates its presence.

denu occasionally appears, principally in the east, south-east and south.

dūn occurs occasionally, except in the north-east and east. It is present as the generic in nine (poss. 10) township names.

ecg is very infrequent, only occurring in f.ns., 4 in Sparkenhoe Hundred.

ēg has given rise to 4 township names and occurs occasionally in f.ns. in Guthlaxton and Sparkenhoe Hundreds.

ellern is common, esp. in the north.

elm is found occasionally throughout the county, but especially in Sparkenhoe Hundred.

ende is very freq. in both minor names and f.ns. The compound *town(s)end* is ubiquitous. Note also the recurring **lane-ende** *infra.*

eng is very freq. throughout the county, used as the generic in f.ns. with pers.ns., els. defining size, shape, the nature of the soil. In Framland, often compounded with *sléttr* 'level'. May also be used as a specific in f.ns.

eorð-burh is only certainly represented by Burrough on the Hill (**2** 231). Six other poss. instances are more likely to be examples of **erber**.

feld is in widespread use in minor p.ns. and in medieval and modern f.ns., but rare in major p.ns., there being only 3 township names with **feld** in compound, all of which appear in DB. Three great open-fields were the norm for each township in the medieval period through to the Enclosures of the 18th century.

fenn is used occasionally, esp. in the south and west.

fisc is rarely used alone in f.ns., but in the compound *fisc-pōl* are 15 instances, in *fisc-ponde* 12 instances and in *fisc-pytt* 3 instances.

flat is commonly used in f.ns. in Guthlaxton, Sparkenhoe and West Goscote. Difficult to distinguish from the adj. **flatr** when used as a specific.

flode-gate is used occasionally throughout the county except perhaps in Gartree where no instances are recorded.

foot-road is usual in f.ns. in Framland, East Goscote and Sparkenhoe, while **fote-path** appears confined to Sparkenhoe and West Goscote; **fote-waye** occurs throughout the county, but **fote-gate** is rare with only one instance noted, that in Framland Hundred.

ford is common in major names, minor names and f.ns. It is compounded in 8 township names. Of these, 5 appear in DB, 2 in the LeicSurv of c.1130.

foss is rare, all 8 instances in f.ns. alluding to the Roman Fosse Way.

fox and **fox-hol** are common throughout, esp. to be found in the Hundreds of East Goscote, Gartree and Sparkenhoe.

Frīsa, **Frísi** occurs with certainty only 3 times, these compounded with **bȳ**: Frisby on the Wreake in East Goscote, Frisby in Gartree and the lost *Frysseby* (**6** 141) beside Fosse Way in Sparkenhoe. Freizeland in Carlton (**6** 63) is likelier to be with **fyrs** 'furze'.

furh occurs frequently, very often in combination with *wæter*, *wæterig* and *wēt*. The 4 instances of *le rennindeforu* (**2** 37, **3** 280, **7** 191, **7** 138, with *rinnende*, *rennandi*) appear to allude to major drainage ditches.

furlang is a very common older f.n. element, often combined with words for crops or descriptive of the soil.

fyrhð is an infrequent term, occurring only in the south and west, chiefly in Sparkenhoe Hundred.

fyrs is very common in f.ns. except in West Goscote; **fyrsig** 'growing with furze', giving spellings with *furry*, occurs occasionally, but not before the middle of the 17th cent. while **fyrsen** with the same meaning is found once only.

galga appears regularly throughout the county, but with the same incidence of OE **galg-trēow** and ON **galga-tré**.

galla is common, with higher incidence in Guthlaxton Hundred.

gang is rare, appearing only in the north-east and east.

gap is frequently used throughout the county, many later instances compounded with township names, presumably indicating gaps in parish boundary hedges through which roads ran.

garðr is rare and used principally in the north. Plungar (**2** 204) appears to be the sole instance of its use in a township name.

gata is extremely common and is usual in the old street names of the principal townships. It outnumbers **weg** in frequency at a ratio of 2:1, although the latter is used commonly for the names of long-distance routes.

geard is frequent, esp. compounded with surns. indicative of ownership in later examples.

gibet is rare; of the 6 instances recorded, 5 are located in the south and south-west beside the principal roads.

golet is rare, occurring only in Sparkenhoe Hundred.

gorst is very common throughout the county, but **gorstig** is much less so, apart from in Sparkenhoe, while **gorst** is freq. compounded with township names. Dialectal **goss** and **gossy** occur only occasionally.

grāf is common and is compounded in 3 surviving township names. The related **grǣfe** is only present significantly in the south-west in Sparkenhoe and in the west in West Goscote.

grange is ubiquitous throughout all hundreds, usually compounded in minor names with a township name prefixed to convey a pretence of antiquity. The el. is rare in f.ns. Of early monastic granges, 7 are first recorded in the 12th cent., 6 in the 13th, 4 in the 14th, 3 in the 15th and 12 in the 16th cent. Of the 20 recorded before 1500, 9 are known to have belonged to Garendon Abbey, 4 to Croxton Abbey, 2 to Leicester Abbey and one to Norton Priory, Cheshire.

gravel, **gravel-hol**, **gravel-pytt** occur throughout in f.ns., but **gravel** compounded with **pytt** exceeds the instances of the el. compounded with **hol** at a ratio of 3:1.

grein is infrequent, but is present principally in the east.

grendel is rare and present only in the south and south-east.

gryppe occurs occasionally in f.ns. in the north-east and south-west.

haga[1] is very difficult to distinguish from ON **hagi** with the same meaning. Freq. occurs in f.ns. in Sparkenhoe, West Goscote and in the Borough of Leicester. A minimal presence only in the north-east in Framland and in the south in Guthlaxton.

hām, an early p.n.-forming generic, is infrequent when compared with other habitative elements. It occurs 7 times only in surviving township names, with another 5 lost instances. Each example is situated close to a Roman road or to ancient trackway or to a Romano-British *vicus* or villa site.

haugr is very common in f.ns. in the north-east in Framland and East Goscote and in the north-west in West Goscote. It is absent from the east and the south of the county. Difficult to distinguish from OE **hōh** when used as a generic.

(ge)hæg is common in f.ns. throughout the county, but its principal concentrations in Sparkenhoe and West Goscote presumably represent fenced-in clearances at the south-east and north-west margins of Charnwood Forest.

hǣð is freq. in minor names and f.ns. in the regions south and west of Charnwood in Sparkenhoe and West Goscote. In the north-east in Framland and in the south in Guthlaxton, the el. is infrequent. The east of the county in Gartree and East Goscote is largely devoid of it.

hlāw is freq. in f.ns., principally in the east, south-east and south-west. Rare in the north-east, esp. in Framland Hundred.

hōh is common in f.ns. throughout the county, but is sometimes difficult to distinguish from ON **haugr**. It is compounded as both specific or generic in 6 township names and in the hundred name Sparkenhoe.

holmr is very freq. in f.ns. throughout the county: as a simplex or with a prefixed pers.n. or surn. Soil type may be specified or wild flora, livestock, produce or (agricultural) buildings. Shape may be indicated or a topographical feature alluded to.

holt is widely distributed in minor names and f.ns., but is commonest in the north-east and east, with only a few instances in the south.

hrycg OE and **hryggr** ON are both commonly used in f.ns., the Scandinavian form often replacing the OE element.

hvin, the Scandinavian word for 'gorse' is occasionally found in f.ns., particularly in the north-east and east, but its ME adjectival derivative **whinny** 'gorsy' is by far the principal usage.

hyll is very freq. in minor names and f.ns. throughout the county in comparison with the less present **berg**, **dūn** and **wald**.

hyrne is used occasionally in f.ns., but is especially to be found in Sparkenhoe and West Goscote in the south and west.

ing and its derivative **ingel** are both rare; the former occurs twice but what appear to be the latter's four instances may disguise **ing** compounded with **hyll**.

-ingas is rare, only 2 certain instances occurring, both in compound with pers.ns. (**-inga-** gen.pl. is also rare, with only one instance (Bringhurst, **4** 18), while 2 others (Theddingworth, **4** 268 and Kilworth, **5** 155) are constructed in their earliest recordings with gen.sg. composition-joints.)

-ingtūn (**-ing**[4] + **tūn**) is a compound generic which occurs 17 times throughout the county, except in Framland in the north-east and Guthlaxton in the south. A large group of such township names is located in the north-west in West Goscote. Invariably, these p.ns. have as their specifics an OE monothematic masculine pers.n. (sometimes occurring several times), suggesting both the antiquity of such a p.n. type, possibly continuing into the later half of the 8th cent. and perhaps indicating the development of multiple estate holdings of powerful individuals.

innām OE, **inntak** ON. The OE el. is rare, recorded principally in the f.ns. of the years 1484 to 1601, but the earliest instance being *le Innome* of 1245 (Long Whatton, **7** 121); the Scand. term of the same meaning, i.e. 'a piece of land taken in or enclosed' is fairly common, but with the various instances belonging invariably to the mid 19th century.

kirkja is common in f.ns. and street names, appearing principally in Framland in the north-east and in Sparkenhoe and West Goscote in the south-west and west.

kirkju-bý(r) appears only three times, in Kirby Bellars (**3** 84), Kirby Muxloe (**7** 150) and Kirkby Mallory (**7** 210).

kjarr is fairly common in f.ns., principally in the south-west and west in Sparkenhoe and West Goscote. It is absent from Framland in the north-east.

land is freq. in f.ns. in ME and modern instances, especially when used of 'lands' in the great open-fields.

lane-ende is a compound appearing freq. in f.ns., but less so in the south-west and west. Its meaning(s) 'a lane-end' and/or '(at) the end of a lane' need further study, *v.* Löfvenberg 117 and EPNS Vol. 54 (1 ii) 262–3.

launde is fairly common in minor names and f.ns., appearing principally in the south-west, west and east. In Guthlaxton in the south it is rare. It is recorded once only as a simplex major p.n., the site of Launde Abbey (**3** 160).

lǣs is frequent in f.ns. throughout the county, but is difficult to distinguish from the Anglian nom.pl. **lǣs** (of **lēah**), except where the dat.sg. **lǣswe** is present.

lēah is rare in the names of townships, but common in f.ns. in the west. Of the township names, nine appear in Sparkenhoe and West Goscote. Of the 368 township names of the county, only 12 (i.e. 3¼ %) are formed with **lēah** as their generics.

līn occurs only 12 times, principally in Sparkenhoe and West Goscote. 5 instances are compounded with **croft**.

lind is rare, appearing only a few times in the south-west, west and north-west. Apart from (Newtown) Linford (**7** 55), the few minor names with the adjective **linden** are modern recordings.

lundr is fairly common, but only in the north-east, south-west and west. In West Goscote, it has given the township names of Lount and Swithland and in the north-east, the name of Framland Hundred. The element occurs 15 times as a simplex, in major names, minor names and f.ns.

lyme-pytt and **lim-kilne** occur occasionally throughout the county, except in Guthlaxton where no eamples are recorded.

lyng is common in f.ns. in the north-east and east in Framland and East Goscote and in the eastern portion of West Goscote. It is scantily recorded in the south-east, south and south-west.

mareis is rare, only appearing in the north-east in Framland and East Goscote.

marr occurs in f.ns. only in the north-east and east.

mere is common in f.ns. throughout the county, except in Framland, but is difficult to distinguish from **(ge)mǣre**.

mersc is freq. in f.ns. throughout the county except in Guthlaxton Hundred where no instances are recorded.

mönïð is a PrW el. possibly found in the north-west in an area of British survival, as in Mantle (**3** 57, 274, **7** 214) and Mindhill (**7** 44).

mōr is extremely common in minor names and f.ns., esp. in the north-east, east, south-east and south of the county in Framland, East Goscote, Gartree and Guthlaxton. As a generic, it may be prefixed by the name of a township or by the surn. of an owner of a stretch of moorland or by an el. indicating shape or size or direction from a township. It is freq. as a simplex and particularly with **dēad** as the specific, indicating infertile wasteland. The specific **wælisc/welisc** appears compounded with **mōr** 4 times in the north-east and south, indicating British survival, presumably on poor land.

mos is infrequent, appearing principally in the south-east in Gartree Hundred.

mōt is rare, but occurs compounded with the elements **hlāw**, **hōh** and **hyll**, indicating raised, conspicuous sites.

mylde is absent from the south-west and west, but occurs occasionally in the north-east, east, south-east and south, no doubt alluding to very fertile soil. Of the 20 instances recorded, 18 are compounded with **blæc**, 2 with **rēad**, of which one is the township name Redmile (**2** 194).

mýrr is common in f.ns., noticeably in the north-east, east and south-east. The adjective **myry** is less well evidenced.

Norðman is sparsely recorded, but is present in the township names Normanton le Heath and Normanton Turville. It is possible in 2 road names, *Normangatt* (**2** 30) and *Normans way* (**7** 65) and 2 f.ns., *Normantoftes* (**4** 85) and *Normanescroft* (**5** 85).

oyser is frequent, usually compounded with **bedd**.

parting occurs occasionally in f.ns., principally in the north-east and east. Of the 14 instances recorded, 8 define grassland.

plain occurs on occasion in f.ns., principally in the north-east in Framland, in the north-west in West Goscote and in the south-west in Sparkenhoe.

port[2] is freq., but is recorded mostly compounded in a road name; 21 instances of *portway* occur, 11 of *portgate*, 1 of *portstreet*. Of the 12 instances of **port**[2] compounded with other elements, 7 are with **hyll**.

quarrelle and **quarrere** occur occasionally in f.ns., especially in Sparkenhoe and West Goscote, **quarrelle** appearing earlier and in three times the number of instances of **quarrere**.

quarter is rare, but appears from c.1500, while **quarterne** is found only in a few late instances in Gartree Hundred.

rein appears occasionally in f.ns., principally in East Goscote Hundred.

rokke is rare and limited to minor names in Sparkenhoe and West Goscote Hundreds.

ryding appears sporadically in f.ns., with a concentration of instances in the woodlands of West Goscote Hundred.

rynel is infrequent, appearing principally in the north-east and east, usually in the dialectal forms **rundle** and **rindle**.

salh is common in f.ns., especially in the north of the county.

sc(e)aga is rare, appearing principally in Sparkenhoe and West Goscote.

scēp-cot is common in f.ns., but **scēp-hūs** is rare.

skáli is rare in f.ns., appearing principally in the north of the county.

slæd is very common in f.ns. throughout the county.

sōg is infrequent in f.ns., appearing principally in Framland and East Goscote in the north-east.

spell appears sporadically in all of the hundreds, except in West Goscote. Usually compounded with **hlāw**.

spitel occurs throughout the county, always alluding to local charitable institutions and not to properties of the military order of Knights Hospitallers; (*v.* **temple** *infra*).

stoc is common in f.ns. and is present in the township names Ibstock, Stoke Golding and Stoughton. Difficult to distinguish from **stocc**.

stōw occurs occasionally, principally in the north-east and east, giving only one major p.n., Wistow (**4** 295).

strēam is rare, occurring only in the east and south-east. It is absent from the south-west and south.

temple occurs 12 times in both minor names and f.ns., in each instance with reference to a Preceptory or properties of the military order of Knights Templars.

toft is common in f.ns. except in Sparkenhoe in the south-west; only 3 extant p.ns. have it as their generics. In Framland, OE, ON and OFr pers.ns. are occasionally compounded with it, but the el. is usually prefixed by a significant word or is recorded as a simplex. Scraptoft (**4** 229) is initially recorded in 1043 (15) and Knaptoft (**5** 122) in 1086.

tōt-hyll is found only in 7 instances, 5 of which are in the south-west and west.

tūn is the commonest habitation el. in the county with 194 recorded instances compounded in township names, of which 65 are no longer extant. (The 17 instances of the compound -**ingtūn** are included in these numbers as well as the 3 known examples of **burh-tūn** and the 5 instances of **bere-tūn**). Of the 194 examples, 59 have OE pers.ns. as their specifics, 28 have ON pers.ns., while only 2 late instances have OFr pers.ns. (Ogier in Redmile and Bochard in Botcheston); 101 have an OE significant word as specific, but only 2 (plus one poss.) have an ON significant word as specific. Only 4 instances are initially recorded in pre-Conquest documents, but 72 in DB, 18 in 12th-cent. records and 13 in those of the 13th century. Of the so-called Grimston hybrids, those names in **tūn** having an ON pers.n. as specific and thought to represent early appropriation of land by Scandinavian settlers after the dispersal of a Viking army hereabouts in 877, distribution in the county is significant. 10 lie in the north-east in Framland and East Goscote around the valley of the river Wreake, while 11 are situated to the south-west and west of the inhospitable Charnwood Forest and the heathland dome in Sparkenhoe and West Goscote. Guthlaxton Hundred in the south has only 3 of the type, while Gartree has 4 of them, 2 lying together on the Roman Gartree Road far to the south-east, near to the county boundary with Northants., these perhaps belonging with Scandinavian settlement in that area. The el. **tūn** is also widespread throughout the county in f.ns. in the names of closes and furlongs. The compound *town*(*s*)*end* is especially common.

tūn-stall occurs rarely, except in Sparkenhoe and West Goscote where 8 instances are recorded.

þing is recorded only 6 times, all in the areas of Scandinavian settlement. In Framland and East Goscote, 3 instances are compounded with **hyll** and one in the compound **þing-haugr** 'an assembly mound'. In West Goscote, the 2 instances are as **þing-haugr**. Gartree and Guthlaxton have no examples of the element or compounds.

þorp is common in the north-east, east and north-west of the county. Sparkenhoe in the south-west is singularly lacking in names of this type. 67 instances are recorded, of which 28 are still extant as the names of townships and 39 are lost. Of these names with **þorp**, 16 are compounded with ON pers.ns., 9 with OE pers.ns. and 4 with ContGerm pers.ns. (these last first recorded in 1086 (x 2), c.1200 and 1271). 15 are compounded with common significant words, especially directional adjectives which are difficult to apportion to either OE or ON in their later development. 15 names with **þorp** are simplex. One **þorp** is recorded as early as 967. In DB, 21 names appear and 6 are first recorded in 12th-cent. documents. Their distribution is significant. Framland has 15 instances, East Goscote 11 and West Goscote/Repton and Gresley 21, mirroring the spread of p.ns. with **bȳ** and the Grimston hybrids on the Wolds, in the Wreake Valley and in High Leicestershire and Scandinavian settlement from the river Trent in the north-west of the county. While earlier names with **þorp** with both ON and OE pers.ns. in compound suggest the establishment of substantial settlements, but later than those with names with **bȳ** and the Grimston hybrids, the numerous instances as simplex names or with significant words as specifics indicating directional/locational sites, point to the later relationship of such farmsteads to three great open-fields cultivation.

vangr is very freq. in f.ns. throughout the county, especially in Framland, East Goscote, West Goscote and Sparkenhoe, less so in the south-east and south. Pers.ns., both masc. and fem. and surns. are commonly compounded, indicating ownership.

wald is common in f.ns., often compounded with the name of a township and also freq. as a simplex, both singular and plural. Frequent in the north-east. 3 township names with **wald** are extant, all initially recorded in 1086.

walh is recorded in the names of 4 townships, of which 3 appear in DB and one in a 12th-cent. document. Rare in f.ns.

wella. The Anglian form **wella** is very common throughout the county, but the Mercian form **wælla** occurs occasionally in the Sparkenhoe and West Goscote Hundreds near the county boundary with Derbyshire.

wīc is rare. As a generic and a simplex, it occurs 7 times (plus 1 poss.) and in the early compound **wīc-hām** once (plus 1 poss.). It survives 3 times in a township name (recorded once (possibly) in an Old English document and twice in DB).

worð is infrequent. Only 22 instances are recorded, 14 with OE masc. pers.ns. compounded, of which 13 are monothematic; one instance is compounded with an OE stream-name, while 7 are prefixed by OE significant words. 2 have an **-inga-** construction. Of these names, 11 became those of townships, 10 with OE pers.ns. Of these, one is recorded initially in a document of 969 and 10 in DB. Their distribution is significant. A large group in the south line the rivers Avon, Swift and Welland. In the south-west, 2 more relate to the river Sence. A group of 4 recorded as later f.ns., each compounded with an OE significant word rather than an OE pers.n., lie in the extreme north-east in the Bottesford/Redmile area, unrelated to major waterways but away from the Norse settlements of the Wreake Valley. Names in **worð**

compounded with pers.ns. appear to be early, certainly dating to before the initial Scandinavian settlements in the county.

wudu is very common, often compounded with the names of townships. Freq. in f.ns. Only in Guthlaxton Hundred in the south is the element sparsely present.

wulf is rare. Only 9 instances are recorded in f.ns., 2 compounded with **pytt**, 3 with **hyll**.

Phonetic Symbols

p	*p*ay	j	*y*ou	ɔ	p*o*t
b	*b*ay	χ	lo*ch* (Scots)	ɔ:	s*a*w
t	*t*ea	h	*h*is	ɔi	*oi*l
d	*d*ay	m	*m*an	e	r*e*d
k	*k*ey	n	*n*o	ei	fl*ay*
g	*g*o	ŋ	si*ng*	ɛ	jam*ais* (French)
ʍ	*wh*en	r	*r*un	ɛ:	th*ere*
w	*w*in	l	*l*and	i	p*i*t
f	*f*oe	tʃ	*ch*ur*ch*	i:	b*ea*d
v	*v*ote	ʤ	*j*u*dg*e	ou	l*ow*
s	*s*ay	ɑ:	f*a*ther	u	g*oo*d
z	*z*one	ɑu	c*ow*	u:	b*oo*t
ʃ	*sh*one	a	m*a*nn (German)	ʌ	m*u*ch
ʒ	a*z*ure	ai	fl*y*	ə	ev*er*
þ	*th*in	æ	c*a*b	ə:	b*ir*d
ð	*th*en				

Phonetic symbols are enclosed in square brackets: [ ], thus ['krousən] Croxton, ['musən] Muston, ['lʌfbʌrə] Loughborough. The sign < ' > indicates that the following syllable is stressed and the sign < : > indicates that the preceding vowel is long.

Notes on the Phonology of Leicestershire Place-Names

The language of the place-names of Leicestershire is that of the Midlands. The Old English once spoken in the county was of the Anglian dialect, although in the place-names of the far west near the border with Derbyshire, evidence of features of the Mercian dialect of Old English may be traced. The forms occurring in surviving Old English charters do not generally reflect local phonological types, as these documents were mostly written in the standard late West Saxon orthography. During the Middle English period (c.1150 to 1450), the dialect of the county was that of the East Midlands.

1. OE *a* before nasals (except in the north and north-west of the county where some *o* spellings appear) remains, as in Branston, Hamilton, Langley, Shangton etc. Spellings in *au* due to AN influence are frequent from the early 13th century in forms for Branston (*Bran-* 1086–1612, *Braun-* 1362–1462), with the eventual disuse of [ɔ:] in the 17th cent. Occasional spellings in *au* also appear in Shangton. In the north and north-west of the county, OE *a* before nasals commonly becomes ME *o*, as in Long Whatton (*Long-* 1357), Long Mere (*Longe-* 1287, **7** 118), West Wong (*-wong* 1424, **2** 8). Flitlands (*-londys* l.13, **7** 219) and Langley (*Long-* e.Hy2, 1244, 1376) both have early spellings in *o*.

2. OE, ON *a* remains as in Gaddesby, Knaptoft, Maplewell, Saxelby, Stathern etc. A few AN spellings with *e* for *a* appear in early forms, as in Saxby (c.1130-c.1250) and Packington (1225–1291). In later ME spellings, *e* occasionally appears before *r* as in Barkby (1442–1553) and Barsby (1344–1502).

3. OE, ON *al* followed by a consonant usually remains in ME, except in some cases AN spellings in *au* are found, as in the forms for Dalby (2), Galby, Saltby and Walton on the Wolds. Diphthongization to *awl* [ɔ:l] appears in the 16th cent. as in Galby (*Gal-* 1549, *Gaul-* 1576), with occasional vocalization or loss of *l* (to *aw*) as in Old Dalby (*Dal-* 1535, *Daw-* 1543).

4. OE (Angl) *a* before *ld* in *ald* remains spelled *a* in the ME forms for Aldeby, Alderman's Haw and Alton (with loss of *d* in Alton). The same development is found in Halstead and Scalford (both with loss of *d*). Both show some AN spellings an *au*. In *cald*, *a* remains in ME in Chadwell, Colborough, Cord Hill and Langton Caudle. Diphthongization to *awl* (modern [ɔ:l]) with vocalization or loss of *l* appears from the 15th cent. in Chadwell (*Cald-* 1353, *Cawd-* 1440), Colborough (*Cal-* 1539, *Caw-*

1586), Halstead (*Hawl-* 1604, *Haw-* 1607), Langton Caudle (*Cauld-* 1806) and Cord Hill (*Cald-* 13th). In the south-east of the county, *o* develops in ME as in Cold Overton (*Cald-* 1201, *Cold-* 1212), Cold Newton (*Cold-* 1279), *Coldham* 1594 (**4** 131). In *wald*, OE *a* shows normal development to ME *o* as in Horninghold, Prestwold, Wymeswold etc. Spellings in *would* from the early 16th cent. (retained in Ashby Woulds) indicate the raising of ME *ō* to [u:] in the north of the county, a pronunciation still retained in Groby, Hoby and Hoton. Cf. also §22 *infra*.

5. ME *a* before *ks*, *x* is occasionally diphthongized to *aw* [ɔ:] in the 16th cent. with loss of the consonant, as in Clawson (*Clax-* 1534, *Claux-* 1564, *Claws-* 1539) and Saxby (*Saws-* 1577). A similar development takes place in Slawston with the vocalization and loss of *g* (*Slages-* 1086, *Slaughes-* 1546, *Slaws-* 1550), but in this case vocalization begins much earlier (*Slaws-* 1232–1583). Cf. also §42 *infra*.

6. OE, ON *ā* usually develops to ME *ō*. Occasionally it remains, with eventual shortening as in Anstey, Bradgate, Bradley, Scraptoft and Stanton (2). When it retained its length, *ā* in open syllables was ultimately diphthongized to [e:], as in Blaby (*Blay-* 1518) and Cadeby (*Cayt-* 1517). Occasional forms for Cranoe (*Crayn-* 1486, *Creyn-* 1487) and Staunton (*Stayn-* 1542) also show this feature. Anstey has two early forms which show the northern diphthong developing (*Ain-* 1203 × 06, *Ayn-* 1329). In the north-west of the county, a few names show a late rounding of *ā*; thus Oakley (*Ac-* l.12–1440, *Ake-* 1291–1603) which has only a few forms in *o* between 1235 and 1480 and Stoneywell (*Stany-* 1623, *Stony-* 1754). Bradgate, also in the north-west, has a similar late rounding in some 16th-cent. forms (*Brad*(*e*)- 1238–1610, *Brod*(*e*)- 1512, 1613, *Broad-* c.1545, 1612), but the rounding does not survive. There are four place-names with OE *stān* as specific: Stanton (2), Staunton and Stonton. All have spellings in *a* and *au* from DB to the 17th cent. (only Stonton in the south-east showing *o* forms developing from the 14th cent.) and this may indicate that in each case *a* (and *o* in Stonton) was shortened late (cf. Bradgate *supra*). Place-names with OE *stān* often indicate interchange of OE *ā* with the cognate ON *ei* in some forms, as Staunton (*Stain-* c.1291), Wigston Parva (*-stain* 1195, 1197, 1202), Humberstone (*-stain* 1229, *-stayn* c.1291, *-stein* 1205). Such an interchange of cognate OE *ā* and ON *ei* may explain late forms for Gatehouse Hill (**7** 59) (*Got-* 1605, *Goat-* 1673, *Get-* 1605, *Gate-* 1754).

7. OE *ā* before *w*, as in *hlāw*, appears as *o* in the modern form except in instances in the south of the county. In ME, the forms are *lawe* and *lowe*. Until the late 13th cent., *a* forms alone are found. During the 14th cent., the rounded forms begin to predominate. In the south of the

county, *-lowe* is reduced to *-ley* in the 16th and 17th cents. in such names as Rowley (*-lowe* c.1290, *-ley* 1590), Tomley (*-lowe* 1543, *-ley* 1606), Tooley (*-lowe* 1630, *-ley* c.1545), Wakeley (*-low* p.1638, *-ly* 1712).

8. OE *æ* usually becomes *a* in ME (with sporadic *e* forms), as in Allexton, Appleby, Asplin (**7** 35), Atterton, Blackbrook etc. Occasional *ei* spellings are found into the early 13th cent. as in Ashby Folville and Ashby Magna and *ai* into the 15th cent. in Ashby de la Zouch and Ashby Magna. Numerous forms with *e* spellings occur into the mid 14th cent. in Ashby (3). These may be due to the influence of ON *eski* 'a place growing with ash-trees'.

9. OE (Mercian) *wælla*, (Anglian) *wella* appear as *wall* and *well* in ME. Modern forms are in *well* except in Pinwall. In lost field-names, *wall* is found in parishes in the extreme west, as *Crasswal* and *Fulwal* (Appleby), *Swetewalle* (Donisthorpe), *Pippall*, *Sandwalls*, *Smithwalls* (Orton on the Hill) and *Swynewall* (Swepstone).

10. OE *ǣ* appears in ME as *ē*, as in Budgmere, Donington le Heath, Ridgemere, Streethill etc. Shortening of *ē* takes place in Stretton (2) and Glenfield. In Claybrooke and Whatborough in the south and east, *a* forms predominate and have remained in ModE.

11. ON *au* appears in ME as *ou*, as in Goadby (2), Oadby and *Thynghou* (Finger Fm, **7** 118). During the second half of the 15th cent. [ɑu] is raised to [ou]: thus Goadby Marwood (*Goud-* 1428, *God-* 1464), Goadby (*Gowd-* 1465, *God-* 1509) and Oadby (*Oud-* 1518, *Od-* 1508).

12. OE, ON *e* normally remains, as in Hemington, Fleckney, Swepstone etc., but is raised to *i* before dentals in forms for Freeby (*Frith-* 1275–1477) and before [ŋ] in early forms for Shenton where an intrusive *g* develops. Spellings in *ei*, *ey* occur in Freeby (1415–96) and in Shenton (1195–1541). In the west of the county, *a* spellings develop in Markfield from 1235 and from the early 16th cent. in Potters Marston and Breedon Brand (**7** 255).

13. OE *ea* becomes ME *a* in Barrow, Marefield, Sharnford, Sparkenhoe etc., *e* in Evington, Skeffington and *Windesers* (**7** 124). Marefield has many *e* spellings (1086–1523) as has Sharnford (1086–1608). Evington and Skeffington have a few *a* forms to the early 13th cent.

14. OE *ēa* becomes ME *ē* in Great Easton, Eastwell, Seagrave, Sheepy, Sheet Hedges (**7** 157) etc.; *e* (with shortening) in Redhill (3), Redmile etc. (Shepshed shows late shortening (*Sheap-* 1553, *Sheep-* 1604)). Redmile has spellings in *ai* (1350–1531) and Seagrave AN *a* for *e* in early forms (1086–1225)); *a*, particularly in the south-west in

Aston, Ratcliffe (3), Sapcote, Shackerstone etc. For Aston, Ratcliffe Culey and Sapcote, a few *e* forms have been noted.

15. ON *ei*, which is normally retained with ME spellings in *ai*, *ay*, *ei*, *ey* and occasionally *a*, is often simplified to ME *e*, as in Enderby, Gelscoe (**7** 93), Heather and early forms for Gartree, Rearsby, Rotherby etc.

16. OE *eo* (together with ON *ja*, *jǫ*) becomes ME *e* in Arnesby, Burrough on the Hill, Peckleton, Wellsborough etc. Occasional *o* forms have been noted and very rarely *u*.

17. OE *ēo* becomes ME *ē* as in Leesthorpe, Peatling etc. Desford, *Prestgrave* (**4** 203), Prestwold, Redmore Plain (**6** 290) and Theddingworth also have *e* spellings throughout but in all of these early shortening has taken place.

18. ME *er* becomes *ar* as in Arnesby, Bardon, Barlestone, Hardwick (**4** 233), Quorndon etc. With very rare exceptions in the late 13th cent., spellings in *ar* do not appear in any number until the mid 14th cent. and they become common from the beginning of the next.

19. OE, ON *o* normally remains as in Cosby, Cropston, Crossburrow (**4** 65), Foxton, Nevill Holt etc. In place-names which contain a Scandinavian personal name with *Þor-*, *o* becomes ME *u* (with occasional *o* spellings) as in Thrussington, Thurcaston, Thurlaston and Thurmaston.

20. ME *o* is often lengthened in the 16th cent., as in Croxton (2) (*Crows-* c.1530), Cotes (*Coates* 1558) etc. Lengthening appears to have occurred much earlier in Rothley (12th cent.) and in Stonesby (13th cent.), in each case with loss of a following consonant. In the south-west of the county, ME *o* occasionally becomes *a* as in Brascote (*Bros-* 1429), Ratby (*Rot-* 1540, *Rat-* 1549) and Narborough (*Nor-* 1526, *Nar-* 1518). A group of names in a small area in the west shows a 17th-cent. change of *-ston* to *-stone*, namely Barlestone, Bilstone, Congerstone, Nailstone, Odstone, Ravenstone, Shackerstone, Snarestone, Snibstone, Swepstone and Thringstone.

21. OE, ON *ō* remains, as in Hose, Noseley, Owston, Rolleston, Sproxton etc., except when shortened in compounds, as in Market Bosworth, Bottesford, Foston and Gopsall.

22. ME *ō* was often raised to [u:] in the north of the county during the 16th cent., which accounts for the local pronunciation of Groby, Hoby and Hoton (cf. the modern spellings of Ashby Woulds, Boothorpe, Hoo Ash (**7** 180), Zouch Bridge (**7** 84)). It is occasionally raised and shortened to [u] before a back consonant, as in Brooksby, Tugby and Wooden Nook (**7** 118) and before a dental as in Stud Brook

(**7** 49). There is evidence for lowering to [ɔ:] in the east of the county, as in Noseley (*Naw(e)s-* 1430 *et passim* to 1540), Foston (*Fors-* 1493, 1539, *Faws-* 1693), Sproxton (*Spraws-* 1539, 1603), Houghton (*Haw-* 1430, 1435, 1468, *Haugh-* 1518, 1610). Cf. Stoughton (*Staw-* 1631, *Staugh-* 1610) and Knossington (*Knaws-* 1622).

23. OE, ON *u* remains, as in Buckminster, Bushby, Hugglescote, Hungarton etc. with frequent *o*, *ou* spellings, in some cases surviving into the 16th cent. (as in Hugglescote and Plungar). An *o* spelling in the modern form sometimes represents [u] as in Somerby, but spelling-pronunciations are now often present as in Cossington, Donington (2), Loddington etc.

24. ON *lundr*, when the final element of a compounded place-name, eventually becomes *-lond*, as in Framland and Swithland (with frequent *o* spellings until the early 16th cent., *a* spellings from the early 13th cent.). As a simplex it is diphthongized to [au] about the 14th cent., as in Lount and Osbaston Lount (cf. the occasional *ou* spellings in Framland and Swithland c.1250–1350).

25. OE *ū* is often shortened early in compounds, as in Dunton Bassett, Humberstone, Huncote, Lutterworth, Muston etc. Otherwise it remains in ME and by the early 16th cent. is diphthongized to [au] as in Breedon Cloud (**7** 36), Mowsley, Rowley (**5** 190) etc.

26. OE, ON *y* appears in ME as *i* or (*y*), *e* and *u*, although *i* is almost universal in the modern forms (*u* in Thurnby and Tur Langton, *e* in Hathern and Stathern). Spellings in *e* are less common than those in *i* but occur in place-names throughout the county. Spellings in *u* generally appear in place-names in the south and east. They are much less common than *i* or *e*.

27. OE *ȳ* is shortened to ME *i* (or *y*) in compounds, as in Bringhurst. It retains its length in Kite Hill (**7** 57) and The Mythe (**6** 258).

28. **Inorganic Vowels**. Svarabhaktic *e* was inserted medially between consonants by the Normans to avoid combinations that were unfamiliar to them. It appears in Leics. material as follows: (i) between a consonant and a nasal as in forms for Nanby (*Nauen-* c.1240 < *Nafni*), Ravenstone (*Raven-* 1086 < *Hrafn*), Stonesby (*Stouen-* 1086 < *Stofn*) and Thornton (*Toren-* 1201 < OE *þorn*); (ii) in initial consonant groups as in forms for Sketchley (*Sekeites-* 1236, *Sketes-* 1287), Thringstone (*Terenges-* 1249, *Trenges-* c.1200); (iii) in groups of two consonants, as in forms for Osbaston (*Osebernes-* 1276, *Osbernes-* 1194), Galby (*Galeby* 1242, *Galby* 1232). AN prosthetic *e* is occasionally found before *s* in forms for Smeeton (*Esmed-* 1086), Stapleford (*Estapel-* 1223) and Stonton Wyville (*Estan-* c.1200).

29. OE *c* [tʃ] before front vowels normally becomes ME *ch*, as in Charley, Charnwood, Chilcote etc. but it is replaced by ON *k* in Kilby. OE *ceorl* is replaced by ON *karl* in Carlton Curlieu (*Cherl-* 1081 (c.1131), *Carl-* 1086). Cf. §55 *infra*.

30. OE (Anglian) *cald* gives forms in [k] in ME and ModE, as in Langton Caudle, Colborough (**3** 249), *Coldham* (**4** 131), Cold Newton, Cold Overton etc. Chadwell is a modern palatalization (*Cald-* 1831, *Chad-* 1932).

31. OE *sc* (usually before front vowels) remains as ME *sh*, as in Shangton, Sharnford, Sheepy, Shellbrook, Earl Shilton etc., but as with OE *c* [tʃ] replaced by ON *k*, there are examples of the substitution of ON *sk*, as in Scalford (forms in *Schal-* to 1527) and Skeffington (forms in *Scheff-* to 1406). OE *sc* [ʃ] becomes [s] in Sapcote (*Scepe-* 1086, *Sape-* 1086). Cf. §32 *infra*.

32. ME *sh* occasionally gives ModE [s] as in River Sence (*Sheynch* 1307, *Sence* 1610) and Seal, Nether-, Over- (*Shele* 1549, *Seale* 1576). Cf. Sapcote in §31 *supra*.

33. ME *s* occasionally gives ModE *sh*: (i) initially as in Shelthorpe (*Serl-* 1490, *Sherl-* 1499), Sewstern (*Sheus-* 1412, *Shewes-* 1609); (ii) medially as in Dishley (*Disse-* 1359, *Dix-* 1518, *Dyssh-* c.1530); (iii) finally as in river Gwash (*Wasse* 1307, *Washe* c.1545).

34. ME *k* in a medial position is occasionally voiced to *g* in early ME, as in Shangton, Wigston Magna and forms for Buckminster, Hinckley, Packington and Snarestone. ME [k] initially is voiced to *g*, as in Glenfield (*g* spellings from 1254) and Gynsills (after 1323). In the 16th cent., [k] medially is voiced to *g* in Hugglescote.

35. ME *-ct-* becomes *-ht-*, *-ght-* usually by the 13th cent., as in Broughton Astley (*Broct-* 1269, *Broght-* 1286), Nether Broughton (*Broct-* 1243, *Broght-* 1258), Houghton (*Hoct-* 1210, *Hoght-* 1220), Loughborough (*Lucte-* 1230, *Lughte-* 1239) and Stoughton (*Stoct-* 1320, *Stoght-* 1320).

36. OE *hw* normally remains as ME *wh*. There is little trace of the northern tendency to over-aspiration, though a single ME *Qu-*, *Qw-* form is found in both Wellsborough and Whitwick. OE *cw* appears as *Qu-*, *Qw-* in Quenby, Queniborough and Quorndon. There is one *c* form in Queniborough.

37. OE, ON *d* normally remains. By 1086 it is unvoiced medially to *t* in Loughborough and Waltham on the Wolds and in some forms for Gaddesby and Donisthorpe. Unvoicing takes place in the 15th cent. in Ratcliffe (2). Finally, *d* becomes *th* from the 12th cent. to the 16th cent. in forms for Bottesford, Linford, Scalford, Sharnford, Stapleford,

Swinford and Twyford. It is unvoiced to *t* finally in occasional early forms for Newbold (3), Prestwold and Swithland.

38. OE, ON *t* when initial appears occasionally as ME *d*, as in the various examples of *tūn-stall* (**4** 89, 150, **6** 130, 135, 229, 262, **7** 103, 137, 208, 272) and also when medial as in Kilwardby and in early forms for Branston, Braunstone, Peatling and Whatborough.

39. ME *t* is regularly lost in the 16th-, 17th- and 18th-century forms of *-ton*, as in Aylestone (*Elson* 1725), Branston (*Branson* 1611), Blaston (*Blason* 1594), Coston (*Coson* 1576), Grimston (*Grimson* 1537) etc. Such loss remains in the ModE forms of Long Clawson, Sibson, Wilson (cf. also Sysonby) and in the local pronunciation of Croxton Kerrial ['krousən], Muston ['musən] and Sproxton ['sprousən].

40. OE, ME medial and final *h* which normally appears as *gh* in later spellings occasionally becomes [k] as in forms for Birstall, Burrough on the Hill, Hallaton, Houghton, Knighton etc. ME *gh* has become [f] in Loughborough ['lʌfbʌrə]. Some 14th-cent. spellings for Loughborough show the fricatives [χ] and [þ] interchanged.

41. OE, ON medial *g* is sometimes unvoiced to [k] by the 12th cent., as in Diseworth, Dishley, Sproxton, Sysonby etc.

42. ME *-ks-*, *-x-* often become later dialect [s, z], spelled *s*, as in Long Clawson (*Clax-* 1534, *Claws-* 1539), Sysonby (*Sixten-* 1428, *Syston-* 1485), Toston Hill (*Tox-* 1314, *Tus-* 1427) and in forms for Barkestone (*Bars-* 1364–1610), South Croxton (*Crows-* c.1530), Saxby (*Saws-* 1577) and Sproxton (*Spraws-* 1539). Cf. §5 *supra*.

43. ME *r* is occasionally lost in the 16th cent. in such place-names as Glooston, Shelthorpe and in forms for Rearsby etc.

44. OE, ON *þ* usually remains (as ME *th*) but develops to *d* medially from 1086 to the 17th cent. in many forms for Guthlaxton, Rothley, Shawell, Stathern etc.

45. OE, ON *ð* is usually lost in later ME due to contraction, being retained in ModE only in Rotherby and Swithland. It is commonly represented by ME *d* in early forms of place-names such as Blaston, Enderby, Freeby etc. ME *d* (< *ð*) is retained in the ModE form of Oadby. Occasionally early *t* forms appear in Oadby, Somerby and Swithland.

46. OE, ON *f*, ME *v* medially is often vocalized to *w* in early forms for Owston, Ravenstone, Rolleston, Shearsby, Stockerston etc. It is commonly lost through contraction or assimilation as in Illston, Kilworth, Naneby, Rolleston, Shearsby, Shepshed etc. Finally, it is occasionally vocalized in early forms for *Prestgrave* (**4** 203) and Belgrave.

47. Prosthetic consonants *s* and *w* are occasionally found; examples of *w* include Wanlip (*Won-* 1439), Welby (*Wel-* 1371), the DB form for Orton on the Hill and many 16th-cent. forms for Ullesthorpe and Ulverscroft. Prosthetic *s* is present in forms for Thringstone (*Strenges-* c.1160–1278) and Thurnby (*Sturne-* 1267).

48. Of intrusive consonants, the most common is *g* which appears when *-ing-* spellings are created by analogy with place-names derived from *-inga-* and *-ing*[4] constructions. It is found early in forms for Bromkinsthorpe, Cossington, Knighton, Markfield, Thrussington etc. Such spellings also occur late in forms for Garendon (*Garrington* 1708), Holywell Hall (*Hallinghall* 1656), Normanton le Heath (*Normington* 1572) and Sparkenhoe (*Sparkingho* 1610). In the 13th cent., an intrusive *d* develops occasionally as in Lindley (*Lynd-* 1233) and in forms for Ingarsby and Wanlip.

49. Assimilations of various types occur, including: (i) the voicing of voiceless consonants before voiced consonants, such as *p* to *b* in Debdale(s) (3), *t* to *d* in Cadeby and Goadby (2), *k* to *g* in Tugby; (ii) the unvoicing of voiced consonants before voiceless consonants, such as *d* to *t* in Ratcliffe (3), *g* to *k* in Strancliffe (*Strangcliff* 1544, *Strankcliffe* 1544), cf. (iii) *infra*, *b* to *p* in early forms for Ab Kettleby, Lubbesthorpe and Ibstock; (iii) the loss or change of one consonant to the form of the following one, as *bg* to *gg* in Baggrave, *lg* to *gg* as in forms for Hallgate (*Holgates* 1753, *Hoggates* 1762); (iv) the change of *n* to *m* before labials as in Framland.

50. Dissimilations of various types also occur, including: (i) the voicing of voiceless consonants before voiceless consonants such as *p* to *b* in Snibstone and early forms for Sapcote and Swepstone; (ii) the change of nasal to labial before a following nasal such as *n* to *l* in forms for Kimcote and Swannington.

51. Metathesis, especially with *r*, is frequent as in early forms for Birstall, Enderby, Gumley, Humberstone, Hungarton, Misterton, Thrussington, Thurmaston etc. It remains in ModE in Thrussington. It appears commonly in place-names in *þorp*, usually in the 16th cent. and often accompanied by the change of *th* to *t*, as in Easthorpe, Elmesthorpe, Thorpe Arnold etc. There are also examples of *le* becoming *el*, as in Carlton Curlieu and Welby and *se* becoming *es* as in Lowesby.

52. Stress-shifting to the medial unstressed syllable occurs in Tur Langton (*Tirlington* 1518) by analogy with neighbouring Church ~, East ~ and West Langton. Cf. §56 *infra*.

53. Contractions are very common, as in Gumley, Harby, Noseley, Owston, Sileby, Somerby, Wilson etc. The only cases of loss of medial *ing* are in Kilworth, Peckleton, Wigston Magna and in late forms for Knossington. From the early 16th cent., Quorndon is commonly Quorn.

54. Grammatical forms of interest include: (i) the inflexionless genitive in *Basiltoftes* (**2** 26) and Bondman Hays (**6** 222); (ii) dative singular *berge* (OE *berg*) in Blackberry (**2** 6) and Muckleborough (**4** 106), *bearwe* (OE *bearu*) in Barrow upon Soar; (iii) dative plural *cotum* (OE *cot*) in Coton (2), *hōm* (OE *hōh*) in Lubenham, *wīcum* (OE *wīc*) in Wykin; (iv) present participle *-and* which is possible in river Welland; (v) the northern ME genitive singular ending *-is*, *-ys* which occurs frequently in ME forms; (vi) inflected weak genitival forms in *-an* which survive in Lubenham, Poultney, Sparkenhoe.

55. The substitution and influence of Scandinavian substantives is notable in OE place-names, as in Carlton (2) (ON *karl* for OE *ceorl*), Congerstone (ODan *kunung* for OE *cyning* in many forms) and Plungar (ON *garðr* for OE *gāra* in many forms). Cf. Melton Mowbray (ON *meðal* for OE *middel*). ON *kirkja* is found in ME forms for *Anderchurch* (**7** 34), Burrowchurch (**2** 286), Church Langton and Netherseal (*Kirkesheile* 1362). Where there are early forms available, as for *Anderchurch*, those derived from ON *kirkja* predate those from OE *cirice*.

56. Metanalysis or misdivision of names is rare but occurs for example in Burton Overy (*Burton Noveray* 1259–1727, ~ *Overay* from 1317) and Tur Langton (*Tirlington* 1518, *Tur Langton* 1573). Cf. §52 *supra*.

A Sense of Place:
An Overview of the Place-Names of Leicestershire

Geology and Landscape

Leicestershire consists essentially of two parts, an eastern and a western divided by the valley of the river Soar which runs north to the river Trent. At its centre and on the river lies the county town, Leicester.

In the north-east of the county, the Wolds, a ridge of high land, much of which is over four hundred feet above sea-level, runs from west to east and continues across the county boundary into Lincolnshire. North of the Wolds lies the Vale of Belvoir, low-lying flat clayland drained by streams flowing north to the river Trent. On these streams stand the Leicestershire villages of the Vale. Our earliest view of this landscape is that provided by the Domesday Survey which shows this area to be highly developed. Its population per square mile was at this time one of the densest in the county. Its woodland must have been cleared by 1086 since none is recorded in the Survey.

The soils of the Wolds are lighter than those of the Vale of Belvoir. Its villages for the most part exploited the light soils produced by Marlstone, Northampton Sands, Ironstone and Lincolnshire Limestone. At the eastern end of the Wolds, the Inferior Oolite of the Lias outcrops at Saltby and Croxton Kerrial providing light dry soils. Meadowland is widespread, but as for the Vale of Belvoir to the north, lack of woodland in the Domesday Survey indicates its early clearance.

South of the Wolds is the Wreake Valley with its gravel terraces, the river with its spreads of alluvium flowing west to join the river Soar below Leicester. The upper valley is wide, falling from four hundred feet above sea-level to two hundred feet west of Frisby on the Wreake. The gravel terraces and heavier soils of the upper Wreake Valley are very fertile and especially rich in meadowland, but as with the Vale of Belvoir and the Wolds, the valley of the Wreake appears devoid of woodland by the time of the Domesday Survey.

South of the Wreake Valley, the east of the county is dominated by High Leicestershire which is of Lias and Keuper Marl, mostly covered by glacial beds of Boulder Clays, below which lie gravels and sand. The centre of this upland is six hundred feet above sea-level. Despite its height, it was developed early because of its gravel and sand islands which occur where the overlying Boulder Clay has been weathered away. Its villages are sited in total dependence to these pockets of water-bearing sand and gravel. The eastern area of High Leicestershire maintained some woodland by the time of the Domesday Survey, a continuation of the heavy woodland of western Rutland.

The south-eastern tip of Leicestershire, the South-east Lowland, is much like the Vale of Belvoir in its soils. It is formed by the valleys of the river Welland and its tributary Eye Brook. A district of heavy clay soils, it must originally have been well-wooded but this was largely cleared by the time of the Domesday Survey. It is a region of fine meadowland. By Domesday, its population was as dense as that of the Vale of Belvoir. Its principal township Medbourne took its name from those meadows.

In the south of the county is the Lutterworth Upland, a wedge-shaped area which is almost all over four hundred feet above sea-level. The land is drained south-westwards by the river Swift which runs into the Warwickshire river Avon and northwards by tributaries of the upper Soar.

Separating the two principal divisions of the county is the Soar Valley which runs roughly from south to north and has Leicester at its centre. Its floor is alluvium, above which lie benches of riverine gravel cutting through the Boulder Clay which spreads to east and west. South of Leicester, the valley is narrower than to its north. Here, the river Soar and its tributaries drain a wider area. The valley is rich in arable and meadowland.

The most northern parishes of western Leicestershire lie in the valley of river Trent, a low-lying area with deposits of alluvium and river terrace gravels, giving freely draining soils. To their south are the Langley Lowlands where Keuper Marl has developed clay loams in a countryside of gently undulating land forms. Large stands of ancient woodland survive here. East and south-east of the Langley Lowlands lie the parishes of the lower Soar Valley, another region of alluvium, giving clay soils on the slopes and clayey soils and gravel patches on the plateaux.

South and south-west of the lower Soar valley is Charnwood Forest, all of which lies over four hundred feet above sea level but which in part rises to over nine hundred feet. This is a rugged, craggy, ridged landscape composed of some of the oldest rocks in Britain. The great outcroppings of Pre-Cambrian volcanic rock, once islands in Triassic and Carboniferous seas, thrust through surrounding beds of Triassic Marl. It is a landscape of rolling hills and boggy valleys. Around the edges of Charnwood are younger igneous deposits which are now extensively quarried for roadstone, slate and granite. The soils of Charnwood are often acidic and infertile. Although considerable areas of woodland survive, jagged outcrops of rock are characteristic of the landscape.

From Charnwood Forest south-west and westwards to the county boundary with Derbyshire lies The Coalfield, a large area of moderately undulating high land, part of a great heath which once stretched north-west from the Roman road Fenn Lanes. Its extensive coal measures include layers of fireclays and brick clays. The soils are generally light, sandy and dry but of poor quality, formed from the Keuper and Bunter Sandstone and Carboniferous Limestone. The coalfields were eventually exploited from mines at Bagworth, Ibstock and Nailstone, while the clay gave rise to brickworks around Ibstock and Heather. The coal, of course, has given us the names of Coleorton and Coalville.

The south-west of the county is dominated by the watershed of the river Sence and its tributaries and that of the river Mease. The Mease and Sence Lowlands form a gently rolling agricultural landscape of intensive arable farming. The underlying Triassic Mercia Mudstone has given reddish clay soils, while outcrops of sandstone support free-draining sandy soils. The river Sence flows westward and south-west to enter the river Anker between Ratcliffe Culey and Atherstone at the county boundary with Warwickshire. South-east from Fenn Lanes, patches of sand and gravel provided soils for early settlement at Burbage, Higham on the Hill and Hinckley and to its north at Market Bosworth.

In general, the eastern portion of Leicestershire provided easily worked, fertile soils for early settlers while the west's difficult terrain and poor quality soils, apart from those in its south-west, discouraged early occupation.

The Territorial Boundaries

Leicestershire's county boundaries were given their modern forms as late as 1897 in an exchange with Derbyshire of parishes of the Repton and Gresley Hundred. But many of the bounds are ancient. The south-western reach of the county bounds is formed by the Roman Watling Street, beginning where the boundary swings northwards at the Romano-British settlement of *Manduessedum* (at Mancetter, beside Witherley). It runs south-east along Watling Street to the Romano-British settlement of *Venonis* at High Cross in Claybrooke Magna parish where the Roman Fosse Way crosses Watling Street. Thence, following Watling Street, it turns further south-east past the settlement of *Tripontium* at Cave's Inn in Shawell parish to meet the southernmost point of the county at the Warwickshire river Avon. The boundary then follows the north-eastward course of the river Avon from which it removes north-east to meet a headwater of the river Welland. The Welland is followed to Caldecott where the boundary turns north-west and runs along Eye Brook, a tributary of the Welland, which forms Leicestershire's common boundary with Rutland.

It is noteworthy that both *Manduessedum* and *Venonis*, although related to Roman Watling Street, are sites with British place-names. The Romans in Britain often settled small towns (*vici*) on tribal boundaries. Such sites were regularly British religious centres. There is evidence for such practice on Leicestershire's border with Rutland. The latter is an ancient land unit marked along its boundaries by funerary barrows. As such, it may be argued that it had its origins even in the Bronze Age. Almost certainly it kept its unity through the Iron Age into Roman Britain and on into the Anglo-Saxon period, becoming 'Rota's land', following which it survived as a unit as an English possession without any Danish settlement after the dispersal of the great Viking army in 877 (presumably by agreement with Ceolwulf II who retained the territory intact). Its unity continued to survive thereafter for it to become the dower land of Eadgyth, queen of Edward the Confessor, a queen whose name survives there in Edith Weston.

Where the boundary formed by Eye Brook reaches Stockerstone, we find Holyoaks (*Haliach* 1086 DB), a pagan Anglo-Saxon religious boundary site, possibly holy to the god Thunor whose especial tree was the oak. The location was later reinforced in its sanctity by the medieval hermitage of *Mirabel* from at least 1232, the guardianship of this boundary thus continuing from the pagan Anglo-Saxon period into the Middle Ages.

Further north, the boundary leaves Eye Brook and continues north between Leicestershire's Knossington and Rutland's Braunston. The latter was no doubt also a sacred border site, the impressive monolithic Romano-British figure of a mother goddess found re-used in the fabric of the Norman parish church emphasizing the antiquity of the border. A temple no doubt existed at this point. The bounds between Leicestershire and Rutland turn east, south of Wymondham and run on to meet the prehistoric trackway of Sewstern Lane. At this point where the boundary meets the track lies Thistleton, its name taken from a Romano-British boundary *vicus* whose residual phosphates fertilized the post-Roman thistles there. More significantly in establishing the antiquity of this stretch of border, the Romano-British temple at this site was dedicated to a British deity, *Vheterus* or *Veteris*, seemingly a companion of the nameless goddess at Braunston as a guardian of the boundary.

From Thistleton, the Leicestershire county boundary follows the ancient trackway of Sewstern Lane north-westwards before meeting the river Devon for a short reach below Belvoir Castle and continues northwards to the most northerly point of the county at Three Shire Oak (earlier *Shire Bush* 1777, *Three Shire Bush* 1824) at the meeting of Leicestershire, Nottinghamshire and Lincolnshire. The northern escarpment of the Wolds was possibly a major territorial demarcation prior to the Anglo-Saxon settlements, but from Three Shire Oak south-westwards to Fosse Way the county boundary is now formed by the parish bounds of a series of single townships below the escarpment, from Bottesford through Muston, Redmile, Barkestone, Plungar, Stathern, Harby, Hose, Long Clawson to Broughton and Old Dalby (formerly *Wold Dalby*). Where the Roman Fosse Way meets the escarpment of the Wolds lies yet another important Romano-British religious site, *Vernemetum* 'the great sacred place or temple' near Willoughby on the Wolds.

After *Vernemetum*, the county boundary follows the foot of the escarpment of the Wolds to meet the river Soar at Stanford whence it follows the Soar north to the river Trent and thence along the Trent below Hemington, Lockington and Castle Donington. Leaving the river Trent at King's Mills, the boundary runs south-west to Breedon, the great hill with the British name which carries one of the most important Iron Age hill-forts in Leicestershire.

From Breedon on the Hill south-west to No Man's Heath near Appleby, the boundary with Derbyshire was ill-defined until the late nineteenth century when the parishes of Chilcote, Measham, Netherseal, Oakthorpe and Donisthorpe, Overseal, Packington, Ravenstone, Stretton en le Field, Willesley and parts of Appleby were exchanged between the counties. The reason for the disposal of these ill-defined limits and 'island' parishes beyond principal county boundaries is uncertain but may have been the result of definite divisions in the Danish army with headquarters at Derby and Leicester in the late ninth century intermingling in this agriculturally less than attractive area.

After No Man's Heath, an ancient trackway forms the county boundary for a mile before it turns south along minor streams to north of Atherstone where it meets the river Anker which forms its final three miles to *Manduessedum* on Watling Street.

Corieltavi, Romans and Romano-British

When, following their invasion of 43 A.D., the Romans arrived in the territory which is now Leicestershire, they encountered an Iron Age folk called the Corieltavi who occupied not only the area of the modern county but also most of Lincolnshire and Nottinghamshire. What became modern Leicestershire was presumably land held by a recognized sub-group of such an extensive tribe. Before the early 1980s, this folk was believed to have been called the Coritani, as mentioned in Ptolemy's *Geography* of c.150 A.D., but the discovery of a scratched tile at *Tripontium* in Shawell parish on Watling Street provided first hand, contemporary and local evidence for the Corieltavi. This tribal name is reinforced by the consecutively listed names *Ratecorion* and *Eltavori* in the *Ravenna Cosmography*, names which it is argued represent *Rate Corieltavoron* (for the usually given *Ratae Corieltavorum*).[1]

A tribal caput for the southern Corieltavi was established by the Romans at what is now the site of Leicester on the line of the great Fosse Way which eventually ran from Lincoln to Exeter in Devon. Evidence of a military ditch suggests that there was a Roman army fortress previously on the site, but there is no evidence for Iron Age fortifications. The earliest recorded instance of the name of this civitas caput is *Ratis*, a singular form, a British **rātis* 'an earthen rampart, a fortification', to be compared with Irish *rāth* 'a fort, a rath'. The later style of the name, Romano-British *Ratae*, is plural, hence 'ramparts'. Whether the caput's name was transferred from what was obviously a major stronghold of the tribe, the majestic hill-fort at Burrough on the Hill, twelve miles to the north-east, or from Bury Camp, Ratby, five miles to the west, is uncertain. *Ratis* is first recorded in a decree of 106 A.D. granting Roman citizenship to Marcus Ulpius Novantico of the First Cohort of Britons, found in Dacia (what is now north-west Romania and annexed to the Roman empire by Trajan in that year). He was a foot-soldier (*peditus*) in a vexillation of British auxiliaries which was serving at the Roman frontier there. He was 'RATIS', i.e. 'from *Ratis*'. Of a little later date, the name of the civitas capital is found on a milestone of the reign of Hadrian at Thurmaston on Fosse Way, this

[1] R. S. O. Tomlin, 'Non Coritani sed Corieltauvi', *Antiquaries Journal* 63 (1983), 353–5.

dating to 119–120 A.D., proclaiming 'A RATIS M II', i.e. 'to *Ratis* two miles' (*milia passuum II*).

While coin evidence suggests the spread of the Corieltavi as far as Old Sleaford in Lincolnshire, their heartland was probably Leicestershire whose natural boundaries could well have been the rivers Avon and Welland to the south-east, the border of the ancient territory that became Rutland to the east and the escarpment of the Wolds across the north, followed by the course of the river Trent, and on to the Iron Age hill-fort of Breedon as a north-western stronghold. The line of Roman Watling Street to the south-west may have imposed a new tribal boundary, especially as the name of the settlement of *Venonis* at the crossing of Watling Street with Fosse Way appears to mean 'the place of the tribe or kindred', from British **ueni-* 'kindred', thus making a tribal statement of demarcation. It is possible, however, that the dense woodland of what was to become the Forest of Arden provided in any case a natural frontier. Woodland clearance as late as the early Anglo-Saxon period as evidenced by *lēah* names on the line of Watling Street here, as Hinckley, Lindley and Witherley, appears to record the forest's northward extent. St Edith's Church at Orton on the Hill, a little north-west of Witherley, is recorded as *ecclesia de Overton subtus Ardern* in 1294 and 1342. That it spread further east is indicated by the name of the medieval church of St Mary in Arden at Great Bowden by Market Harborough, the style still recorded there as late as 1526.

Ratae has left little of note in local place-names. Concretely, the Jewry Wall representing the west side of a Roman basilica survives, having been incorporated in the narthex of an early Anglo-Saxon church on the site of the later St Nicholas's. It was so named from a meeting house of the Jurats, the medieval town councillors of Leicester, while Raw Dykes was a name given to another Roman survivor, an aqueduct. There appears to be nothing else; but the rectangular shape of the Roman walls which surrounded the town from the end of the third century survived intact to be clearly discerned in Thomas Roberts' town plan of 1741 and that of J. Fowler of 1828.

The Roman road system in Leicestershire presents itself as the spokes of a wheel radiating from the caput *Ratae* at its hub. From *Lindum Colonia* in the north-east comes Fosse Way to *Ratae* and from *Ratae* continues south-west to cross Watling Street at *Venonis*. From *Ratae*, even more to the south-west to *Manduessedum* on Watling Street runs what is now Fenn Lanes. The road is lost between Leicester and Kirkby Mallory but its line is remembered by such field-names as *Strathawe* in Cadeby and *Strathow* in Kirby Muxloe. This was no doubt the road taken by Richard III, his army and cannon, on his way to meet Henry Tudor at the Battle of Bosworth in 1485.

From *Ratae* south-east ran '*Via Devana*' (Gartree Road) to meet Ermine Street south of *Durobrivae* (Water Newton). From Ermine Street south of Ancaster a road crossed the Wolds south-west to meet Fosse Way just south of *Vernemetum* (near Willoughby on the Wolds) and continued to Barrow upon Soar and thence across Charnwood Forest where its route is lost, but is surmised by being remembered in the name of Stretton en le Field, presumably to meet Watling Street at *Letocetum* (at Wall in Staffordshire). A minor road in the north-east, now called King Street Lane, joined the Roman *vicus* at Goadby Marwood with that at Thistleton on the Rutland border. A lost minor road, later called *Barnsdale Strete*, ran east from Gartree Road at Medbourne to *Durobrivae* on Ermine Street. Of all these roads, only Fosse Way, named from its ditched and agger construction (OE *foss* 'a ditch') has a name relating to its physical presence. The earliest reference to it is in a doubtful fourteenth-century copy of a charter of 705 A.D. relating to land in Somerset, where we find it as an item, *anlang foss*.

The names of several of the Romano-British settlement sites in the county are recorded. On Watling Street, the name of the *vicus* of *Manduessedum* (Latin from Brit **Manduessedo*) survives only as the first element of the later Mancetter, the name in origin a Brit **mandu-* 'horse' and **essedo-* 'chariot'. Further south-east on Watling Street is *Venonis* at High Cross in Sharnford, a name from a British base **ueni-* 'family, kindred', hence as observed above, a Corieltavi tribal marker '(place of) the kindred, tribe'. The *territorium* of this important township appears to be represented by the lines of the present parish boundaries of Bittesby, Ullesthorpe, Claybrooke, Sharnford and Wigston Parva on the Leicestershire side of Watling Street and those of Copston Magna, Wibtoft and Willey on its Warwickshire side. *Tripontium* lies even further south-east on Watling Street in Shawell parish. This name is from Latin *tri-* 'three' and *pont-* 'bridge', hence '(place of) three bridges', but since there are no major streams at the location, perhaps a series of causeways over marshy ground was indicated. Possible also is a name alluding to a longer stretch of road containing three proper bridges, the most south-easterly at what is now Dow Bridge carrying the road over the river Avon at Catthorpe, a lost bridge over the stream at Shawell and what is now Bransford Bridge carrying Watling Street across the river Swift in Cotesbach parish further north-west. The major border settlement of *Vernemetum* (a Latin form from Brit *Vernemeton*) began as a holy site, 'the great or very sacred temple', from **uer-* 'very, great' and **nemet* 'sacred place, sanctuary' (cf. *Aquae Arnemetiae*, the Roman spa at Buxton, Derbyshire). The names of the small *vici* at Medbourne, Goadby Marwood and Ravenstone are unknown, although that at Ravenstone is noteworthy for its exploitation of the local clays for its potteries. There was a settlement at Barrow upon Soar where a Romano-British cemetery has been discovered but the habitation site remains elusive. There must have been a very important bridge here (as there was in the medieval period) carrying the road from across the Wolds on its way via Charnwood and the *vicus* at Ravenstone, past Stretton en le Field, presumably to *Letocetum*. Villas are known only through archaeological remains at Medbourne (3), Hallaton, East Langton, West Langton, Rothley and Shangton, mostly in the fertile South-east Lowland area.

Names of Leicestershire's pre-English rivers remain: the Anker, Avon, Chater, Devon, Saffron, Soar, Trent, Welland and *Glene* (which survives in the place-names Great ~ and Little Glen). To these may be added the lost **Legra* (cf. the French river Loire) which, via an Anglo-Saxon folk-name **Legora* 'the dwellers on the river Legor', became compounded in the name of Leicester itself. It survives as the place-name Leire. Minor streams with pre-English names appear to be a lost **Severne* running through Walton on the Wolds (**3** 213) and Seagrave (**3** 270), a lost **Dove* in Oadby (**5** 168) and a lost **Lugge* in Lutterworth (**5** 143). The river Tweed may be pre-English, but no forms before the late eighteenth century are recorded.

Apart from Leicester and Mancetter, place-names which suggest the survival of the Romano-British inhabitants of the area in the Anglo-Saxon period are to be found principally in the north and the north-west of the county, with a small group in the far south. Place-names with OE *walh* 'a Briton' are Walton on the Wolds in the north, Isley Walton in the north-west, Walton and Walcote in the south. The east is devoid of such names except for the lost *Walworthehow* (**2** 41) in Muston, to be compared with Walworth in Surrey. The township names with *walh* are surrounded by groups of lost minor names whose bases are most likely British but are uncertain of interpretation because of the limited material surviving, usually as single forms. Only Breedon, with Brit **brigā* (PrW **breȝ*) 'a hill', and Charley/Charnwood with PrW **carn* 'a heap of stones' are well documented. (One may add to them the place-names Leire and Great Glen with Glen Parva as former river-names.) Charnock Hill in Castle Donington (**7** 47) and *Charnell Wood* in Belton (**7** 28) may also be from PrW **carn*. High Cademan in Whitwick (**7** 73) may be from PrW **cadeir* 'a chair, a seat', as may Chitterman Hill(s) in Ulverscroft (**7** 237). A further hill-name which could be very early and from Brit **barro-* 'a top, a summit' is Barom Hill in Gilmorton (**5** 98). From PrW **creig* 'a steep hill, a cliff' appear to be *Creake Hill* in Stonton Wyville (**4** 256) and *Gricke* in Kibworth Beauchamp (**4** 134). From PrW **mönïð* may well be *Mantyll* in Swannington (**7** 214), Mindhill in Wilson (**7** 44) and *Munetil* in Burton on the Wolds (**3** 57). Names such as Pen Hill perhaps contain PrW **penn* 'a head, a hill' rather than OE *penn* 'a fold, a pen for livestock', but *Panhill* in Lockington (**7** 106) and Pen Hill in Whitwick (**7** 75) and in Enderby (**6** 88) may be considered of British origin. To these may be added *Pennyston* in Ibstock (**6** 149). In Seagrave, *Finchit* (**3** 208) and *Trunchit* **3** 213) perhaps contain PrW *cę̄d* 'a wood', with respectively PrW **fin* 'a boundary' and PrW *trūm* 'a nose', the latter in some transferred topographical sense.

As well as OE *walh*, English minor names which refer to the British are *Cumberdale* in Wymeswold (**3** 279) and *Cumberlea* in Seagrave (**3** 211), both with OE *Cumbre* 'the Cymry, the British' and *Bretterhul* in Wigston Magna (**5** 227) with OE *Bretta* (gen.pl. *Brettas*) 'Britons'. OE *wælisc* 'British' appears in a series of repeated minor names, as *Walchemore* in Burton Lazars (**2** 76) and Skeffington (**3** 21), *Walsemore* in Leesthorpe (**2** 240), *Walschemore* in Cosby (**5** 72) and *Welchmore* in Leire (**5** 136). It is worthy of note that the instances of such names in Burton Lazars, Leesthorpe and Skeffington are unusually isolated in the extreme east of the county. All are compounded with OE *mōr* 'a moor', alluding to unattractive ground. *Walsshecroft* in Shepshed (**7** 205) and *Welchwod* in Swannington (**7** 217), with OE *croft* 'a small enclosed field' and OE *wudu* 'a wood' respectively are further instances, although *Welsh Slade* in Barton in the Beans (**6** 238), with OE *slæd* 'a valley' as a late recording of 1840, is less convincing. In general, names which indicate Romano-British survival are confined to the agriculturally less attractive west of the county with only a few surviving peripherally in the east.

The Anglo-Saxon Settlement

It is to be presumed that Anglo-Saxon settlers arrived in what became Leicestershire by the middle of the fifth century, but perhaps more likely by the early sixth. The British had appealed to Flavius Honorius, Roman Emperor of the West (393–423), for help against invading barbarians from the north but his reply sent c.410 told the *civitates* that they must take care of themselves. Effectively, this marked the end of Roman rule in Britain. Gildas in *De Excidio et Conquestu Britanniae* of c.545 tells of a *superbus tyrannus* inviting Germanic mercenaries to help with the defence of the eastern part of the island. Bede in his *Historia Ecclesiastica Gentis Anglorum* of c.730 cites the date of 449 for this event, naming a Vortigern (or Vertigern, probably a title rather than a personal name, from Brit **uer-* 'over, great' and **tigern* 'lord') as the *superbus tyrannus* of Gildas and the Anglo-Saxon leaders of the warrior bands arriving to help defend the country as Hengist and Horsa. This marked the *Adventus Saxonum*, after which the floodgates of Germanic immigration opened. The process of settlement must have been gradual. We know that a British leader, one Ambrosius Aurelianus, was stemming the Anglo-Saxon tide towards the west, especially at the Battle of Mount Badon (*Mons Badonicus*) c.493.

Bede was to define the major groups of Germanic settlers as Angles, Saxons, Jutes and Frisians but there must have been initially a complex intermingling of disparate folk groups. The pagan Anglo-Saxon burial sites in Leicestershire, of which some forty are known, lie principally around Leicester itself, to its north along the river Soar, to its east in East Goscote and Gartree Hundreds and in the Wreake Valley to its north-east in Framland Hundred. Pagan burials are noticeably absent from the south and west of the county. Burial practices confirm an early mixture of Germanic tribes. Cremation cemeteries are known, for example, at Loughborough and Rowley Fields (Shearsby), inhumation cemeteries at Birstall, Foxton, Glen Parva, Medbourne, Melton Mowbray, Oadby, Shawell, Sysonby, Thurmaston, Twyford, West Cotes (Leicester), West Langton, Wigston Magna, Willoughby on the Wolds and Wymeswold and mixed rite cemeteries at East Gate (Leicester) and Stapleford Park (Saxby). To these should be added a large number of isolated inhumation burials which, of course, could be the remains of pagan Anglo-Saxon cemeteries destroyed by ploughing as later expanding populations demanded the agricultural exploitation of the limits of the parishes. At the time of writing, some six thousand pagan Anglo-Saxon inhumation burials are well recorded in England. To these inhumations may also be added some sites recorded only in later field-names as *Deadman* (e.g. in Gumley (**4** 90), Laughton (**4** 157), Little Stretton (**4** 161) etc.) and *Deadmans Grave* (South Croxton (**3** 74), Hallaton (**4** 102) etc.) of which the earliest known in the county is *Dedmanysgraue* 1467 × 84 in Skeffington (**3** 223). Some such names, however, no doubt allude to the long-held custom of burying village outcasts at the parish boundaries which were also the usual location of townships' pagan English cemeteries.

Do such archaeological sites throw light on the development of early Anglo-Saxon place-name types? We have no reliable English records before a charter of c.672 to inform us of their nature. The first two hundred years of Anglo-Saxon place-name giving is specifically lost to us. An analysis of the earliest authentic records of c.672 to c.731 isolates a range of place-name types current in Britain in those sixty years and so presumably before, but the nature of much of the material's being from ecclesiastical sources no doubt gives a skewed presentation of what was typical and current.[2] The topographical generics of that collection are *burna*, *dūn*, *ēg*, *feld*, *ford* and *lēah*; habitative generics are *burh*, *ceaster*, *hām* and *wīc*. To these is to be added the folk-name-forming suffix *-ingas*. The townships with associated pagan Anglo-Saxon burials and with names incorporating such generics in Leicestershire are in type as follows: of nature names, *burna* one instance – Medbourne; *dūn* one instance – Billesdon; *ford* two instances – Stapleford, Twyford; *lēah* one instance – Rothley; habitation names, *burh*, two instances – Loughborough, Queniborough; *ceaster*, two instances (one township) – Leicester; *hām* one instance (if the lost *Badlow* on the boundary of Higham on the Hill be accepted as a burial mound after the style of Taplow in Buckinghamshire); *tūn* eight instances – Cossington, Foxton, Hungarton, Knipton, Melton Mowbray, Thurmaston, West Langton, Wigston Magna; and *worð* three instances – Husbands Bosworth, Kegworth, Lutterworth. These amount to approximately 50% of the pagan burial site townships. A notable exception to English-named townships with pagan Anglo-Saxon burial sites are those which now have Scandinavian habitative generics in *bȳ*. They significantly outnumber any type of English place-name generic except *tūn*, with eleven instances. These townships are Beeby, Enderby, Ingarsby, Kirby Bellars, Lowesby, Oadby, Old Dalby, Saxby, Shearsby, Sysonby and Tugby. They will be considered below.

An important Old English place-name-forming generic of the pagan period is *hām* 'a village, an estate'. Place-names with *hām* are closely related to the network of Roman roads and ancient trackways and to major and minor Romano-British settlements and villas in the east of England and in the Midlands.[3] It may be that a number of these names

[2] Barrie Cox, 'The place-names of the earliest English records', *JEPNS* 8 (1975–6), 12–66.

[3] Barrie Cox, 'The significance of the distribution of English place-names in *-hām* in the Midlands and East Anglia', *JEPNS* 5 (1973), 15–73. Reprinted in *Place-*

represent Romano-British estates which were appropriated by Germanic settlers in the north-east of the county in what became Framland Hundred.

Closely positioned to the Roman road Margary 58a across the Wolds is Wycomb, a *wīc-hām* beside the Roman *vicus* at Goadby Marwood. Close by is Waltham on the Wolds, a *wald-hām* which eventually became a royal (hunting) estate. In Wycomb and Chadwell parish was the lost *Hygham* (with OE *hēah* 'high') and in Ab Kettleby, also beside the Roman road, was the lost *Whenham* 'the *hām* at the *wenn* or barrow'. The furthest east in this region is Wymondham 'the *hām* of a man called Wīgmund' beside the ancient trackway now called Sewstern Lane (Margary 580); a branch from Ermine Street, the 'lane' forming the county boundary here. Wymondham, a villa site, is the only place-name with *hām* in the county compounded with an OE dithematic masculine personal name. The pattern of compounding in *hām* names is either with a significant word relating to topography or a monothematic OE masculine personal name or a river-name used as the specific. In general, monothematic personal names in OE place-names appear to be earlier than dithematic personal names. It may be that Wīgmund's personal name replaced an earlier specific. He was perhaps the magnate after whom a portion of the Wolds a little further west was called Wymeswold 'Wīgmund's high forested land'.

In East Goscote Hundred, only two names with *hām* as their generics are known, Keyham, either 'the *hām* of a man called Cǣga' or having *cǣg* 'a key' used of a narrow ridge of land as specific, and the lost *Luffnam* in Humberstone parish, 'the *hām* of a man called Luffa'. Whether he was the *Luffa* of the lost *Luffewyke* (in Manton) and Luffenham, some fifteen and eighteen miles respectively to the east in Rutland is not recorded. Both Keyham and *Luffnam* lie on the ancient trackway that branched from the Anglo-Saxon *Ferdgate* 'the army or military road' near Burrough on the Hill, an offshoot of which ran south-west to Leicester.

In Gartree Hundred, the principal Roman road was the so-called *Via Devana* ('the road to *Deva*', i.e. Chester; Margary 57a), also known as Gartree Road, running south-east to the important Romano-British complex at Medbourne where a small town and several villas are known. Welham 'the *hām* of a man called Wēola' lies just south of the

Name Evidence for the Anglo-Saxon Invasion and Scandinavian Settlements, ed. K. Cameron (1975), 55–98.

road, while the lost *Coldham* (with OE *cald* 'cold, exposed') in Illston on the Hill parish stood slightly to its north.

Sparkenhoe Hundred's Higham on the Hill (with OE *hēah* 'high') lies beside Watling Street (here Margary 1g), while Repton and Gresley Hundred's Measham (with the specific the name of the river Mease) is given credibility as a name with *hām* by the presence of the lost Roman road from the major bridge at Barrow upon Soar (and thus a continuation of Margary 58a across the Wolds) remembered in the township name Stretton en le Field, with OE *strǣt* (Anglian *strēt*). Measham is unusual as an early *hām* site in its location in the more inhospitable west of Leicestershire, but the Romano-British *vicus* at nearby Ravenstone was exploiting the local clays for pottery before the arrival of the Anglo-Saxons, and the earliest known Anglo-Saxon pottery industry centred in the Charnwood Forest area was in production before 600 A.D. Measham no doubt related to these.

The Domesday Survey records a lost *Legham*, the property of Hugo de Grentemaisnil, listed with Desford and the lost *Bromkinsthorpe* (**1** 218). These townships are close to Roman Leicester so that the specific of *Legham* may be a reduced form of an English river-name **Legor* (from pre-English **Legra*), the river-name eventually compounded in the name of the folk living around the *ceaster*, the **Legore*. The element *hām* as generic continued to be used to create place-names in Christian Anglo-Saxon England as evidenced by the two Bisphams in Lancashire, both with *biscop* 'a bishop', signifying ecclesistical estates.

Leicestershire has only two early sites named with the OE generic *ceaster*, used to describe an important Roman town and fortification. These are Leicester itself and Mancetter on Watling Street. The present-day village of Mancetter lies just south of Watling Street in Warwickshire and the name is treated in the place-name survey volume for that county. However, the archaeological site lies both north and south of Watling Street, with considerable remains in Leicestershire's Witherley parish to its north. Earliest evidence is of a small Roman fort of 50–60 A.D. The Roman arterial road ran through a large *vicus*, eventually having defences of the late third or early fourth century. It possessed an extensive industrial complex, principally for the production of pottery. A villa was also located close by. Coinage of Magnus Maximus (383–8) found here suggests British continuity to the late fourth century and beyond, as does the survival of first syllable *Man-* of *Manduessedum*, its Romano-British name. The name of the township, as noted above, is from Brit **mandu-* 'small horse' and **essedo-* 'war chariot'. The reason for the name 'horse chariot' given to a place appears obscure. Kenneth Jackson (*Britannia* I (1970), 76) has suggested that some local legend may be at its root. Graham Webster in his *Boudica* of 1978 argues that this was the site of the defeat of the British queen Boudicca with tribesmen of both Iceni and Trinovantes by Suetonius Paullinus in 60 A.D., who with the Fourteenth Legion and part of the Twentieth and auxiliary cavalry had waited in vain near the crossing of Fosse Way with Watling Street, at what became *Venonis*, for reinforcement by the Second Legion which failed to move from the south-west. Tacitus (*Annals* XIV xxxiv) tells of a battle, with numbers no doubt exaggerated, of 400 Roman soldiers killed in contrast with the deaths of 80,000 Britons who were slaughtered against their wagon-lines. Thus a possible source of the name *Manduessedum* is the folk-memory of the Roman battle against British opponents renowned for their mastery of chariots in battle as witnessed by Julius Caesar in his earlier invasions of the island.

The place-name Leicester also comprises a generic *ceaster* with an echo of a British name, this the river **Legra* which survives in the place-name Leire. As noted above, the pre-English river-name lived on as an OE **Legor* which in turn gave an OE folk-name, the **Legore* 'the dwellers on the river Legor', which was incorporated in the place-name Leicester. That portion of the river upon which Leicester stands is now called the Soar, itself a British river-name, the name **Legra* having retreated along its course to its south-eastern reaches. As late as c.1125, William of Malmesbury in his *Gesta Regum* tells us that Leicester was named *a Legra fluvio prœterfluente*, i.e. 'from the river Legra which flows past the town'. However, Geoffrey of Monmouth writing c.1145 in his *Historia Regum Britanniae* notes that Leicester was built on the river *Sora* (i.e. the Soar). Calling the town both *Kairleir* and *Leircestre*, he believed that it was named from the early legendary king of Britain, King Lear. This is echoed by Gervase of Tilbury as late as c.1210 in his *Otia imperalia* where Leicester is styled *Caerleir super Soram*.

Until the mid 1960s, OE place-names in *-ingas* denoting 'the people of …' were thought to derive from the earliest phase of Anglo-Saxon immigration and settlement. Such names were constructed with the monothematic masculine personal names of men supposed to be the leaders or founders of incoming folk groups. The folk-name was believed to have extended to the territory in which the folk lived and then to have become attached to a settlement site that they occupied. As late as 1962, Eilert Ekwall in the second edition of his *English Place-Names in -Ing* maintained this position. However, a seminal paper by John Dodgson published in 1966 demonstrated that such place-names were separate in place from pagan Anglo-Saxon burial sites and were thus evidence for a later phase of settlement.[4] Such names have survived rarely in Leicestershire. Foremost is Peatling (Magna and Parva) in Guthlaxton Hundred in the far south of the county, representing the **Pēotlingas*, named from the folk of *Pēotla*. A lost field-name (*on*) *Peatling* in nearby Claybrooke Parva may indicate an extent of the territory of this folk. Also in Guthlaxton Hundred is the lost *Lilinge* of the Domesday Survey, 'the folk of Lilla'. He was a leader also recorded in Lilbourne, 'Lilla's stream', now the name of a village just over the county boundary with Northamptonshire. The **Lillingas* were settled in the Ullesthorpe/Westrill and Starmore area, also in the extreme southern reach of the county. The only other possible surviving *-ingas* name in Leicestershire is in the extreme north-east, in Stathern parish in Framland Hundred, where the field-name *Bebing* is recorded once only in 1292. This may represent the **Bebbingas* 'the folk of Bebba'.

Only one certain instance of a name with *-inga-*, the genitive plural form of *-ingas*, survives in the county. This is Bringhurst, an OE **Brȳningahyrst* 'the wooded hillock of Brȳni's folk', in the far south in Gartree Hundred. The hill may once have been a territorial boundary marker. The only other probable instances of this type of name, Kilworth and Theddingworth, alluding respectively to men called *Cyfel* and *Þēoda*, have simple *-es-* genitival composition-joints in their earliest spellings, but each when next recorded one hundred years later indicates a name in *-inga-*. Theddingworth and Kilworth, both names with *worð*, rub shoulders at the south-eastern boundary of Leicestershire and conform with most *-ingas* (*-inga-*) names as being at the periphery of things and unrelated to the archaeological evidence of earliest settlement, the Anglo-Saxon pagan burials. Nevertheless, they remain English place-names of a very early period.

Place-names with *worð* 'an enclosure (with a homestead)', form a considerable body of township names in the county surveys, but no systematic work on them has yet been undertaken. No example of the name-type is recorded before c.730. In the Midlands, the form *worð* of their generics is usual in Derbyshire, Leicestershire, Nottinghamshire and Warwickshire, but in Staffordshire and the south-west the forms for the same feature are *worðig* and *worðign*. In Leicestershire, there are twelve *worð* names surviving as those of townships, while ten more such names are recorded but lost. Of the surviving township names, ten

---

[4] J. M. Dodgson, 'The significance of the distribution of the English place-name in *-ingas*, *-inga-* in south-east England', *Medieval Archaeology* 10 (1966), 1–29.

have OE masculine personal names as specifics, while one has an OE river-name and one the element *lȳtel* 'little'. Of the lost names with *worð*, only one (plus two possible) are compounded with OE masculine personal names, while six (plus two possible) have significant elements as specifics. The masculine personal names, except for one, are the early monothematic type: *Bacga*, *Bār*, *Bōsa*, *Cagga*, *Cybba*, *Cyfel*, *Digoð*, *Godel*, *Storm*, *Þēoda*, *Wina* (and probably *Cran* and *Fulla*). The one compounded later dithematic personal name is *Frēoðuwulf* in Frolesworth. The OE river-name is **Hlūtre* in Lutterworth, an older name for the river Swift and meaning 'the clear one, the pure one'. *Hlūtre* appears to have approximated to in meaning and replaced a pre-English river-name **Lugge*, which is from an Indo-European base **lewk-* 'gleam, light', to be compared with Welsh *llug* 'light, radiance'. Not only are the compounded OE personal names of an early type, but Husbands Bosworth, Kegworth and Lutterworth have associated pagan Anglo-Saxon burial sites. Both Kilworth and Theddingworth are possibly names compounded with the early folk-name-forming element *-inga-*. Ten of the names with *worð* lie in the far south and south-west of the county. They are almost without exception riverine settlements, beside the rivers Swift, Avon and Welland. In the north, Kegworth and Diseworth (and the lost *Fullworth* (**6** 232) in Thurcaston) relate to the river Soar. A small group of lost names with *worð* lies in the extreme north-east of the county, the hilltop situations of two recorded as *Langwrth hill* and *Stonewrth hill* (**2** 203, 204) in Barkestone. *Nythingworth* (**2** 16) in Knipton, with OE *nīðing* 'an outlaw, a villain', is beside the river Devon. Such an unlikely name echoes the unusual Shackerstone in Sparkenhoe Hundred, with OE *scēacere* 'a robber'. *Walworthehow* (**2** 41) in Muston appears to record with its *walh* 'a Briton, a serf' Romano-British survival here. Kibworth, Bagworth and the Scandinavianized *Steynwordhoc* (**2** 237) in Burrough on the Hill are raised sites. The survival of *Steynworth* provides an isolated instance of the generic *worð* in the east of the county. It was surely not a lone instance in this region in the past. It indicates much renaming by the English and Norse hereabouts and rural settlement shift may in part explain the high rate of name changing. What we have in many cases in the east are names given in the last phase of this process, with relocation tied in with changes of use, ownership and social context.

The relationship of these *worð* sites to rivers and hills, together with their typical compounded early monothematic personal names, occasional possible *-inga-* constructions, occasional late dithematic personal names and the time taken for the replacement of a pre-English river-name by an English one of approximately similar meaning all suggest early formation, but perhaps as a type with significant continuity after the earliest land-taking. Their lack of presence in documents before c.730 need not indicate their formation only after that date. As with archaeological materials, absence of evidence is not necessarily evidence of absence.

The example of Tamworth, only four miles to the west of Leicestershire's county boundary, may be relevant in helping to provide a chronological range for the formation of names with *worð*, since it is a rare instance of a place-name of this type with some recorded history. The generic *worð* of the final form of the name Tamworth is recorded only from the Domesday Survey of 1086. Previously it had as its generic the south-western version of the element as *worðig*, but even earlier the place may have been styled as a *tūn*. In each of these compounds the specific is the pre-English river-name Tame. A memorandum written at Peterborough records a transaction of 675 × 92 in which King Æðelrǣd sold land to the newly created monastery at Breedon on the Hill. This transaction was confirmed at a place called *Tomtun*. It is generally considered that *Tomtun* was an earlier name for Tamworth. It was early styled a *vicus*, the transaction having been confirmed by 'King Æðelrǣd in his chamber in his vicus called Tomtun'. A charter of King Offa dated 781 records a changed form of the place-name as *in regali palatio in Tamworðige* and in one of King Coenwulf of 799 as *in vico regio æt Tomeworðige*. Thus at some time during the eighth century, the generic *tūn* was replaced by *worðig*, presumably indicating a change in the nature of the royal *vicus* from something simply fenced to something more strongly defended. Certainly by the time the *worðig* had conformed to the usual Midland style *worð*, strong defences had been created by Æðelflǣd in 913, but importantly these have been shown by excavation to lie above a ditched and palisaded enclosure of the eighth century.

In sum, at Tamworth a *worð*, typically on raised ground beside a river, appears to have developed from a *tūn* when its importance demanded its enclosing in some sort. The Leicestershire sites with names in *worð* echo its riverside / hilltop location. A few of these place-names may belong to the eighth century, but their absence from documents before c.730 does not negate their much earlier presence. Certainly the notion of an enclosure in an early Leicestershire place-name indicates the need for protection and thus defended land-taking. Such names as **Stoneworth* in Barkestone and **Steynworth* in

Burrough on the Hill (both originally with *stān* 'stone') suggest some important investment in time and effort.

A *burh* was the style given to an Anglo-Saxon major defended site from its beginning. Only four instances of *burh* have given township names in the county; Burrough on the Hill, Loughborough, Narborough and Queniborough. Burrough on the Hill records a great Iron Age hill fort in the east. The present settlement with this name lies on a hill across the valley from the earthwork which was also styled an *eorð-burh* from the thirteenth to the early seventeenth century. Although having evidence of Romano-British occupation, there is none to indicate an early Anglo-Saxon settlement inside its ramparts. Loughborough, however, was a major stronghold on the river Soar of a man called *Luhhede*. An early OE place-name on the north-eastern edge of the wilds of Charnwood Forest is indicated. By contrast, Narborough is not recorded until 1205 A.D. It is 'the north stronghold', but a south stronghold in relation to it is at present unidentified. Queniborough (with *cwēn*) belonged to a queen, but to which queen is uncertain. By the Domesday Survey, when it is first recorded, it is a wealthy vill. Since a queen is signified as possessing the *burh*, it may be that this is either a restyled 'fortification' name with a replaced specific or that the generic is used in a late sense 'a (fortified) manor'. The location of the vill does not suggest a name for a fortification created in the early Anglo-Saxon period, although, as with Loughborough, Queniborough has an associated pagan Anglo-Saxon burial site. This may well indicate a renaming of the place.

Place-names with *tūn* 'a farmstead, a village' as generic feature rarely in the earliest English documents to c.730. Only six are so recorded but they are otherwise omnipresent in England. In Leicestershire, they are one of the commonest place-name type. The *tūn* was surely part of the place-name-forming vocabulary of the earliest Anglo-Saxon settlers in the county, but the precise meaning of the word in the early years of the *Adventus Saxonum* is uncertain. In Primitive Germanic **tūnaz* meant 'fence', hence a development to 'something fenced in' may be surmised and the relationship of *tūn* with *worð* in the case of Tamworth explicable.

There are 129 such township names surviving, while 65 *tūn* names more are lost, these appearing only among field-names in later documents. Of these 194 instances, 101 have OE significant words as specifics while 59 have OE masculine personal names in compound. Of these OE personal names, 45 are of the earlier monothematic type, while only 14 are of the later dithematic kind. It is uncertain whether place-names in *tūn* with OE dithematic personal names represent renaming of more prosperous settlements by individuals higher in the social hierarchy. Two place-names with *tūn* were formed with post-Norman Conquest personal names, Botcheston in Sparkenhoe Hundred (with OFr *Bochard*) and the lost *Ogerstone* (**2** 206) in Framland Hundred (with OFr *Ogier*). Such names indicate that formations with *tūn* were being created in the county well into the eleventh century. Botcheston is first recorded in 1265 and *Ogerstone* only by 1410.

There are 23 names with *tūn* which have Scandinavian personal names as specifics – the so-called Grimston hybrids. These for the most part indicate renaming of desirable Anglo-Saxon settlement sites through appropriation by Danes of the Great Army of 877 and will be discussed below.

While apportioning dates in general for the formation of names with *tūn* is difficult, a group of names in which the generic is combined with the OE connective particle *-ing*[4], linking a personal name to the generic (as *-ingtūn*) and signifying a place associated with that individual is of particular interest. In Leicestershire, such place-names occur principally in the west, forming a swathe running from Castle Donington in the north-west to Dadlington in the south-west, but especially sited in West Goscote Hundred to the north and west of Charnwood Forest. The compounded OE masculine personal names are all monothematic, as *Dædel*(*a*), *Dēora*, *Dunn*(*a*), *Hemma*, *Hwīta*, *Loc*(*a*), *Pac*(*c*)*a*, *Swan* and *Weorð*. It is noteworthy that even with the possibility of loss through renaming or failure, that within a radius of twenty miles of Tamworth, place-names of this type contain recurring masculine personal names, as for example *Dunn*(*a*) in the Doningtons, *Hwīta* in the Whittingtons and *Pac*(*c*)*a* in the Packingtons (three instances of this name). It may be that such recurring place-names record series of estates held by wealthy thegns and are related to the growth of Tamworth as the civil centre of the kingdom of Mercia. An eighth-century date may be indicated generally for this type of place-name. But when attempting to date the formation of types of place-name, it would be of course wrong to build a chronology of settlement on the basis of place-names that can be dated. Place-name formation is not to be confused with place formation.

When Anglo-Saxon settlers arrived in the territory which became Leicestershire, they would have given their own names to significant features of the landscape as well as borrowing those of the Romano-British population. Just when such various topographical names became attached to settlements situated close by them is lost to us. However, in the place-names present in the earliest English records of c.675 to c.730, names with generics in *dūn*, *ēg*, *ford* and *lēah* are the most noticeable types. Of names with *dūn* 'a large hill, a tract of hill country' in Leicestershire, only seven have given township names. In the east and south-east, Billesdon and Bowden survive, both with OE monothematic masculine personal names, *Bil(l)* and *Bug(g)a* respectively, both recorded initially in the Domesday Survey. At Billesdon, pagan Anglo-Saxon inhumation burial is known. There are five more major names with *dūn*, these lying in the later-settled north-west and west of the county: Breedon on the Hill, first recorded in the *Anglo-Saxon Chronicle* for the year 675 or thereabouts, a major monastic site with a pre-English hill name *Bre* (from Brit **brigā* 'a hill', Bardon, recorded only from the late twelfth century and having as its specific OE *berg*, presumably in the sense 'a burial mound, a barrow', Garendon, initially recorded c.1130 with an OE dithematic masculine personal name *Gærwald*, Quorndon, with OE *cweorn* 'a quern (stone)', also recorded late, this in the reign of Henry II (1154–89) and Sibson, a Domesday Survey vill with the OE dithematic masculine personal name *Sigeberht* (or *Sigebed*) as specific. To these may be added Atterton in Witherley parish, if the record *æt Æþeredes dune* of 967 belongs to the township, *tūn* having replaced an earlier generic.

Only two names with *ēg* 'land partly surrounded by water, a piece of dry ground in fen, an island' as generic are known to have become those of townships: Fleckney and Poultney, both in the south of the county and both with OE monothematic masculine personal names, *Flecca* and *Pulta* respectively. Both vills are recorded initially in the Domesday Survey, though Poultney no longer survives as a settlement.

Seven names with *ford* as generics have given settlement names, four in the east and north-east of the county, three in the south and south-west. While names with *ford* obviously depend on ford locations, it is interesting to note that six of the settlements so named lie within two miles or less of a Roman road or early trackway. It is as if the importance of these particular ford settlements was dependent on the immediate relationships of the fords with the roads. In the east and north-east, Bottesford is beside Sewstern Lane, Scalford beside the Roman road Margary 58a across the Wolds and the trackway running south via Melton Mowbray to Burrough on the Hill and beyond and Twyford also beside this same ancient track. In the south and south-west, Desford is sited a short distance from Fenn Lanes (Margary 57b) from Leicester to Mancetter, while Sharnford relates to both Fosse Way and Watling Street and Swinford also to Watling Street. Six of these township names compounded with the generic *ford* have significant words as specifics: Bottesford with *botl* 'a dwelling', Scalford with *sceald* 'shallow', Twyford with *twi-* 'double', Sharnford with *scearn* 'muck, dung', Stapleford with *stapol* 'a post' (here marking a stream's crossing place) and Swinford with *swīn* 'swine'. Only Desford is problematical, since the specific could be either the substantive *dēor* 'deer' or the OE masculine personal name *Dēor*.

That Desford is constructed with a genitive singular composition-joint does not necessarily indicate a personal name in the possessive as the specific. An animal name in the singular in such a construction may represent a genus. Hence *Deresford* of 1086 'the ford of the deer' (i.e. singular) may indicate 'the ford frequented by deer'. It is worthwhile noting that the initial recording of 'deer' as an antlered animal as opposed to an animal of any kind is in King Alfred's translation of Orosius's *Historiae adversum Paganos Libri Septem* of c.893 where is found *þa deor hi hatað hranas*, i.e. 'these deer they call reindeer'. But even though *dēor* as an antlered animal is only recorded late, the context of the Desford site beside the forest of *Hereswode* (**6** 158), together with the Leicestershire pattern of such names constructed typically with a significant word plus *ford* and also that the style of personal name plus *ford* is not common in English place-names, all may favour the animal as the specific. However, *Dēor* as a masculine personal name was known as that of the *scop* 'the poet, the singer' in the heroic elegy *Deor's Lament*:

ic hwile wæs Heodeninga scop
drytne dyre. Me wæs Deor noma.

'I was once the poet-singer of the Heodeningas (i.e. 'the folk of Heoden'), dear to my lord. Dēor was my name'.

The elegy relates the personal name *Dēor* to the period of the *-ingas* folk constructions in place-names and may indicate an early date for the origin of Desford, with the specific as a personal name. Also perhaps of significance in estimating the antiquity of the Leicestershire names with *ford* is the pagan Anglo-Saxon mixed rite cremation/inhumation cemetery discovered at Stapleford.

Two other ford sites have associated settlements, Blackfordby in the extreme north-west (with *blæc* 'black' alluding to surface coal deposits) and Wyfordby in the north-east. Both have Scandinavian *bȳ* 'farmstead, village' added to an OE name of a ford, but whether the sites at the fords were already settlements with ford-names of their own or whether the

Scandinavian farmsteads were newly settled at fords without previous related habitation sites is uncertain, though **Wīgford* appears to have been the location of a pagan Anglo-Saxon holy place, a *wīg* rather than a village.

Some 125 place-names with *lēah* (Angl *lǣh*) as generics are recorded in Leicestershire. Of these, 12 became the names of townships. They probably represent 'a clearing in woodland'. Such names are largely absent from the north-east of the county, but otherwise, surviving township names with this element as generic fall into three groups, each of which has numerous surrounding recorded minor names of this formation. In the south-east are Gumley and Noseley, with the OE dithematic masculine personal names *Gōdmund* and *Nōðwulf* repectively and Mowsley with OE *mūs* 'mouse'. In the south-west and lining Watling Street are Hinckley, with the OE masculine personal name *Hinca*, Witherley with the OE feminine personal name *Wīgðrȳð* and Lindley, probably with a tree name, either *lind* 'lime-tree' or *hlin* 'maple' as specific. These appear to reflect woodland clearance at the north-eastern edge of the Forest of Arden. The largest group of township names with *lēah* as generic lies in the north-west of the county: Charley, with PrW **carn* 'a heap of stones', alluding to the rocky outcrops of Charnwood, Dishley, with the OE masculine personal name *Digoð* of a man who also features in his nearby *worð* of Diseworth, Isley, with the OE masculine personal name *Isa*, Langley, with lang 'long', Rothley, probably with the OE masculine personal name *Hrōða* and Willesley, with the OE masculine personal name *Wifel*. All of these names indicate the process of woodland clearance, especially in the north-west and south-west of the county, but are also noteworthy for their proportion of compounded later dithematic personal names, *Gōdmund*, *Noðwulf* and especially the feminine *Wīgðrȳð*. Of note too is *Digoð* whose homestead was his *worð* of Diseworth and *Wifel* with his *tūn* at Wilson (**Wifelestūn*) and his outlying settlement of *Wifeles þorp* nearby. Although hinting at an eighth-century and later formation for a number of these *lēah* names, some may well be earlier, as suggested by the pagan Anglo-Saxon inhumation burial at Rothley. What is remarkably evident in Leicestershire is the degree of separation between names with *lēah* and those with *tūn*, especially in the west. It suggests that *lēah* replaced *tūn* as a settlement generic as woodland clearance progressed.[5] However, if

[5] Margaret Gelling, 'Some notes on Warwickshire place-names', *Transactions of the Birmingham and Warwickshire Archaeological Society* 86 (1974), 65–9.

any settlements with names in *tūn* are of Romano-British origin on land cleared of woodland before the *Adventus Saxonum*, there is scant material evidence to show that this is the case.

The OE element *wella* 'a spring, a well, a stream' does not feature as a place-name generic in the earliest English records to c.730. It occurs once only, but in the river-name Cherwell. However, it is the most prolific of the place-name-forming substantives in Leicestershire, with some 200 instances recorded. It has given the names of seven townships, in each of which the generic *wella* is combined with a significant word rather than with a personal name. The distribution of these township names mirrors those of settlements with *ford* to a remarkable degree. In the extreme north-east are Chadwell, Eastwell and Holwell lining the Roman road Margary 58a across the Wolds, with *cald* 'cold', *ēast* 'east' and *hol* 'deep, lying in a deep hollow' respectively. Beside the ancient trackway running past the Iron Age hill fort at Burrough on the Hill is Pickwell, with *pīc* 'a (conical) hill'. The three others probably relate to Watling Street in the south, as Bitteswell and Shawell, with *bytme* 'a valley bottom' and possibly *scēað* 'a boundary' respectively and Barwell with *bār* 'a boar'. These townships occupied prime sites and, like those with *ford* relating to Roman roads and early trackways, were established early in the English settlement of the territory.

As a place-name-forming element, *wella* produced new toponyms well into the eleventh century and beyond as evidenced by compounded personal names. OE personal names with *wella* are usually of the later dithematic type, as *Hildebald* in *Hyldbaldwell* (**2** 18), *Ōsgār* in *Osgarrwell* (**3** 17), *Wulfrīc* in *Wolfrichwell* (**3** 143) and *Wulfmǣr* in *Wulmereswell* (**4** 12). Where monothematic pre-Conquest personal names appear, it is sometimes difficult to distinguish Old English from Scandinavian, as in *Apewell* (**6** 32, with *Aba* or *Ápi*), *Grimmeswell* (**3** 39, with *Grīm* or *Grímr*), *Strykeswell* (**2** 131, with *Stric* or *Stríkr*), *Ravens Well* (**6** 8, with *Hræfn* or *Hrafn*), but occasional OE monothematic forms are clear, as *Gylla* in *Gilwel* (**7** 185) and *Iola* in *Yolwell* (**4** 131). OFr and ContGerm personal names indicate late formations, such as *Alein* in *Allenwell* (**2** 197), *Gawain* in *Gueyne Well* (**2** 228), *Roger* in *Rogerwell* (**4** 26), *Ogbert* in *Ogberdeswell* (**2** 9) and *Pippin* in *Pippines well* (**5** 8). The Mercian form *wælla* of *wella* occurs in minor names and field-names in Appleby, Donisthorpe, Kilwardby, Orton on the Hill, Sheepy and Swepstone in the extreme west of the county bordering Derbyshire.

Toponyms recording religious sites of the pagan Anglo-Saxons are very few in the county. *Alfletford* (**3** 281) with *alh* 'a heathen temple' and Arrow Hill (**3** 278) with *hærg*, also meaning 'a heathen temple', both in Wymeswold, are likely instances particularly since *Vernemetum* 'the great sacred place or temple' of the Romano-British near Willoughby on the Wolds was adjacent to them. It may well be that there was continuity in the sanctity of its immediate area. Other *hærg* sites may be *Arrow* (**5** 42) in Broughton Astley, *Harrowe* (**2** 214) in Scalford, Harrow (Brook) (**6** 123) in Hinckley, *Harrow hole* (**4** 115) in Houghton on the Hill and *harrow slade* (**5** 180) in Peatling Parva. Another ford-side holy site was probably at the **Wīgford* (**2** 142) of Wyfordby, with *wīg* 'a holy place, a shrine', to be compared with Weeford in Staffordshire. Waterside locations for Anglo-Saxon sanctuaries may be assumed, as in the Kentish *Alhfleot* 812 (9) BCS 341 (S 169), 815 (9) BCS 353 (S 178), with *alh* and *flēot* 'a river', to be compared with *Alfletford* above and perhaps the Harrow Brook. Apart from these, the worship of the Germanic god *Tīw* is remembered at Tysoe Hill (**6** 93) in Glenfield and that of the god *Þunor* who may have been venerated at the site of his sacred tree, the oak, at *Haliach* 'the holy oak' (**4** 250) in Stockerstone. *Thunderbush* (**7** 39) in Breedon on the Hill may also have related to him, but this instance is uncertain.

As for place-names recording early Anglo-Saxon Christianity, churches have given the names Buckminster and Misterton, both with *mynster* 'a mother church', the lost *Andreschirch* (**7** 34) in Breedon on the Hill and the lost *Burrowchurch* (**2** 286) in Wymondham, both with OE *cirice* 'a church', but forms varying with ON *kirkja*. Kirby Bellars, Kirby Muxloe and Kirkby Mallory, each from the appelative *kirkju-býr* 'a village with a church', may also record pre-Scandinavian English churches. To these should be added Wistow, 'St Wigstan's holy place', with OE *stōw* 'a sacred site'. *Wīgstān*, a member of the Mercian royal family, was murdered in 849 at *Wistanstowe* and his body taken for burial at the Mercian royal mausoleum at Repton where he was subsequently revered as a martyr. The church at Wistow is dedicated to St Wistan and is the traditional site of his death.

The Scandinavian Settlements

The Danelaw, whose southern borders formed by Watling Street and the river Welland also became those of Leicestershire, originated in the ninth-century settlements of Danes and others of the Great Army (the *micel here* of the *Anglo-Saxon Chronicle*) who had marauded through the island from 865 onwards. In 877, this army disbanded: *gefor se here on Miercna lond ond hit gedeldon sum ond sum Ceolwulfe seldon* ('the host departed into Mercia and some of it they shared out and some they gave to Ceolwulf'). The English Ceolwulf II, a puppet ruler subject to the Danes, had replaced Burgred, the last independent king of the Mercians in 874. In Leicestershire, Danes of the *micel here* appropriated land in the east and north-east, principally in the valley of the river Wreake, on the Wolds and on the sand and gravel spreads of the western and southern slopes of High Leicestershire. Such was the density of Scandinavian settlement in the Wreake Valley that the name of its river, formerly the Eye (OE *ēa* 'a river, a stream') throughout its length, was changed in its lower reaches to Scandinavian Wreake (ON *vreiðr* 'crooked, twisted', hence 'the winding one'). Leicester with its attendant territory became one of the Danish strongholds of the Five Boroughs.

The principal marker of Danish appropriation of land in the county is the habitative generic *bȳ* 'a farmstead, a village'. So many of the sites of settlements with *bȳ* are very desirable for farming that such Scandinavian place-names appear to indicate wholesale replacement of those that had been given formerly by Anglo-Saxons. It is significant, for instance, that in Framland Hundred, a pagan Anglo-Saxon inhumation cemetery is known at Sysonby and a mixed rite cremation/inhumation cemetery at Saxby. In East Goscote Hundred, pagan Anglo-Saxon inhumations are known at Beeby, Kirby Bellars, Lowesby, Old Ingarsby and Tugby and an inhumation cemetery on the county boundary at Old Dalby. In Guthlaxton Hundred, a pagan Anglo-Saxon inhumation cemetery at Oadby and a cremation cemetery at Shearsby may be added. The density of place-names with *bȳ* in the north-east and east of the county may suggest even further Scandinavian immigration in the years immediately following the initial appropriations of 877 and perhaps also settlement from the Viking army which arrived in 892 and disbanded in 896. Also, later came the disbanding of Cnut's army in 1018 after his conquest of England. If with a new name, any such later settlement is almost impossible to distinguish. But that the majority of names with *bȳ* are early, belonging to the late ninth and early tenth centuries, may perhaps be indicated by their compounded personal names. So, for example, *Auði* (Oadby), *Berg-Skáld* (Bescaby), *Blár* (Blaby), *Brók* (Brooksby), *Eindriði* (Enderby), *Frethi* (Freeby), *Gaddr* (Gaddesby), *Iarund* (Arnesby), *Kani* (*Canby*, **3** 217), *Lauss* (Lowesby), *Nafni* (Naneby), *Sigulfr* (Sileby), *Skeifr* (Shearsby) and *Stofn* (Stonesby) do not appear in the Domesday Survey. *Áli* (Welby and *Alby*, **4** 130), *Asfrøðr* (Asfordby), *Barkr*

(Barkby), *Saxi* (Saxby) and *Sigsteinn* (Sysonby) are rare in that record. While such absence is not evidence that they were only current early, the stratum of Scandinavian personal names with *bȳ* does have an archaic character. Only where a Scandinavian personal name, such as ODan *Ketelfrith* in Kilwardby (**7** 16) in West Goscote Hundred has been strongly anglicized, or where as in Blackfordby, also in the far west, the generic *bȳ* was added to an existing English topographical name is there a sense of its continuity as a place-name-forming generic in the county later than the initial land-taking by the Great Army of 877 and maybe that of 896. But occasionally, names such as Galby (with the ON specific *gall* 'barren, poor') at a place where the soil is of stiff clay and loam and Ratby (with ON *rót* 'a root') among the roots of cleared woodland in *Hereswod*e, suggest later exploitation of ground not immediately desirable.

There are some 80 recorded names with Scandinavian *bȳ* in the county, of which 16 are of lost settlements. Of these, 34 (plus 8 possible) have Scandinavian personal names as specifics and only two have OE personal names. The rest are mostly compounded with ON significant words, including three instances of *Frísir* (Frisby on the Wreake, Frisby by Galby) and the lost *Frysseby* (**6** 141) in Huncote indicating the presence of Frisians in the Viking armies. There are 11 instances of OE significant words as specifics with *bȳ* which may signal place-names where OE *tūn* was replaced by its Scandinavian equivalent generic. Of these are the common Appleby (with *æppel* 'an apple-tree'), Ashby (with *æsc* 'an ash-tree'), Willoughby (with *wilig* 'a willow-tree') and Hoby (with *hōh* 'a spur of land'). The curious Beeby (with *bēo* 'bee') suggests the continuity of an Anglo-Saxon settlement specializing in the production of honey. That it was not a later foundation is indicated by the pagan Anglo-Saxon inhumations there.

No doubt there was great disruption in the colonized areas after 877 and many places would have become separately owned and indeed separately named for the first time. This would have been conducive to the formation of place-names in which the specifics were personal names. Although names given to habitation sites were no doubt often formed by folk who lived in the neighbourhood rather than those who lived in the places themselves as will be seen in an examination of the so-called Grimston hybrids, one notes from *Landnámabók*, the book of the settlement of Iceland by the Norse, that some settlers there who came in the wake of Ingólfr in 874 gave their own personal names to their new homes. Many of the personal names in the Leicestershire place-names with *bȳ* may well be those of the initial appropriators of 877.

In distribution, the Grimston hybrids, those place-names with an English generic *tūn* in compound with a Scandinavian personal name, are peripheral in the north-east and east of the county to those place-names with *bȳ* that form the main body of the settlements of the Vikings of the *micel here* of 877 and perhaps of the army of 896 who appropriated land. Simply, in the eastern half of the county, Grimston hybrids are present where names with *bȳ* are not present. In the west and south-west, the Grimston hybrids form a group to the west of Charnwood Forest and south-west of the great dome of the heathland. Here these hybrids occupy good sites of equal quality with those of the surrounding *tūn* villages which have wholly English names. The Grimston hybrids were presumably named in general by Anglo-Saxons in areas where the English population was strongly represented. In the north-east and east of the county, the Scandinavian personal names in these Grimston hybrids may well have belonged to members of the disbanded Danish army of 877, just as many of those did in place-names with *bȳ*. Here the Grimston hybrid settlements are all on prime sites with light soils from sand and gravel spreads above the Boulder Clay.[6] Whether Scandinavian appropriation in the west was contemporary with that in the east or whether settlement was later is uncertain. It is interesting to note that the settlements of the Viking Norwegians (Normanton in Bottesford (**2** 41), Normanton Turville in Thurlaston (**6** 304) and Normanton le Heath) are all with *tūn* and occupy sites similar in quality to those of the Grimston hybrids, whereas the three settlements of Frisians are all styled *bȳ*. It may have been that the Norwegians were able to appropriate better *tūn* sites because of their greater standing in the *here* compared with Frisians who only acquired *bȳ* sites. Or the disparity may have been simply because of date of settlement and availability of land. Note that Frisby by Galby is in an area of poorer soil (hence neighbouring Galby's ON *gall* 'barren (spot), poor (ground)' while the lost *Frysseby* in Huncote failed.

In the north-east, Grimston, Long Clawson, Barkestone, Toston, Croxton Kerrial, Sproxton, Coston, South Croxton and Thrussington encircle the *bȳ* townships of the Wolds and the Wreake Valley. In the south-east, Illston, Rolleston, Slawston and Blaston lie south of the English-named villages of the High Leicestershire uplands and were

[6] Kenneth Cameron, 'Scandinavian settlement in the territory of the Five Boroughs: the place-name evidence. Part III, the Grimston-hybrids', *England Before the Conquest, Studies...presented to Dorothy Whitelock* (1971), 147–63.

presumably settled south-east via the Roman Gartree Road. North of Leicester, Thurmaston with its pagan Anglo-Saxon cemetery, Thurcaston, Cropston and the lost *Grimyston* (**7** 177) in Quorndon parish lie on the desirable sands, gravels and Keuper Marl surrounding the river Soar and its tributary Rothley Brook. West of Charnwood Forest and south-west of the great heath, the Grimston hybrids form a compact chain surrounded by English-named villages. From the north, they are Thringstone, the lost *Flamston* (**7** 76) in Whitwick, Ravenstone, Snibstone, Odstone, Bilstone, Osbaston and Thurlaston. The Scandinavian personal names in Osbaston and Thurlaston became anglicized, *Ásbjǫrn* to *Ōsbern* and *Þorleifr* to *Þorlāf*. Adjacent to these two settlements, the English-named villages of Carlton and Congerstone had their name Scandinavianized, Carlton with OE *ceorl* 'a free peasant' to ON *karl* 'a freeman of the lower class' and Congerstone with OE *cyning* 'a king' to ODan *kunung* (ON *konungr*) with the same meaning. Finally, south of Leicester on its prime site is Wigston Magna with its pagan Anglo-Saxon cemetery.

While bearing in mind the reservation made concerning the relative age of the stratum of Norse personal names with *bȳ*, of the personal names in the 28 Grimston hybrids in the county, more than half are not found in the Domesday Survey, again suggesting their archaic nature. They are *Blað* (Blaston), *Fleinn* (the lost *Flamston* in Whiwick), *Fótr* (Foston), *Grímr* (Grimston and the lost *Grimyston* in Quorndon), *Iólfr* (Illston), *Kátr* (Coston), *Krókr* (Croxton Kerrial and South Croxton), *Kroppr* (Cropston), *Náttfari* (the lost *Nafferton* in Foston), *Oddr* (Odstone), *Slagr* (Slawston), *Snípr* (Snibstone), *Sprok* (Sproxton), *Þorketill* (Thurcaston), *Þorleifr* (Thurlaston), *Þræingr* (Thringstone). It is noteworthy that the *Þorketill* of Thurcaston is of the early uncontracted form which gave *Þorkell*. In Leicestershire, the very density of place-names of the Grimston hybrid type together with those with *bȳ*, both with an arguably archaic stratum of personal names, suggests early appropriation followed by early colonization on a much greater scale than would have resulted simply from settlement from those relatively small Danish armies whose nature was convincingly advocated by Peter Sawyer in his seminal publications of 1958 and 1962.[7] The dating of the Grimston hybrids is still disputed, however, whether as part of the appropriations of the late ninth century or whether perhaps even continuing in creation into the reign of Cnut (1016–1035).

[7] P. H. Sawyer, 'The diversity of the Danish settlement in England', *University of Birmingham Historical Journal* 6 (1958), 1–17 and P. H. Sawyer, *The Age of the Vikings*, 1962.

Of the place-names in the county relating to the Scandinavian appropriations, colonization and any subsequent settlement, those with *þorp*, either as a generic or as a simplex are second in recorded numbers (67) only to those with *bȳ* (80). In Denmark from which a great majority of Scandinavians came, the element was very productive of place-names in the Viking period and it was naturally part of their word-hoard when settling in England. When relating to early single settlements, the word means 'a farm belonging to a township, a dependent outlying farmstead or hamlet, a secondary settlement'. Of the recorded 67 thorpes, early and later, 28 survive as township names (42%) and 39 are lost (58%). In the Domesday Survey, 21 are recorded, of which 17 have survived as township names, while only 4 are lost. The only *þorp* name recorded in the county to predate Domesday is *æt Wifeles þorpe* of c.967 in Breedon on the Hill parish, this in a fourteenth-century copy of a Breedon charter. Of these 22 thorpes, 8 are compounded with Scandinavian personal names, 8 are with OE personal names, one is with a ContGerm personal name while 5 are simplex. More largely, of the 67 recorded instances of *þorp*, 29 (43%) are compounded with personal names (16 Scand, 9 OE, 4 ContGerm) and 16 (24%) are simplex.

The majority of Domesday Survey thorpes appear to have been settled as separate habitation sites, as were those of the Grimston hybrids and the *bȳ*s. That such Continental Germanic personal names as *Durand* (Donisthorpe), *Serlo* (Shelthorpe), *Ricolf* (*Ringlethorpe*, **2** 208) and *Hubert* (*Huberetorp*, **7** 167) are specifics with *þorp* indicates post-Conquest place-name creation. And indeed, the balance of the Scandinavian and OE personal names of the Domesday thorpes also suggests later settlement, with movement away from the areas of initial Danish appropriations into English-speaking areas.

The distribution of the Domesday Survey thorpes is interesting. Those in the north-east, east and south line the county boundaries. In sequence from the north-east, they are Edmondthorpe (OE *Ēadmǣr*), Leesthorpe (OE *Lēof*), Keythorpe (ON *Keia*), Othorpe (ON *Áki*), Hothorpe (OE *Hūda*) and Ullesthorpe (ON *Ulfr*). In the north-west and perhaps echoing original Scandinavian settlement via the river Trent are *Wifeles þorp* (**7** 43, OE *Wifel*), Boothorp (ON *Búi*), Donisthorpe (ContGerm *Durand*) and Oakthorpe (ON *Áki*). The more central Domesday thorpes located towards Leicester are the lost *Bromkinsthorpe* (**1** 218, OE *Brūncyng*) and Lubbesthorpe (OE *Lubb*).

Late simplex thorpes appear to have been so styled because of local or limited importance. Some have subsequently added the name of a parent village, as Barkby Thorpe, Thorpe Langton and *Redmylthorp* (**2** 196, Redmile). Others have subsequent prefixing or suffixing of a personal or manorial name or a significant word to the original simplex, as Countesthorpe (ME *cuntesse*), *Erlesthorpe* (**2** 277, ME *earl*), Knight Thorpe (ME *knyght*), Elmesthorpe (OE *Æilmar*), Primethorpe (OE or ContGerm *Prim*), Littlethorpe, Woodthorpe, *Thorp on le Toftis* (**3** 52), Catthorpe (*le Cat*) and Thorpe Satchville (*Secheville*).

Some townships show numbers of thorpes related to them, sometimes recorded in threes. Hence in Kirby Bellars were *le Esthorp*, *le Midulthorp* and *le Westhorp*. In Ashby de la Zouch were *Netherthorpe*, *Overthorpe* and *Littlethorpe*. Associated with Long Whatton were *Thorpes* and *Westhorpe*. In Knipton, the *Thorpes* occur again. Each of such small late thorpes presumably had a specialized function related in some sort to the great open-fields of a township's three field system of arable farming. The well-defined physical layouts of those located are often replicated.[8]

Late Anglo-Saxon Leicestershire

The shire system in the Midlands developed in the course of the tenth century. Leicestershire as we know it, apart from late minor parish adjustments in the far west, originated as the territory of the Danish borough of Leicester, although its natural boundaries of upland, river and forest suggest that it may well have been a land unit recognized as early as the late Iron Age. With the shire system of the tenth century came the hundreds, the local administrative units of Anglo-Saxon England, each served by a hundred court. The hundreds are first mentioned in the mid tenth-century *Hundred Ordinance* of Edmund (939–46, the first king to succeed to all England) which set out the duties of the hundred court which was to meet monthly, the shire court meeting only twice a year. A hundred traditionally was assessed at about 100 hides, a hide commonly consisting of 120 acres, a typical hide supporting a single family in the eighth century but by the mid tenth, four, eight or more. In the Danelaw, a wapentake was substantially the equivalent of a hundred and was so called from ON *vápnatak* 'a taking of weapons'. Tacitus in his *Germania* describes how consent at gatherings for legal business in Germanic tribes was once shown by the brandishing of weapons. Leicestershire's earliest recorded administrative system is that presented in the Domesday Survey of 1086 where we find the county divided into four wapentakes, those of

[8] P. Cullen, R. Jones and D. N. Parsons, *Thorps in a Changing Landscape*, 2011.

Framland, Goscote, Gartree and Guthlaxton. Framland is recorded as a wapentake to 1227 and occasionally so to 1509, but most frequently as a hundred from c.1130; Goscote is so styled to 1242 and occasionally so to 1509 but as a hundred from 1230; Gartree as a wapentake to 1227 but as a hundred from c.1130, with Guthlaxton a wapentake to 1203 and as a hundred from 1184 onwards.

In extent, both Goscote Hundred and Guthlaxton Hundred were twice the size of Framland and of Gartree. Framland Hundred comprises the north-east of the county. The name Framland is a Scandinavian **Frœnalundr*, the specific an ODan personal name *Frœna* and the generic ON *lundr* 'a small wood, a grove, a clump of trees'. This was the name of the wapentake's moot site, that of an isolated grove which lay on a high ridge two miles from the Roman road (Margary 58a) across the Wolds, joining Ermine Street via Fosse Way eventually to Watling Street at *Letocetum* (Wall) in Staffordshire and beside an ancient trackway also used in the Roman period, later called by the Anglo-Saxons *le Ferdgate* 'the military or army road' which entered the county near Harby in the Vale of Belvoir and ran south to Melton Mowbray and beyond.

Goscote Hundred once stretched from the borders of Rutland in the east across the north of the county to meet the Nottinghamshire and Derbyshire boundaries in the north-west. The poor soils of western Leicestershire were exploited later than those of the east and the size of the original wapentake doubtlessly reflected its more sparsely spread population. The hundred moot eventually assembled on a spur of land lying between Barkby and Queniborough at a spot one mile east of Syston and one and a half miles from Fosse Way. The site appears as *Mute Bush* 1609 (*Moote Bush* in 1635) (**3** 24). The name of the wapentake is no doubt a rare OE **gōsacot* 'a shelter for geese'. The Goscote Wapentake was eventually divided into the East and West Goscote Hundreds, the boundary between the two parts being the river Soar. Nichols, citing a lost taxation roll, claims the division to have occurred in 1346, but as late as 1553 in the *Calendar of Patent Rolls* it is still presented as a unity. Otherwise, the Hundred of *East Goscott* appears earliest recorded in 1571 and *West Goscott* in 1607. No open-air moot site is known for West Goscote Hundred. It is doubtful that it ever had one. The original moot site of the Goscote Wapentake may have been further north than the Barkby *Mute Bush*, still on Fosse Way but at a point where the territories of Willoughby on the Wolds, Wymeswold, Burton on the Wolds, Walton on the Wolds, Seagrave, Thrussington, Ragdale and Old Dalby (*Wold Dalby*) meet as at the hub of the spokes of a wheel. At this point on the Roman road there used to be a small extra-parochial patch of land which may have been the location of the moot. At the extreme limit of Wymeswold at the Fosse in the early thirteenth century is recorded a unique *Gosefot* (surely rectius *Gosecot*). The radial configuration of the eight wedge-shaped parishes, appearing like the segments of a halved orange and centring on the small extra-parochial plot on Fosse Way, suggests a place of former and perhaps contemporary importance in the early medieval period. Was this the original location of the Romano-British sacred *Vernemetum* but with continuity as an Anglo-Saxon moot site?

The moot of the Gartree Wapentake was held at *Gartre Bush* in Shangton parish beside the so-called *Via Devana* or Gartree Road (Margary 57a). Its name is Scandinavian *geirtré* 'a tree with a gash in the trunk'. There is also a Gartree Wapentake in Lincolnshire in the South Riding of Lindsey and the name is found too as an assembly place-marker in Kärnbo and Kloster in Sweden. The names reflect the Scandinavian custom of using marked trees for meeting places.

The Guthlaxton Wapentake of the Domesday Survey was approximately the same size as that of Goscote and like Goscote its large area (twice that of Framland or Gartree) may be accounted for by the early relative sparseness of the population in the west of the county at the time of the tenth-century formation of the wapentakes. The original wapentake stretched from the boundary of Gartree Wapentake in the east of the county to those of the old Goscote Wapentake and Derbyshire's Repton Wapentake to the north-west and west. By the date of the *Leicestershire Survey* of c.1130, some two thirds of the former Guthlaxton Wapentake north-west of Fosse Way had been separated from it to form Sparkenhoe Hundred. The name Guthlaxton is OE **Gūðlācesstān* 'Gūðlāc's stone'. The moot site of the early wapentake lay beside Fosse Way at Guthlaxton Gap (**5** 67) near *Guthlaxton Bridge* and beside *Guthlakestonfelde* in Cosby parish. The site is six Roman miles from Roman Leicester, so that the stone may have been a Roman milestone used as a moot site marker. Whether the stone was used as an estate boundary mark of a local landowner called *Gūðlāc* or whether this relatively rare OE masculine personal name alluded to land held by a minster dedicated to St Gūðlāc who died in 714 and whose cult became extensive in eastern Mercia is uncertain.

The Sparkenhoe Hundred is initially recorded c.1130. It is never styled as a wapentake. Its name is probably an OE **spearcanhōh* 'broom-covered spur of land', with *spearca* 'spark' alluding to the small yellow flowers of the broom. Taken from the original Guthlaxton

Wapentake, its territory was roughly coextensive with that of the Sparkenhoe Deanery first recorded in the *Rotuli Hugonis de Welles* of 1209 × 35. There are three possible locations for its moot site, each lying in close proximity to the Roman Fenn Lanes (Margary 57b) which ran from Leicester to Mancetter on Watling Street. Towards the south-west boundary of the county in Upton is to be found a recent Sparkenhoe, a site so recorded only from 1855 but with local non-toponymic evidence to suggest an earlier date of at least 1745 (**6** 1–6). The site, in its close proximity to a Roman road and to an ancient trackway running north-westwards from it, conforms to the pattern of the locations of Framland, Goscote, Gartree and Guthlaxton moot sites in relation to Leicester. A site proposed by Peter Foss for the moot site is a *Sparkloe* of 1621 in Cadeby parish, central to the hundred and also close to Roman Fenn Lanes, but this demands a metathesized *spearca* to *spræc* 'speech', with OE *hlāw*, hence 'speech mound', thus signifying a moot site. However, such is not the pattern of the names of the local moots in the county. The third site is that originally proposed in 1972, that of *Sherakehilles* in Peckleton parish, one mile from Fenn Lanes. *Sherake-* is OE *scīr-āc* 'the district oak, the shire oak'. It lay on Broom Hills, a headland above the Roman road at the foot of which was *Shirrevesbrigge* 'the shire-reeve's bridge', which suggests its former association with a visiting shire-reeve based at Leicester who presumably attended each respective hundred moot as it was held. This site would conform to what appears to have been a deliberate organization of the hundred moots in relation to the radial Roman roads throughout the county. An early twelfth-century date for such a patterning seems probable.[9]

The county court or moot with its shire-reeve was held in *le Mothall* in Leicester, recorded only from 1301. In addition to the shire-moot and the hundred moots, a series of local moot-sites for less formal business are recorded. They are of three types only: (i) those with OE *mōt* 'a meeting, an assembly', (ii) those with OE *spell* 'speech, discourse', (iii) those with ON *þing* 'an assembly'. As well as *le Mothall* in Leicester are Moat Hill (Cotes, **3** 70), Motlow Hill (Ratby, **6** 224), *Mouthill* (Swannington, **7** 215), *Mute Bush / Mothowes* (Barkby, **3** 24), Muttley (Blackfordby, **7** 15) and *motthoryn* (with *þorn* 'a thorn-bush', Illston on the Hill, **4** 131). Swannymote Rock (with OE *swān* 'a herdsman, a peasant', Charley, **7** 58) was an open-air local moot-site before the court was moved indoors to Whitwick by the Earl of Huntingdon. OE *spell*,

[9] Barrie Cox, 'Leicestershire moot-sites: the place-name evidence', *Transactions of the Leicestershire Archaeological and Historical Society* 47 (1971–2), 14–21.

as in *Spellow* (Appleby Magna, **6** 21, Asfordby, **3** 24, Husbands Bosworth, **4** 126), Speland (also with *hlāw* 'a mound, a hill', Kirkby Mallory, **6** 213) is usual in the county. OE *spræc* 'speech' does not appear to occur in names of Leicestershire moot sites, which gives grave doubt to identifying *Sparkloe* in Cadeby as that of the Sparkenhoe Hundred. The Scandinavian *þing-haugr* 'assembly mound' is found at Finger Farm (Diseworth, **7** 118), *Fingoe* (Kegworth, **7** 99), *Fyngehow* (Measham, **7** 266) and *Tingoe* (Saxelby, **3** 110). A variant, *Dingil* (with *hyll*), occurs in Somerby (**2** 229).

Medieval Leicestershire

The Norman Conquest gave rise to few major place-names in the county, although some forty or so French elements are to be found compounded in medieval and later field-names. The range of French words in the major names is very limited. In the north-east, Belvoir (OFr *bel*, *vedeir*) describes the 'beautiful view' from its castle across the Vale of Belvoir. North of Leicester, Beaumanor (OFr *beau*, *maner*) proclaims a splendid building or hall, while Belgrave, originally an OE **mearð-grāf* 'grove frequented by marten', developed as *Merdegrave*, but since the specific became identical with OFr *merde* 'excrement, filth', it was replaced in the late eleventh century by OFr *bel* 'beautiful'. Also just north of Leicester is Beaumont (OFr *beau*, *mont* 'beautiful hill'), recorded as a place-name from 1276 to 1523. While Robert de Beaumont, Count of Meulan, gained possession of nearby Leicester Forest in 1101 at the death of Ivo de Grentmaisnil, it may well be that the local name Beaumont was created on a French model, referring to the high ground north of Beaumont Leys rather than transferred from Beaumont-le-Roger in Normandy, the home of Robert's family. Also north of Leicester, the castle site of Mountsorrel (OFr *mont*, *sorel*) is 'the sorrel-coloured hill', a name which perhaps describes the pinkish-brown colour of its hill's granite. While the name may have been transferred from either Mont-Sorel near Rennes or from Montsoreau near Saumur, a local creation (forms from 1152) for a local feature as a Norman memory of such a site on the Loire in north-western France is just as likely.

In Leicester itself, two transferred names from northern France are recorded, *Normandy*, a small district in St Margaret's parish, presumably once alluding to a significant Norman population there and *Fremantel* (OFr *freid*, *mantel* 'cold cloak'). This curious name also occurs in Kingsclere in Hampshire and Truro in Cornwall. Its use as the name of a tenement in Leicester is unexplained. Also, in the town's environs, the lost Abbey of St Mary de Pratis was occasionally in the fifteenth century styled *St Marie de la Pré*, with French *pré* ‘meadow, meadowland’. Otherwise, the names of two priories are of note, Launde (OFr *lande* ‘a woodland glade’) in the extreme east at the edge of Rutland Forest, with forms from c.1160 and Grace Dieu (OFr *grace, dieu* ‘Grace of God’) in Belton in the north-west, with forms from 1241.

The Norman Conquest brought castles to Leicestershire, building of which commenced as early as 1068 by Hugh de Grentmaisnil in Leicester itself which had been granted to him by William the Conquerer and continued to c.1830 when the last major works at Belvoir Castle were completed. Thirteen castles are recorded, eight of them in the north-west quarter of the county which presented more immediately favourable sites for defensive structures.

Belvoir Castle, high on the Wolds in the extreme north-east, was begun in the late eleventh century by Robert de Todenei. It is recorded variously as a location from 1130 and as a castle from 1146, as *castrum de Belvedeire* 1146 to *Bevercastell* 1439 to *Belvoir Castle* in 1849. Such minor names as *le Ward* 1292, *le Mote* 1356, *Hallgarth* 1425 and *le Gatehouse* 1542 belong to it. Manorial courts were held here in *le Courthous* 1531. Further south at the eastern boundary with Rutland is Sauvey Castle (*castrum de Sauueie* 1211). It was built by King John in the years immediately following 1211 and is the finest motte and bailey castle in the county. Sauvey is perhaps ‘willow island’, with OE *salh, ēg*. Ravines with streams which meet at the eastern end to form an ‘island’ make the site easily defensible. It was abandoned by 1373. Its *Castell hill* 1620 is one of several such minor names relating to the county’s castle sites. In the far south-east in Hallaton are the earthworks of another motte and bailey, probably built in the reign of Stephen (1135–54). It is recorded as *le castil* in 1327, while *Hallaton Castle Hill* is a late reference of 1798 by John Nichols. Another outlier, this in the south of the county, is at Sapcote. Here *Castle Close* contains the earthworks of an early fortification of the Bassetts.

Apart from Leicester Castle, eight castles lie in the west and north-west. Kirby Muxloe Castle is really a brick-built fortified manor house, work upon which was begun in 1480 by William, Lord Hastings. He was beheaded on the orders of Richard III in 1483, after which any work ceased. Moat Banks (*le mot* 1484) relates to it. In Leicester, a castle begun by Hugh de Grentmaisnil immediately after the Norman Conquest in the south-west angle of the old Roman town walls was rebuilt by Robert de Beaumont, first Earl of Leicester, as a motte and bailey early in the twelfth century. The great hall of the mid twelfth century survives (*aula comitis Leycestrie ad castrum* 1273) as does the motte. The motte gave *Castle Mount* 1645. An inner bailey is now Castle Yard (*the Castle yarde* 1612). Also recorded are *the Barbycan in the castle* 1607, *atte Posterneyate* 1467 × 84 and a later defensive ditch called *Gunne dyke* 1385. The Church of St Mary de Castro (*la Eglise de seynt Marie iuxte le Chastiel* 1385) was built within the precincts of the castle. The Newarke ('the new work') was created as an extension to an outer bailey to the south of the motte c.1330. The now isolated Newarke Gate (c.1410) survives, surrounded by city roads.

To the immediate north-west of Leicester once lay Groby Castle, originally a Norman motte and bailey slighted in 1176 on the orders of Henry II. Castle Hill (*le Tourhull* 1343, the original motte, still 22 ft high) and *the old castelle* 1540 remember it. To its north in Charnwood Forest stood Bawdon Castle (in Ulverscroft parish). It crowned an isolated conical hill. Nothing remains apart from the name on the map. Recorded late as *Bawdewyncastell* 1477 and *Baudewyn Castell* in 1481, it is a rare example in England of a castle with its builder's or custodian's personal name attached. In this case, this is ContGerm Baldwin. Its style may be compared with that of Goodrich Castle in Herefordshire (*castellum Godric* 1102, *Goderychescastell* 1372) with the name of Godric Mapson, the holder of the estate in 1086 and perhaps with that of the twelfth-century Pendragon Castle in Westmorland, known thus from 1309 and incorporating the name of Uther Pendragon, father of King Arthur of medieval romance. Nothing is known of Baldwin. Another castle in the Charnwood area was at Whitwick. Only the modern Castle Street there remembers it (otherwise it is recorded as *castr' de Witewich* 1205, *the Castell* 1427 and *Whitwick Castel* 1545).

Two castles controlled passage along the Soar Valley, at Mountsorrel and at Quorndon. The castle at Mountsorrel was built by the Earl of Leicester and destroyed in 1217. Earthworks including the bailey ditch are visible. It is earliest recorded as *castelli de Muntsorel* in 1199 and was still known by Leland as *the castel of Mountsorelle* c.1545. The familiar Castle Hill is current, but *Castelwro* 1284, *Castelwong* c.1474 and *Castelgrene* 1481 (with ON *vrá* 'a corner of land', ON *vangr* 'an in-field' and OE *grene* 'a grassy spot') survive in records. In Quorndon in 1752 a *Castle Hill* was evident and a *Castlelowe* (with OE *hlāw* 'a mound, a hill') in local deeds of 1608 and 1670, but nothing otherwise remains.

In the far west and north-west are Ashby Castle at Ashby de la Zouch and Donington Castle at Castle Donington. Ashby Castle was begun by the Beaumonts, Earls of Leicester, in the mid twelfth century. It passed c.1160 to the Breton La Zouch family which gave their name to the town. William, Lord Hastings was granted the manor in 1464, gained licence to crenellate in 1474 but, as with Kirby Muxloe Castle, enjoyed his fortification only until 1483 when he was beheaded. The castle was slighted in 1648 following the English Civil War. Castle Donington is one of a few townships, such as Castle Bytham in Lincolnshire, in which *castel* has been incorporated in its name. Its castle was probably built in the eleventh century, was demolished in 1216 and rebuilt in the late thirteenth century, with additions in 1409 (as *castr' de Duninton* 1214, *castro de Doninton* 1242 to *Donnington Castelle* c.1545 and *Dunyngton cast'* 1579). It was finally demolished in 1595. The deep ditch surrounding the castle, known locally as The Moat, survives while a *Castelorchard* is listed in a deed of 1482.

Two of the military orders of knights founded to protect and succour pilgrims to Jerusalem and the Holy Land held lands in Leicestershire from the twelfth century. The Knights of the Hospital of St John of Jerusalem or the Knights Hospitallers founded c.1120 held a Commandery under the rule of the *Magister Hospitalis Jerlm' de Daubi* in 1206 at Old Dalby, the manor having been gifted to them by Robert Bossu, Earl of Leicester, in the reign of Henry II (1154–89). Dalby is defined as ~ *Hospitali* in 1254 and 1314 and ~ *Pital* c.1258 in place-name forms. No other toponymic evidence for their properties in the county survives. The Poor Knights of Christ and of the Temple of Solomon or Knights Templars, established in 1118, held three Preceptories in the county, at Misterton, Rothley and Wellsborough. At Misterton, *Minstreton Temple* is recorded in 1322. The Templars were given the manor of Rothley by Henry III c.1231 when *Rothley Temple* was established. Here *le tempulle de Rotheley* is recorded from 1410 to the present day. Rothley Court Hotel now occupies the site of the Preceptory or *Temple Hall*, the chapel of which survives. *The Temple* at Wellsborough is recorded from 1261 but the date of its establishment is uncertain. As with Rothley, its *Temple Hall* is on the site of the Preceptory. A range of personal names, as ~ *del Temple*, ~ *de la Temple* from 1261 to 1365 relates to *The Temple* at Wellsborough. In addition to the various preceptories, a number of Templar lands are recorded in the county. In Bottesford was *Templewong* 1253 to 1374 (with *vangr* 'an in-field'); in Baggrave were *Temple clos* and *Templelands*, both of c.1505; in Gaddesby, *Templeland* of 1502 to 1523; in Melton Mowbray, *le Templegore* 1329 to 1550 (with *gāra* 'a point of land, a triangular plot of ground'). Many lands of the Templars were transferred to the

Hospitallers after the former Order's suppression by Pope Clement V in 1312.[10]

Medieval Leicestershire was home to seventeen monastic and conventual houses. Beyond the north gate of Leicester's town walls, St Mary de Pratis Abbey was founded in 1143 by Robert le Bossu for the Order of Augustinian Canons, as was Owston Abbey, established c.1160 by Robert Grimbald, Justice of England, to the east near the border with Rutland. At Croxton Kerrial to the north-east on the Wolds, Croxton Abbey was founded in 1162 by William, Earl of Montaigne, originally as a priory of Premonstratensian Canons. The great Garendon Abbey at the northern edge of Charnwood Forest housed Cistercian Canons from its foundation in 1133 by Robert le Bossu.

Of the priories, Launde (founded in 1199 by Richard Bassett and his wife Maud), Breedon (a.1122, by Robert de Ferrers), Ulverscroft (1134, by Robert le Bossu), Bradley in Nevill Holt (c.1200) and Kirby Bellars (1359) all housed Augustinian Canons. St Mary's Priory, established c.1076 by Robert de Todenei below his castle at Belvoir, was a house of Benedictine Canons. Hinckley Priory, an alien foundation of the late twelfth century, once belonged to the Benedictines of the Abbey of St Mary in Lyre, Normandy. In 1399, it was transferred to the Carthusians of Mountgrace Priory in Yorkshire. Alderman's Haw in Woodhouse in Charnwood became a cell of the Abbey of Bermondsey in Southwark from c.1220. There were two houses for nuns in the county. Grace Dieu Priory in Belton was founded c.1240 by Roesia de Verdon for Augustinian Canonesses, while Langley Priory was established c.1154 by William Pantulf, lord of neighbouring Breedon, for Benedictine Canonesses.

Of houses for friars, Charley Priory was established in Charnwood Forest by Robert Blanchmains, Earl of Leicester, in 1164 for Augustinian Friars, otherwise Friars Eremites or White Friars. There were three houses in Leicester itself. The Black Friars, otherwise Dominican Friars or Friars Preachers, came to the town c.1253 and settled in its north-west corner. Their priory church was originally the ancient parish church of St Clement, granted to them by the Abbey of St Mary de Pratis. Their name lived on as a toponym until the early nineteenth century. The White Friars established themselves in 1254 outside the west gate on an island between two arms of the river Soar. The Grey Friars, otherwise Franciscan Friars or Friars Minor, built their priory church c.1255 just within the southern wall of the town near *the*

[10] N. Morton, *The Medieval Military Orders 1120–1314*, 2013.

Saturday Market. Their name survives in Friar Lane, but they have become known principally for the burial within their church of the body of Richard III after his death at the Battle of Bosworth in 1485 and its subsequent discovery in 2012.

To the seventeen monastic and conventual houses dating from the medieval period may be added Mount St Bernard Abbey or the Abbey of St Bernard, founded in Charnwood in 1835 for Cistercian Canons, following the tradition of Garendon Abbey established there in 1133.

The titles of abbots, priors, monks and nuns of these religious communities are compounded not only in the minor names and field-names of both the immediate areas of their abbeys and priories but also in those of their far-flung grange estates. In contrast to the names of the minutiae of the land as illustrated later in the Glebe Terriers, recorded so because of their significance in the everyday minor workings of medieval and post-medieval agriculture, names related to ownership of ground by the religious houses tend to feature larger aspects of the landscape. The following examples illustrate their nature. For *abbat* 'an abbot': *Abbottesmede* (**3** 15, Garendon Abbey), *Abbotispoole* (**3** 51, Leicester Abbey), *Abbotte gate* and *Abbott tonge* (**2** 70, Burton Lazars, Burton Grange being an outlier of Vaudey Abbey, Lincolnshire). For *prior* 'a prior of a religious house': *Le Pryours Close* (**3** 162, Launde Priory), *Priourscroft* (**2** 183, Kirby Bellars Priory), *le Priouresgores* (**2** 198, Belvoir Priory), *the Pryer wood* (**4** 150, Owston Abbey), *Priors slade* (**3** 225, Croxton Abbey). For *munuc* 'a monk': *Monkesdam* (**3** 40, Leicester Abbey), *Monkkewode* (**3** 20, Garendon Abbey), *the Monkes wonges* (**2** 115, Croxton Abbey). For *nunne* 'a nun': *Nuncraftes* (**7** 122, Langley Priory), *Nunnesti* (**7** 95, Langley Priory).

Although *grange* is ubiquitous in the county's place-names, the majority of such are modern, usually prefixed by an older name to convey the pretence of antiquity. However, abbeys and priories held granges as outlying farms, each of which was worked by lay brothers. The granges feature significantly in medieval field-names. Croxton Abbey held granges at Beeby, Branston, Coston, Croxton Kerrial, Hose, Nether Broughton and Saltby. Garendon Abbey had granges at Alton (Ravenstone), Burton on the Wolds, Goadby Marwood, Horsepool (Stanton under Bardon), Ringlethorpe (which later became Goldsmith Grange), Sysonby and Welby. Leicester Abbey held Eaton and later from Garendon Abbey, Horsepool Grange. Kirby Bellars Priory owned a grange at Buckminster. (The Templars held *Temples Grange* at Wellsborough.) The granges of eight religious houses of other counties were situated in Leicestershire. Merevale Abbey (Warwickshire) held

Moor Barn Grange, Newhouse Grange and Pinwall Grange in Sheepy. Norton Priory (Cheshire) held Wartoft Grange in Isley cum Langley parish. Nuneaton Priory (Warwickshire) owned a grange called *The Nuns* at Waltham on the Wolds. Peterborough Abbey held the lost *Prestgrave* in Nevill Holt as a grange. To Sempringham Priory (Lincolnshire) belonged a grange at Thrussington on the site of the present Thrussington Grange. (Husbands) Bosworth Grange was the property of Sulby Abbey (Northamptonshire). Tutbury Priory (Staffordshire) owned the grange of Wymondham (which is now represented by Grange Farm there), while Vaudey Abbey (Lincolnshire) held both The Grange at Burton Lazars and Sewstern Grange at Sewstern.

Chaucer's monk in *The Canterbury Tales* was the Keeper of a grange but he also loved hunting, not only the hare on foot but also deer by horseback, for which pursuit he kept a pack of hounds. Monasteries and priories in the county maintained their own parks for such recreation and supplies of game as did its lords and gentry. Medieval parks recorded in Leicestershire date from c.1140 to 1486. Of these, there are twenty-eight, with ten more of the period 1525 to 1575. Breedon Priory, Croxton Abbey, Garendon Abbey and Launde Priory each had its own hunting park, while Belvoir Priory may well have enjoyed such rights in Belvoir Castle's Old Park, since both castle and priory were early established by Robert de Todenei. One assumes that the Great Park in Belton was the purlieu of Grace Dieu Priory and the park at Isley Walton that of Langley Priory, houses of Augustinian and Benedictine nuns respectively and dependent on lay brothers for the game from them for their tables. As for castles, as well as that at Belvoir, those at Ashby de la Zouch, Castle Donington, Kirby Muxloe and possibly Groby had associated parks for the hunt, while the park at Rothley recorded in 1270 was that of the Knights Templars before their suppression in 1312.

Seventeen of the medieval parks lay in Charnwood and its environs and the heathland to its south in the western half of the county, while seven were on the Wolds in the north-east and at the edges of High Leicestershire bordering the Rutland boundary in the east. The south is markedly without medieval parks except for mention of a lone instance in Kimcote in a record of 1467 × 84 in the *Liber de Terris Dominicalibus* of Leicester Abbey. Of parks first mentioned in the period 1525 to 1559, six lie in the west. All such parks used for hunting would have been enclosed by a pale (ME *pale* 'a fence or enclosing barrier'), but only the early park pales of Burleigh Park (*park-side pale* 1628, **7** 147), Great Park at Ashby de la Zouch (*Ashbie parke pale* 1598, **7** 13) and Croxon Park (*the parke pale* 1612, **2** 103) have survived in records. Old Park Pale (**7** 3), that of *le Newe Parke de Byrdesnest* of 1550 in Anstey, is a linear embankment, significant enough in presence to appear on modern O.S. maps.

As well as the formal Christianity of the great religious houses and the parish churches, medieval Leicestershire's countryside was liberally endowed with a range of sacred sites of its peasant folk, principally in the form of holy springs or wells. Waters welling from the ground would early have been venerated as sources of life. Hence perhaps their frequent female dedications, as for example, the various instances of St Ann's Well and Our Lady's Well or Lady Well. St Ann, the supposed mother of Our Lady, the Blessed Virgin Mary, was thought to intercede for the childless, hence her patronage of wells as sources of fertility. Whether such sacred springs had their origins in pre-Roman and Roman Britain, with continuity into medieval England, can only be speculative, as is such suggested derivation of the various St Ann's Wells from the Celtic goddess Anu or Annis. Sacred springs are recorded in Old English sources before the Norman Conquest, as Gloucestershire's Cold Aston instance of Seven Wells (737 × 40 (11)) or Tichbourne's in Hampshire (938 (12)) and the Midlands example of Showell in Staffordshire (985 (12)). Nothing so early is known from ancient Leicestershire, but of the thirty examples of holy springs which have survived in its written sources, twelve date from the late twelfth century through to 1487. Ten are first recorded between 1550 and 1700, with eight post 1700. Most instances are evenly spread across the west of the county, together with a band of six across the south-east. Noticeable, however, is what appears to be a dearth of examples in the north-east and east where only three are known, absent that is from precisely those areas of heavy Scandinavian settlement. It is as if holy springs of any kind did not feature in Norse tradition and that those of the appropriated lands of the Anglo-Saxons were ignored and forgotten.

A sacred spring which did survive in the north-east was *Annwell* (**2** 65) or *Annie well* (**2** 143) which one assumes to have lain on the boundary between Burton Lazars and Wyfordby and not to be two discrete examples, one in either parish. The Ann here is not graced as a saint, but the survival remembered at Burton Lazars in 1550 is accorded a cross, an *Annwell Cross*. Adjacent Wyfordby is one of the very few sites where Anglo-Saxon paganism has left its mark in the toponymy of the county as a **wīg ford*, so that it may be that a spring relating to an Ann lived on here in folk memory, especially if there is any validity in her doubtful association with the Celtic goddess of fertility called Anu or Annis.[11] Two other sacred springs are known to have been marked by standing crosses, *Croswell* (**3** 26) in Barkby and *Cross-well* (**6** 172) in Market Bosworth.

Only three springs specifically styled as saintly have survived in record, St Ann's Well (**4** 37) in East Langton, the possible instance at *St An Hill* (**6** 171) in Market Bosworth and *St Morrills well* (**4** 104) in Hallaton. Morrill or Morrell was possibly St Merewald of Symeon of Durham's *Historia Regum* or Merewala, brother of Wulfhere, king of Mercia (657–74), instrumental in the gift of local lands to St Peter's Minster at *Medeshamstede* (Peterborough) at the beginning of Wulfhere's reign. This holy spring is not recorded as that of St Morrill until 1601 but no doubt it was the *Stowe Welle* (**4** 104) of 1318 (with OE *stōw* 'a sacred place'). It may be more than a coincidence that Hallaton is the site of a most elaborate shrine of the pre-English Corieltavi which continued to receive large deposits of votive treasures until near the end of Roman rule in Britain.[12]

Eleven instances of *Haliwell* / *Holywell* are known in the county, the earliest first recorded in the late twelfth century at Holywell Hall (*Halliwellehage* 'the enclosure of the holy well' (**7** 146)), a property of Garendon Abbey. At this date, the enclosure boasted a hermitage. The remaining examples of sacred springs in the county are those called Seven Wells.[13] Of these seven instances are known, the earliest *Sevenewelles* (**6** 214) of c.1280 in Kirkby Mallory, an Anglo-Saxon church site. Developed forms of the name type appear as *Schowell* (**7** 106) in Lockington and *Showell* (**5** 15) in Ashby Parva. It is difficult to conceive of seven springs occurring together in one limited location and especially of seven such instances in one county. Whatever the original significance of the number seven in compound with *wella* may have been, it appears to have become a norm for a type site. Seven is traditionally a lucky number in folk lore, just as thirteen is an unlucky one. Water from these springs may have thought to be in some sort sacred and to possess curative properties.

Perhaps the township name Shawell (**5** 182) in Guthlaxton Hundred needs to be reconsidered as a possible instance of a Seven Wells. It is commonly thought to be a name formed with *scēað* 'a boundary', with *wella* taken as 'a stream' because of forms *Schadewelle* and *Shathewelle* recorded from 1224 to 1518. However, the earliest spellings are *Sawelle* from 1086 to 1235 and *Sewell* from 1203 to 1230.

---

[11] A. L. F. Rivet and Colin Smith, *The Place-Names of Roman Britain*, (1979), 250.
[12] F. Hargrave, 'The Hallaton Treasure', *Current Archaeology* 236 (2009).
[13] Keith Briggs, 'Seven Wells', *JEPNS* 39 (2007), 7–44.

The obvious boundary here is formed by Watling Street through which the local stream runs at right angles. If the stream was the 'boundary' of an original name, it is unclear what sort of demarcation it formed. A stream running *through* a boundary seems unlikely to have given such a toponym as 'boundary stream'. But an early Seven Wells here may have been refashioned because of the notion of the boundary created by Watling Street. The site is also that of the Romano-British town of *Tripontium*. Could Shawell as a Seven Wells remember a Romano-British sanctuary at this location, just as the *Annwell* of Wyfordby may?

Richard III's precipitate cavalry charge with his chosen knightly companions from the ridge of Ambion Hill to be killed in the boggy ground of *Fennes Hole* (**6** 279) beside Fenn Lanes, as the last English king to die in battle, marked the end of medieval England. The Plantagenet kings were replaced by the Tudors.[14] The Battle of Bosworth should perhaps be better styled the Field of Redmoor ('reed moor'), so called in the municipal records of York only one day after the battle in August 1485, or even the Battle of Brown Heath, the heath being the probable site of Henry Tudor's encampment at Higham on the Hill on the night before the encounter. Very little surviving local toponymy relates to the conflict. The area was much altered by eighteenth-century drainage for agricultural improvement. Crown Hill in Stoke Golding may well be that where Henry received the crown lost from Richard's helmet in the melée. The hill provides a superb panorama of the battlefield and was presumably the place where Henry paused on his withdrawal to an encampment on Brown Heath (**6** 111), a name surviving until the early nineteenth century. Otherwise, the few minor names relating marginally to the battle are late folklore creations. King Richard's Well in Sutton Cheney, now roofed in stone, is reputed to have been where the king drank before the battle and Dicken's Nook (**6** 288) the place where he harangued his troops. The latter, however, is much more likely to contain a local surname rather than Dickon, a pet-form of Richard, which Shakespeare used of him in his *Richard III*:

> *Jockey of Norfolke, be not so bold*
> *For Dickon thy maister is bought and sold.*

As for King Dick's Hole, a bathing place at the river Anker in Pinwall, a little to the west of the battle site, nothing is known to explain its immediate relevance.

---

[14] Barrie Cox, 'The Battle of Bosworth and related toponyms', *The Place-Names of Leicestershire* Part 6, EPNS 90 (2014), xiv–xviii.

Modern Leicestershire

The last major township names of medieval Leicestershire are the latecomers Newtown Unthank, first recorded in 1282 and Newtown Linford in 1325, both villages on poorer soils to the south of Charnwood. No new township names were created until those introduced during the industrial exploitation of the coal, stone, slate and fireclays of the north-west of the county in the reigns of William IV and Victoria, as Coalville 1838, Moira 1831, named from the Earl of Moira, a developer of the local coalmines and Ellistown 1875, from John Ellis, a railway entrepreneur and colliery owner.

The treasure house of medieval field-names provided by the Glebe Terriers for Leicestershire parishes survives principally in documents from 1601 to the middle of the eighteenth century. But it is with the Enclosures of the eighteenth century that new names arrived in an altered landscape, the great open-fields being replaced by fenced and hedged closes. There had been piecemeal enclosures of parts of common fields in the late sixteenth century for sheep and cattle farming, as at Barleythorpe, Belton and Foston, heavy clay soils encouraging pastoralism. By 1640, twenty-five per cent of the county was enclosed. However, it was the eighteenth century which brought a significant tranche of new minor names to the county. The first Parliamentary Act of Enclosure for Leicestershire was passed in 1730 for Horninghold in Gartree Hundred. There were twelve Enclosure Awards in the 1750s and eleven in 1760. The 1760s saw forty-one parishes enclosed. Large farms were established, especially for beef cattle bred for the London market. Those at Sileby and neighbouring Seagrave in East Goscote Hundred are typical and named from important national events. In Sileby parish were erected Belle Isle (**3** 215), built after the Enclosure of 1760 and named from Belle Isle Strait in Canada which featured in General James Wolfe's victorious campaign against Montcalm in the Seven Years War with France (1756–63). Quebec House (**3** 216) was named from Wolfe's victory and death at Quebec after his feats at the Heights of Abraham. Hanover Lodge (**3** 216) celebrated the reign of the Hanoverian King George II who died in 1760, the year after the victories at Belle Isle and Quebec. In Seagrave, Bunker Hill Farm (**3** 207) was named from the Battle of Bunker Hill of 1775 in the American War of Independence, while New York Farm (**3** 207) also relates to events in that conflict.

The mining and transportation of coal were next to affect names in the landscape in a major way, with the cutting of canals and a short time later the development of railways which largely superseded them. The earliest toponymical evidence for coal extraction in the county is the township name Coleorton. Its earliest spelling prefixing *col* 'coal' is *Colloverton* of 1443. In 1498, two *collyers* are recorded here, indicating the establishment of professional hewers in a significant occupation. At this date, outcrops of coal seams were exposed at the surface to the north of Whitwick, as at Coleorton and Swannington. Colliers at such villages as Coleorton, Staunton Harold, Swannington and Worthington worked small open bell-pits. A *Colpitt close* is recorded in Coleorton in 1539. For this township, the *Collpit Book* and the *Synkinge Book* of 1572 are evidence of the development of the deeper gin-pits served by horse-driven gin-wheels for lifting the coal. Such coal was distributed by pack horse on the numerous routes called *Colepitt way* listed in the section 'Early roads and ways' *supra*. As the sinking of shafts to reach deeper seams developed, as at Swannington Common in 1760, routes described as *Colecart way* reflected increasing volume in the transport of coal, wagons replacing pack horses. Even deeper mines followed in the earlier nineteenth century, as at Whitwick in 1824, Ibstock in 1825, Bagworth in 1826 and Snibstone in 1831.

The need to transport coal more effectively was accommodated by the development of a system of waterways. In the years shortly after 1778, the river Soar was canalized from the river Trent to Loughborough and by 1794 had been made navigable to Leicester. The county's first artificial canal, a waterway one and a half miles in length, was opened in 1778 joining Loughborough to the navigable river Soar. The Charnwood Forest Canal was opened in 1794 to transport coal for Leicester. It ran from Thringstone to Nanpantan but lasted only three years because its feeder reservoir, *Blackbrook* in Shepshed parish, was severely damaged by a hard frost which burst its embankment. Two-and-three-quarter miles of horse-drawn wagon way connected Nanpantan to Loughborough as a Charnwood Forest railway. The Ashby de la Zouch Canal opened in 1804, running south-west from Moira to carry coal and limestone to Hinckley and beyond to the Coventry Canal south of Nuneaton. Its server in Moira called *The Reservoir* is recorded from 1807. The Leicester and Swannington Railway which opened in 1832 eventually proved its nemesis. To the east, the Union Canal was driven south and south-eastwards via Fleckney and Saddington (with their tunnel and server reservoir of 1796) to reach Debdale Wharf (*Depdale Wharf* 1846) at its southern terminus in Gumley. Such field-names as *Tunnel Meadow* in Fleckney and *Basin Meadow* in Saddington are typical on these canal sides. The Union Canal reached Market Harborough by 1809 to become part of the

Grand Union Canal in 1814. A well-known landmark of this canal is Foxton Locks, the staircase of ten locks at Foxton built in 1812. In the north-east of the county, the Wreake and Eye Navigation to Melton Mowbray was also part of the canal mania of the early 1790s, with construction of an extension to Oakham in Rutland via Saxby and Stapleford begun in 1794 and opened in 1802. Further north-east, the Grantham Canal joined the river Trent at Nottingham via Saxby and Stapleford with their wharves to the river Witham at Grantham.

Along the lines of the canals, bridges and wharves were named from the gang-masters of the navvies who built them and from the local landowners and farmers through whose fields the canals were cut. Those on the Ashby de la Zouch Canal from Moira south as far as Hinckley are typical of all the canals: Cockspur Bridge (Donisthorpe), Steam Mill ~ (Oakthorpe), Pegg's Close ~ (Measham), Timms ~, Hill's ~, Turn ~ (all Shackerstone), Bates Wharf ~, Bates ~, Dakin's ~ (all Congerstone), Iliffe ~ (Carlton), King's ~, Bosworth Wharf ~, Jackson's ~, Deakin's ~, Fox ~, Hook's ~ (all Market Bosworth), Sutton Wharf ~ (Sutton Cheney) and Nutt's Bridge (Hinckley). Of these, only Turn Bridge is untypical, a 'turnover' bridge being one which allowed a horse to cross the canal while still drawing a barge and without the need to unhitch the towrope.

The industrial development of north-west Leicestershire demanded further growth in modes of transportation. The canals gave way to the expansion of railways for ease of movement and carrying capacity. Coal was the prime mover, with the advent of deep mines, but granite, limestone, gravel, slate, sand and pottery clay all needed carriage. William Stenson, a colliery owner of Whitwick and John Ellis, who gave his name to Ellistown where he opened a colliery in 1876, promoted a railway from the coalfields to Leicester. Ellis was a friend of George Stephenson whose Stockton and Darlington Railway provided the stimulus. Stephenson's son, Robert, was appointed engineer for the venture. The Leicester and Swannington Railway opened in 1832 from Moira via the Glenfield Tunnel of more than one mile in length to its West Bridge terminus. This cut the cost of Derbyshire coal brought by the river Soar Navigation to the county town. The 1835 first edition (with mid nineteenth-century additions) of the one inch Ordnance Survey map of Leicestershire shows the Midland Counties Railway running from the north to Leicester and on to the southern county boundary, the Leicester and Burton Branch Railway from Ashby de la Zouch which had taken over part of the Leicester and Swannington line and the Syston and Peterborough Branch Railway running to Leicester from the north-east along the Wreake Valley. In the south-east, the Leicester and Hitchin Branch of the Midland Railway is shown running from the junction near Wigston Magna to Kettering in Northamptonshire. In the south, the Rugby and Stamford Branch Railway is serving such towns as Market Harborough and Husbands Bosworth, while the Nuneaton and Leicester Railway belies its name, running from Nuneaton only as far as Hinckley. The short Mount Sorrel Railway which was established principally to carry granite from Mountsorrel runs to a Midland Counties Railway wharf south of Barrow upon Soar. Deep mines were opened in 1876 at Hugglescote and Nailstone as well as at Ellistown, with the last two sunk at Desford in 1900 and Lount in 1924. The railways added significantly to the name stock of the county. Those along the short Leicester and Swannington Railway are typical of all lines: as Ashby de la Zouch's *Coal Wharf*, Swannington's *Inclined Plane*, *Railway Close* and *Tunnel Close*, Bagworth's *Incline Field* and *Signal Box Field* and Glenfield's *Glenfield Tunnel* and *Station Field*. The scale of Victorian building of railways in Leicestershire, while creating a range of minor names and field-names related to them, promises a significant loss of such names now that lines have been closed and dismantled in favour of motorized transport.

Loss is also continuing apace with the names of inns and taverns in the face of social change. Such names are as much a part of the historical toponomy of the county as the clearing of Hinca 'the limper' at Hinckley, Ulf's croft at Ulverscroft or Baldwin's fortification at Bawdon Castle (**7** 237). Although many names of inns and taverns are national, such as those presenting the Red Lion coat of arms of John of Gaunt or the White Hart of King Richard II, there are many which record people, both public figures and obscure and industries, trades and events belonging specifically to Leicestershire.[15] There are such dignitaries remembered as the Earl of Cardigan in the *Cardigan Arms* in Cranoe, where the earl was Lord of the Manor, Francis, Lord Carington in the *Carington Arms* in Ashby Folville who founded the almshouses there in 1673 for seven poor men, the *Denbigh Arms* in Lutterworth where the Earls of Denbigh were Lords of the Manor or the *Hastings Arms* in Ashby de la Zouch of which William, Lord Hastings, was granted the manor and licence to crenellate in 1474, only to be beheaded in 1483 on the orders of King Richard III. On a grander scale was the *Marquis of Granby*, heir of the Duke of Rutland of Belvoir

[15] Barrie Cox, *English Inn and Tavern Names*, 1994.

Castle. John Manners, Marquis of Granby from 1721 to 1770, became a popular hero as leader of the victorious cavalry at Warburg against the French in the Seven Years War. Ten hostelries in the county record him. Less heroic but perhaps as large in scale and repute was one Daniel Lambert (1770–1809). The *Daniel Lambert* was named from the former keeper of Leicester town jail who made money out of his huge bulk by touring the country, exhibiting himself rather in the manner of the Durham Ox of the days of early nineteenth-century livestock development. At his death, he weighed some fifty-three stones. The tavern named after him is no more. In terms of trade and industry, the *Fish and Quart* remembered the former porters of Leicester's fish market who habitually drank their ale from quart pots. Also in Leicester, the *Heanor Boat* recalled coal brought by canal barge from the area of Heanor in the Derbyshire coalfield via the Soar Navigation before coal delivered from the Leicestershire coalfield by railway led to that route's demise. The *Union* at Glen Parva was the tavern of the bargemen of the Union Canal before it became part of the Grand Union Canal in 1814. The *Crispin's Arms* in Leicester was so called from Crispin, patron saint of shoemakers and cobblers, an appropriate protector of the important footwear manufactory of the town in the nineteenth century. The *Tailors' Arms* was named from *the Company of Taylers of the Borough of Leicester* of 1689. Likewise the *Woolcombers' Arms* and the *Woolstaplers' Arms* reflected Leicester's wool-yarn industry of the nineteenth century. Leicester's the *Iron Founders' Arms* and the *Foundry Arms* both related to the former Court and Company's iron foundry which appears at *Gass Street* (sic) on Fowler's town map of 1828. On a more intimate scale is a tavern name given by a hostelry's mine host. Hence the *Bakers' Arms* of Thorpe Langton was that of Thomas Smith, its publican from 1846 to 1863 who was also a baker, the *Chandlers' Arms* of Shearsby that of Richard Botterill, also a chandler in 1846, the *Bricklayers' Arms* of Bagworth that of William Dikes, also a bricklayer in 1863. The *York Castle* in Leicester was so named by its innkeeper of 1846, John York. Of the *Butchers' Arms* in Husbands Bosworth, Francis Groocock, a butcher, was husband of its tenant Lucy Groocock.

The four most modern major names in Leicestershire relate to transportation. Three of these are to do with motorways, the M1 Motorway which divides the county in two, running north to south, the ancient *Hereswode* or Leicester Forest through which it cuts remembered popularly nowadays only by its well-known Leicester Forest East Service Station — and the later M69 Motorway from

Leicester to Coventry. The fourth name is that of East Midlands Airport, the presence of which bears heavily upon Castle Donington's old-world ambience.

The eastern half of Leicestershire long provided the most favourable soils for early farming and was exploited by Anglo-Saxons and Scandinavians alike, as well as by later medieval and Tudor pastoralists. With the development of industry from the early eighteenth century onwards, the prosperity of the western half of the county burgeoned and with it came the growth of large towns such as Loughborough, Ashby de la Zouch, Coalville, Hinckley and Shepshed, while the east remains in general the countryside of villages and agriculture.

INDEX, PART **8**

This index includes all river-names, names of major roads and ways and those place-names, minor names and field-names noted in the concluding section 'A Sense of Place: an Overview of the Place-Names of Leicestershire'. Lost field-names are in italics and identified by townships. References are not given to names appearing in the analyses or to the listed personal names or family names.

Abbotte gate (Burton Lazars) 132
Abbottesmede (Asfordby) 132
Abbotispoole (Belgrave) 132
Ab Kettleby 105
Alby (Illston on the Hill) 118
Alderman's Haw 131
Alfletford (Wymeswold) 116
Allen well (Redmile) 116
Almeshouses, The
(Ashby Folville) 140
Alton 132
Ambion Hill 136
Andreschirch
(Breedon on the Hill) 117
Anker, R. 2, 97
Annie well (Wyfordby) 134
Annwell (Burton Lazars) 134
Apewell (Bagworth) 116
Appleby 116
Arnesby 118
Arrow (Broughton Astley) 117
Arrow Hill (Wymeswold) 116
Asfordby 118, 126
Ashby Castle 129
Ashby de la Zouch 140
Ashby de la Zouch Canal 138
Ashby Folville 140
Atterton 113
Avon, R. 2, 94
Badlow (Higham on the Hill) 104
Bagworth 95, 109
Bakers' Arms (P.H.) 141
Bardon 113
Barkby 118, 124
Barkby Thorpe 122
Barkestone 109
Barleythorpe 137
Barnsdale strete (Great Easton) 100
Barom Hill 102
Barrow upon Soar 101
Barwell 116
Basin Meadow (Saddington) 138
Bates Bridge (Congerstone) 139
Bawdon Castle 129
Bates Wharf Bridge 139
Beaumanor 127
Beaumont 127
Beaumont Leys 127
Bebing (Stathern) 108
Beeby 119
Belgrave 127
Belle Isle 137
Belton 128
Belvoir 127
Belvoir Castle 128
Belvoir Priory 131
Bescaby 118
Billesdon 104, 113

Bilstone 121
Birstall 103
Bittesby 100
Bitteswell 116
Blaby 118
Blackbrook Reservoir 138
Blackfordby 114
Black Friars Priory 131
Blaston 120
Boothorpe 122
Bosworth Grange 133
Bosworth Wharf Bridge 139
Botcheston 112
Bottesford 113
Bradley Priory 131
Bransford Bridge 100
Branston 132
Breedon on the Hill 97, 99
Breedon Priory 131
Bretterhull (Wigston Magna) 102
Bricklayers' Arms (P.H.) 141
Bringhurst 108
Bromkinsthorpe (Leicester) 122
Brooksby 118
Broom Hills 126
Brown Heath 136
Buckminster 117
Bunker Hill Farm 137
Burbage 95
Burleigh Park 133
Burrough on the Hill 98
Burrowchurch (Wymondham) 117
Burton Lazars 102
Burton on the Wolds 124
Bury Camp (Ratby) 98
Butchers' Arms (P.H.) 141

Cadeby 126
Canby (Sileby) 118
Cardigan Arms (P. H.) 140
Carington Arms (P.H.) 140
Carlton 121, 139
Castelgrene (Mountsorrel) 129
Castell hill (Withcote) 128
Castelorchard (Castle Donington) 130
Castelwong (Mountsorrel) 129
Castelwro (Mountsorrel) 129
Castle Close 128
Castle Donington 112, 129
Castle Hill (Groby) 129
Castle Hill (Mountsorrel) 129
Castle Hill (Quorndon) 129
Castlelowe (Quorndon) 129
Catthorpe 123
Cave's Inn 96
Chadwell 116
Chandlers' Arms (P.H.) 141
Charley 101, 115
Charley Priory 131
Charnell Wood (Belton) 101
Charnock Hill 101
Charnwood Forest 94
Charnwood Forest Canal 138
Chater, R. 2, 101
Cherwell, R. 116
Chilcote 97
Chitterman Hills 101
Claybrooke Magna 95
Coalfield, The 95
Coalville 137
Coal Wharf (Ashby de la Zouch) 140
Cockspur Bridge 139
Coldham (Illston on the Hill) 105
Coleorton 95
Colpitt close (Coleorton) 138
Congerstone 121
Cosby 102
Cossington 104
Coston 120
Countesthorpe 122
Cranoe 140
Creake Hill (Stonton Wyville) 102
Crispin's Arms (P.H.) 141
Cropston 120
Croswell (Barkby) 135
Cross-well (Market Bosworth) 135
Crown Hill 136
Croxton Abbey 131
Croxton Kerrial 93, 131
Croxton Park 133
Cumberdale (Wymeswold) 102
Cumberlea (Seagrave) 102

Dadlington 112
Dakins Bridge 139
Daniel Lambert (P.H.) 141
Deadman (Gumley) 103
Deadmans Grave
(South Croxton) 103
Deakin's Bridge 139
Debdale Wharf 138
Dedmanysgraue (Skeffington) 103
Denbigh Arms (P.H.) 140
Desford 114
Devon, R. 3, 97
Dicken's Nook 136
Dingil (Somerby) 127
Diseworth 109, 115
Donington Castle 129
Donisthorpe 116
Dove, R. (Oadby) 101
Dow Bridge 100

East Gate 103
East Goscote Hundred 124
East Langton 135
East Midlands Airport 141
Eastwell 116
Eaton 132
Edmondthorpe 122
Ellistown 137
Elmesthorpe 122
Enderby 118
Erlesthorpe (Thorpe Arnold) 122
Esthorpe (Kirby Bellars) 123
Eye Brook 3, 96
Eye, R. 3, 118

Fennes Hole (Stoke Golding) 136
Fenn Lanes 13, 99, 136
Ferdgate, le 14, 105
Finchit (Seagrave) 102
Finger Farm 127
Fingoe (Kegworth) 127
Fish and Quart (P.H.) 141
Flamston (Whitwick) 121
Fleckney 113
Forest of Arden 99
Fosse Way 13, 98
Foston 137
Foundry Arms (P.H.) 141
Fox Bridge 139
Foxton 103
Foxton Locks 139
Framland 124
Framland Hundred 123
Freeby 118
Fremantel (Leicester) 127
Frisby by Galby 120
Frisby on the Wreake 93
Frolesworth 109
Frysseby (Huncote) 119
Fullworth (Thurcaston) 109
Fyngehow (Measham) 127

Gaddesby 118
Garendon 113
Garendon Abbey 131
Gartre Bush (Shangton) 125
Gartree Hundred 125
Gartree Road 13, 100
Gilmorton 102
Gilwel (Nailstone) 116
Glenfield 117
Glenfield Tunnel 140
Glen Parva 101, 103
Goadby Marwood 100
Goldsmith Grange 132
Gosefot (Wymeswold) 124
Grace Dieu Priory 131
Grand Union Canal 139
Grange, The (Burton Lazars) 133
Grange Farm (Wymondham) 133
Grantham Canal 139
Great Bowden 99
Great Glen 101
Grey Friars Priory 131
Great Park (Ashby de la Zouch) 133
Great Park (Belton) 133
Gricke (Kibworth Beauchamp) 102
Grimmeswell
(Barrow upon Soar) 116
Grimston 120, 121
Grimyston (Quorndon) 121
Groby Castle 129
Gueyne Well (Somerby) 116
Gumley 115

Guthlakestonfelde (Cosby) 125
Guthlaxton Bridge (Cosby) 125
Guthlaxton Gap 125
Guthlaxton Hundred 125
Gwash, R. 4

Hallaton 128, 135
Hallaton Castle Hill (Hallaton) 128
Hanover Lodge 137
Harby 97, 124
Harrow Brook 117
Harrowe (Scalford) 117
Harrow hole
(Houghton on the Hill) 117
Harrow slade (Peatling Parva) 117
Hastings Arms (P.H.) 140
Heanor Boat (P.H.) 141
Heather 95
Hemington 97
Hereswode 114
Higham on the Hill 105, 136
High Cademan 101
High Cross 95, 100
High Leicestershire 93
Hill's Bridge 139
Hinckley 115
Hinckley Priory 131
Hoby 119
Holwell 116
Holyoaks 96
Horninghold 137
Horsepool Grange 132
Hose 97
Hothorpe 122
Huberetorp (Osgathorpe) 122
Hugglescote 140
Humberstone105
Huncote 119
Hungarton 104
Husbands Bosworth 109
Hygham
(Wycomb and Chadwell) 105
Hyldebaldwell (Knipton) 115

Ibstock 138
Iliffe Bridge 139
Illston on the Hill 120
Inclined Plane (Swannington) 140
Incline Field (Bagworth) 140
Iron Founders' Arms (P.H.) 141
Isley Walton 115, 133

Jackson's Bridge 139
Jewry Wall 99

Kegworth 104, 109
Keyham 105
Keythorpe 122
Kibworth Beauchamp 109
Kilwardby 119
Kilworth 109
King Dick's Hole 136
King Richard's Well 136
King's Bridge 139
King's Mills 97
King Street Lane 14, 100
Kirby Bellars 117, 118
Kirby Bellars Priory 132
Kirby Muxloe 117
Kirby Muxloe Castle 128
Kirkby Mallory 117
Knight Thorpe 122
Knipton 104
Knossington 96

Langley Lowlands 94
Langley Priory 131, 133
Langwrth hill (Barkestone) 109
Laughton 103
Launde Priory 132, 133
Leesthorpe 122
Legham 106
Legra, R. 106
Leicester 98
Leicester Abbey 133
Leicester and Burton
Branch Railway 139
Leicester and Hitchin
Branch Railway 140
Leicester and Swannington
Railway 138
Leicester Castle 128
Leicester Forest East
Service Station 141

Leicestershire 1
Leire 101
Lilinge (Ullesthorpe) 108
Lindley 115
Lipping, R. 4
Little Stretton 103
Littlethorpe 123
Littlethorpe (Ashby de la Zouch) 122
Lockington 97
Long Clawson 120
Long Whatton 122
Loughborough 104, 111
Lount 140
Lowesby 118
Lubbesthorpe 122
Luffnam (Humberstone) 105
Lugge, R. (Lutterworth) 109
Lutterworth 104, 109
Lutterworth Upland 94

Mancetter 106
Manduessedum 106
Mantyll (Swannington) 102
Market Bosworth 95
Market Harborough 138
Marquis of Granby (P.H.) 140
Mease and Sence Lowlands 95
Mease, R. 4, 95
Measham 106
Medbourne 94, 103
Melton Mowbray 103, 139
Mercia 125
Midland Counties Railway 139
Midland Railway 140
Midulthorp (Kirby Bellars) 123
Mindhill (Wilson) 103
Minstreton Temple (Misterton) 130
Mirabel (Great Easton) 96
Misterton 117
Moat, The (Castle Donington) 130
Moat Banks (Kirby Muxloe) 128
Moat Hill 126
Monkesdam (Barrow upon Soar) 132
Monkeswonges (Croxton Kerrial) 132
Monkkewode (Welby) 132
Moira 137
Moor Barn Grange 132
Moote Bush (Barkby) 124
Mothall (Leicester) 126
Mothowes (Barkby) 126
Motlow Hill (Ratby) 126
Motthoryn (Illston on the Hill) 126
Mount St Bernard Abbey 132
Mountsorrel 129
Mount Sorrel Railway 140
Mouthill (Swannington) 126
Mowsley 115
Munetil (Burton on the Wolds) 102
Muston 101
Muttley (Blackfordby) 126

Nafferton (Foxton) 121
Nailstone 140
Naneby 118
Nanpantan 138
Narborough 111
Nether Broughton 132
Netherseal 97
Netherthorpe (Ashby de la Zouch) 122
Newarke The 129
Newarke Gate 129
Newe Parke of Byrdesnest (Anstey) 133
Newhouse Grange 132
Newtown Linford 137
Newtown Unthank 137
No Man's Heath 97
Normandy (Leicester) 127
Normanton 120
Normantom le Heath 120
Normanton Turville 120
Noseley 115
Nuncraftes (Long Whatton) 132
Nuneaton and Leicester Railway 140
Nunnesti (Langley) 132
Nuns, The (Waltham on the Wolds) 132
Nutt's Bridge 139
Nythingworth (Knipton) 109

Oadby 103
Oakthorpe 122

Odstone 121
Ogberdeswell (Belvoir) 116
Ogerstone (Redmile) 112
Old Dalby 124
Old Ingarsby 118
Old Park (Belvoir) 133
Old Park Pale (Anstey) 133
Orton on the Hill 99
Osbaston 121
Osgarwell (Asfordby) 116
Othorpe 122
Overseal 97
Overthorpe (Ashby de la Zouch) 122
Owston Abbey 131

Packington 112
Panhill (Lockington) 102
Peatling (Claybrooke) 108
Peatling Magna 108
Peatling Parva 108
Peckleton 126
Pegg's Close Bridge 139
Pen Hill (Whitwick) 102
Pennyston (Ibstock) 102
Pickwell 116
Pinwall Grange 132
Pippines well (Arnesby) 116
Plungar 97
Poultney 113
Prestgrave 133
Primethorpe 122
Priors slade (Skeffington) 132
Priouresgores (Belvoir) 132
Priourscroft (Kirby Bellars) 132
Pryer wood (Knossington) 132
Pryours Close (Launde) 132

Quebec House 137
Queniborough 111
Quorndon 129

Ragdale 124
Railway Close (Swannington) 140
Ratae Corieltavorum 98
Ratby 98
Ratcliffe Culey 95
Ravenstone 106, 121
Ravens Well (Arnesby) 116
Raw Dykes 99
Redmile 97
Redmylthorp (Redmile) 122
Repton and Gresley Hundred 95
Ringlethorpe (Scalford) 132
Rogerwell (Burton Overy) 116
Rolleston 120
Rothley 130, 133
Rothley Brook 5
Rothley Temple (Rothley) 130
Rowley Fields 103
Rugby and Stamford
Branch Railway 140

Saddington 138
Saffron Brook 5
St Ann's Well (East Langton) 135
St Morrills Well (Hallaton) 135
Saltby 93, 132
Sauvey Castle 128
Saxby 104
Saxelby 127
Scalford 113
Seagrave 124, 137
Sence, R. (1) 5, 95
Sence, R. (2) 6
Severne (Seagrave) 101
Sewstern Grange 133
Sewstern Lane 14, 97
Shackerstone 109
Shangton 125
Sharnford 100
Shawell 98, 135
Shearsby 118
Sheepy 116
Shelthorpe 122
Shepshed 138
Sherakehilles (Peckleton) 126
Shirrevesbrigge
(Kirkby Mallory) 126
Sibson 113
Signal Box Field (Bagworth) 140
Sileby 137
Skeffington 103
Slawston 120
Smite, R. 6

Snibstone 138
Soar, R. 6, 93
Soar Navigation 139
Soar Valley 94
South Croxton 120
South-east Lowland 94
Sparkeloe (Cadeby) 126
Sparkenhoe 126
Sparkenhoe Hundred 125
Speland (Kirkby Mallory) 127
Spellow (Appleby Magna) 126
Spellow (Asfordby) 126
Spellow (Husbands Bosworth) 126
Sproxton 120
Stapleford 139
Stapleford Park 103
Starmore 108
Stathern 108
Station Field (Glenfield) 140
Staunton Harold 138
Steynwordhoc
(Burrough on the Hill) 109
Stockerstone 96
Stoke Golding 136
Stonesby 118
Stonton Wyville 102
Stonwrth hill (Barkestone) 109
Stowe Welle (Hallaton) 135
Stretton en le Field 106
Strykeswell (Freeby) 116
Sutton Cheney 136
Sutton Wharf Bridge
(Sutton Cheney) 139
Swannington 140
Swannington Common 138
Swannymote Rock 126
Swepstone 116
Swift, R. 7, 109
Swinford 114
Sysonby 103
Syston 124
Syston and Peterborough
Branch Railway 139

Tailors' Arms (P.H.) 141
Temple, The (Wellsborough) 130
Temple clos (Baggrave) 130
Templegore (Melton Mowbray) 130
Temple Hall (Rothley) 130
Temple Hall (Wellsborough) 130
Templeland (Gaddesby) 130
Templelands (Baggrave) 130
Temples Grange (Wellsborough) 132
Templewong (Bottesford) 130
Theddingworth 108
Thorpe Langton 122
Thorp on le Toftis (Belgrave) 123
Thorpe Satchville 123
Three Shire Oak 97
Thringstone 121
Thrussington 124
Thrussington Grange 133
Thunderbush
(Breedon on the Hill) 117
Thurcaston 120
Thurlaston 121
Thurmaston 98, 103
Timms Bridge 139
Tingoe (Saxelby) 127
Toston 120
Trent, R. 7, 97
Tripontium 98, 100
Trunchit (Seagrave) 102
Tugby 118
Tunnel Close (Swannington) 140
Tunnel Meadow (Fleckney) 138
Turn Bridge 139
Tweed, R. 8
Twyford 114
Tysoe Hill 117

Ullesthorpe 122
Ulverscroft 140
Ulverscroft Priory 131
Union (P.H.) 141
Union Canal 138
Upton 126

Vale of Belvoir 93
Venonis 99, 107
Vernemetum 100, 116
Via Devana 13, 105

Walchemore (Burton Lazars) 102

Walchemore (Skeffington) 102
Walcote 101
Walschemore (Cosby) 102
Walsemore (Leesthorpe) 102
Walsshecroft (Shepshed) 102
Waltham on the Wolds 105
Walton 101
Walton on the Wolds 101, 124
Walworthehow (Muston) 101
Wartoft Grange 132
Watling Street 14, 95, 107
Welby 132
Welchemore (Leire) 102
Welchewod (Swannington) 102
Welham 105
Welland, R. 8, 96
Wellsborough 130
Welsh Slade
(Barton in the Beans) 102
West Bridge 139
West Cotes 103
West Goscote Hundred 124
Westhorp (Kirby Bellars) 122
Westhorpe (Long Whatton) 123
West Langton 103
Westmanway 15
Westrill 108
Whenham (Ab Kettleby) 105
White Friars Priory 131
Whitwick 138
Whitwick Castel (Whitwick) 129
Wigford (Wyfordby) 117
Wifeles þorp
(Breedon on the Hill) 122
Wigston Magna 103, 121
Wigston Parva 100
Willesley 97
Wilson 115
Wistow 117
Witherley 106
Wolds, The 93, 97
Wolfrichwell (Humberstone) 116
Woodthorpe 123
Woolcombers' Arms (P.H.) 141
Woolstaplers' Arms (P.H.) 141
Worthington 138
Wreake, R. 9
Wreake and Eye Navigation 139
Wreake Valley 93, 103, 118
Wulmereswell (Billesdon) 116
Wycomb 105
Wyfordby 117, 134
Wymeswold 103, 105
Wymondham 105

Yolwell (Illston on the Hill) 116
York Castle (P.H.) 141

INDEX OF THE PLACE-NAMES OF LEICESTERSHIRE

This index includes all the major names and minor names treated in volumes **1**–**7**, the Introduction to each volume, and in the main body of the work but not in the sections The Elements. Field-names in lists (a) and (b) are not indexed. The names of the townships are printed in capitals. Lost names are printed in italic.

Abbey Fm
(Launde) **3** 161
(Lubbesthorpe) **6** 160
Abbey Ford Fm **7** 26
Abbey Gate **1** 13
Abbey Gate Close **1** 182
Abbey Grange **7** 56
Abbey Inn (P.H.)
(Whitwick) **7** 74
(Wood Gate) **1** 121
Abbey Lands **1** 213
Abbey Lane
(Belgrave) **3** 46
(Newton Linford) **7** 155
Abbey Meadow **1** 196
Abbey of St Mary de Pratis **1** 90
Abbey Park **1** xiii, 223
Abbey Rd **7** 56
Abbey St.
(Coalville) **7** 72
(Leicester) **1** 13
(Market Harborough) **4** 171
Abbey Wood **4** 209
Abbot Lodge **2** 149
Abbots Oak Drive **7** 62
Abbot's Close **1** 182
Abbot's Oak **7** 61
Abbot's Spinney **3** 29
Abell's Wood **7** 155
Abington **5** 224
Abraham's Bridge **6** 127
AB KETTLEBY **2** xii, 157
Acacia Ho. **2** 23
Acrelands Lane **2** 23
Acresford **7** 279
Acresford Plantation **7** 279
Acresford Rd **7** 282
Adam and Eve (P.H.)
(Loughborough) **7** 132
(Market Harborough) **4** 173
Adam and Eve St. **4** 171
Adam's Gorse **3** 264
Admiral Duncan (P.H.) **1** 121
Admiral Nelson (P.H.) **4** 173
Admiral Nelson (P.H.)
(Leicester) **1** 121
(Kibworth Harcourt) **4** 138
Admiral Rodney (P.H.) **1** 121
Agar Nook **7** 61
Agar Nook Fm **6** 35
Ainsloe Spinney **5** 156
Airedale Fm **5** 130
Albert (P.H.) **1** 121
Albert Inn **7** 20
Albert Rd
(Coalville) **7** 62
(Hinckley) **6** 117
Albert St.
(Bottesford) **2** 23
(Fleckney) **4** 50

(Ibstock) **6** 144
(Kibworth Harcourt) **4** 138
(Loughborough) **7** 126
(Syston) **3** 227
Albert St. **1** 13
Albert Village **7** 20
Albion (P.H.) **7** 132
Albion (P.H.) **1** 121
Albion Cottages **7** 21
Albion Hill **1** 13
Albion St.
(Anstey) **7** 2
(Leicester) **1** xiv, 13
(Oadby) **5** 163
(Wigston Magna) **5** 219
Albion Tepid Baths **1** 142
ALDEBY ST JOHN **6** 86
Alder Hall **6** 206
Alder Spinney **6** 98
Alderman Newton's School **1** 112
Alderman Newton's School **6** 120
Alderman's Haw **7** xi, 245
Alders, The **7** 156
Aldersgate St. **1** xv, 14
Aldgate **7** 130
Alexander St. **1** 14
Alfred St. **1** 14
All Saints' Church
(Asfordby) **3** 11
(Beeby) **3** 42
(Blaby) **5** 32
(Cadeby) **6** 58
(Cossington) **3** 60
(Dunton Bassett) **5** 83
(East Norton) **3** 177
(Gilmorton) **5** 96
(Hoby) **3** 113
(Husbands Bosworth) **4** 119
(Isley cum Langley) **7** 93
(Keyham) **3** 158
(Kimcote) **5** 112
(Kirkby Mallory) **6** 211
(Knipton) **2** 14
(Leicester) **1** 82
(Long Whatton) **7** 112
(Loughborough) **7** 126
(Lowesby) **3** 168
(Lubenham) **4** 164
(Nailstone) **6** 182
(Narborough) **6** 186
(Newtown Linford) **7** 156
(Peatling Magna) **5** 174
(Pickwell) **2** 241
(Ragdale) **3** 128
(Ratcliffe Culey) **6** 330
(Rotherby) **3** 122
(Sapcote) **6** 226
(Scraptoft) **4** 229
(Seagrave) **3** 207
(Shawell) **5** 182
(Sheepy Magna) **6** 252
(Slawston) **4** 240
(Somerby) **2** 226
(Swinford) **5** 200
(Theddingworth) **4** 269
(Thorpe Acre) **7** 144
(Thurcaston) **7** 229
(Thurlaston) **6** 300
(Wigston Magna) **5** 224
All Saints' Opening **1** 14
All Saints' School **1** 112
ALLEXTON **3** 2,4
Allexton Field Rd **4** 251
Allexton Hall **3** 4
Allexton Lane **4** 106
Allexton Lodge **3** 4
Allexton Rd **4** 95
Allexton Wood **3** 4
Allhallows **2** 195
Allotment Covert **6** 166
Allotment Gardens **3** 261
Allsopp's Lane **7** 126
Alma Ho. **5** 61
Alma Lodge **3** 11
Alma Rd **6** 117
Alma Villas **7** 12
Almey's Lane **6** 133
Almshouse, The **3** 100
Almshouses, The
(Coleorton) **7** 78
(Congerstone) **6** 241
(Frolesworth) **5** 90

(Netherseal) **7** 267
(Osgathorpe) **7** 163
(Sutton Cheney) **6** 287
(Woodhouse) **7** 248
Alton Cottages **7** 180
Alton Grange **7** 180
Alton Hill **7** 180
Alton Lodge **7** 12
Alton Wood **7** 180
Altons, The **7** 180
Amberdale Spinney **5** 107
AMBION **6** 287
Ambion Hill **6** xiii, xiv, xvi, 287
Ambion Hill Fm **6** 287
Ambion Wood **6** 288
Ambro Hill **7** 43
Ambro Mill **7** 43
America Fm **4** 204
America Lodge **4** 204
America Wood **4** 204
Amos Lodge **5** 205
Anchor (P.H.)
(Burbage) **6** 52
(Hathern) **7** 83
(Snarestone) **3** 268
Anchor (P.H.)
(Charles Street) **1** 121
(Kegworth) **7** 96
(Loughborough) **7** 132
(Market Harborough) **4** 173
(Mountsorrel) **7** 152
(Woodhouse) **7** 248
Anchor Fm **7** 210
Anchor Ho. **7** 210
Anchor Inn **2** 45
Anchor Inn **2** 205
Anchor Lane
(Coleorton) **7** 78
(Hathern) **7** 83
(Swannington) **7** 210
Anchorage, The **7** 279
Anderchurch **7** 34
Andrew's Lane **4** 65
Angel (P.H.)
(Market Harborough) **4** 173
(Oxford St.) **1** 121
Angel (P.H.)
(Gallowtree Gate) **1** 121
(Hallaton) **4** 97
(Loughborough) **7** 132
(Lutterworth) **5** 137
(Waltham on the Wolds) **2** 272
(Wymondham) **2** 287
Angel Inn **7** 78
Angel Inn **2** 59
Angel St. **4** 171
Angel Yard **7** 126
Anker Hill **6** 257
Ankle Hill **2** 180
Ann street **2** 170
Anne of Cleve's Ho. **2** 178
ANSTEY **7** 2
Anstey Frith **6** 92
Anstey Grange **6** 92
Anstey High Leys **7** 2
Anstey Lane
(Anstey) **7** 2
(Groby) **6** 98
(Thurcaston) **7** 229
Anstey Mill **7** 2
Anstey Pastures **7** 3
Antelope (P.H.)
(Humberstone Gate) **1** 121
(Silver St.) **1** 121
Antelope Bridge **1** 72
Apesgate **7** 47
Apiary Gate **7** 47
Apple Orchard Fm **6** 288
Appleby Field **6** 9
Appleby Hall **6** 9
Appleby Hill **6** 9
APPLEBY MAGNA **6** xii, xiii, 7
Appleby Park **6** 9
APPLEBY PARVA **6** 9
Appleby Rd **6** 268
Applegate **1** xii, 14
Aqueduct Fm **6** 166
Aqueduct Spinney **4** 80
Arbor Rd **6** 67
Arbour **2** 162
Archdale St. **3** 227
Archdeacon Lane **1** xv, 14

Archer's Close **1** 182
Archway Cottage **5** 212
Arkwright Cottages **5** 38
Arlick Fm **7** 285
ARNESBY **5** xiv, 4
Arnesby Lodge **5** 5
Arnesby Lodge Cottages **5** 5
Arnesby Rd **4** 50
Arnold Lodge **2** 23
Arnold's Fm **6** 232
Artilleryman (P.H.) **1** 121
ASFORDBY **3** xiv, xv, 9, 10
Asfordby: unindexed modern street-names **3** 11
Asfordby Hall **3** 11
Asfordby Hill
(Asfordby) **3** 11
(Sysonby) **2** 191
Asfordby Ho. **3** 11
Asfordby Old Hall **3** 11
Asfordby Rd **2** 168
Ash Close **1** 182
Ash Close Meadow **1** 196
Ash Hill Plantation **2** 284
Ash Lane **1** xii, 15
Ash Leigh **5** 193
Ash Plantation
(Burton Lazars) **2** 63
(Walton on the Wold) **3** 268
(Welby) **3** 18
Ash Pole Spinney **2** 239
Ash Spinney
(Blaby) **5** 32
(King's Norton) **4** 142
(Little Stretton) **4** 159
(Long Whatton) **7** 112
(Thurlaston) **6** 305
Ash Tree Fm **3** 85
Ash Tree Ho. **5** 27
Ash Yard Closes **1** 182
Ashburton Rd **7** 62
Ashby Arms (P.H.) **3** 144
Ashby Castle **7** 7
ASHBY DE LA ZOUCH **7** xi, xii, xiii, 7
Ashby de la Zouch Canal **6** xiii, **7** xiii
(Ashby de la Zouch) **7** 8
(Donisthorpe) **7** 279
(Market Bosworth) **6** 166
(Moira) **7** 23
(Shackerstone) **6** 232
Ashby de la Zouch Free School **7** 12
ASHBY FOLVILLE **3** xiv, 10, 98
Ashby Folville Lodge **3** 100
Ashby Grange **3** 100
Ashby Ho. **5** 27
Ashby Lane
(Bitteswell) **5** 27
(Blackfordby) **7** 14
(Swepstone) **7** 218
Ashby Lodge
(Ashby Folville) **3** 100
(Ashby Parva) **5** 12
(Staunton Harold) **7** 207
ASHBY MAGNA **5** xiv, 9
Ashby Magna Station **5** 9
ASHBY PARVA **5** xiv, xv, 12
Ashby Pastures
(Ashby Folville) **3** 100
(Kirby Bellars) **3** 85
Ashby Rd
(Belton) **7** 26
(Breedon on the Hill) **7** 35
(Coalville) **7** 62
(Coleorton) **7** 78
(Donisthorpe) **7** 279
(Gilmorton) **5** 96
(Hinckley) **6** 117
(Loughborough) **7** 126
(Markfield) **6** 176
(Measham) **7** 264
(Normanton le Heath) **6** 197
(Osgathorpe) **7** 163
(Packington) **7** 285
(Peatling Parva) **5** 178
(Shepshed) **7** 194
(Stapleton) **6** 215
(Swannington) **7** 210

(Twycross) **6** 307
(Ullesthorpe) **5** 205
(Wood Gate) **1** 15
(Worthington) **7** 255
Ashby Road Cottages **5** 178
Ashby Shrubs **6** 159
Ashby Square **7** 126
Ashby way **5** 139
Ashby Woulds **7** 20
Ashclose Spinney **5** 126
Ashfield
(Frisby on the Wreake) **3** 80
(Knighton) **5** 126
Ashfield Ho. **7** 269
Ashlands **4** 129
Ashlands, The **6** 186
Ashleigh
(Thorpe Arnold) **2** 278
(Wartnaby) **2** 166
Ashley Rd **4** 188
Ashpole Spinney
(Cosby) **5** 67
(Fenny Drayton) **6** 328
(Higham on the Hill) **6** 109
Ashpole Spinneys **6** 211
Ashtree Holding **7** 21
Ashwell St. **1** 15
Asletts Yard **7** 130
Asplin Cottages **7** 35
Asplin Wood **7** 35
Assage Wood **7** 180
Assebygate **2** 170
Assembly Rooms **1** 142
Assheton Ho. **6** 307
Aston Firs **6** 22
ASTON FLAMVILLE **6** 22
Aston Lane
(Burbage) **6** 50
(Sharnford) **6** 246
Aston Oaks **6** 50
Asylum St. **1** 15
Athenaeum, The **1** 142
Atherstone **6** xi, xiv
Atherstone House Fm **6** 291
Atherstone Rd
(Appleby) **6** 9
(Atterton) **6** 326
(Norton juxta Twycross) **6** 312
(Pinwall) **6** 257
Atherstone Road Plantations **6** 9
Athestone Rd **7** 264
Atkin St. **1** xv, 15
ATTERTON **6** 326
Atterton Lane **6** 261
Atterton Rd **6** 322
Auburn Place **5** 139
Auburn Place Lodge **5** 139
Augustine Friars **1** 202
Austen Dyke **3** 113
Austen Dyke Bridge **3** 113
Austin Friars **1** 90
Austrey Rd **6** 9
Ave Maria lane **7** 130
Avenue Fm **2** 284
Avenue Rd **7** 62
Avenue Villas **5** 61
Avenue, The
(Belvoir) **2** 7
(Nevill Holt) **4** 204
(Noseley) **4** 209
Aviary, The **7** 26
Axe and Square (P.H.) **1** 121
Axe and Square (P.H.) **5** 79
AYLESTONE **5** 18
Aylestone: unindexed modern street-names **5** 20
Aylestone Grange **5** 104
Aylestone Hall **5** 18
Aylestone Holt **5** 104
Aylestone Lane **5** 219
Aylestone Lane Park **5** 224
Aylestone Mill Lock **5** 18
Aylestone Park **5** 19
Aylestone Rd **1** 16
Ayre's Close **1** 182

Babelake St. **7** 285
Babington Rd **7** 185

Back Brook **1** 225
Back Brook Close **1** 182
Back Lane
(Castle Donington) **7** 47
(Leire) **5** 130
(Long Clawson) **2** 90
(Old Dalby) **2** 50
(Prestwold) **3** 180
(Shearsby) **5** 188
(Sileby) **3** 215
(Thorpe Acre) **7** 144
Back Lane
(Ashby de la Zouch) **7** 10
(Hinckley) **6** 118
(Leicester) **1** 16
(Lutterworth) **5** 139
Back Rd **3** 244
Back Side **5** 113
Back Side **1** 16
Back Soar **1** 225
Back St.
(Bottesford) **2** 23
(North Kilworth) **5** 156
Back Street **2** 170
BAGGRAVE **3** xiii, 150
Baggrave Park **3** 150
Baggrave Hall **3** 150
BAGWORTH **6** xi, xii, 25
Bagworth and Ellistown Station **6** 25
Bagworth Colliery **6** 25
Bagworth Heath **6** 25
Bagworth Lane **6** 27
Bagworth Moats **6** 25
Bagworth Park **6** 25
Bagworth Rd
(Barlestone) **6** 39
(Newbold Verdon) **6** 194
Bailiff's Close, The **1** 182
Bailiff's Mead **7** 47
Bailiffs Covert **3** 268
Bakehouse Lane
(Leicester) **1** xii, 16
(Loughborough) **7** 130
(Lutterworth) **5** 139
Baker St.
(Coalville) **7** 62
(Lutterworth) **5** 139
Baker St. **1** 17
Baker's Arms (P.H.) **5** 32
Bakers' Arms (P.H.) **4** 276
Bakers' Arms (P.H.) **1** 121
Bakers' Row **1** 17
Bakewell St. **7** 62
Bakewell's Lane **7** 78
Bakhous Lane **2** 170
Baldwin Lane **1** xii, 17
Baldwin's Spinney **5** 205
Balk, The **6** 92
Ball's Lane **6** 50
Balldike street **5** 220
Bally Fm **5** 130
Bambury Lane **5** 212
Bandalls Fm **3** 54
Bank Fm
(Carlton) **6** 63
(Ratcliffe Culey) **6** 330
Bank St. **5** 139
Bank, The **4** 133
Banks, The
(Burton Overy) **4** 21
(Sileby) **3** 215
Banky Mdw **6** 50
Bantlam Lane **6** 87
Baptist Chapel
(Appleby Parva) **6** 9
(Arnesby) **5** 5
(Billesdon) **4** 4
(Cosby) **5** 67
(Hathern) **7** 83
(Hose) **2** 99
(Sutton in the Elms) **5** 39
(Walton) **5** 113
(Wymeswold) **3** 275
Baptist Church
(Earl Shilton) **6** 133
(Netherseal) **7** 269
(Sketchley) **6** 57
Baptist College **1** 112
Baptist Lane **7** 264

BARDON **6** 35
Bardon Hall **6** 35
Bardon Hill **6** xi, 35
Bardon Hill Quarry **6** 35
Bardon Hill Wood **6** 35
Bardon Park **6** 35
Bardon Park Chapel **6** 36
Barfoot Lodge **4** 224
Barford House Fm **4** 224
BARKBY **3** xiv, xv, 2, 10, 21
Barkby Arms (P.H.) **1** 121
Barkby Brook **3** 21
Barkby Grange **3** 21
Barkby Holt **3** 21
Barkby Holt Fm **3** 21
Barkby Holt Lane **3** 21
Barkby Lane **1** xiii, 17
Barkby Lane
(Humberstone) **3** 133
(Syston) **3** 228
Barkby Lodge **3** 21
Barkby Rd **3** 42
BARKBY THORPE **3** 21, 29, 157
Barkby Thorpe Lane **3** 21
Barkby Thorpe Rd **3** 133
Barkby Thorpe Spinney **3** 29
BARKESTONE **2** xii, 199
Barkestone Bridge **2** 200
Barkestone Lane **2** 23
Barkestone Wharf **2** 200
Barkestone Wood **2** 200
Barkhouse, The **1** 145
BARLESTONE **6** xiii, 39
Barlestone Field **6** 39
Barlestone Lodge (x2) **6** 39
Barlestone Rd
(Bagworth) **6** 25
(Newbold Verdon) **6** 194
Barley Croft **7** 35
Barley Hill Ho. **3** 34
Barley Leas **3** 144
Barley Mow (P.H.)
(Granby St.) **1** 121
(Loughborough) **7** 132
Barley Mow (P.H.)
(Cadeby) **6** 58
(Thorpe Langton) **4** 276
Barley Sheaf (P.H.) **6** 121
Barley Sheaf (P.H.)
(Higham on the Hill) **6** 109
(Huncote) **6** 139
Barlow's Lodge **2** 94
Barn Close Spinney **4** 129
Barn Closes **1** 183
Barn Fm
(Grimston) **3** 106
(Illston on the Hill) **4** 129
(Newton Burgoland) **7** 224
(Ratcliffe Culey) **6** 330
(Shawell) **5** 182
(Stapleton) **6** 215
(Woodhouse) **7** 248
(Wymeswold) **3** 275
Barn Gate **1** 17
Barn, The **5** 224
Barncroft **6** 151
Barnes Hill Plantation **3** 108
Barns Heath **6** 9
Barnsdale **4** 74
Barnstaple Ho. **3** 130
Barr Lane **6** 109
Barrack Cottages **3** 275
Barracks, The
(Barwell) **6** 127
(Slawston) **4** 240
Barratt Mill Fm
(Moira) **7** 23
(Overseal) **7** 282
Barratt Pool
(Moira) **7** 23
(Overseal) **7** 282
Barrel Inn **6** 25
Barron Park **6** 79
Barron Park Fm **6** 80
Barroon, The **7** 47
Barrow Barn **3** 34
Barrow Hill
(Barrow upon Soar) **3** 34
(Worthington) **7** xiii, 255
Barrow Hill Fm **7** 255
Barrow Hill Quarry **6** 133
Barrow Lock **3** 34

Barrow Lodge **3** 34
Barrow Mill **3** 34
Barrow Rd
(Sileby) **3** 215
(Quorndon) **7** 170
Barrow St. **7** 126
BARROW UPON SOAR
3 xi, xiii, xv, 33
Barrowcliffe **3** 34
Barrowcliffe Fm **3** 183
Barrowcliffe Spinney **3** 101
Barrowhill Lodge **7** 255
Barrows Lane **6** 92
BARSBY **3** xiv, 101
Barsby Spinney **3** 102
Barstable's Leys **1** 202
Barston St. **1** xv, 17
BARTON IN THE BEANS **6** 236
Barton Lane
(Congerstone) **6** 241
(Nailstone) **6** 182
Barton Rd
(Barlestone) **6** 39
(Carlton) **6** 63
(Market Bosworth) **6** 166
BARWELL **6** xiii, 126
Barwell: unindexed modern
street-names **6** 128
Barwell Fields **6** 127
Barwell Fields Fm **6** 127
Barwell Footpath **6** 123
Barwell Ho. **6** 127
Barwell Lane
(Barwell) **6** 127
(Hinckley) **6** 117
Basin Bridge **6** 109
Basin Bridge Fm **6** 109
Bassett Fm **6** 305
Bassett House **6** 304
Bassett Lane **6** 226
Bassett's Hill Spinney **4** 70
Bateman House Fm **6** 9
Bateman's Row **1** 17
Bates Bridge **6** 241
Bates Wharf Bridge **6** 241
Bath Gardens **1** 176
Bath Grounds **7** 8
Bath Ho. **7** 61
Bath Hotel **5** 188
Bath House Spinney **6** 109
Bath Lane
(Bruntingthorpe) **5** 49
(Leicester) **1** 18
(Moira) **7** 23
Bath Spinney **4** 62
Bath St.
(Ashby de la Zouch) **7** 8
(Market Harborough) **4** 172
(Syston) **3** 228
Bath St.
(Carlton St.) **1** 18
(Jewry Wall St.) **1** 18
Bath, The **1** 142
Battle Flat **6** 273
Battle of Bosworth **6** xii, xiii, xiv
Battlefield Line **6** xiii
Battleflat Lodge **6** 273
Battleflat Lodge Fm **6** 273
Battling Brook **6** 123
Battram Ho. **6** 144
Battram Rd **6** 144
Baulk Lane
(Arnesby) **5** 5
(Walton on the Wolds) **3** 268
Bawdon Castle **7** 237
Bawdon Cottage Fm **7** 248
Bawdon Lodge **7** 56
Bawdon Rough **7** 56
Baxter Gate **7** 126
Baxter's Ct. **1** 18
Baxterlane **2** 170
Bay St. **1** 18
Baytlane **2** 170
Beacon Cottage **7** 248
Beacon Cresc. **7** 62
Beacon Hill
(Bottesford) **2** 23
(Woodhouse) **7** 248
Beacon Lodge **7** 250
Beacon Plantation **7** 248
Beacon Rd **7** 126
Bean Hill Fm **5** 188

Beanfield Covert **6** 233
Beanfield Ho. **6** 233
Bear (P.H.) **1** 122
Bear Garden **1** 176
Bear on the Hoop (P.H.) **4** 173
Beast Market **5** 139
Beauchamp Fm **4** 54
Beauchamp Grange **4** 133
Beaumanor **7** 247
Beaumanor Arms (P.H.) **7** 74
Beaumanor Park **7** xii, 248
Beaumont Arms (P.H.)
(Coleorton) **7** 78
(Whitwick) **7** 74
Beaumont Hamel **4** 281
Beaumont Hey **1** 202
Beaumont Ho. **7** 78
Beaumont Leys **1** 202
Beaumont Park **1** xiii, 223
Beaumont Walk **1** 203
Beaumont Wood **1** 224
Becebrigge **2** 174
Beck Mill **2** 179
Beck Mill St. **2** 168
BECKINGTHORPE **2** 22
Beckingthorpe Fm **2** 23
Becks Fm **6** 211
Becks, The **6** 211
Bedale Cl. **7** 62
Bedehouse Garden **1** 176
Bedehouse Meadows **1** 196
Bedehouses **2** 139
Bedford St.
(Leicester) **1** xv, 18
(Loughborough) **7** 126
Bedlam Barn Fm **7** 83
Bee Hive (P.H.) **1** 122
BEEBY **3** xiii, xiv, 42
Beeby Ho. **3** 42
Beeby Rd
(Barkby) **3** 21
(Scraptoft) **4** 229
Beeby Spring **3** 42
Beeby Spring Grange **3** 42
Beech Spinney
(Kirkby Mallory) **6** 211
(Noseley) **4** 209
Beeches, The
(Appleby) **6** 9
(Kirby Muxloe) **6** 151
(Little Dalby) **2** 84
(Melton Mowbray) **2** 178
Beehive Cottage **7** 78
Beehive lane **7** 130
Bees Well Lane **4** 21
Beeson's Barn
(Gaddesby) **3** 94
(Rearsby) **3** 197
Beggar's Lane **6** 160
Beggars Lane **6** 87
Belcher's Bar **6** 182
Belcher's Hill **4** 106
Belchers Lodge **4** 106
BELGRAVE **3** xiv, xv, 46
Belgrave: unindexed modern
street-names **3** 47
Belgrave Gate **1** xi, xii, xiv, 18
Belgrave Hall **3** 46
Belgrave Lock **3** 46
Belgrave Mill **3** 46
Bell (P.H.)
(Burton Overy) **4** 21
(Gumley) **4** 88
(Narborough) **6** 186
(Wigston Magna) **5** 222
Bell (P.H.)
(Humberstone Gate) **1** 122
(Market Harborough) **4** 173
(Swinesmarket) **1** 122
Bell and Crown (P.H.) **7** 50
Bell and Swan (P.H.) **2** 177
Bell Dip Fm **3** 72
Bell Dip Lodge **3** 72
Bell Hotel (P.H.) **2** 177
Bell Inn
(Frisby on the Wreake) **3** 80
(Husbands Bosworth) **4** 119
Bell Inn **4** 38
Bell Lane
(Burton Overy) **4** 21
(Husbands Bosworth) **4** 119
(Narborough) **6** 186

Bell St.
(Claybrooke Magna) **5** 58
(Wigston Magna) **5** 219
Bell's Plantation **2** 133
Belle Isle **3** 215
Bellemere Fm **2** 126
Bellfields Lane **4** 185
Bellow's Clump **6** 233
Belper Arms (P.H.) **7** 224
Belt, The
(Castle Donington) **7** 47
(Eastwell) **2** 121
(Newtown Linford) **7** 156
(South Kilworth) **5** 193
(Stathern) **2** 261
(Walcote) **5** 149
BELTON **7** 25
Belton St. **7** 195
Belton Rd **3** 163
BELVOIR **2** xiii, 4
Belvoir Castle (P.H.) **1** 122
Belvoir Castle **2** xiii, 6
Belvoir Lodge **4** 188
Belvoir St. **1** 19
Belvoir St. Chapel **1** 89
Ben's Cottage **2** 163
Bend, The **6** 27
Bendbow Spinney **6** 44
Benford St. **1** 19
Benn Hill **6** 252
Benn Hill Fm **6** 252
Bennington's Close **1** 183
Bennyer's Walk **1** 203
Benscliffe **7** 156
Benscliffe Hay **7** 156
Benscliffe Wood **7** 156
Benskin's Barn **3** 197
Bent's Close **1** 183
Bent's Corner **1** 19
Bent's Farm **1** 180
Bent's Hospital **1** 96
Bentley St. **2** 169
Berehill **1** 19
Berehill Cross **1** 102
Beresford Ho. **6** 104
Berlea **2** 166
Berlea Fm **2** 166
Berners' Arms (P.H.) **3** 5
Berridge Lane **3** 47
Berrisford St. **7** 62
Berry Ave **7** 35
Berry Covert **2** 139
Berry's Lane **6** 222
Berrycott Lane **3** 207
Berryhill Lane **7** 64
Berryhills Fm **7** 64
BESCABY **2** xiii, 249
Bescaby Ho. **2** 250
Bescaby Oaks **2** 250
Bess Bagley **7** 56
Bethell Ct. **1** 19
Betty Henser's Lane **7** 152
Beveridge Lane **7** 66
Beveridge St. **3** 34
Beverley Cottage **7** 255
Bewicke Arms (P.H.) **4** 97
Big Clump **3** 268
Big Gunsel **3** 254
Big Hill **7** 47
Big Lane
(Sapcote) **6** 226
(Seagrave) **3** 207
Big Lawn Covert **7** 47
Big Ling Spinney **3** 180
Biggin St. **7** 126
Biggin, The **7** 47
Bigging, The **1** 181
Biggs Lodge **3** 183
Billa Barra **6** 176
Billa Barra Fm **6** 273
Billa Barra Hill **6** 176
Billa Barrow **6** 176
Biller's Close **1** 183
BILLESDON **4** xii, 4
Billesdon Brook **4** 4
Billesdon Coplow **4** 4
Billesdon Coplow Lodge **4** 4
Billesdon Lodge **4** 5
Billesdon Lodge South **4** 5
Billesdon's Hollow **6** 161
Billhedge Cottages **3** 34
Billington Rough **6** 83

BILSTONE **6** xii, 238
Bilstone Hill Fm **6** 239
Bilstone Rd **6** 307
Bingham's Cottage **6** 322
Birch Coppice **7** 78
Birch Hill **7** 56
Birch Tree (P.H.) **7** 66
Birch Tree Fm **4** 290
Birchcroft **6** 159
Birchwood Hill **7** 56
Bird Hill **7** 248
Bird in Hand (P.H.) **1** 122
Birds Hill Cottage **6** 9
Birds Hill Gorse **6** 9
Birkley St. **1** 19
Birmingham road **2** 170
Birmingham Tavern (P.H.) **1** 122
BIRSTALL **7** x, 29
Birstall: unindexed modern street-names **7** 30
Birstall Hill Park **7** 29
Bishop Blaize (P.H.)
(Barrow upon Soar) **3** 36
(Causeway Lane) **1** 122
(Loughborough) **7** 132
Bishop Blaze (P.H.) **2** 177
Bishop Meadow Bridge **7** 126
Bishop Meadow Fm **7** 126
Bishop Meadow Lock **7** 126
Bishop Ryder's School **5** 138
Bishop St. **1** 19
Bishop St. **1** 20
Bishop's Barn Close **1** 183
Bishop's Cottage **7** 78
Bishop's Fee **1** xi, 12
Bishop's Water **1** 225
BITTESBY **5** xi, xii, xiv, xv, 25
Bittesby Cottages **5** 25
Bittesby Spinney **5** 25
BITTESWELL **5** xiii, 27
Bitteswell Aerodrome **5** 27
Bitteswell Fields **5** 28
Bitteswell Grange **5** 27
Bitteswell Hall **5** 27
Bitteswell Hall Park **5** 27
Bitteswell Ho. **5** 27
Bitteswell Lodge **5** 27
Bitteswell Rd **5** 139
BLABY **5** xiv, 32
Blaby: unindexed modern street-names **5** 33
Blaby Bridge **5** 32
Blaby Hall **5** 32
Blaby Hill **5** 32
Blaby Hospital **5** 32
Blaby Lane **5** 219
Blaby Mill **5** 32
Blaby Station **5** 32
Black Boy (P.H.)
(Albion St.) **1** 122
(Hungarton) **3** 144
Black Brook **7** 194
Black Bull (P.H.)
(Applegate) **1** 122
(Bottesford) **2** 23
Black Cliff **7** 237
Black Ditches **7** 8
Black Dog (P.H.) **5** 164
Black Friars **1** 91
Black Friars Lane **1** 20
Black Hill **7** 237
Black Holt **2** 10
Black Horse (P.H.)
(Appleby) **6** 10
(Aylestone) **5** 19
(Blaby) **5** 32
(Foxton) **4** 54
(Grimston) **3** 106
(Hinckley) **6** 121
(Houghton) **4** 109
(Market Bosworth) **6** 166
(Sheepy Magna) **6** 252
(Tugby) **3** 254
(Walcote) **5** 149
(Whitwick) **7** 74
Black Horse (P.H.)
(Belgrave Gate) **1** 122
(Castle Donington) **7** 50
(Frisby on the Wreake) **3** 80
(Granby St.) **1** 122

(Hose) **2** 99
(Loughborough, High St.) **7** 132
(Loughborough, Wood Gate) **7** 132
(Melton Mowbray) **2** 177
(Scalford) **2** 209
(Slawston) **4** 240
(Thorpe Acre) **7** 144
(Thurmaston) **3** 238
(Ullesthorpe) **5** 205
Black Horse Hill **6** 10
Black Hovel Spinney **7** 185
Black Lane **3** 268
Black Lion (P.H.)
(Blackfordby) **7** 14
(Loughborough) **7** 132
Black Lion (P.H.)
(Belgrave Gate) **1** 122
(Gallowtree Gate) **1** 122
Black Moor's Head (P.H.)
(Melton Mowbray) **2** 177
(Syston) **3** 229
Black Pool **1** 225
Black Spinney
(Blaby) **5** 32
(King's Norton) **4** 142
(Swithland) **7** 227
Black Swan (P.H.)
(Belgrave Gate) **1** 123
(Melton Mowbray) **2** 177
(Shepshed) **7** 198
Black Swan (P.H.)
(Church Gate) **1** 123
(Grimston) **3** 106
(Ibstock) **6** 145
(Kilby) **5** 107
(Market Harborough) **4** 173
(Mountsorrel) **7** 152
(Syston) **3** 229
Black-a-Moors Spinney **3** 130
Blackberry Fm **7** 64
Blackberry Hill **2** 6
Blackberry Lane
(Coalville) **7** 64
(Cossington) **3** 60
Blackbird's Nest **7** 146
Blackbrook Drive **7** 62
Blackbrook Fm **7** 194
Blackbrook Mill **7** 194
Blackbrook Reservoir **7** xiii
(Charley) **7** 56
(Shepshed) **7** 194
BLACKFORDBY **7** xi, 14
Blackfordby Fields **7** 14
Blackfordby Hall **7** 14
Blackfordby Ho. **7** 14
Blackfriars St. **1** 20
Blackmile Spinney **7** 242
Blackpool **3** 197
Blacksmith's Arms (P.H.) **6** 127
Blacksmith's Lane **2** 261
Blacksmith's Shop
(Edmondthorpe) **2** 298
(Scalford) **2** 209
Blacksmith's Shop
(Cossington) **3** 60
(Gaddesby) **3** 94
(Keyham) **3** 158
(Loddington) **3** 163
(South Croxton) **3** 72
(Tugby) **3** 254
Blacksmiths' Arms (P.H.)
(Cosby) **5** 67
(Desford) **6** 72
(Loughborough) **7** 132
(Whitwick) **7** 74
Blacksmiths' Arms (P.H.) **3** 36
Blackspinney Lane **4** 170
Blackthorn Lane **5** 164
Blackwell Lodge **2** 103
Blackwood Rd **7** 62
Blaise's Inn **2** 59
Blake Fm **7** 286
Blakenhall Fm **5** 27
Blakeshay Fm **7** 156
Blakeshay Wood **7** 156
Blankwell **1** 228
Blankwell Lane **1** 20
BLASTON **4** xii, 13
Blaston Hall **4** 14
Blaston Hill **4** 14

Blaston Hollows **4** 14
Blaston Lodge **4** 14
Blaston Pastures **4** 14
Blaston Rd **4** 240
Bleach Mill Cottages **7** 264
Bleak Hills **2** 45
Bleak Ho.
(Diseworth) **7** 117
(Fleckney) **4** 50
(Illston) **4** 129
(Knossington) **4** 147
(Whitwick) **7** 72
Bleak Moor **3** 197
Blenheim Plantation **4** 221
Bliss's Close **1** 183
Blobbs, The **6** 10
Bloods Hill **6** 151
Bloomhills Fm **5** 83
Blower's Brook
(Normanton le Heath) **6** 197
(Ravenstone) **7** 180
Blowpool Spinney **2** 63
Blue Ball (P.H.) **7** 170
Blue Bank Lock **5** 104
Blue Bell (P.H.)
(Ashby de la Zouch) **7** 11
(Blackfordby) **7** 14
(Desford) **6** 72
(Shepshed) **7** 198
(Stoney Stanton) **6** 282
Blue Bell (P.H.)
(Arnesby) **5** 5
(Catthorpe) **5** 54
(Claybrooke Magna) **5** 58
(Coalville) **7** 62
(Glooston) **4** 65
(Hinckley) **6** 121
(Melton Mowbray) **2** 177
(Sharnford) **6** 246
(Syston) **3** 229
Blue Bell Inn
(Asfordby) **3** 11
(Hoby) **3** 114
Blue Boar (P.H.) **7** 132
Blue Boar (P.H.)
(High Street) **1** 123
(Hinckley) **6** 121
(South Gates) **1** 123
(Thrussington) **3** 232
Blue Boar Lane **1** xiv, 20
Blue Bull (P.H.) **2** 55
Blue Cow (P.H.) **2** 55
Blue Dog (P.H.) **2** 59
Blue Lion (P.H.)
(Thrussington) **3** 232
(Witherley) **6** 322
Blue Lion (P.H.)
(Granby St.) **1** 123
(Slawston) **4** 240
Blue Pig (P.H.) **2** 149
Blue Point (P.H.) **2** 287
Blue Pot (P.H.) **6** 151
Blunt's Lane **5** 219
Board Inn (P.H.) **5** 137
Boat (P.H.) **7** 132
Boat (P.H.)
(Belgrave Gate) **1** 123
(Theddingworth) **4** 269
(Thurmaston) **3** 238
Boat and Engine (P.H.) **1** 123
Boat Inn (P.H.) **2** 177
Boathouse Walk Plantation **7** 47
Bob's Baulk **7** 47
Boden Brook **7** 255
Bodicotes mill **5** 223
Bodkin Fm **7** 194
Bog Spinney **5** 208
Bollard's Shop **1** 118
Bolt Wood **4** 251
Bolus Lodge **6** 72
Bon Croft Fm **7** 276
Bon Hills Spinneys **4** 106
Bond Lane **7** 152
Bond St. **1** 20
Bondgate **7** 47
Bondman Hays **6** 222
Boneham's Lane **5** 96
Bonner's Lane **1** 21

Bonser's Spinney **3** 180
Boot (P.H.)
(Houghton on the Hill) **4** 109
(Hinckley) **6** 121
(Long Whatton) **7** 112
(Loughborough) **7** 132
(Measham) **7** 264
Boot Inn (P.H.) **6** 145
Boot Inn (P.H.) **6** 52
Booth Rd **7** 70
Booth Wood **7** 144
BOOTHORPE **7** 21
Boothorpe Fm **7** 21
Boothorpe Hall **7** 21
Boothorpe Lane **7** 14
Bordel, The **1** xi, 142
Bordelhouse Lane **1** 21
Borough St.
(Castle Donington) **7** 47
(Kegworth) **7** 96
Borough, The **6** 123
Borrowdale Gates **6** 176
Boston Lane **2** 99
Boston Lodge **5** 96
Bosworth Gorse **4** 119
Bosworth Grange **4** 119
Bosworth Hall **6** 166
Bosworth Lane
(Barlestone) **6** 39
(Osbaston) **6** 201
Bosworth Lodge **4** 119
Bosworth Mill **4** 119
Bosworth Mill Fm **4** 120
Bosworth Park **6** 166
Bosworth Rd
(Measham) **7** 264
(Snarestone) **6** 268
(Theddingworth) **4** 269
(Walton) **5** 113
Bosworth Tunnel **4** 119
Bosworth Wharf Bridge **6** 166
Botany Bay
(Charley) **7** 56
(Coleorton) **7** 78
(Nether Broughton) **2** 46
(Shepshed) **7** 194
Botany Bay Fox Covert **3** 153
Botany Bay Spinney **6** 194
Botany Spinney **6** 266
BOTCHESTON **6** 78
Botcheston Lodge **6** 79
Botcheston Rd **6** 80
Botney Lodge **5** 193
Bott's Hill Fm **6** 36
BOTTESFORD **2** 21
Bottesford Nursery **2** 23
Bottesford School **2** 23
Bottesford Vineries **2** 23
Bottesford Wharf **2** 23
Bottle Neck **6** 166
Bottleacre Lane **7** 126
Bottom Barn **7** 47
Bottom End Bridge **5** 212
Bottom Fm **7** 78
Bottom Park **2** 63
Bottom Plantation **2** 55
Bottom Round Spinney **5** 156
Botts Lane **6** 10
Bouch's Covert **2** 180
Boundary **7** 16
Boundary Fm **6** 226
Boundary Kennel, The **4** 240
Boundary Rd **5** 139
Bow Bridge **1** 72
Bow Bridge Close **1** 183
Bow Pool Covert **6** 166
Bow St. **1** xv, 21
Bowden Inn Fm **4** 54
Bowden Lane
(Market Harborough) **4** 172
(Welham) **4** 290
Bowden Rd **4** 276
Bowleys Lane **6** 10
Bowling Green **4** 174
Bowling Green **1** 142
Bowling Green (P.H.) **7** 11
Bowling Green (P.H.)
(Earl Shilton) **6** 135
(Measham) **7** 264
(St Peter's Lane) **1** 123
Bowling Green Garden **1** 176
Bowling Green Rd **6** 117

Bowling Green Spinney **7** 156
Bowling Green St. **1** 21
Bowmar's Bleach Yard **1** 145
Bowmar's Lane **1** xv, 21
Boyer St. **7** 126
Boyer's Lodge **6** 159
Boyslade Rd **6** 50
Bracknell's Barn **6** 305
Bradfield Bridge **6** 295
Bradgate
 (Newtown Linford) **7** 155
 (Walcote) **5** 149
Bradgate Arms (P.H.) **7** 156
Bradgate Arms (P.H.) **7** 234
Bradgate Drive **7** 62
Bradgate Hall **7** 156
Bradgate Hill **6** 98
Bradgate Ho. **6** 98
Bradgate Home Fm **6** 98
Bradgate Lane **3** 11
Bradgate Park **7** 156
Bradgate Rd
 (Anstey) **7** 3
 (Cropston) **7** 234
Bradley **4** 209
Bradley Lodge **4** 204
Bradley Priory **4** xiii, 202
Bradley's Row **2** 171
Bradshaws, The **6** 215
Brake, The **6** 159
Bramboro Fm **7** 279
Bramborough Fm **7** 23
Bramborough Lane Bridge **7** 276
Bramborough Terrace **7** 276
Bran Hills **3** 85
Brancliff Cottage **3** 72
Brancliff Fm **3** 72
Brand Fm **7** 255
Brand Gate **7** 36
Brand Hills **7** 248
Brand House Fm **7** 255
Brand Lane **7** 248
Brand, The **7** 248
Brandgate Fm **7** 36
Bransford Bridge **5** xii, 75
BRANSTON **2** xiii, 110
Branston Lodge **2** 111
Brant Hill Fm **5** 188
Branting Hill **6** 98
BRASCOTE **6** 193
Brascote Covert **6** 194
Brascote Ho. **6** 194
Brascote Lane **6** 194
Braunston Rd **4** 147
BRAUNSTONE **6** xiii, 44
Braunstone Frith **6** 44
Braunstone Frith Closes **1** 184
Braunstone Gate **1** 21
Braunstone Gate Bridge **1** 72
Braunstone Hall **6** 44
Braunstone Lane **6** 45
Braunstone Park **6** 45
Braunstone Pasture **1** 203
Braybrooke Rd **4** 185
Braziers' Arms (P.H.) **1** 123
Brazil Wood **7** 227
Breach Barn
 (Ullesthorpe) **5** 205
 (Walton) **5** 113
Breach Cottage **7** 210
Breach Fm
 (Packington) **7** 286
 (Saddington) **4** 224
 (Walton) **5** 113
Breach Fm, The **6** 133
Breach Hill **7** 286
Breach Ho. **7** 255
Breach Lands **6** 133
Breach Lane **6** 133
Breach Lane Fm **6** 133
Breach Rd **7** 62
Breach, The **6** 133
Breaches **7** 194
Bread St. **1** xv, 22
Breadcroft Lane **3** 34
Breakback Plantation **7** 248
Breech Spinney
 (Thurcaston) **7** 230
 (Wanlip) **7** 242
Breedon Brand **7** 255
Breedon Brand Fm **7** 255
Breedon Cloud Wood **7** 36

Breedon Hall **7** 36
Breedon Hill **7** x, xii, 36
Breedon Lodge **7** 36
BREEDON ON THE HILL **7** x, 34
Breedon Priory **7** xi, 35
Breedon's Sq. **1** 22
BRENTINGBY **2** xii, 132
Brentingby Lodge Fm **2** 133
Brentingby Road **2** 171
Brentingby Wood **2** 133
Brewery Cottages **3** 42
Brian's Close **4** 154
Brick Kiln Cottage **6** 261
Brick Kiln Fm **6** 288
Brick Kiln Hill **6** 123
Brick Kiln Lane **1** 22
Brick Kiln Lane **7** 194
Brick Kiln Plantation **6** 318
Brick Kilns **1** 145
Brickfield Fm **2** 239
Brickfield Ho. **2** 239
Brickfield Plantation **7** 18
Brickfield Spinney **4** 119
Brickhill Plantation **7** 194
Brickkiln Street **6** 118
Bricklayers Arms (P.H.) **6** 27
Bricklayers' Arms (P.H.) **1** 123
Bricklayers' Arms (P.H.)
(Belgrave) **3** 47
(Castle Donington) **7** 50
(Donington le Heath) **7** 64
(Donisthorpe) **7** 279
(Melton Mowbray) **2** 177
Brickmakers' Arms (P.H.) **1** 123
Brickmans Hill **6** 151
Brickyard Cottage **2** 140
Brickyard Cottages **7** 56
Brickyard Fm
(Ashby Magna) **5** 9
(Burbage) **6** 50
(Glenfield) **6** 92
(Kirkby Mallory) **6** 211
(Owston) **4** 215
(Rothley) **7** 185
(Sapcote) **6** 226
Brickyard Lane
(Ashby Magna) **5** 9
(Kegworth) **7** 96
Brickyard Plantation **2** 139
Bridewell **1** 109
Bridewell, The **6** 120
Bridge Fields **7** 96
Bridge Fm
(Ashby Magna) **5** 10
(Elmesthorpe) **6** 83
(Ibstock) **6** 144
(Kibworth Harbourt) **4** 138
(Shackerstone) **6** 233
Bridge St.
(Barrow upon Soar) **3** 34
(Loughborough) **7** 127
(Shepshed) **7** 194
Bridge St.
(Duns Lane) **1** 22
(Russell St.) **1** 22
Bridgeland Fm **3** 232
Bridgemere Fm **5** 113
Bridget's Covert **2** 50
Bridle Road Spinney **7** 185
Briery Cottage **2** 7
Briery Leys Spinney **3** 254
Briery Wood **2** 7
Briggs's Hospital **3** 80
Brighton Arms (P.H.) **1** 123
Brindles, The **5** 90
BRINGHURST **4** xiv, 18
Britannia (P.H.)
(Queniborough) **3** 183
(Shepshed) **7** 198
Britannia (P.H.)
(Belgrave Gate) **1** 123
(Castle St.) **1** 123
(Great Bowden) **4** 177
Britannia Inn **7** 96
Britannia St. **1** xiv, 22
Briton Lodge **7** 23

Broad Acres **4** 4
Broad Hill
(Kegworth) **7** 96
(Mountsorrel) **7** 152
(Thringstone) **7** 70
Broad Lane **6** 273
Broad Meadow **1** 196
Broad St.
(Coalville) **7** 62
(Syston) **3** 228
Broadgate **4** 74
Broadnook Spinney **7** 242
Broadview
(Great Easton) **4** 74
(Willoughby Waterleys) **5** 235
Brock Hill **2** xi, 90
Brocker Ho. **2** 239
Brockers Cliffe **7** 156
Brockey Farm Cottages **6** 127
Brockey Fm
(Barwell) **6** 127
(Stapleton(x2)) **6** 215
Brockey Lane **6** 127
Brockey, The **6** 127
Brockhill Hall **2** 99
Brockleys **3** 85
Brockleys Fm **3** 85
Brocks Hill **5** 164
Brocks Hill Fm **5** 164
Bromkinsthorpe **1** xi, xiii, 218
Bromkinsthorpe Gate **1** 22
Bromley Ho. **5** 174
Bromley Lane **7** 26
Brook Cottages **7** 78
Brook Fm
(Bardon) **6** 36
(Burton on the Wolds) **3** 54
(Launde) **3** 161
(Nanpantan) **7** 146
(Stoke Golding) **6** 275
(Tonge) **7** 41
(Wilson) **7** 43
(Woodhouse) **7** 248
Brook Hill Fm **6** 127
Brook Ho.
(Rearsby) **3** 198
(Sileby) **3** 215
(Smeeton Westerby) **4** 246
(Stoke Golding) **6** 275
(Swithland) **7** 227
Brook Lane
(Asfordby) **3** 11
(Billesdon) **4** 4
(Great Easton) **4** 74
(Melton Mowbray) **2** 169
Brook Side **3** 228
Brook Spinney **4** 259
Brook St. **1** 22
Brook St.
(Ashby de la Zouch) **7** 8
(Shepshed) **7** 194
(Sileby) **3** 215
(Syston) **3** 228
(Thurmaston) **3** 238
(Walcote) **5** 149
(Whetstone) **5** 212
(Wymeswold) **3** 275
Brook Vale Cottages **6** 98
Brookdale **7** 78
Brooke Fm **6** 109
Brookesby's Closes **1** 184
Brookfield
(Burton on the Wolds) **3** 54
(Medbourne) **4** 188
(Sharnford) **6** 246
(Stoney Stanton) **6** 282
Brookfield **5** 126
Brookfield Fm **7** 185
Brookfield Ho. **3** 21
Brookfield House Fm **4** 34
Brookhill Fm **5** 174
Brooklands
(Anstey) **7** 3
(Worthington) **7** 255
Brooklands Fm
(Barkby) **3** 21
(Barwell) **6** 127
(Overseal) **7** 283
Brooklands, The **5** 212
Brooklet Fm **7** 47
BROOKSBY **3** xiv, 125
Brooksby Grange **3** 125

Brooksby Spinney **3** 125
Brookside
(Shepshed) **7** 194
(Whetstone) **5** 212
Brookside Cottage
(Eye Kettleby) **2** 189
(Glooston) **4** 65
Brookside Fm
(Oadby) **5** 164
(Osgathorpe) **7** 163
(Tonge) **7** 44
Broom Leys Ave. **7** 62
Broom Lodge **3** 198
Broom's Fm **3** 161
Broombriggs Cottage Fm **7** 248
Broombriggs Hill **7** 248
Broombriggs Ho. **7** 248
Broomfields Fm **7** 269
Broomhill Fm **6** 104
Broomhills **6** 206
Broomhills Fm **6** 206
Broomleys Fm **7** 61
Broomwood **2** 278
Broomy Husk **7** 210
BROUGHTON ASTLEY **5** xi, xv, 38
Broughton Astley Lodge **5** 39
Broughton Grange **2** 46
Broughton Hill **2** 46
Broughton Lane
(Leire) **5** 130
(Stoney Stanton) **6** 282
Broughton Lodges **2** 46
Broughton Rd
(Coalville) **7** 62
(Cosby) **5** 67
(Croft) **6** 67
(Frolesworth) **5** 90
(Stoney Stanton) **6** 282
Brown Heath **6** xiv, xv, xvi, xvii
Brown Hill **7** 185
Brown Horse (P.H.) **6** 206
Brown St. (Lower and Upper) **1** 22
Brown's Hay **7** 156
Brown's Hill **2** 163
Brown's lane **7** 130
Brown's Wood
(Skeffington) **3** 221
(Thornton) **6** 27
Broxtowe Fm **5** 10
Bruces Lane **4** 147
Brunsleigh **7** 84
Brunswick Sq. **1** xiv, 23
Brunswick St. **1** 23
BRUNTINGTHORPE **5** xiv, xv, 49
Bruntingthorpe Airfield **5** 49
Bruntingthorpe Hall **5** 49
Bruntingthorpe Ho. **5** 49
Bruntingthorpe Holt **5** 49
Bruntingthorpe Rd
(Peatling Parva) **5** 178
(Shearsby) **5** 188
Brutnall's Lodge **3** 102
Bryan's yard **7** 130
Buck Hill **7** 146
Buck's Head (P.H.)
(Gallowtree Gate) **1** 123
(Newtown Linford) **7** 156
BUCKMINSTER **2** xiii, 54
Buckminster Hall **2** 55
Buckminster Lodge **2** 55
Buckminster Park **2** 55
Bucknall Hill **3** 34
Buckston Lane **1** xii, 23
Buckston's Orchard **1** 176
Buckwell Lodge **5** 149
Buddon Wood **7** 170
Buddon Wood Fm **7** 170
Budgemere Fm **5** 113
Buffalo Lodge **4** 204
Buffalo's Head and Garland (P.H.) **7** 149
Bufton **6** 63
Bufton Lane **6** 63
Bufton Lodge **6** 79
Bufton Lodge Fm **6** 63
Bull (P.H.)
(Ashby de la Zouch) **7** 11
(East Langton) **4** 38
(Enderby) **6** 87
(Lutterworth) **5** 137
(North Kilworth) **5** 156

(South Gates) **1** 124
(Witherley) **6** 322
Bull and Lion (P.H.) **7** 286
Bull and Mouth (P.H.) **7** 152
Bull Head (P.H.) **5** 137
Bull Head St. **5** 219
Bull Hill **7** 255
Bull in the Oak **6** 59
Bull Inn (P.H.) **6** 121
Bull Lane **1** xiv, 23
Bull Pen **1** 196
Bull Pitts **6** 133
Bull Ring **7** 194
Bull Spinney **4** 246
Bull's Head (P.H.)
(Ashby de la Zouch) **7** 11
(Blaby) **5** 32
(Claybrooke Magna) **5** 58
(Cosby) **5** 67
(Countesthorpe) **5** 79
(Desford) **6** 72
(Markfield) **6** 176
(Nailstone) **6** 182
(Quorndon) **7** 170
(Ratby) **6** 222
(Stoney Stanton) **6** 282
(Thringstone) **7** 71
(Tur Langton) **4** 286
(Whetstone) **5** 212
(Whitwick) **7** 74
(Wilson) **7** 43
Bull's Head (P.H.)
(Belgrave) **3** 47
(Burbage) **6** 52
(Diseworth) **7** 117
(Donisthorpe) **7** 279
(Hathern) **7** 84
(High Street) **1** 124
(Hinckley) **6** 121
(Knighton) **5** 126
(Loughborough) **7** 132
(Market Bosworth) **6** 166
(Market Pl.) **1** 124
(Mountsorrel) **7** 152
(Osgathope) **7** 163
(Oxford St.) **1** 124
(Peckleton) **6** 206
(Primethorpe) **5** 41
(Shepshed) **7** 198
(Swannington) **7** 210
(Syston) **3** 229
(Walcote) **5** 149
(Wigston Magna) **5** 222
(Woodhouse) **7** 248
(Woodthorpe) **7** 149
(Wymeswold) **3** 275
Bull's Head Inn **6** 159
Bull's Head Plantation **6** 307
Bull's Head yard **7** 130
Bull's Lane **1** 23
Bullacre Spinney **6** 206
Bullfurlong Lane **6** 50
Bullockhall Fm **6** 72
Bulwarks, The **1** 9
Bulwarks, The **7** 36
Bulwell Barn **6** 197
Bumble-Bee Fm **6** 246
Bumble-Bee Hall **6** 246
Bumper (P.H.) **1** 124
Bunbury Fm **3** 94
Bunde Mead **1** 196
Bungalow Fm
(Bagworth) **6** 25
(Normanton Turville) **6** 305
Bungalow, The **5** 232
Bunker Hill **7** 194
Bunker Hill Fm **3** 207
Bunkers Hill **4** 164
Bunkers Hill Fm **4** 164
Bunkers Wood **2** 111
Bunny's Lodge **2** 84
Bunny's Spinney **2** 84
BURBAGE **6** xi, 50
Burbage Common **6** 123
Burbage Common Rd **6** 83
Burbage Fields **6** 50
Burbage Fields Fm **6** 51
Burbage Hall **6** 50
Burbage Ho. **6** 50
Burbage House Cottages **6** 50
Burbage Nurseries, The **6** 50
Burbage Rd **6** 117

Burbage Wood **6** 123
Burbage's Covert **2** 180
Burchnall Spinney **6** 176
Burgate **2** 176
Burges Lane **1** 23
Burges Pavement **1** 79
Burgess St.
(Leicester) **1** 23
(Wigston Magna) **5** 219
Burgesses' Meadow **1** 197
Burleigh **7** 146
Burleigh Brook **7** 146
Burleigh Hall **7** 146
Burleigh Wood **7** 146
Burley's Garden **1** 176
Burley's Lane **1** 24
Burn Hill **4** 106
Burney Lane **7** 36
Burney Rough **7** 36
Burnmill Hill **4** 177
Burnmill Ho. **4** 174
Burnmill Lane **4** 177
Burnside **4** 188
Burrough Court **2** 232
Burrough Hill **2** xi, 232
Burrough Hill Covert **2** 78
Burrough Hill Ho. **2** 232
Burrough Hill Lodge **2** 232
BURROUGH ON THE HILL **2** xi, 231
Burrough on the Hill:
unindexed dwellings **2** 232
Burrough Rd **3** 261
Burrow Hill Rd **4** 65
Burrow Spinney **5** 76
Burrow Wood **7** 56
Burrowchurch **2** 286
Burton Bandalls **3** 54
Burton Bandalls Fm **3** 54
Burton Bridge **2** 63
Burton Brook
(Burton Lazars) **2** 63
(Burton Overy) **4** 21
(Illston) **4** 129
Burton End **2** 180
Burton End Bridge **2** 174
Burton Grange **4** 21
Burton Hall **3** 54
Burton Hill **2** 180
Burton Lane **7** 210
BURTON LAZARS **2** xiii, 62
Burton Lazars Hall **2** 63
Burton Lodge Cottage **2** 63
Burton Lodge Fm **2** 63
BURTON ON THE WOLDS **3** xii, xv, 54
BURTON OVERY **4** xiii, 21
Burton Rd
(Ashby de la Zouch) **7** 8
(Measham) **7** 264
(Melton Mowbray) **2** 169
(Norton Juxta Twycross) **6** 312
(Oakthorpe) **7** 276
Burton Road Lodge **2** 140
Burton St.
(Loughborough) **7** 127
(Melton Mowbray) **2** 169
Burton Walk **7** 127
Burton Wolds **3** 54
Burton's Tea Gardens **1** 143, 176
Bury Camp **6** 222
Bush Lock **5** 224
BUSHBY **4** xii, 281
Bushby Brook
(Humberstone) **3** 133
(Thurnby) **4** 282
Bushby Ho. **4** 282
Bushby Lodge **4** 282
Bushby Lodge Fm **4** 282
Bushby Spinney **4** 282
Bushes, The **3** 94
Bushley End **5** 221
Bushloe Ho. **5** 222
Bushloe road **5** 220
Bushwell Cottage **7** 78
Bushwell Ho. **7** 255
Bushy Field Wood **7** 237
Busky Ho. **6** 27
Butcher's Arms (P.H.) **7** 234
Butcher's Lane **3** 207

Butchers' Arms (P.H.)
(Croxton Kerrial) **2** 103
(Husbands Bosworth) **4** 119
Butler's Spinney **5** 156
Butlers Cottage **3** 163
Butt Close **1** 184
Butt Close **2** 191
Butt Close Lane **1** 24
Butt Ho., The **7** 12
Butt Lane
(Blackfordby) **7** 14
(Hinckley) **6** 117
(Wymondham) **2** 287
Buttercross, The **2** 175
Buttermilk Hill Spinney **2** 84
Butthole Lane **7** 194
Button's Hill Spinney **5** 76
Butts Fm **5** 147
Butts Lane **4** 119
Butts, The **1** 143
Bybrook Fm **7** 230
Byron St. **1** 24

Cadborough Fm **7** 269
Cadborough Hill **7** 269
CADEBY **6** xiv, 58
Cadeby Hall **6** 59
Cadeby Lane **6** 59
Cademan St. **7** 72
Cademan Wood **7** 72
Cage, The **1** 111
Cage's Garden **1** 176
Calais St. **1** 24
Calcroft's Close **2** 7
Caldicote Spinney **5** 194
Caldwell Place **2** 171
California Cottage **7** 78
Callans Lane **7** 207
Callis, The **7** 8
Calvary Rock **7** 70
Calver Hey **1** 203
Calver Hill **6** 221
Calver Hill Cottages **6** 226
Calver Hill Quarry **6** 226
Cambridge Rd
(Cosby) **5** 67
(Whetstone) **5** 213
Cambridge Spinney **4** 209
Cambridge St. **7** 127
Camden St. **1** xv, 24
Cammas Close **6** 50
Camp Barn **5** 114
Campbell St. **1** 24
Canaan Fm **5** 12
Canal Ho. **7** 264
Canal Lane
(Hose) **2** 99
(Long Clawson) **2** 90
Canal St.
(Aylestone) **5** 19
(Oakthorpe) **7** 276
Canal wharf **7** 130
Canals, Locks and Wharfs **1** 80
Cank St. **1** 25
Cank Well **1** 229
Cank, The **1** 24
Canning Pl. **1** 25
Canning St.
(Hinckley) **6** 117
(Leicester) **1** xv, 25
Cannon (P.H.) **1** 124
Cannon St. **1** xv, 25
Cant's Thorns **2** 166
Cap and Stocking (P.H.) **1** 124
Cap's Spinney **3** 177
Cappe Lane **2** 171
Captain's Gorse **7** 47
Car Hill Rock **7** 70
Cardigan Arms (P.H.) **4** 31
Cardigan Terrace **2** 171
Cardinal's Hat (P.H.) **1** 124
Carington Arms (P.H.) **3** 100
Carington Spinney **3** 100
Carland Spinney **4** 119
Carley St. **1** 25
Carlisle Wood **2** 7
CARLTON **6** xiii, 63
Carlton Bridge **6** 63
Carlton Clump **4** 27
CARLTON CURLIEU **4** 27
Carlton Curlieu Hall **4** 27
Carlton Curlieu Manor Ho. **4** 129

Carlton Gate **6** 63
Carlton Grange **4** 28
Carlton Hayes Hospital **6** 186
Carlton Lodge **3** 94
Carlton Pl. **1** 25
Carlton Rd **4** 138
Carlton St. **1** 25
Caroline St. **1** xiv, 25
Carpenter's Shop **3** 60
Carpenters' Arms (P.H.) **3** 215
Carr Bridge
(Lowesby) **3** 168
(Shepshed) **7** 194
Carr Bridge Spinney **3** 168
Carriageway, The **4** 147
Carrier, The **2** 14
Carrington St. **1** xv, 25
Carrs Hill **6** 127
Carrs Lane **6** 127
Carrygate **4** 62
Cart's Lane **1** 25
Carter's Rough **6** 98
Carter's Windmill **1** 148
Carthegena **3** 60
Cary Hill Quarry **6** 282
Cary Hill Rd **6** 282
Castle (P.H.) **6** 121
Castle (P.H.)
(Ashby de la Zouch) **7** 11
(Castle Donington) **7** 50
Castle Close **6** 226
CASTLE DONINGTON
7 xi, xii, xiii, 46
Castle Fd **2** 90
Castle Fm
(Congerstone) **6** 241
(Kirby Muxloe) **6** 152
Castle Hill
(Castle Donington) **7** 47
(Groby) **6** 98
(Hallaton) **4** 95
(Hinckley) **6** 123
(Mountsorrel) **7** 152
(Withcote) **2** 284
Castle Hill House **6** 122
Castle Inn (P.H.) **1** 124
Castle Inn **2** 119
Castle Inn
(Great Easton) **4** 74
(Hugglescote) **7** 66
Castle Mills **1** 148
Castle Mills Holme **1** 197
Castle Mound **5** 182
Castle Orchard **1** 176
Castle Rock Fm **7** 61
Castle Sq. **1** 25
Castle St.
(Hinckley) **6** 117
(Leicester) **1** 25
(Whitwick) **7** 72
Castle Tavern (P.H.) **1** 124
Castle, The **1** 9
Castle, The (P.H.) **7** 132
Cat Hill Wood **7** 56
Catherine Dalley Ho. **2** 178
Catherine Spinney **5** 104
Catherine St. **1** 26
Catholic Chapel **1** 89
Catholic School **1** 112
Catsick Hill **3** 34
Catsick Lane **3** 34
Cattens Rough **7** 56
Cattesholme **1** 197
CATTHORPE **5** xi, xii, xiv, xv, 53
Catthorpe Barn **5** 200
Catthorpe Hall **5** 54
Catthorpe Rd **5** 182
Catthorpe Towers **5** 54
Cattle Market **4** 174
Cattle Market
(Ashby de la Zouch) **7** 10
(Leicester) **1** 116
Cattows Fm
(Shackerstone) **6** 233
(Swepstone) **7** 218
Caudale Field Fm **3** 169
Cauldwell Fm **5** 27
Cauldwell Lane **5** 27
Causeway Lane
(Leicester) **1** 26
(Cropston) **7** 234
Causeways, The **1** 77

Cavalry St. **1** xiv, 26
Cave's Arms (P.H.) **5** xii, 200
Cave's Arms (P.H.) **7** 279
Cave's Inn **5** 182
Cavendish Bridge **7** 47
Cawdell Fm **4** 276
Cedar Fm **5** 182
Cedar Hill **2** 103
Cedar House Fm **5** 178
Cedar Lodge Fm **4** 224
Cedars, The
(Glenfield) **6** 92
(Hose) **2** 99
(Kirby Muxloe) **6** 152
(Lowesby) **3** 169
(Saddington) **4** 224
(Skeffington) **3** 221
Cedarwood Houses **7** 269
Central Rd **7** 62
CHADWELL **2** 217
Chaff Lane **1** 26
Chain, The **5** 28
Chalk Pool Hill **3** 85
Chalkpit Fm **3** 54
Chamberlain's Ct. **1** 26
Chamberlain's Nether Close **4** 63
Chamberlayne Arms (P.H.) **4** 14
Champion (P.H.) **1** 124
Champion Inn (P.H.) **3** 47
Chancery St. **1** 26
Chandlers' Arms (P.H.) **5** 188
Change Spinney **6** 79
Chantry Ho. **3** 114
Chapel Houses **7** 23
Chapel Lane
(Knighton) **5** 126
(Nether Broughton) **2** 46
(Ratby) **6** 222
(Sharnford) **6** 152
(Walcote) **5** 149
(Walton) **5** 114
Chapel Nook **2** 189
Chapel of Our Lady of the Bridge **1** 88
Chapel of St John **1** 88
Chapel St.
(Barwell) **6** 127
(Blaby) **5** 32
(Bottesford) **2** 23
(Donisthorpe) **7** 279
(Enderby) **6** 87
(Measham) **7** 264
(Melton Mowbray) **2** 169
(Oakthorpe) **7** 276
(Syston) **3** 228
Chapel Street **6** 118
Chapel, The **2** 284
Chaplin's Rough **7** 156
Chapman St. **7** 127
Chapman's Spinney **6** 261
Charity Fm
(Breedon on the Hill) **7** 36
(Stoughton) **4** 259
Charles St.
(Coalville) **7** 62
(Leicester) **1** 26
(Sileby) **3** 215
Charles St. Chapel **1** 89
CHARLEY **7** x, xiii, 55
Charley Hall **7** 56
Charley Knoll **7** 56
Charley Knoll Fm **7** 57
Charley Mill **7** 57
Charley Mill Fm **7** 57
Charley Priory **7** xi, 56
Charley Rd **7** 194
Charlotte St.
(Alexander St.) **1** 26
(Archdeacon Lane) **1** xiv, 26
Charlton St. **1** 27
Charnborough Rd **7** 62
Charnock Hill **7** x, 47
Charnwood **6** xii, 152
Charnwood Cottage **7** 57
Charnwood Fm
(Shepshed) **7** 194
(Thringstone) **7** 70
Charnwood Forest **7** ix, x, xii, xiii, 55
Charnwood Hall **7** 146

Charnwood Heath **7** 57
Charnwood Ho.
(Ashby de la Zouch) **7** 12
(Quorndon) **7** 170
(Sileby) **3** 215
Charnwood Kennels **7** 194
Charnwood Lodge **7** 57
Charnwood Quarries **7** 194
Charnwood St. **7** 62
Charnwood Tower **7** 57
Charnwood Towers **7** 57
Chasewood **7** 93
Chater Fm **6** 194
Chater Ho. **6** 194
Chatham St. **1** xiv, 27
Chaveney Ho. **7** 170
Chaveney Plantation **7** 170
Cheap End **3** 81
Cheapside
(Leicester) **1** xv, 27
(Shepshed) **7** 194
Cheapside **2** 171
Cheatle's Barn **7** 17
Checketts Close **3** 47
Checketts Rd **3** 47
Cheney Arms (P.H.)
(Ashby Folville) **3** 100
(Gaddesby) **3** 94
Cheney Ho. **3** 183
Chequer Close **1** 184
Chequer, The **1** 104
Chequer, The (P.H.) **6** 227
Chequers (P.H.)
(Ashby Magna) **5** 10
(Barkestone) **2** 200
(Burbage) **6** 52
(Swinford) **5** 200
Chequers (P.H.)
(Tur Langton) **4** 286
(Ullesthorpe) **5** 205
Cherry Orchard **1** 176
Cherry Orchard Fm **6** 109
Cherry St. **1** 27
Cherry Tree (P.H.)
(Catthorpe) **5** 54
(Husbands Bosworth) **4** 119
(Market Harborough) **4** 173
Cherry Tree (P.H.)
(Bond St.) **1** 124
(Loughborough) **7** 133
Cheseldyne Spinney **4** 147
Chester Way **1** xii, 27
Chestnut Fm **2** 63
Chestnut Grove **7** 62
Chestnut Villa **3** 183
Chestnuts Fm **4** 95
Chestnuts, The
(Bottesford) **2** 24
(Saddington) **4** 224
Chew's Opening **1** 27
CHILCOTE **7** 261
Chine Ho. **3** 60
Chippingdale Ho. **3** 34
Chitterman Hills **7** 237
Choyce's Rough **6** 222
Christ Church **1** 82
Christ Church
(Coalville) **7** 61
(Mountsorrel) **7** 152
(Smeeton Westerby) **4** 246
Christ Church School **1** 112
Chuckey Hall **5** 205
Chuckey Hall Fm **5** 205
Church Causeway **4** 37
Church Close **4** 264
Church Drive **5** 96
Church End **5** 221
Church Fm
(Appleby) **6** 10
(Ashby Magna) **5** 10
(Aston Flamville) **6** 22
(Barlestone) **6** 39
(Bottesford) **2** 24
(Congerstone) **6** 241
(Croxton Kerrial) **2** 103
(Earl Shilton) **6** 134
(Elmesthorpe) **6** 83
(Humberstone) **3** 133
(Orton on the Hill) **6** 318
(Potters Marston) **6** 218
(Ravenstone) **7** 180
(Scalford) **2** 209

(Stapleton) **6** 215
(Wartnaby) **2** 166
Church Gate
(Hallaton) **4** 95
(Leicester) **1** 27
(Loughborough) **7** 127
(Seagrave) **3** 207
(Shepshed) **7** 194
Church Gate Pavement **1** 79
Church Hill
(Birstall) **7** 29
(Cranoe) **4** 31
(Kibworth Beauchamp) **4** 133
(Lowesby) **3** 169
(Scraptoft) **4** 229
(Swannington) **7** 210
(Woodhouse) **7** 248
Church Hill Fm **5** 90
Church Lane
(Anstey) **7** 3
(Arnesby) **5** 5
(Barwell) **6** 127
(Castle Donington) **7** 47
(Desford) **6** 72
(Dunton Bassett) **5** 83
(East Norton) **3** 177
(Gilmorton) **5** 96
(Hungarton) **3** 144
(Husbands Bosworth) **4** 119
(Narborough) **6** 186
(Old Dalby) **2** 50
(Osgathorpe) **7** 163
(Ravenstone) **7** 180
(Saxelby) **3** 108
(Shearsby) **5** 188
(Stockerston) **4** 251
(Stoughton) **4** 259
(Swannington) **7** 211
(Thrussington) **3** 232
(Whitwick) **7** 72
Church Lane
(Hinckley) **6** 118
(Leicester) **1** 28
Church lane, the **2** 171
CHURCH LANGTON **4** xiii, 37
Church Leys **3** 198
Church of St Dionysius **4** 174
Church of St John Aldeby **6** 87
Church of St Mary in Arden **4** 177
Church of St Peter and St Paul **4** 177
Church Rd
(Aylestone) **5** 19
(Great Glen) **4** 80
(Worthington) **7** 255
Church Spinney
(Kirkby Mallory) **6** 211
(South Kilworth) **5** 194
Church Square **4** 174
Church St.
(Appleby) **6** 10
(Ashby de la Zouch) **7** 8
(Barrow upon Soar) **3** 34
(Belton) **7** 26
(Billesdon) **4** 4
(Blaby) **5** 32
(Bottesford) **2** 24
(Burbage) **6** 50
(Countesthorpe) **5** 79
(Donisthorpe) **7** 279
(Earl Shilton) **6** 134
(Hathern) **7** 84
(Leicester) **1** 28
(Lutterworth) **5** 139
(Market Harborough) **4** 172
(Netherseal) **7** 269
(North Kilworth) **5** 156
(Oadby) **5** 164
(Sapcote) **6** 227
(Scalford) **2** 209
(Shepshed) **7** 194
(Swepstone) **7** 218
(Thurlaston) **6** 300
(Thurmaston) **3** 238
(Twycross) **6** 307
Church Street **6** 118
Church Thorns **2** 195
Church Town **7** 78

Church View **6** 144
Church View Fm **7** 163
Church Walk
(Bruntingthorpe) **5** 48
(Hinckley) **6** 123
(Lubenham) **4** 164
Church Way **7** 283
Churchyard Fm **6** 39
Cinder Hill **7** 163
Cinder Hill Fm **7** 164
Cinquefoil (P.H.) **1** 124
City of Dan **7** 72
City of Three Waters **7** 72
City Wall St. **1** 28
City, The **4** 138
Clack Hill **4** 185
Clapgun St. **7** 48
Clare Fm **6** 144
Clare's Barn **6** 307
Clarence St. **1** 28
Clarence Tavern (P.H.) **1** 125
Clarendon Park **5** 126
Clark's Barn **1** 181
Clark's Fm **6** 307
Clarke's Bush **4** 259
Clarke's Lodge **5** 68
Clarke's Spinney **5** 67
Clawson Hall **2** 90
Clawson Hill **2** 90
Clawson Hill Fm **2** 90
Clawson Lane
(Holwell) **2** 163
(Nether Broughton) **2** 46
Clawson Lodge **2** 90
Clawson Thorns **2** 90
Clay Lane
(Coleorton) **7** 78
(Swannington) **7** 211
Clay Pits **1** 147
Claybrooke Grange **5** 90
Claybrooke Grange Fm **5** 90
Claybrooke Hall **5** 61
Claybrooke Lodge Fm **5** 58
CLAYBROOKE MAGNA **5** xi, xii, xiii, 57
Claybrooke Magna Mill **5** 58
CLAYBROOKE PARVA **5** xiii, xv, 61
Clayfield Fm **2** 209
Claypit Bridge **1** 73
Claypit Moor Wong **1** 184
Clays Mill **5** 223
Clematis Cottage **2** 218
Clements Gate **7** 117
Cliff Cottage **3** 34
Cliff Fm
(Birstall) **7** 29
(Lockington) **7** 103
Cliff Hill **3** 34
Cliff Ho.
(Barrow upon Soar) **3** 34
(Burton on the Wolds) **3** 54
(Twycross) **6** 307
Cliff Rd **7** 29
Cliff Spinney **7** 29
Cliff Terrace **3** 34
Cliff, The **3** 54
Cliffe Hill **6** 273
Cliffe Hill Cottages **6** 273
Cliffe Hill Quarry **6** 273
Cliffe Ho. **3** 192
Cliffe Lane **6** 273
Cliffe Slade Fm **6** 176
Cliffe, The **6** 152
Clifton Rd **7** 269
Clifton Row **7** 269
Clifton's Bridge **5** 222
Cliftonthorpe **7** 8
Clint Hill Quarry **6** 282
Clint's Crest **4** 152
Clock Mill **7** 218
Clock Mill Fm **7** 219
Close Meadow **1** 197
Close Nurseries, The **6** 268
Clothiers' Arms (P.H.) **1** 125
Clotts Fm **6** 273
Cloud Hill Quarries **7** 255
Cloud Hill View **7** 255
Clover Place **7** 70
Clowes Arms (P.H.) **3** 47
Clump Fm **6** 300
Clump Hill **5** 38

Clump, The **3** 54
Coach and Horses (P.H.)
(Anstey) **7** 3
(Kibworth Beauchamp) **4** 133
(Lubenham) **4** 164
(Markfield) **6** 176
Coach and Horses (P.H.)
(Humberstone Gate) **1** 125
(Lutterworth) **5** 137
(Market Harborough) **4** 173
Coach Rd **7** 194
Coach Road Plantation **7** 207
Coal Hill **1** 115
Coal Pit Lane **4** 295
Coal Pitt Lane **2** 171
Coal Wharf **7** 10
Coalbourn Wood **7** 237
Coalepitt way, the **5** 139
Coalfield Fm **6** 104
COALVILLE **7** ix, xiii, 61
Coalville: unindexed
modern street-names **7** 62
Coates's Close **1** 184
Cock (P.H.) **6** 259
Cock (P.H.)
(Belgrave Gate) **1** 125
(Burbage) **6** 52
(Market Harborough) **4** 173
Cock Abingdon Fm **4** 95
Cock Inn **5** 174
Cock Muckhill **1** 108
Cock Muckhill Houses **1** 96
Cock Pit, The **1** 143
Cocklow Wood **7** 170
Cockpit row **7** 130
Cockspur Bridge **7** 279
Cogg's Well **6** 118
Coker's Kitchen **1** 119
Colbaulk Rd **3** 144
Colborough Hill **3** 249
Colby Lodge **3** 238
Colby Rd **3** 238
Cold Comfort Fm **6** 123
Cold Fm **5** 147
COLD NEWTON **3** xi, xv, 172
Cold Newton Grange **3** 173
Cold Newton Lodge **3** 173
COLD OVERTON **4** 151
Cold Overton Grange **4** 152
Cold Overton Park Wood **4** 152
COLEORTON **7** 77
Coleorton Hall **7** 78
Coleorton Lane **7** 286
Coleorton Moor **7** 78
Coleorton Rd **7** 8
Colepitway **5** 220
Coles Barn **5** 38
Coles Lodge **3** 95
Coley Lane **6** 27
College Close **1** 184
College Fm **3** 60
College Rd **5** 213
College St. **5** 205
*Collegiate Church of the
Annunciation of the
Blessed Virgin Mary* **1** 101
Collegiate School **1** 112
Colliers Hill **7** 57
Colliery Cottage **7** 279
Collin's Holme **4** 119
Collinson's Close **1** 184
Colony Reservoir **7** 57
Coltman's Sq. **1** 28
Colton St. **1** 28
Combs Plantation **2** 261
Commissioner's Lane **4** 240
Common Fm
(Ashby de la Zouch) **7** 8
(Market Bosworth) **6** 166
Common Oven, The **1** 119
Common, The
(Barwell) **6** 127
(Evington) **4** 43
Compass Fields Fm **6** 275
Conduit Field **1** 210
Conduit Spinney
(Hardwick) **4** 234
(Old Ingarsby) **3** 153
Conduit St. **1** 28
Conduit, The **1** 108

Coneries, The **7** 127
Conery Lane
(Enderby) **6** 87
(Seagrave) **3** 207
Conery passage **7** 130
Coney Hill Plantation **4** 209
CONGERSTONE **6** 240
Congerstone Bridge **6** 241
Congerstone Lane **6** 237
Congregational Church
(Burbage) **6** 51
(Kilby) **5** 107
(Market Harborough) **4** 174
Consanguinitarium, The **1** 96
Constable Lane **7** 61
Convent Drive **7** 62
Conygear Wood **2** 103
Cook's Lodge **6** 187
Cook's Plantation **7** 227
Cooke's Fm **5** 96
Cooke's Shop **1** 118
Cooks Lane
(Sapcote) **6** 227
(Wigston Magna) **5** 219
Cool Hill Fm **6** 258
Cooper's Lane **5** 83
Cooper's Plantation **2** 103
Copeland Cottages **2** 50
Copeland Lane **1** 28
Coplow Brook **4** 5
Coplow Fm **4** 5
Coplow Ho. **4** 5
Coplow Lane **4** 5
Coplow Lodge **4** 5
Coplow, The **4** 5
Coppice Fm **7** 48
Coppice Plantation **7** 156
Coppice Wood **7** 48
Coppice, The
(Ashby de la Zouch) **7** 8
(Ashby Magna) **5** 10
(Narborough) **6** 187
(Newton Harcourt) **4** 298
(Queniborough) **3** 183
(Quorndon) **7** 170
Copt Oak **6** 175
Copt Oak Fm **6** 187
Copt Oak Ho. **6** 187
Copt Oak Inn **6** 176
Copt Oak Rd
(Markfield) **6** 176
(Narborough) **6** 187
Copt Oak Wood **7** 237
Copthill Fm **3** 163
Copton Ash **6** 307
Corah St. **1** xv, 29
Cord Hill **2** 287
Cordals **5** 194
Cordhill Lane **2** 298
Cordwainers' Row **1** xii, 29
Coriley's Yard **7** 10
Cork Hall **7** 156
Cork Hole **6** 123
Cork Lane **5** 104
Corkscrew Lane **7** 78
Corn Close **4** 259
Corn Close Fm **4** 215
Corn Cross, The **2** 175
Corn Exchange **4** 174
Corner Croft **1** 184
Corner Lodge Fm **5** 174
Cornhill **2** 171
Cornwall, The **1** 116
Cornworthy **7** 8
Coronation Lane **7** 276
Coronation Spinney **4** 209
Coronation Villa **7** 269
Corporation Hotel (P.H.) **7** 133
Corpus Christi Hall **1** 104
Cort and Co.'s Foundry **1** 145
COSBY **5** xi, xiii, xv, 267
Cosby Hall **5** 67
Cosby Hill Fm **5** 67
Cosby Ho. **5** 67
Cosby Lane **5** 235
Cosby Lodge **5** 67
Cosby Lodge Fm **5** 67
Cosby Rd **5** 38
Cosby Spinneys **5** 67
COSSINGTON **3** xv, 59
Cossington Gorse **3** 60
Cossington Grange **3** 60

Cossington Lane **7** 185
Cossington Mill **3** 60
Cossington Old Mill **3** 60
Cossington Rd **3** 215
COSTON **2** xii, xiii, 151
Coston: unindexed dwellings **2** 152
Coston Covert **2** 152
Coston Lodge **2** 152
Coston Lodge East **2** 152
Coston Lodge West **2** 152
Cote Hill Fm **4** 119
COTES **3** 70
Cotes Bridge **3** 70
COTES DE VAL **5** 96
Cotes Rd **6** 51
Cotes Toll Bar **3** 180
COTESBACH **5** xi, xii, 75
Cotesbach Fields Fm **5** 76
Cotesbach Hall **5** 76
Cotesbach Ho. **5** 76
Cotesbach Lodge Fm **5** 76
Coteswick Fm **3** 268
Coton Bridge **6** 166
Coton Ho. **6** 152
Cottage Fm
(Bitteswell) **5** 28
(Brentingby) **2** 133
(Bruntingthorpe) **5** 50
(Burbage) **6** 51
(Enderby) **6** 87
(Ibstock) **6** 144
(Leicester Forest East) **6** 159
(Newbold Verdon) **6** 194
(Normanton le Heath) **6** 197
(Norton juxta Twycross) **6** 312
(Oadby) **5** 164
(Osgathorpe) **7** 164
(Sharnford) **6** 247
(Withcote) **2** 284
Cottage Fm, The **5** 123
Cottage Homes **5** 79
Cottage Inn (P.H.) **7** 11
Cottage Lane
(Broughton Astley) **5** 38
(Markfield) **6** 176
(Norton juxta Twycross) **6** 312
Cottage Park **4** 38
Cottage Plantation **2** 140
Cottage Sq. **1** 29
Cottage, The
(Barwell) **6** 127
(Blaby) **5** 32
(Claybrooke Magna) **5** 58
(Desford) **6** 72
(Hoton) **3** 130
(Husbands Bosworth) **4** 119
(Illston) **4** 129
(Lubenham) **4** 164
(Scalford) **2** 209
(Sysonby) **2** 191
(Whetstone) **5** 213
Cottagers Close **5** 19
Cottages, The **3** 264
Cotterill Fm **4** 264
Cotterill Spinney **4** 159
Cotton's Field Fm **4** 209
Cotton's Field Ho. **4** 209
Cotton's Field Plantation **4** 209
Council Fm **7** 18
Countess of Devonshire's Hospital **1** 97
Countess's Bridge **1** 73
COUNTESTHORPE **5** xiv, xv, 79
Countesthorpe: unindexed modern street-names **5** 80
Countesthorpe Rd **5** 213
County Bridewell **2** 176
County Gaol **1** 109
Court Fm **5** 205
Court, The **4** 278
Courts yard **7** 130
Coventry Rd
(Burbage) **6** 51
(Hinckley) **6** 117
(Lutterworth) **5** 140
(Market Haborough) **4** 172
(Narborough) **6** 187
(Sapcote) **6** 227
(Sharnford) **6** 147
Coventry St. **1** 29
Coventry Street **6** 118
Coventry Way **1** xii, 29

Cover Cloud **7** 156
Covermill Hill **2** 129
Covert Lane **4** 229
Cow Close **1** 184
Cow Drift Lane **1** 29
Cow Hey **1** 203
Cow Hill **7** 194
Cow Hill Bridge **7** 194
Cow Lane
(Leicester) **1** 29
(Lutterworth) **5** 139
Cow Lane **6** 222
Cow Leasows, The **1** 204
Cow Leys **1** 204
Cow Pasture Bridge **1** 73
Cow Pasture Close **1** 184
Cow Pastures **6** 166
Cow Pastures Spinney **6** 166
Cowpen Cottage **6** 98
Cowpen Spinney **6** 98
Cox's Close Spinney **3** 259
Cox's Lane **4** 215
Crab St. **1** 29
Crabtree Close **1** 185
Crabtree Corner **5** 19
Crabtree Fm **6** 127
Crackbottle Lodge **3** 177
Crackbottle Rd **3** 177
Crackbottle Spinney **3** 177
Craddock St. **7** 127
Cradock Arms (P.H.) **5** 126
Cradock's Covert **6** 241
Craggs Fm **7** 146
Craigmore Fm **6** 194
Crailing Ho. **6** 295
Crainmore Fm **6** 194
Crane (P.H.) **1** 125
Crane Close, The **1** 185
Crane's Lock **4** 80
Craneclose Spinney **4** 14
Cranford's Meadow **1** 197
Cranhill Fm **4** 221
Cranmer Lane **5** 156
CRANOE **4** xii, xiii, 31
Cranoe Lodge **4** 31
Cranoe Rd
(Glooston) **4** 65
(Tur Langton) **4** 286
Cranyke Fm **2** 126
Craven Arms (P.H.) **1** 125
Craven Ho. **2** 24
Craven Lodge **2** 178
Craven St. **1** xv, 30
Craven's Rough **7** 156
Cream Gorse **3** 85
Cream Lodge
(Barrow upon Soar) **3** 34
(Kirby Bellars) **3** 85
Crescent St. **1** xiv, 30
Crescent, The **1** xiv, 30
Cresswell Pl. **1** 30
Cresswell Spring Fm **2** 272
Crete Cottages **6** 282
Cribb's Lodge **2** 287
Crick's Lodge **4** 269
Crick's Retreat **4** 80
Cricket (P.H.) **7** 289
Cricket Ground **1** 143
Cricket Ground (P.H.) **1** 125
Cricket Ground Spinney **5** 156
Cricket Players (P.H.) **7** 133
Cricket Players' Arms (P.H.) **1** 125
Cricketers' Arms (P.H.) **4** 246
Cricketers' Inn (P.H.) **7** 269
Cripwell Fm **3** 275
Crispin's Arms (P.H.) **1** 125
Crock's Fm **4** 286
CROFT **6** 67
Croft Bridge **6** 67
Croft Fm **6** 67
Croft Hill **6** 67
Croft Hill Rd **6** 139
Croft Ho. **6** 67
Croft House Fm **4** 119
Croft Lodge **6** 67
Croft Quarry **6** 67
Croft Rd
(Cosby) **5** 67
(Thurlaston) **6** 300
Croft Sidings **6** 67

Croft View Cottages **6** 139
Croft Way **6** 176
Croft, The **1** 185
Croft, The
(Burbage) **6** 51
(Tonge) **7** 41
Crompton's Plantation **2** 50
Crooked Billet (P.H.)
(Dunton Bassett) **5** 83
(Loughborough) **7** 133
Crophurst Hill **7** 194
CROPSTON **7** xi, 234
Cropston Drive **7** 62
Cropston Rd **7** 3
Cropston Reservoir
(Cropston) **7** 234
(Newtown Linford) **7** 156
Cropstone Ho. **7** 234
Crosher's Fm **2** 278
Cross Fm **7** 118
Cross Green **7** 185
Cross Hands, The **6** 255
Cross Hills Baptist Church **6** 25
Cross in Hand Fm **5** xii, 140
Cross Keys (P.H.)
(Barwell) **6** 127
(Burbage) **6** 52
(Castle Donington) **7** 50
Cross Keys (P.H.)
(Cosby) **5** 67
(Highcross St.) **1** 125
(Loughborough) **7** 133
(Market Harborough) **4** 173
(Swinford) **5** 200
(Worthington) **7** 255
Cross Lane **1** 30
Cross Lane **2** 63
Cross Lanes **6** 159
Cross Roads Fm **6** 57
Cross St.
(Breedon on the Hill) **7** 36
(Hathern) **7** 84
(Market Harborough) **4** 172
(Syston) **3** 228
Cross, The
(Diseworth) **7** 117
(Enderby) **6** 87
(Hallaton) **4** 95
(Hathern) **7** 84
Crossburrow Hill **4** 65
Crosshill Lane **7** 127
Crossing Covert **2** 287
Crossing Hand (P.H.) **5** 137
Crossways **6** 51
Crossways Fm **5** 213
Crow Lodge **5** 222
Crow Mill Bridge **5** 222
Crow Spinney
(Little Stretton) **4** 159
(North Kilworth) **5** 156
Crow Wood
(Rolleston) **4** 221
(Skeffington) **3** 221
(Swithland) **7** 227
(Thornton) **6** 27
Crowder's Eaves **7** 48
Crowmilne **5** 223
Crown (P.H.)
(Anstey) **7** 3
(Appleby) **6** 10
(Cotes de Val) **5** 96
(Fleckney) **4** 50
(Great Glen) **4** 80
(Heather) **6** 104
(Shepshed) **7** 198
(Sproxton) **2** 246
(Theddingworth) **4** 269
(Tur Langton) **4** 286
Crown (P.H.)
(Asfordby) **3** 11
(Castle Donington) **7** 50
(Great Easton) **3** 74
(Great Easton) **4** 74
(Hinckley) **6** 121
(Market Pl.) **1** 126
(Medbourne) **4** 188
(Melton Mowbray) **2** 177
(Mountsorrel) **7** 152

(Stanton under Bardon) **6** 273
(Swinesmarket) **1** 125
(Walcote) **5** 149
Crown and Anchor (P.H.)
(Belgrave Gate) **1** 126
(Hinckley) **6** 121
(Millstone Lane) **1** 126
Crown and Cushion (P.H.) **7** 133
Crown and Cushion (P.H.)
(Belgrave Gate) **1** 126
(Church Gate) **1** 126
Crown and Dolphin (P.H.) **1** 126
Crown and Magpie (P.H.) **1** 126
Crown and Plough (P.H.) **2** 90
Crown and Sceptre (P.H.) **4** 246
Crown and Thistle (P.H.)
(Dunton Bassett) **5** 83
(Loseby Lane) **1** 126
Crown and Thistle (P.H.)
(Loughborough) **7** 133
(Mountsorrel) **7** 152
(Northgate St.) **1** 126
(Townhall Lane) **1** 126
Crown Hill
(Great Dalby) **2** 78
(Stoke Golding) **6** xvi, xvii, 275
Crown Hills **4** 43
Crown Hotel (P.H.) **5** 138
Crown Inn
(Old Dalby) **2** 50
(Ullesthorpe) **5** 205
Crown Inn
(Barlestone) **6** 39
(Snarestone) **6** 268
Crown Inn (P.H.) **6** 145
Crown St. **1** 30
Croxfield Spinney **4** 286
Croxton Abbey **2** xiii, 103
Croxton Banks **2** 103
CROXTON KERRIAL **2** xii, xiii, 102
Croxton Lodge **2** 103
Croxton Park **2** xiii, 103
Croxton Rd **3** 42
Crusoe's Plantation **7** 207
Cuckoo Hill **2** 140
Culloden Fm **6** 312
Cumberland Lodge **2** 209
Cumberland Spinney **2** 144
Cumberland St. **1** 30
Curzon Arms (P.H.) **7** 248
Curzon Arms Inn **6** 307
Curzon St. **1** xv, 30
Cut End **7** 10

DADLINGTON **6** xii, xiii, xiv, xv, xvi, xvii, 291
Dadlington Ho. **6** 291
Dadlington Lane **6** 215
Dag Lane **4** 197
Dairy Cottages **5** 156
Dairy Fm
(Burbage) **6** 51
(Normanton Turville) **6** 305
(Peatling Parva) **5** 178
Dairy Fm, The
(Barkby) **3** 21
(Twyford) **3** 261
(Ullesthorpe) **5** 205
Daisy Plantation **7** 180
Dakins Bridge **6** 241
Dalby Brook **2** 50
Dalby Covert **7** 48
Dalby Lane **2** 46
Dalby Lodges **2** 50
Dalby Rd
(Anstey) **7** 3
(Melton Mowbray) **2** 169
Dalby Wolds **2** 50
Dale Covert **6** 166
Dale Hill **3** 95
Dale Ho. **3** 133
Dale Spinney
(Misterton) **5** 147
(Newton Linford) **7** 156
Daleacre Fm **7** 103
Daleacre Hill **7** 103
Dales Spinney **3** 180
Dales, The **4** 5
Dalls, The **7** 8
Dam Dyke **2** 99
Dam's Spinney **4** 259

Damside Spinney **4** 269
Dan's Barn **6** 206
Dan's Lane **6** 206
Dandees, The **6** 176
Dane Hill Closes **1** 185
Dane Hills **1** 221
Daniel Lambert (P.H.) **1** 126
Dannett's Close **1** 185
Dannett's Garden **1** 176
Dannett's Hall **1** 154
Dannett's Meadow **1** 197
Dawson's Lane
(Barwell) **6** 127
(Marefield) **4** 170
(Newbold) **4** 219
Day's Plantation **2** 287
De Lisle Arms (P.H.) **7** 198
Deacon's Cottages **6** 67
Deacon's Meadow **4** 164
Dead Lane **7** 127
Dead Lane
(Leicester) **1** 30
(Lutterworth) **5** 139
(Melton Mowbray) **2** 171
Deadman's Lane **1** 31
Deakin's Bridge **6** 166
Deakin's Close **1** 185
Dean Cottage **4** 38
Dean's Lane **7** 248
Deane Bank Fm **4** 215
Deansgate Fm **6** 39
Debdale **6** 72
Debdale Fm
(Muston) **2** 35
(Scalford) **2** 210
(Smeeton Westerby) **4** 246
Debdale Hill **2** 50
Debdale Lane
(Foxton) **4** 54
(Gumley) **4** 88
(Smeeton Westerby) **4** 246
Debdale Lodge
(Little Dalby) **2** 84
(Scalford) **2** 210
Debdale Spinney **2** 84
Debdale Wharf **4** xiii, 88
Debdales **2** 24
Decoy **7** 264
Decoy Cottage **2** 140
Deep Holme **1** 197
Deepdale **7** 211
Deepdale Fm **6** 51
Deeping Lane **6** 59
Deeping, The **6** 59
Deer Park Spinney **7** 156
Delph, The **7** 36
Delven Lane **7** 48
Demoniac Plantation **7** 180
Denbigh Arms (P.H.) **5** 138
Dene, The **3** 269
Denman St. **1** 31
Dennis St. **7** 66
Denton's Yard **7** 10
Dent's Meadow **1** 197
Dent's Spinney
(Blaston) **4** 14
(Medbourne) **4** 188
Denyer's Barn **5** 200
Depdale Wharf (P.H.) **4** 88
Derby Lane
(Newton Burgoland) **7** 224
(Shackerstone) **6** 233
Derby Rd
(Ashby de la Zouch) **7** 8
(Kegworth) **7** 96
(Loughborough) **7** 127
Derby Road **6** 118
Derby Spinney **6** 328
Derne Ford **1** 226
DESFORD **6** 72
Desford Colliery **6** 25
Desford Cross Roads **6** 159
Desford Grange **6** 72
Desford Hall **6** 72
Desford Hill **6** 72
Desford Junction **6** 80
Desford Lane
(Kirkby Mallory) **6** 211

(Newtown Unthank) **6** 80
(Peckleton) **6** 206
(Ratby) **6** 222
Desford Rd
(Kirby Muxloe) **6** 152
(Lubbesthorpe) **6** 161
(Narborough) **6** 187
(Newbold Verdon) **6** 194
(Thurlaston) **6** 300
Desford Station **6** 72
Devana Ave. **7** 62
Devil's Elbow **7** 97
Devon Fm
(Belgrave) **3** 47
(Bottesford) **2** 24
Devon Lane **2** 24
Devon, The **2** 7
Devonshire Square **7** 127
Devonshire St. **1** 31
Dewes Barn Fm **7** 21
Diamond Jubilee Covert **5** 19
Diamond Spinney **3** 173
Dick Hills Spinney **4** 106
Dicken Bridge **5** 213
Dicken's Nook **6** 288
Digby Fm **3** 244
Dimmingsdale **7** 207
Dimmingsdale Spinney **7** 156
Dingle Fm **6** 10
Dingle Lane **6** 10
Dingley Rd **4** 178
DISEWORTH **7** x, xi, xii, 117
Diseworth Brook **7** 118
Diseworth Gorse **7** 118
Diseworth Rd **7** 48
DISHLEY **7** 139
Dishley Fm **7** 219
Disraeli St. **5** 19
Dixie Arms (P.H.) **6** 166
Dixie Spinney **6** 307
Dixon's Square **5** 139
Dobb Hall **4** 159
Dockey Fm **3** 4
Doctor's Lane **7** 36
Doctors Fields **6** 134
Doebanks Spinney **6** 233
Dog and Gun (P.H.)
(Earl Shilton) **6** 135
(Enderby) **6** 87
(Hinckley) **6** 121
(Keyham) **3** 158
(Kilby) **5** 107
(Thurlaston) **6** 300
(Walton) **5** 114
Dog and Gun (P.H.)
(Belvoir St.) **1** 126
(Blaby) **5** 32
(Loughborough) **7** 133
(Mountsorrel) **7** 152
(Owston) **4** 215
(Pearling Parva) **5** 178
Dog and Gun Lane **5** 213
Dog and Hedgehog (P.H.) **6** 291
Dog Inn **7** 269
Dog Kennel Plantation **4** 209
Dog Kennel Spinney **6** 201
Dog Lane
(Burton Lazars) **2** 63
(Netherseal) **7** 269
(South Kilworth) **5** 194
Dogkennel Pool **7** 207
Doles Fm **7** 8
Dolphin (P.H.)
(Hinckley) **6** 121
(Jewry Wall St.) **1** 126
(Market Harborough) **4** 173
(Market Pl.) **1** 126
Dominion Estate **6** 92
Donington Arms (P.H.) **7** 64
Donington Hall **7** 48
DONINGTON LE HEATH **7** xi, 63
Donington Park **7** xiii, 48
Donington Park Fm **7** 48
DONISTHORPE **7** 278
Donisthorpe Lane **7** 23
Dorian Lodge **2** 178
Double Gate Lane **1** 31
Double Rail Lock **5** 224
Douse's Wong **1** 185
Dovecoat Ho. **2** 90
Dovecot Nook Hill **2** 144
Dovecote **7** 194

Dovecote Close
(St Margaret's) **1** 186
(The Newarke) **1** 185
Dovecote Fm **7** 84
Doveland **1** 221
Doveland Closes **1** 186
Doveland Lane **1** 32
Doveland Wood **1** 224
Dover Castle (P.H.) **1** 126
Dover St. **1** 32
Dow Bridge **5** xii, 54
Dowell's Barn **7** 97
Dowry Cottage **2** 284
Dragon Lane **6** 194
Dragwell, The **7** 97
Drapery, The **1** 119
DRAYTON **4** xii, xiv, 34
Drayton Barn Fm **6** 322
Drayton Grange Fm **6** 328
Drayton Ho. **4** 34
Drayton Rd **4** 19
Drift Fm **7** 21
Drift Hill
(Redmile) **2** 195
(Wymondham) **2** 287
Drift Side **7** 14
Drift Way, The **2** 172
Drift, The
(Burton Lazars) **2** 63
(Sewestern) **2** 59
(Sproxton) **2** 246
(Stonesby) **2** 256
Druid St. **6** 117
Druids' Arms (P.H.) **7** 133
Druids' Arms (P.H.) **1** 126
Dry Brook **7** 57
Drybrook Wood **7** 57
Dryden St. **1** 32
Drypot Lodge **2** 51
Duchess Garden **2** 8
Duchess of Kent (P.H.) **1** 127
Duck Holmes **1** 186, 198
Duck Lake **6** 10
Duck Paddle **6** 118
Duck's Nest **7** 48
Duckery, The **6** 166
Duckpond Covert **6** 308
Duke of Cumberland (P.H.)
(Church Gate) **1** 127
(Cumberland St.) **1** 127
Duke of Devonshire (P.H.) **1** 127
Duke of Newcastle (P.H.) **7** 74
Duke of Northumberland (P.H.) **1** 127
Duke of Rutland (P.H.) **6** 121
Duke of Rutland (P.H.) **1** 127
Duke of Wellington (P.H.)
(Market Harborough) **4** 173
(Markfield) **6** 176
(Wellington St.) **1** 127
Duke of York (P.H.) **3** 215
Duke of York (P.H.)
(Loughborough) **7** 133
(Mountsorrel) **7** 152
(South Gates) **1** 127
Duke St. **1** xiv, 32
Duke's Fm **2** 35
Duke's Lane **6** 118
Duke's Wharf **7** 130
Dumbles
(Netherseal) **7** 269
(Swannington) **7** 211
Dumps Plantations, The **7** 93
Dumps Rd **7** 72
Dumps, The **7** 103
Dun Cow (P.H.)
(Fleckney) **4** 50
(Knighton) **5** 126
Dun's Lane Fm **3** 169
Dungehill Fm **3** 275
Dunkirk St. **1** 32
Dunn's Corner **1** 32
Dunn's Lock **5** 104
dunninc wicon **5** xv, 65, 204
Duns Lane **1** 32
Dunster Barn **7** 103
DUNTON BASSETT **5** xv, 83
Dunton Lane
(Ashby Parva) **5** 12
(Leire) **5** 130
Dunton Lodge **5** 84
Dunton Mill **5** 83

Durham Ox (P.H.)
(Belgrave Gate) **1** 127
(Buckminster) **2** 55
(Old Dalby) **2** 51
(Wigston Magna) **5** 222
Durham St. **1** xv, 32
Dysart Arms Hotel **2** 55
Dyson's Close **7** 264

Eady Fm **2** 24
Eagle (P.H.) **7** 133
Eaglesfield Fm **5** 130
Earl de Grey's Arms (P.H.) **6** 52
Earl Howe (P.H.) **1** 127
Earl Howe's Arms (P.H.) **1** 127
Earl of Rutland's Hospital **2** 24
Earl of Stamford's Arms (P.H.) **1** 127
EARL SHILTON **6** 133
Earl Shilton: unindexed modern street-names **6** 134
Earl Shilton Rd **6** 305
Earl St. **1** 32
Earlesmere **7** 180
Early Mills **1** 153
Early Taverns and Breweries **1** 141
East End **2** 90
East Field
(Husbands Bosworth) **4** 119
(Netherseal) **7** 269
East Fm **2** 63
East Gate **4** 95
East Gates **1** xiii, xiv, 7, 32
East Gates Bridge **1** 73
East Gates Pavement **1** 79
EAST LANGTON **4** xi, 38
East Langton Grange **4** 38
East Langton Station **4** 293
East Midlands Airport **7** xiii, 48
EAST NORTON **3** xi, 177
East Norton Hall **3** 177
East Norton Rd **4** 95
East Norton Station **3** 177
East Park **3** 259
East Plantation **2** 152
East Quarter **1** 11
East St. **1** 33
East St.
(Royal East St.) **1** 33
(Wymeswold) **3** 275
East Suburb **1** 11
East Way **1** 33
Eastfield **5** 126
EASTHORPE **2** 33
Easthorpe Cottage **2** 33
Easthorpe Lodge **2** 33
Easthorpe Mill **2** 33
EASTWELL **2** 121
Eastwell Lodge **2** 121
EastWest **2** 218
EATON **2** xi, 118
Eaton Grange **2** xiii, 119
Eaton Lodge **2** 119
Eaton St. **1** 33
Ebenezer Chapel **1** 89
Ebenezer Chapel **6** 121
Ebury **3** 21
Edenhurst **3** 47
Edgell Spinney **5** 208
EDMONDTHORPE **2** 297
Edmondthorpe Drift **2** 298
Edmondthorpe Hall **2** 298
Edmondthorpe Mere **2** 298
Edward Cottages **7** 78
Egate **2** 171
Egerton Lodge **2** 178
Egerton Park **2** 180
Eggleston Fm **3** 54
Egypt Lodge Fm **3** 54
Egypt Plantation **2** 251
Eight Acre Covert **6** 233
Eight Bells (P.H.) **2** 177
Eight Lands **6** 330
Eightlands Fm **6** 330
Elbow Close **1** 186
Elbow Lane **1** 33
Elder Lane **7** 255
Elder Plantation **7** 157
Eldon St. **1** 33
Elephant (P.H.) **7** 219
Elephant and Castle (P.H.) **6** 300
Elephant and Castle (P.H.) **1** 127

Eleven Acre Covert **6** 295
Elford street **7** 10
Elizabeth Plantation **4** 209
Elizabeth Rd **4** 50
Elkington Lodge **4** 119
Ellaby's Spinney **2** 63
Eller's Fm **3** 275
Eller's Gorse **3** 275
Ellernestub Wong **1** 186
Elliot's Lane **6** 273
Ellis Park **6** 92
Ellistown **6** 144
Ellistown Fm **6** 144
Elm Cottage **3** 114
Elm Fm
  (Barrow upon Soar) **3** 34
  (Swannington) **7** 211
Elm Grove **6** 118
Elm Line **7** 48
Elm Tree (P.H.) **7** 207
Elm Tree Fm **6** 92
Elm Tree, The **1** 117
Elmcroft **6** 152
ELMESTHORPE **6** 82
Elmesthorpe Estate **6** 83
Elmesthorpe Lane **6** 134
Elmesthorpe Plantation **6** 83
Elmesthorpe Station **6** 83
Elms Cottages **3** 86
Elms Farm Cottages **3** 133
Elms Fm
  (Evington) **4** 43
  (Humberstone) **3** 133
  (Kirby Muxloe) **6** 152
  (Narborough) **6** 187
  (Norton juxta Twycross) **6** 312
  (Osgathorpe) **7** 164
  (Sheepy Magna) **6** 252
  (Shenton) **6** 296
  (Worthington) **7** 255
Elms, The
  (Barwell) **6** 127
  (Bitteswell) **5** 28
  (Blaby) **5** 32
  (Bottesford) **2** 24
  (Earl Shilton) **6** 134
  (Fleckney) **4** 50
  (Hathern) **7** 84
  (Hoby) **3** 114
  (Kirby Bellars) **3** 86
  (Normanton Turville) **6** 305
  (Oadby) **5** 164
  (Peckleton) **6** 206
  (Quorndon) **7** 170
  (Ratcliffe Culey) **6** 330
  (Saxby) **2** 135
  (Scalford) **2** 210
  (South Kilworth) **5** 194
  (Stapleton) **6** 215
  (Thorpe Satchville) **3** 264
  (Whetstone) **5** 213
  (Wymeswold) **3** 275
Elmside Fm **6** 182
Elmstead **6** 152
Elstead Lane **7** 14
Elton St. **1** 33
Ely Gate **5** 138
Emmanuel Church **7** 127
Emscote **7** 264
ENDERBY **6** xi, xii, xiii, 86
Enderby: unindexed
  modern street-names **6** 88
Enderby Bridge
  (Enderby) **6** 87
  (Whetstone) **5** 213
Enderby Grange **6** 87
Enderby Hall **6** 87
Enderby Hill Quarries **6** 87
Enderby Ho. **6** 87
Enderby Lodge **6** 161
Enderby Quarry **6** 87
Enderby Rd
  (Thurlaston) **6** 300
  (Whetstone) **5** 213
Enderby Warren Quarry **6** 87
Enderbys Lane **3** 173
Engine (P.H.) **7** 62
Engine (P.H.)
  (Coleorton) **7** 78
  (Donisthorpe) **7** 279
  (Queen St.) **1** 127
  (Worthington) **7** 255

Engine House **1** 104
Engine, The (P.H.) **5** 205
Engineers' Arms (P.H.) **7** 62
Englands Fm **6** 300
Ervin's Lock **5** 224
Ettington **4** 133
EVINGTON **4** 43
Evington: unindexed
modern street-names **4** 44
Evington Brook **4** 43
Evington Gate **1** xii, 33
Evington Grange **4** 44
Evington Hall **4** 44
Evington Ho. **4** 44
Evington Lane **4** 44
Evington Lodge **4** 44
Evington Park **4** 44
Evington Pl. **1** 33
Ewells Fm **5** 83
Exchange, The **1** 104
Exhibition (P.H.) **7** 152
Exning Spinney **7** 234
Eye Brook **4** 74
EYE KETTLEBY **2** xii, 188
Eye Kettleby Hall **2** 189
Eye Kettleby Hall Fm **2** 189
Eye Kettleby Ho. **2** 189
Eye Kettleby Lodge **2** 189
Eye Kettleby Mill **2** 189
Eye Mills **2** 179

Factory Lane **5** 5
Factory St. **7** 127
Fair Haven **7** 79
Fair Lawn **4** 174
Fairfield
(Ashby de la Zouch) **7** 8
(Ibstock) **6** 144
Fairfield Bridge **6** 241
Fairfield Rd
(Coalville) **7** 62
(Market Harborough) **4** 172
Fairham Brook **2** 51
Fairhaven Fm **7** 3
Fairholme **3** 130
Falcon (P.H.) **7** 112
Falcon (P.H.) **1** 127
Falcon Ho. **3** 130
Falconer's Nook **7** 237
Far Barn **2** 205
Far Coton **6** xiii, 165
Far Hill Fm **5** 130
Far Meadow **1** 198
Far Park lane **7** 130
Far St. **3** 275
Fargate Fm **4** 286
Farm Lane **7** 64
Farm Lodge **6** 308
Farm Orchard **1** 176
Farm Town **7** 79
Farm, The **6** 215
Farm, The **1** 180
Farmer's Close **1** 186
Farmer's Leys **1** 204
Farmery Sq. **1** 33
Farnham Bridge **7** 185
Fazeley Glebe Fm **6** 307
Fealer Fm **2** 90
Fearn Farm Cottages **4** 95
Fearn Fm **4** 95
Fearnedock Covert **7** 21
Feather Bed Lane **7** 10
Featherbed Lane **4** 133
Feathers (P.H.) **6** 121
Feeding Brook
(Huncote) **6** 139
(Thurlaston) **6** 300
Felding Ford **1** 226
Felding Way **1** 33
Felstead's Spinney **2** 63
Female Asylum, The **1** 97
Fenn Lane Cottage **6** 261
Fenn Lane Fm **6** xvi, 261
Fenn Lanes **6** xi, xii, xv
(Dadlington) **6** 291
(Upton) **6** 262
Fennel St. **7** 127
Fennell St. **1** 34
Fennes Hole **6** xvi, xvii
Fenney Hill **7** 194
Fenney Spring **7** 194
Fenney Windmill **7** 194

FENNY DRAYTON **6** xi, xv, 328
Fenton Cottage **7** 57
Fenton St. **1** 34
Fern Lea Ho. **6** 57
Ferny Wong **1** 186
Ferrers' Arms (P.H.) **7** 207
Fiddle Spinney **6** 305
Fiddlers Green **3** 177
Field Barn **3** 216
Field Fm
(Ashby de la Zouch) **7** 8
(Bitteswell) **5** 28
(Dadlington) **6** 291
(Measham) **7** 264
(Osbaston) **6** 201
(Wymeswold) **3** 275
Field Head **6** 176
Field Head Fm **7** 157
Field Lane **7** 41
Field St. **7** 194
Fielding Rd **7** 29
Fieldon Bridge **6** 258
Fields Cottages **6** 22
Fields Farm Ho. **7** 164
Fields Fm
(Barlestone) **6** 39
(Burbage) **6** 51
(Sapcote) **6** 227
(Sutton Cheney) **6** 288
Fields Fm, The **7** 224
Fields, The
(Lutterworth) **5** 140
(Newbold Verdon) **6** 194
Finchley Bridge **3** 177
Finger Fm **7** 118
Finney Hill **7** 194
Finney Spring Fm **7** 194
Fir Holt **2** 8
Fir Tree Lodge **5** 28
Firs Fam, The **4** 119
Firs Fm **4** 278
Firs, The **3** 183
First Hill **2** 78
Fish and Quart (P.H.) **1** 127
Fish House, The **1** 119
Fish Pond **4** 264
Fish Ponds **2** 103
Fish Stews Covert **6** 166
Fish's Plantation **6** 10
Fisher's Mill **1** 148
Fishley Belt **6** 92
Fishpond
(Waltham on the Wolds) **2** 272
(Wartnaby) **2** 166
Fishpond Cottage **7** 73
Fishpond Ho. **2** 166
Fishpond Plantation
(Burton on the Wolds) **3** 54
(Old Dalby) **2** 51
Fishpond Spinney
(Cotes) **3** 70
(Nevill Holt) **4** 204
(Stockerston) **4** 251
Fishponds Spinney **3** 18
Fishpool **7** 36
Fishpool Brook
(Barrow upon Soar) **3** 34
(Seagrave) **3** 207
Fishpool Grange **7** 195
Fishpool Spinney
(Enderby) **6** 87
(Tugby) **3** 254
Five Tree Plantation
(Charley) **7** 57
(Shepshed) **7** 195
Flagstaff Butts **3** 60
Flash Fm **6** 187
Flat Hill **7** 57
Flat Ho. **5** 10
Flat House Fm **5** 10
Flat Spinney **5** 164
Flax Dressers (P.H.) **7** 11
Flaxhill Bungalow **5** 5
Flaxman's Spinney **4** 298
FLECKNEY **4** 50
Fleckney Lodge **4** 50
Fleckney Rd
(Arnesby) **5** 5
(Kibworth Beauchamp) **4** 133
(Kilby) **5** 107
(Saddington) **4** 224
Fleckney Tunnel **4** 224

Fleet St. **1** 34
Fleet, The **6** 282
Fleming's Almshouses **2** 24
Fleming's Bridge **2** 24
Fleur de Lis (P.H.) **1** 127
Flitlands **7** 218
Floodgates **3** 4
Floodmill **1** 148
Flude Lodge **5** 235
Fludes Lane **5** 164
Flying Childers (P.H.) **3** 86
Flying Horse (P.H.)
  (High Street) **1** 127
  (Kegworth) **7** 97
  (Loughborough) **7** 133
  (Markfield) **6** 176
  (Wellington St.) **1** 128
Foan Hill **7** 211
Foleville brigge **2** 175
Folly Bridge **5** 174
Folly Cottages, The **6** 206
Folly Fm **6** 206
Folly, The **5** 157
Fomer **6** xvi
Fomer Fm **6** 295
Forest Closes, The **1** 186
Forest Edge
  (Kirby Muxloe) **6** 152
  (Thringstone) **7** 70
Forest Field **7** 26
Forest Fm **6** 152
Forest Gate
  (Anstey) **7** 3
  (Belton) **7** 26
  (Shepshed) **7** 195
Forest Hill Fm **6** 72
Forest Ho.
  (Desford) **6** 72
  (Leicester Forest East) **6** 159
Forest Lane **7** 26
Forest of Ardern **6** xii
Forest Rd
  (Coalville) **7** 62
  (Huncote) **6** 139
  (Loughborough) **7** 127
  (Narborough) **6** 187
  (Woodhouse) **7** 248
Forest Road Fm **6** 139
Forest Rock (P.H.) **7** 248
Forest Rock Inn (P.H.) **7** 74
Forest Rock Quarry **7** 73
Forest Terrace **7** 255
Forest View
  (Desford) **6** 72
  (Hinckley) **6** 123
  (Kirby Muxloe) **6** 152
Forest, The **6** 72
Foresters (P.H.) **1** 128
Foresters' Arms (P.H.) **7** 198
Foresters' Arms (P.H.) **7** 133
Fortune of War (P.H.) **1** 128
Forty Foot Lane **7** 48
Fosse Cottage **5** 39
Fosse Fm
  (Croft) **6** 67
  (Frolesworth) **5** 90
Fosse Way **1** xi, 34
Fosse Way **6** xi
Fossefield Fm **6** 282
FOSTON **5** xiv, 109
Foston Cottages **5** 109
Foston Hall Fm **5** 109
Foston Ho. **5** 109
Foston Lodge **5** 109
Foston Rd **5** 79
Fostongate **5** 220
Foundry Arms (P.H.) **1** 128
Foundry Lane **1** xv, 34
Foundry Sq. **1** 34
Fountain (P.H.)
  (Humberstone Gate) **1** 128
  (Sileby) **3** 216
Fountain Inn, The **7** 211
Four Acre Wood **3** 55
Foursladegate **5** 220
Fourteen Acre Spinney **4** 129
Fox (P.H.)
  (Hallaton) **4** 97

(Higham on the Hill) **6** 109
(Lutterworth) **5** 138
(Thorpe Satchville) **3** 264
Fox (P.H.)
(Barrow upon Soar) **3** 36
(Croxton Kerrial) **2** 103
(Humberstone Gate) **1** 128
(Kibworth Harcourt) **4** 138
(Loughborough) **7** 133
(Market Harborough) **4** 173
(North Gate) **1** 128
(Oadby) **5** 164
(Stonesby) **2** 256
(Thringstone) **7** 71
(Wymeswold) **3** 275
Fox and Goose (P.H.) **4** 129
Fox and Goose (P.H.)
(Coalville) **7** 62
(Great Glen) **4** 80
(Humberstone Gate) **1** 128
(Ratcliffe on the Wreake) **3** 192
Fox and Hounds (P.H.)
(Congerstone) **6** 241
(Knossington) **4** 147
(Skeffington) **3** 221
(Syston) **3** 229
(Tugby) **3** 254
Fox and Hounds (P.H.)
(Burrough on the Hill) **2** 232
(Humberstone Gate) **1** 128
(Melton Mowbray) **2** 177
(Wilson) **7** 43
(Witherley) **6** 322
Fox and Hounds Fm **4** 255
Fox Bridge **6** 166
Fox Cottages **3** 73
Fox Covert
(Bitteswell) **5** 28
(Kirkby Mallory) **6** 211
(Newbold Verdon) **6** 194
(Wistow) **4** 295
Fox Covert Fm **6** 241
Fox Croft Spinney **3** 130
Fox Earths Spinney **5** 156
Fox Holes **2** 163
Fox Holes Spinney **3** 144
Fox Inn (P.H.) **2** 177
Fox Lane
(Kirby Muxloe) **6** 152
(Leicester) **1** 34
Fox Yard **6** 118
Fox's Monument **6** 328
Fox's St. **1** 34
Foxcover Fm **6** 109
Foxcovert Ho. **3** 55
Foxhill Fm **3** 34
Foxhole Spinney **4** 129
Foxholes **4** 95
Foxholes Spinney **6** 45
Foxley Hay **7** 157
FOXTON **4** xii, xiii, 54
Foxton Locks **4** 54
Foxton Lodge **4** 54
Foxton Rd
(Gumley) **4** 88
(Lubenham) **4** 164
Framland gate **2** 171
Framland Hundred **2** xi, xiii, 1
Framlands farm **2** 180
Frances Walthoms Farm **2** 180
Francis Dixon Lodge **3** 134
Francis Lane **7** 224
Franks Lane **5** 149
Freake's Ground **1** 186
Freake's Ground Windmill **1** 148
Free Grammar School **1** 112
Free Lane **1** 35
Freeboard Spinney **6** 161
FREEBY **2** xii, 129
Freeby Fox Earth **2** 129
Freeby Lodge **2** 129
Freeby Wood **2** 129
Freehold Ho. **2** 78
Freehold St. **7** 127
Freeholt Lodge **6** 227
Freeholt Wood **6** 227
Freeman's Arms (P.H.)
(Archdeacon Lane) **1** 128
(Aylestone Rd) **1** 128
Freeman's Lane **6** 51

Freemasons' Arms (P.H.)
(Archdeacon Lane) **1** 128
(Great Bowden) **4** 177
Freemen's Meadow **1** 198
Freemen's Pasture **1** 204
Freeschool Lane **1** 35
Freezeland Lodge **3** 261
Freizeland **6** 63
Fremantel **1** 155
Freshfields **6** 59
Friar House Fm **6** 123
Friar Lane **1** 35
Friar Lane Chapel **1** 89
Friars Rd **1** 35
Friars Well **2** 166
Friars Well Fm **2** 166
Friars' Causeway **1** 35
Friars' Meadow **1** 198
Friars' Mill **1** 149
Friars' Pl. **1** 35
Friday St. **1** xv, 35
Friends' Meeting House **1** 89
FRISBY **4** xii, 58
Frisby Fm **4** 58
Frisby Grange **3** 81
Frisby Hags **3** 81
Frisby House Fm **4** 58
Frisby Lodge
(Frisby on the Wreake) **3** 81
(Frisby) **4** 58
Frisby Lodge Fm **4** 58
FRISBY ON THE WREAKE **3** xiv, 80
Frisby's Croft **1** 186
Frisby's Spinney **4** 106
Friswell's Fm **6** 127
Frith Closes, The **1** 186
Froane's Hill **6** 87
Frog Hall **6** 252
Frog Island **1** 35
Frog Island **6** 118
Frogmire **1** 227
Frogmire Bridge **1** 73
FROLESWORTH **5** xi, xiii, xv, 90
Frolesworth Hill **5** 91
Frolesworth Ho. **5** 91
Frolesworth Lane **5** 58
Frolesworth Lodge **5** 91
Frolesworth Rd
(Ashby Parva) **5** 12
(Broughton Astley) **5** 38
(Ullesthorpe) **5** 205
Front Park **2** 180
Front St. **7** 29
Froune's Hill **6** 87
Fulewellegate **5** 220
Full Moon (P.H.)
(East Bond St.) **1** 128
(Russell Sq.) **1** 128
Furlong's Barn **3** 130
Furlongs, The **7** 14
Furnace Plantation **7** 23
Furnace, The **7** 23
Furze Hill **4** 215
Furze Hill Fm **4** 215

Gables Fm
(Claybrooke Magna) **5** 58
(Frolesworth) **5** 91
Gables, The
(Ashby de la Zouch) **7** 8
(Barwell) **6** 127
GADDESBY **3** xiv, xv, 10, 94
Gaddesby Grange **3** 95
Gaddesby Hall **3** 95
Gaddesby Lane **3** 86
Gaddesby Lodge **3** 95
Gainsborough, The **1** 104, 110
Galby Lane
(Frisby) **4** 58
(Houghton) **4** 109
Galby Rd
(Frisby) **4** 58
(Illston) **4** 129
GALBY(or GAULBY) **4** xii, 62
Gallard's Hill **6** 45
Gallaway's Sq. **1** 36
Gallow Field Rd **4** 54
Gallow Hill **4** 54
Gallow Lodge **4** 178
Gallow Windmill **1** 149
Gallows Field **1** 212

Gallows Flesh Wood **7** 48
Gallows Lane **7** 264
Gallows, The **1** 111
Gallowtree Butt Wong **1** 187
Gallowtree Gate **1** xii, 36
Galtree Spinney **5** 164
Gamber's Hill Lodge **3** 275
Gamble's Close **1** 187
Gap Cottages **3** 221
Garat's Hay **7** 248
Garbrodfelde **6** xvi, xvii
Garden Cottage, The **7** 57
Garden Fm **6** 39
Garden Ho., The **4** 210
Garden St.
(Leicester) **1** 36
(Thurmaston) **3** 238
Gardiner St. **4** 172
GARENDON **7** xi, 140
Garendon Hall **7** 141
Garendon Lodge **7** 195
Garendon Park **7** xii, 141
Garendon Rd
(Coalville) **7** 62
(Loughborough) **7** 127
Garland Lane **6** 39
Garland Lane Fm **6** 39
Garth, The **7** 230
GARTHORPE **2** 148
Gartree Hill **2** 78
Gartree Hill Covert **2** 78
Gartree Hill Lodge **2** 78
Gartree Ho. **5** 164
Gartree Hundred **4** xi, xii, xiii, 1
Gartree Road
(Oadby) **5** 164
(Shangton, Stoughton) **4** xii, 234, 259
Gartree Stud **2** 63
Gas Lane **5** 219
Gas St. **1** xv, 36
Gas Works **1** 145
Gate (P.H.)
(Osgathorpe) **7** 164
(Ratcliffe Culey) **6** 330
(Syston) **3** 229
Gate (P.H.)
(Gaddesby) **3** 95
(Sutton Cheney) **6** 288
Gate Cottages **5** 174
Gate Inn
(Carlton) **6** 63
(Osbaston) **6** 201
Gate Inn **7** 276
Gate Lodge **2** 210
Gatehouse Lane **4** 74
Gateside **7** 93
GAULBY **4** 62
Gaulby Lane **4** 259
Gaulby Lodge **4** 63
Gawney Lane **5** 96
Gee's Lock **5** 104
Gelscoe Fm **7** 118
Gelscoe Lane
(Breedon on the Hill) **7** 36
(Isley cum Langley) **7** 93
Gelscoe Lodge **7** 36
Gelscoe Plantation **7** 93
Gelsmoor **7** 255
Gelsmoor Fm **7** 255
General Baptists Meeting House **6** 121
General Elliott (P.H.) **5** 235
General News Room and Library **1** 143
Generous Briton (P.H.) **2** 177
Generous Briton (P.H.)
(Loughborough) **7** 133
(Wharf St.) **1** 128
Generous Heart (P.H.) **1** 128
Gentle Lane **1** 36
George (P.H.) **5** 32
George (P.H.)
(Belton) **7** 26
(Friar Lane) **1** 128
(High St.) **1** 129
(Hinckley) **6** 121
(Loughborough) **7** 133

(Lutterworth) **5** 138
(Market Harborough) **4** 173
(Shepshed) **7** 198
George and Dragon (P.H.)
(Newbold Verdon) **6** 194
(Osgathorpe) **7** 164
(Primethorpe) **5** 41
(Stoke Golding) **6** 276
(Thringstone) **7** 71
George and Dragon (P.H.)
(Kent St.) **1** 129
(Loughborough) **7** 133
(Melton Mowbray) **2** 177
(Waltham on the Wolds) **2** 272
George Hotel (P.H.) **2** 177
George Hotel (P.H.) **1** 129
George III (P.H.)
(Haymarket) **1** 129
(Mountsorrel) **7** 152
George Inn **6** 176
George Inn (P.H.)
(Ashby de la Zouch) **7** 11
(Coleorton) **7** 79
George Inn (P.H.) **6** 135
George IV (P.H.)
(Abbey Gate) **1** 129
(Loughborough) **7** 133
(Wharf St.) **1** 129
George St.
(Hinckley) **6** 117
(Leicester) **1** xiv, 36
(Lutterworth) **5** 140
George yard **7** 130
George's Spinney **3** 150
Gibbet Hill **5** 182
Gibbet Lane
(Bilstone) **6** 239
(Shawell) **5** 182
(Twycross) **6** 308
Gibbet Post **6** 239
Gibbet, The **1** 111
Gibson's Lane **2** 51
Gilbert's Fm **6** 194
Gillethorp' **2** 226
GILMORTON **5** xiii, 95
Gilmorton Ho. **5** 97
Gilmorton Holt **5** 96
Gilmorton Lane **5** 235
Gilmorton Lodge
(Ashby Magna) **5** 10
(Gilmorton (×2)) **5** 97
Gilmorton Lodge Fm **5** 10
Gilmorton Rd **5** 10, 140
Gilmorton Spinney **5** 97
Gilroes **1** 221
Gilwiscaw Brook **6** 268
Gilwiskaw Brook
(Ashby de la Zouch) **7** 8
(Measham) **7** 264
(Packington) **7** 286
Gimbro Fm **7** 48
Gin Stables **7** 276
Ginn Stables **7** 255
Gipsey Lane **7** 185
Gipsy Lane
(Belgrave) **3** 47
(Humberstone) **3** 134
(Seagrave) **3** 207
Gipsy Nook **2** 149
Gisborne's Gorse **7** 57
Gladstone St.
(Anstey) **7** 3
(Fleckney) **4** 51
(Ibstock) **6** 144
(Loughborough) **7** 127
(Lutterworth) **5** 140
(Market Harborough) **4** 172
(Wigston Magna) **5** 219
Gladstone Terrace **6** 122
Glebe Barn **6** 215
Glebe Cottages **7** 93
Glebe Farm Cottage **5** 140
Glebe Fm
(Barwell) **6** 127
(Billesdon) **4** 5
(Bitteswell) **5** 28
(Blaby) **5** 32
(Broughton Astley) **5** 38
(Burton Overy) **4** 21
(Claybrooke Parva) **5** 61
(Cossington) **3** 60
(Countesthorpe) **5** 79

(Fenny Drayton) **6** 328
(Fleckney) **4** 51
(Gaddesby) **3** 95
(Glenfield) **6** 92
(Goadby Marwood) **2** 126
(Groby) **6** 98
(Higham on the Hill) **6** 109
(Hoby) **3** 114
(Hugglescote) **7** 66
(Husbands Bosworth) **4** 119
(Keyham) **3** 158
(Kirkby Mallory) **6** 211
(Little Stretton) **4** 159
(Long Clawson) **2** 90
(Long Whatton) **7** 112
(Lutterworth) **5** 140
(Markfield) **6** 176
(Nailstone) **6** 182
(Normanton le Heath) **6** 197
(Oadby) **5** 164
(Orton on the Hill) **6** 318
(Pearling Parva) **5** 178
(Ravenstone) **7** 180
(Redmile) **2** 195
(Saxelby) **3** 108
(Scalford) **2** 210
(Sibson) **6** 258
(Skeffington) **3** 221
(Stoney Stanton(x2)) **6** 282
(Thringstone) **7** 70
(Thurlaston) **6** 300
(Wigston Magna) **5** 224
Glebe Fm, The **6** 295
Glebe Ho.
(Leire) **5** 130
(Plungar) **2** 205
Glebe Lodge
(Brentingby) **2** 133
(Freeby) **2** 129
Glebe Rd
(Asfordby) **3** 11
(Broughton Astley) **5** 38
(Hinckley) **6** 117
Glebe St. **1** 36
Glen Ford **5** 104
Glen Gorse **4** 80
Glen Hill Fm **5** 164
Glen Hill Lodge **5** 104
Glen Hills Nursery **5** 104
Glen Oaks **4** 80
GLEN PARVA **5** xiii, xv, 103
Glen Parva: unindexed modern street-names **5** 104
Glen Parva Lodge **5** 104
Glen Rd **5** 164
Glen Water Mill **4** 80
Glen, The **7** 8
Glendale Fm **6** 79
GLENFIELD **6** xii, 92
Glenfield: unindexed modern street-names **6** 93
Glenfield Fm **5** 149
Glenfield Frith **6** 92
Glenfield Frith Hall **6** 92
Glenfield Frith Park **6** 92
Glenfield Lane **6** 152
Glenfield Mill **6** 93
Glenfield Tunnel **6** 93
Glenfields Fm **7** 195
Glengate **6** 72
Glengate **5** 220
Glenmore Park **7** 195
Glenn Ho. **4** 80
Glenn Manor Fm **4** 81
Glenn Valley Fm **4** 80
Glenworth Fm **3** 34
Globe (P.H.) **6** 268
Globe (P.H.)
(Hinckley) **6** 121
(Horninghold) **4** 106
(Silver St.) **1** 129
(unlocated) **1** 129
GLOOSTON **4** xiii, 65
Glooston Lodge **4** 65
Glooston Wood **4** 65
Glossoms, The **2** 210
Glover's Fm **3** 55
Glovers' Stalls, The **1** 119
Gnarley Cottage **6** 201
Gnarley Ho. **6** 201
GOADBY **4** xii, 70
Goadby Gorse **2** 126

Goadby Grange **2** 125
Goadby Hall **2** 126
Goadby Hall Fm **2** 126
Goadby Hill **4** 70
Goadby Home Fm **4** 70
GOADBY MARWOOD **2** xi, xii, xiii, 125
Goadby Rd **4** 95
Goadby's Close **1** 187
GOATHAM **6** 300
Goatham Spinneys **6** 201
Goddard's Pl. **1** 37
Goddard's Sq. **1** 37
Godtorp
(Cold Overton) **4** 151
(Somerby) **2** 226
Golden Ball (P.H.)
(Bakehouse Lane) **1** 129
(Blaby) **5** 32
Golden Fleece (P.H.)
(Melton Mowbray) **2** 177
(South Croxton) **3** 73
Golden Fleece (P.H.)
(Loughborough) **7** 133
(Wood Gate) **1** 129
Golden Gate **7** 207
Golden Lion (P.H.) **1** 129
Golden Square **7** 84
Golden Well **6** 227
Goldhill **5** 19
Goldhill Fm **5** 126
Goldhill Spinney **5** 126
Goldsmith Grange **2** 208, 210
Good's Lane **3** 228
Goodacre St. **1** 37
Goodman's Fm **5** 97
Goodrich street **2** 171
Goodwin's Plantation **7** 261
Goose Barn **6** 22
Goose Holme **1** 198
Goose Lane **6** 127
Goose Pen **7** 17
Goosehills Rd **6** 51
Goosewell Gate **1** 37
GOPSALL **6** 311
Gopsall Hall **6** 308
Gopsall Hall Fm **6** 308
Gopsall Ho. **6** 308
Gopsall Park **6** 308
Gopsall Wharf **6** 268
Gopsall Wood **6** 308
Gore Lodge **4** 164
Gores Lane **4** 185
Gorse Close Plantation **2** 55
Gorse Covert **7** 112
Gorse End **6** 206
Gorse Fm **3** 130
Gorse Hill **7** 3
Gorse Lane
(Moira) **7** 23
(Oadby) **5** 164
(Seagrave) **3** 207
Gorse Plantation **2** 55
Gorse Spinney
(Chilcote) **7** 261
(Enderby) **6** 87
(Hoton) **3** 130
(Newton Harcourt) **4** 298
Gorse, The **6** 59
Gorsey Lane **7** 269
Gorsey Leys **7** 283
Gorsey Leys Fm **7** 283
Goscote Hall Rd **7** 29
Goscote Hundred **3** xi, xii, xiii, xiv, xv, 1, 2, 3
Gosling Closes **1** 187
Gosling Croft **1** 187
Gosling Meadows **1** 198
Goswell St. **1** 37
Goward St. **4** 172
Goward's Spinney **4** 70
Grace Dieu Brook
(Belton) **7** 26
(Thringstone) **7** 70
Grace Dieu Cottages **7** 26
Grace Dieu Hill **7** 26
Grace Dieu Manor **7** 26
Grace Dieu Priory **7** xi, 25
Grace Dieu Warren **7** 26
Grace Dieu Wood **7** 26
Grafton Pl. **1** 37
Grammar School Fm **2** 180

Granby (P.H.) **2** 24
Granby Ct. **1** 37
Granby Hotel **2** 272
Granby Pl. **1** 37
Granby Row **1** 37
Granby St.
(Leicester) **1** xiv, 37
(Loughborough) **7** 127
Granby Wood **2** 14
Grand Union Canal **4** xiii, 54
Grange Cottage
(Barrow upon Soar) **3** 34
(Netherseal) **7** 269
(Nevill Holt) **4** 204
(Thrussington) **3** 232
(Welby) **3** 18
Grange Cottages
(Higham on the Hill) **6** 110
(Old Dalby) **2** 51
Grange Fm
(Arnesby) **5** 5
(Barton in the Beans) **6** 237
(Broughton Astley) **5** 38
(Bruntingthorpe) **5** 50
(Buckminster) **2** 55
(East Langton) **4** 38
(Higham on the Hill) **6** 110
(Husbands Bosworth) **4** 120
(Ibstock) **6** 144
(Leicester Forest East) **6** 159
(Netherseal) **7** 269
(Newton Burgoland) **7** 224
(North Kilworth) **5** 156
(Oadby) **5** 165
(Overseal) **7** 283
(Owston) **4** 215
(Scalford) **2** 210
(Sibson) **6** 258
(Snibstone) **7** 182
(Sutton in the Elms) **5** 39
(Swepstone) **7** 224
(Willoughby Waterleys) **5** 235
(Woodthorpe) **7** 149
(Wymondham) **2** 287
Grange Ho., The **2** 191
Grange Lane
(Coston) **2** 152
(Leicester) **1** 38
(Nailstone) **6** 182
(Thurnby) **4** 278
Grange Lodge **3** 134
Grange Spinney
(East Norton) **3** 178
(Glen Parva) **5** 104
Grange Wood **7** 269
Grange Yard **1** 172
Grange, The
(Burton Lazars) **2** 63
(Claybrooke Magna) **5** 58
(Coston) **2** 152
(Cranoe) **4** 31
(Donisthorpe) **7** 279
(Earl Shilton) **6** 134
(Foxton) **4** 55
(Freeby) **2** 129
(Great Bowden) **4** 178
(Hoby) **3** 114
(Hose) **2** 99
(Hungarton) **3** 144
(Leesthorpe) **2** 239
(Little Dalby) **2** 85
(Netherseal) **7** 269
(Newbold) **4** 219
(North Kilworth) **5** 156
(Saddington) **4** 224
(Saxby) **2** 135
(Saxelby) **3** 108
(Shepshed) **7** 195
(Sileby) **3** 216
(South Croxton) **3** 73
(Stapleford) **2** 140
(Thorpe Langton) **4** 276
(Thurmaston) **3** 238
(Walcote) **5** 149
(Woodhouse) **7** 248
(Woodthorpe) **7** 149
Grange, The **3** 47
Grangewood Cottage **7** 269
Grangewood Fm **7** 269
Grangewood Hall **7** 269

Grangewood Lodge **7** 269
Granite Quarry **6** 67
Granitethorpe Quarry **6** 227
Granville Ho. **3** 198
Granville Lodge **6** 123
Granville St. **4** 172
Grape St. **1** 38
Grapes (P.H.) **2** 177
Grapes (P.H.) **7** 152
Grassy Lane
(Markfield) **6** 176
(Measham) **7** 264
Gravel Hill **5** 209
Gravel Hole Spinney **2** 64
Gravel Pit **1** 147
Gravel Pit Spinney **4** 120
Gravel St. **1** 38
Gravelhole Spinney **7** 242
Gray Sq. **1** 38
Gray St.
(Leicester) **1** 38
(Loughborough) **7** 127
Graziers' Arms (P.H.) **4** 120
GREAT BOWDEN **4** xiii, 175
Great Bowden Hall **4** 178
Great Bowden Inn (P.H.) **4** 177
Great Bowden New Inn (P.H.) **4** 177
Great Bowden Rd **4** 172
Great Central Hotel (P.H.) **7** 133
Great Central Rd **7** 127
Great Close Plantation **2** 64
GREAT DALBY **2** xii, 77
Great Dalby Lodge **2** 78
Great Dalby Station **2** 78
GREAT EASTON **4** xii, xiii, xiv, 73
Great Easton Lodge **4** 74
Great Easton Park **4** 74
Great Easton Rd **4** 34
Great Fox Covert **6** 25
Great Framlands **2** xiii, 180
GREAT GLEN **4** xii, 79
Great Glen Ho. **4** 80
Great Glen Manor **4** 80
Great Glen Station **4** 80
Great Holme St. **1** 38
Great Lane **3** 81
Great Lane Hill **3** 81
Great Merrible Wood **4** 74
Great Peatling Covert **5** 174
Great Peatling Lodge **5** 174
Great Poultney Fm **5** 149
Great Spinney **4** 251
GREAT STRETTON (or STRETTON MAGNA) **4** 264
Great Wood **6** 27
Greaveley Fm **7** 164
Green Acres **4** 70
Green Close Lane **7** 127
Green Clump **6** 308
Green Dragon (P.H.)
(Market Harborough) **4** 173
(Market Pl.) **1** 129
Green Ford **4** 178
Green Hill
(Billesdon) **4** 5
(Charley) **7** 57
(Coalville) **7** 61
(Hathern) **7** 84
(Nether Broughton) **2** 46
(Ulverscroft) **7** 238
Green Lane
(Barwell) **6** 127
(Billesdon) **4** 5
(Breedon on the Hill) **7** 36
(Coalville) **7** 73
(Eaton) **2** 119
(Great Bowden) **4** 178
(Humberstone) **3** 134
(Isley cum Langley) **7** 93
(Orton on the Hill) **6** 318
(Overseal) **7** 283
(Owston) **4** 215
(Shackerstone) **6** 233
(Slawston) **4** 240
(Snarestone) **6** 268
(Stapleton) **6** 215
(Whitwick) **7** 73
(Wilson) **7** 43
Green Lane Coverts **6** 233
Green Lane Fm **6** 127

Green Lane Spinney **5** 183
Green Leys **7** 79
Green Man (P.H.) **7** 133
Green Rd **5** 41
Green Spinney
(Kirkby Mallory) **6** 211
(Little Dalby) **2** 85
(Shawell) **5** 183
Green St. **1** 38
Green, The
(Anstey) **7** 3
(Ashby de la Zouch) **7** 8
(Bitteswell) **5** 28
(Bottesford) **2** 24
(Diseworth) **7** 118
(Donington le Heath) **7** 64
(Great Dalby) **2** 78
(Hathern) **7** 84
(Leire) **5** 130
(Lubenham) **4** 164
(Markfield) **6** 176
(Mountsorrel) **7** 152
(Newton Burgoland) **7** 224
(North Kilworth) **5** 156
(Oadby) **5** 164
(Old Dalby) **2** 51
(Swepstone) **7** 219
(Syston) **3** 228
(Thringstone) **7** 70
Green's Close **1** 187
Green's Closes **1** 187
Green's Crofts **1** 187
Green's Lane **1** 38
Green's Lodge **6** 139
Greenacres
(Nether Broughton) **2** 46
(Normanton le Heath) **6** 197
(Shawell) **5** 183
Greendale **6** 152
Greenfield
(Ashby de la Zouch) **7** 8
(Bottesford) **2** 24
Greenfields Drive **7** 62
Greengate Lane **7** 29
Greenhill **6** 252
Greenhill Belt **6** 288
Greenhill Covert **6** 288
Greenhill Fm
(Nether Broughton) **2** 46
(Sutton Cheney) **6** 288
Greenhill Lodge Fm **7** 57
Greenhill Rd **7** 62
Greenkirtle Meadow **1** 198
Greenlea Fm **6** 51
Greenwood Rd **6** 276
Gregory St. **7** 127
Grendon Plantation **6** 252
Grenegate, le **5** 220
Gresley Fm **6** 252
Grey Close **7** 157
Grey Friars **1** 39, 91
Grey Lodge **6** 98
Greyfriars **6** xvii
Greyhound (P.H.)
(Great Glen) **4** 80
(Hinckley) **6** 121
(Little Bowden) **4** 185
(Loughborough) **7** 133
(Lutterworth) **5** 138
Greyhound (P.H.)
(Burbage) **6** 52
(Knossington) **4** 147
(South Gates) **1** 129
(Thames St.) **1** 129
Greyhound Inn
(Botcheston) **6** 79
(Burton on the Wolds) **3** 55
Greyhound Inn
(Sutton Cheney) **6** 288
(Wigston Parva) **5** 232
Greyhound Inn (P.H.) **7** 62
Greyhound lane **5** 139
Greystones
(Ashby de la Zouch) **7** 8
(Markfield) **6** 176
Griffin (P.H.)
(Loughborough) **7** 133
(Swithland) **7** 227
Griffin (P.H.)
(Belgrave Gate) **1** 129

(Glenfield) **6** 93
(Mountsorrel) **7** 152
(Worthington) **7** 255
Griffy Hill Ho. **7** 256
Griffydam **7** 256
Grimes Gate **7** 118
Grimley's Rock **7** 70
Grimmer, The **2** 24
Grims Lane **6** 118
GRIMSTON **3** xi, xiii, 106
Grimston Gap **3** 106
Grimston Gorse **3** 106
Grimston Station **3** 108
Grimston Tunnel **3** 106
GROBY **6** xii, 98
Groby Lane **7** 157
Groby Lodge **6** 98
Groby Lodge Fm **6** 98
Groby Nurseries **6** 98
Groby Old Quarry **6** 98
Groby Parks **6** 176
Groby Pool **6** 98
Groby Quarries **6** 98
Groby Rd
(Anstey) **7** 3
(Glenfield) **6** 93
(Leicester) **1** 39
Groby Upper Park **6** 176
Grooby St. **1** 39
Grosvenor St
(Belgrave Gate) **1** xiv, 39
(Welford Rd) **1** xiv, 39
Grove Fm **6** 87
Grove Lane **3** 34
Grove Rd **6** 51
Grove St. **1** 39
Grove Street **6** 118
Grove, The
(Asfordby) **3** 11
(Cossington) **3** 60
(Loughborough) **7** 127
(Quorndon) **7** 170
(Somerby) **2** 226
Guardhouses **1** 105
Guildhall Orchard **1** 176
Guildhall, The **1** 105
Gullet Lane **6** 152
GUMLEY **4** xiii, 87
Gumley Covert **4** 88
Gumley Hall **4** 88
Gumley Lodge **4** 88
Gumley Rd
(Foxton) **4** 55
(Laughton) **4** 154
(Smeeton Westerby) **4** 246
Gumley Wood **4** 88
Gun Hill **7** x, 57
Gunby Fm **7** 269
Gunby Hill **7** 269
Gunby Lea **7** 269
Gunhill Rough **7** 57
Gunpowder Spinney **4** 210
Gurney Lane **5** 113
Guthlaxton Gap **5** 67
Guthlaxton Hundred **5** xi, xii, xiii, 1
Gutteridge St. **7** 62
Gwens Gorse **5** 10
Gynsill Lane **7** 3
Gynsills, The **6** 93

Half Moon (P.H.) **2** 177
Half Moon (P.H.) **7** 133
Half Moon Spinney **5** 164
Halford road **2** 171
Halford St. **1** 39
Halford Terrace **7** 12
Halfway Cottages **2** 191
Halfway Ho.
(Hemington) **7** 107
(Sysonby) **2** 191
Halfway House (P.H.) **7** 62
Halifax **6** 194
Halifax Fm **6** 194
Hall Close **4** 138
Hall Cottages **6** 218
Hall Croft **7** 195
Hall Farm Cottages **5** 178
Hall Fd **6** 134
Hall Fm
(Appleby) **6** 10
(Bitteswell) **5** 28
(Broughton Astley) **5** 38

(Burton Lazars) **2** 64
(Castle Donington) **7** 48
(Charley) **7** 57
(Coleorton) **7** 79
(Coston) **2** 152
(Cotes) **3** 70
(Cotesbach) **5** 76
(Dadlington) **6** 291
(Diseworth) **7** 118
(Donisthorpe) **7** 279
(Earl Shilton) **6** 134
(East Norton) **3** 178
(Eastwell) **2** 121
(Edmondthorpe) **2** 298
(Foston) **5** 109
(Frolesworth) **5** 91
(Heather) **6** 104
(Higham on the Hill) **6** 110
(Holwell) **2** 163
(Huncote) **6** 139
(Knaptoft) **5** 123
(Leire) **5** 130
(Lockington) **7** 103
(Loddington) **3** 163
(Netherseal) **7** 270
(Osabaston) **6** 201
(Packington) **7** 286
(Peatling Parva) **5** 178
(Ravenstone) **7** 180
(Scraptoft) **4** 229
(Seagrave) **3** 207
(Shangton) **4** 234
(Snarestone) **6** 268
(Swithland) **7** 227
(Thorpe Arnold) **2** 278
(Wanlip) **7** 242
Hall Fm, The **5** 10
Hall Gate **7** 61
Hall Lane
(Aylestone) **5** 19
(Bitteswell) **5** 28
(Coalville) **7** 61
(Packington) **7** 286
(Ullesthorpe) **5** 205
(Walton) **5** 114
(Whitwick) **7** 73
Hall Meadow **1** 198
Hall Moor Meadow **1** 198
Hall Orchard **3** 81
Hall Plantation **2** 51
Hall Rd **6** 322
Hall Spinney **3** 151
Hall Yard Garden **1** 177
Hall, The
(Ashby de la Zouch) **7** 12
(Barkby) **3** 21
(Brentingby) **2** 133
(Brooksby) **3** 125
(Broughton Astley) **5** 38
(Claybrooke Magna) **5** 58
(Cold Overton) **4** 152
(Cosby) **5** 67
(Cossington) **3** 60
(Donisthorpe) **7** 279
(Drayton) **4** 34
(Eastwell) **2** 121
(Glooston) **4** 65
(Great Glen) **4** 80
(Houghton) **4** 109
(Husbands Bosworth) **4** 120
(Illston) **4** 129
(Knaptoft) **5** 123
(Leesthorpe) **2** 239
(Little Dalby) **2** 85
(Medbourne) **4** 188
(Nevill Holt) **4** 204
(Newbold Verdon) **6** 194
(Quorndon) **7** 170
(Rotheby) **3** 122
(Shangton) **4** 234
(Sileby) **3** 216
(Somerby) **2** 226
(Stretton en le Field) **7** 289
(Sutton Cheney) **6** 288
(Thorpe Satchville) **3** 264
(Tur Langton) **4** 286
(Walton) **5** 114
Hall, The **6** 122
Hall's Fm **6** 123
Hallam's Close **1** 187
Hallam's Fm **7** 29
Hallam's Wood **2** 103

HALLATON **4** xi, xiii, xiv, 94
Hallaton Grange **4** 95
Hallaton Hall **4** 95
Hallaton Manor **4** 95
Hallaton Rd
(Allexton) **3** 4
(Blaston) **4** 14
(Medbourne) **4** 188
(Tugby) **3** 255
Hallaton Spinneys **3** 259
Hallaton Wood **4** 95
hallegate, le **7** 130
Hallfield Close **6** 72
Hallfields
(Desford) **6** 72
(Twycross) **6** 308
Hallfields Lane **7** 185
Hallgate Fm **7** 157
Hallgates **7** 157
HALSTEAD **3** 248
Halstead Cottages **3** 249
Halstead Grange **3** 249
Halstead Ho. **3** 249
Halstead Lodge **3** 249
Ham Bridge **2** 144
HAMILTON **3** 30
Hamilton Grounds **3** 31
Hamilton Lane **4** 229
Hammer and Pincers (P.H.) **3** 36
Hammercliffe Lodge **7** 238
Hamner' s Lodge Fm **3** 173
Hampton St. **1** 39
Hamwell Spring **2** 250
Hancock's Fm **6** 206
Hanging Hill **7** 21
Hanging Hill Fm **7** 21
Hanging Stone
(Charley) **7** 57
(Woodhouse) **7** 248
Hangingstone Fm **7** 248
Hangingstone Hills **7** 248
Hangingstone Lodge **7** 248
Hangland Spinney **5** 149
Hangman Lane **1** xii, 40
Hangman's Hall **6** 288
Hangman's Lane **6** 117
Hanover Fm **3** 216
Hanover St. **1** xv, 40
Happy Valley Cottage **5** 205
Harboro Cottage **7** 195
Harboro Pit **7** 195
Harborough Arms (P.H.) **2** 177
Harborough Cottage **3** 95
Harborough Hill Rd **4** 251
Harborough Rd
(Foxton) **4** 55
(Glooston) **4** 65
(Kibworth Harcourt) **4** 138
(Leicester) **1** 40
(Oadby) **5** 164
Harbrook Fm **3** 255
HARBY **2** 93
Harby and Stathern Station **2** 261
Harby Colston Bridge **2** 94
Harby Hall **2** 94
Harby Hill **2** 95
Harby Lodge **2** 95
Harcourt St. **1** 40
Hard Arse **1** 198
Hardwick **2** 23
HARDWICK **4** 233
Hardwick Bridge **4** 234
Hardwick Ho. **6** 152
Hardwick Lodge **6** 187
Hardwick Lodge Fm **6** 187
Hardwick Wood **4** 234
Hardy's Ct. **1** 40
Hardy's Gunsel **3** 178
Hare and Hounds (P.H.)
(Anstey) **7** 3
(Whitwick) **7** 74
Hare and Hounds (P.H.)
(Ashby de la Zouch) **7** 11
(Conduit St.) **1** 129
(Loughborough) **7** 133
(Theddingworth) **4** 269
Hare and Pheasant (P.H.) **1** 129
Hare Pie Bank **4** 95
Harolds Lane **6** 87
Harp Orchard **1** 177

Harper's Hill
(Higham on the Hill) **6** 110
(Stapleton) **6** 215
Harper's Hill Fm **6** 291
Harrington Bridge **7** 103
Harris Bridge **6** 308
Harris Bridge Fm **6** 121
Harrison's Barn **3** 255
Harrison's Nurseries **1** 177
Harrow (P.H.) **3** 238
Harrow (P.H.)
(Hinckley) **6** 121
(Shepshed) **7** 198
Harrow Bridge **6** 123
Harrow Brook **6** 123
Harrow Fm
(Burton on the Wolds) **3** 55
(Hinckley) **6** 123
HARSTON **2** 10
Harston Wood **2** 10
Hartfield Lodge **3** 151
Hartopp Arms (P.H.) **4** 88
Harts Fm **3** 130
Hartshorne Turnpike Road **7** 10
Harvey Lane **1** 40
Harvey Lane Chapel **1** 89
Harwood Nurseries **3** 153
Haslyn Walk **7** 62
Hastings Arms (P.H.)
(Ashby de la Zouch) **7** 11
(Breedon on the Hill) **7** 36
(Ibstock) **6** 145
(Whitwick) **7** 74
Hastings Ho. **7** 127
Hastings Hotel (P.H.) **7** 11
Hastings St. **7** 127
Hastings St. **1** xv, 41
Hat and Beaver (P.H.) **1** 129
Hat Cottages **6** 161
Hat Fm **6** 161
HATHERN **7** xii, 83
Hathern Hill **7** 84
Hathern Lounds **7** 84
Hathern Turn **7** 84
Hatton Lodge **2** 46
Haughley Ho. **2** 226
Haunch of Venison (P.H.) **1** 129
Haunch of Venison (P.H.) **6** 206
Hawcliff Hill **7** 152
Hawcliff Quarry **7** 152
Hawethorngathe **5** 220
Hawkes Hill **5** 19
Hawley's Lane **1** 41
Hawthorn Bridge **5** 222
Hawthorn Ho. **7** 270
Hawthorn Rd **5** 156
Hawthorne Ho. **3** 86
Hawthorns, The **5** 156
Hayhill Lane **3** 34
Haymarket, The **1** 115
Haynes farme **2** 180
Haynes Rd **3** 134
Hays Lane **6** 117
Hays, The **3** 269
Hazel St. **6** 72
Hazlerigg Fm **3** 255
Hazletongue Lodge **2** 90
Headland Ho. **3** 100
Heanor Boat (P.H.) **1** 129
Heath End **7** 207
Heath End Fm **7** 8
Heath Fm
(Bagworth) **6** 25
(Croxton Kerrial) **2** 103
(Osbaston) **6** 201
Heath Ho. **6** 10
Heath Lane
(Blackfordby) **7** 15
(Earl Shilton) **6** 134
Heath Lodge Fm **6** 39
Heath Rd **6** 25
Heath Road Villas **6** 25
Heath Wood **6** 110
Heath, The
(Earl Shilton) **6** 134
(Newton Burgoland) **7** 224
Heathcote Arms (P.H.) **6** 67
HEATHER **6** xi, xiii, 104
Heather Close Fm **6** 27
Heather Fm **7** 180
Heather Hall **6** 104
Heather Lane **6** 197

Heatherfield Cottage **7** 157
Heatherfields **7** 157
Heathfield **6** 134
Hecadeck Lane **2** 46
Hedgerow Lane **6** 152
Heg Spinney **4** 106
Helm (P.H.) **1** 130
Help Out Mill **6** 244
HEMINGTON **7** 107
Hemington Fields **7** 107
Hemington Fields Ho. **7** 107
Hemington Hall **7** 107
Hemington Hill **7** 107
Hemington Hole **7** 107
Hemington Lane **7** 107
Hemmings's Close **1** 187
Hemp Pit Hill **7** 248
Hen and Chickens (P.H.) **1** 130
Henshaw St. **1** xv, 41
Henson's Lane **7** 70
Hercules (P.H.) **6** 288
Hercules Monument **6** 166
Hercules Plantation **6** 166
Hereswode **6** xii, xiii, 158
Hering Holme **1** 199
Hermitage Brook **7** 128
Hermitage Cottage **7** 195
Hermitage Inn (P.H.) **7** 74
Hermitage Rd **7** 73
Hermitage, The **1** 92
Hermitage, The
(Kegworth) **7** 97
(Shepshed) **7** 195
(Stockerston) **4** 251
(Thorpe Satchville) **3** 264
Heron (P.H.) **1** 130
Herrick Rd **7** 248
Herring Gorse **2** 251
Hervey Wood **7** 73
Hethilegh **6** 151
Heyday Hays **7** 157
Heygate St. **4** 172
Hickling's Spinney **7** 185
Hickling's Sq. **1** 41
High Barn **7** 93
High Barns Fm **7** 93
High Bridge **4** 298
High Bridge Plantation **4** 298
High Cademan **7** 73
High Croft
(Oadby) **5** 164
(Stapleton) **6** 215
High Cross
(Claybrooke Magna) **5** xi, xiv, 58
(Sharnford) **6** 247
High Cross Fm **6** 247
High Cross, The **1** xiv, 102
High Fm **3** 4
High Leas **4** 44
High Lees **6** 247
High Leigh **5** 194
High Leys **7** 3
High Leys Fm **2** 111
High Leys, The **2** 15
High Meres **3** 134
High Robey **7** 238
High Sharpley **7** 73
High St.
(Barwell) **6** 127
(Bottesford) **2** 24
(Castle Donington) **7** 48
(Coalville) **7** 62
(Desford) **6** 72
(Earl Shilton) **6** 134
(Enderby) **6** 87
(Evington) **4** 44
(Fleckney) **4** 51
(Great Easton) **4** 74
(Great Glen) **4** 80
(Hallaton) **4** 95
(Husbands Bosworth) **4** 120
(Kegworth) **7** 97
(Kibworth Beauchamp) **4** 133
(Loughborough) **7** 128
(Lutterworth) **5** 140
(Market Harborough) **4** 172
(Measham) **7** 264
(Melton Mowbray) **2** 169
(North Kilworth) **5** 156
(Oadby) **5** 164
(Packington) **7** 286
(Sileby) **3** 216

(Stoke Golding) **6** 276
(Syston) **3** 228
(Whetstone) **5** 213
High St. **1** xiii, 41
High Street (later Highcross St.) **1** xiii, 41
High Tor Fm **7** 57
High Town Pasture **1** 204
High View **2** 178
Higham Fields **6** 110
Higham Gorse **6** 110
Higham Grange **6** 110
Higham Hall **6** 110
Higham Lane **6** 276
HIGHAM ON THE HILL **6** xi, xii, xiii, xiv, xv, 109
Higham Thorns **6** 110
Highbank **7** 15
Highbury **3** 216
Highcroft Fm **4** 120
Highcroft Lodge Fm **4** 120
Highcross St. **1** 42
Highfield **6** 152
Highfield Fm
(Barrow upon Soar) **3** 35
(Chilcote) **7** 261
(Cold Newton) **3** 173
(Ibstock) **6** 144
(Kegworth) **7** 97
(Twyford) **3** 261
(Walcote) **5** 149
(Wigston Magna) **5** 224
Highfield Ho.
(Freeby) **2** 129
(Heather) **6** 104
(Husbands Bosworth) **4** 120
(Kegworth) **7** 97
(Market Harborough) **4** 174
(Melton Mowbray) **2** 178
(Stoney Stanton) **6** 283
(Swannington) **7** 211
(Wigston Magna) **5** 222
Highfield Spinneys **3** 259
Highfield St. **4**
(Anstey) **7** 3
(Coalville) **7** 62
(Fleckney) **4** 51
(Market Harborough) **4** 172
Highfields
(Albert Village) **7** 20
(Ashby de la Zouch) **7** 8
(Barwell) **6** 127
(Castle Donington) **7** 48
(Hinckley) **6** 123
(Leicester) **1** 221
(Osgathorpe) **7** 164
(Sheepy Magna) **6** 252
(Snibstone) **7** 183
(Thornton) **6** 27
Highfields Fm
(Albert Village) **7** 20
(Blaby) **5** 32
(Croxton Kerrial) **2** 104
(Kimcote) **5** 113
(Kirby Bellars) **3** 86
(Normanton le Heath) **6** 197
(Quorndon) **7** 170
(Rotherby) **3** 122
(South Kilworth) **5** 194
(Stoke Golding) **6** 276
(Stoney Stanton) **6** 283
(Walcote) **5** 149
Highfields Ho. **7** 112
Highfields Spinney **2** 64
Highgate Lodge **3** 216
Highland Close Spinney **4** 264
Highland Fm
(Broughton Astley) **5** 39
(Sharnford) **6** 247
Highland Spinney **4** 14
Highlands, The **7** 8
Highthorn Fm **3** 275
Highway Rd **3** 238
Highway Spinney **6** 45
Hill Close **1** 187
Hill Cottage
(Lubenham) **4** 164
(Queniborough) **3** 183
Hill Croft **6** 176
Hill Field Fm **5** 67

Hill Fm
(Atterton) **6** 326
(Barlestone) **6** 39
(Botcheston) **6** 79
(Bottesford) **2** 24
(Charley) **7** 57
(Cotesbach) **5** 76
(Countesthorpe) **5** 79
(Fenny Drayton) **6** 328
(Goadby) **4** 70
(Launde) **3** 161
(Packington) **7** 286
(Shawell) **5** 183
(Sheepy Parva) **6** 255
(Sketchley) **6** 57
(Smeeton Westerby) **4** 246
(Thurlaston) **6** 300
(Walcote) **5** 149
(Willesley) **7** 18
(Willoughby Waterleys) **5** 235
(Witherley) **6** 322
Hill Fm, The **5** 67
Hill Foot Fm
(Croft) **6** 67
(Potters Marston) **6** 218
Hill Ho.
(Cold Newton) **3** 173
(Coleorton) **7** 79
(Hoby) **3** 114
(Husbands Bosworth) **4** 120
(Snarestone) **6** 268
Hill House **5** 138
Hill House Fm **6** 10
Hill Lane
(Blaby) **5** 32
(Markfield) **6** 177
Hill Parks Fm **7** 26
Hill Rise **6** 72
Hill St.
(Ashby de la Zouch) **7** 8
(Croft) **6** 67
(Leicester) **1** 42
Hill Tamborough **4** 58
Hill Top
(Castle Donington) **7** 48
(Earl Shilton) **6** 134
(Great Glen) **4** 80
Hill Top Fm
(Barkby Thorpe) **3** 29
(Castle Donington) **7** 48
(Marefield) **4** 170
(Normanton le Heath) **6** 197
(Oadby) **5** 164
(Old Dalby) **2** 51
(Owston) **4** 215
(Walcote) **5** 149
(Walton) **5** 114
(Wellsborough) **6** 266
Hill Top Lodge **5** 114
Hill View **6** 134
Hill, The **6** 39
Hill's Barn **5** 157
Hill's Bridge **6** 233
Hillclose Fm **4** 215
Hillcrest
(Normanton le Heath) **6** 197
(Old Dalby) **2** 51
(Shawell) **5** 183
(Ullesthorpe) **5** 205
(Walcote) **5** 149
Hillcrest Fm
(Glenfield) **6** 93
(Kirby Bellars) **3** 86
(Leire) **5** 130
(Market Harborough) **4** 174
(Osgathorpe) **7** 164
Hillcroft Holt **4** 5
Hills Barn Fm **2** 133
Hillside
(Drayton) **4** 34
(Stanton under Bardon) **6** 273
(Ullesthorpe) **5** 205
Hillside Cottage **7** 57
Hillside Fm **2** 104
Hilltop Fm **7** 207
Hilltop Ho. **7** 207
HINCKLEY **6** xi, xii, xiii, 116
Hinckley: unindexed
modern street-names **6** 120
Hinckley Fields **6** 123
Hinckley Fields Fm **6** 123
Hinckley Lane **6** 110

Hinckley Priory **6** 121
Hinckley Rd
(Aston Flamville) **6** 22
(Burbage) **6** 51
(Cadeby) **6** 59
(Dadlington) **6** 291
(Kirby Muxloe) **6** 152
(Leicester) **1** 42
(Nailstone) **6** 182
(Sapcote) **6** 227
(Stoke Golding) **6** 276
(Stoney Stanton) **6** 283
Hinckley Station **6** 123
Hincks's Sq. **1** 42
Hind (P.H.) **5** 138
Hind (P.H.) **4** 173
Hind Inn (P.H.) **1** 130
Hind Leys **7** 157
Hindle Top Fm **2** 278
Hissar Ho. **6** 127
Hissar House Fm **6** 127
Hive, The **5** 67
Hoarstone Meadow **1** 199
Hob's Hole **7** 57
Hobbes Hole **7** 36
Hobbs Hayes **6** 227
Hobby Hall **6** 177
Hobday Hills Plantation **7** 280
HOBY **3** xi, xiv, xv, 113
Hoby Barn **3** 114
Hoby Ho. **3** 114
Hockley Fm **6** 45
Hoctonegate **5** 220
Hodson's Ct. **1** 42
Hoeback Spinney **4** 106
Hoefields **6** 300
Hog Lane **4** 95
Hog Lane
(Hinckley) **6** 118
(Lutterworth) **5** 139
Hogue Hall **6** 51
Hogue Hall Cottages **6** 51
Hogue Hall Spinney **6** 51
Holegate **1** 42
Holgate Hill Spinney **7** 157
Holland St. **7** 128
Hollier's Walk **6** 123
Hollies, The
(Burbage) **6** 51
(Frolesworth) **5** 91
(Hoton) **3** 130
(Kirby Bellars) **3** 86
(Markfield) **6** 177
(Sheepy Magna) **6** 252
(South Kilworth) **5** 194
(West Langton) **4** 293
Hollis Fm **6** 318
Hollow Fm
(Nailstone) **6** 182
(Netherseal) **7** 270
Hollow Lane **2** 64
Hollow Rd
(Anstey) **7** 3
(Breedon on the Hill) **7** 37
Hollow, The
(Bagworth) **6** 182
(Earl Shilton) **6** 134
(Normanton le Heath) **6** 197
Hollow, The **1** 42
Holloway Spinney **4** 88
Hollows Fm, The **6** 152
Hollows, The **6** 137
Holly Bush (P.H.)
(Breedon on the Hill) **7** 37
(Hinckley) **6** 121
(Netherseal) **7** 270
Holly Bush (P.H.)
(Belgrave Gate) **1** 130
(Netherseal) **7** 286
Holly Cottage **3** 163
Holly Croft **6** 123
Holly Croft Fm **6** 123
Holly Croft House **6** 122
Holly Croft Park **6** 123
Holly Hayes Fm **7** 73
Holly Hayes Wood **7** 73
Holly Hays **7** 29
Holly Hedges **6** 72
Holly Ho. **6** 139
Holly Plantation **7** 157
Holly Walk Spinney **5** 76
Holly Wood **7** 48

Hollygate **2** 140
Hollytree Fm **5** 114
Hollytree Ho. **3** 130
Holme Fm **2** 90
Holme St. **1** 42
Holme's Fm **4** 164
Holmes's Mill **1** 149
Holmfield **5** 83
Holmfield Rd **6** 73
Holmlea **3** 275
Holmwood **6** 152
Holt Farm Cottage **5** 50
Holt Fm
(Ashby Magna) **5** 10
(Bruntingthorpe) **5** 50
(Gilmorton) **5** 97
(Shangton) **4** 234
Holt Ho. **5** 83
Holt Lane
(Ashby Magna) **5** 10
(Great Easton) **4** 74
Holt Rd **7** 29
Holt Spa **4** 204
Holt Wood **4** 204
Holt Yard **4** 34
Holt, The
(Aylestone) **5** 19
(Kirby Muxloe) **6** 152
(Loughborough) **7** 128
(Thurlaston) **6** 300
(Thurnby) **4** 278
Holt's Lane **7** 64
Holt's Leys **1** 204
Holton Fm **5** 114
HOLWELL **2** 162
Holwell Huts **2** 163
Holwell Mouth **2** 163
Holwell Mouth Covert **2** 90
Holy Bones **1** xii, 42
Holy Rood Church
(Bagworth) **6** 25
(Packington) **7** 286
Holy Rood Lane **1** 43
Holy Trinity Chapel **7** 207
Holy Trinity Church **1** 82
Holy Trinity Church
(Ashby de la Zouch) **7** 8
(Barrow upon Soar) **3** 35
(Hinckley) **6** 120
(Leicester) **1** 82
(Normanton le Heath) **6** 197
(Norton juxta Twycross) **6** 312
(Sewstern) **2** 59
(Thrussington) **3** 232
Holy Well
(Ashby de la Zouch) **7** 8
(Nanpantan) **7** 146
(Nevill Holt) **4** 204
(Ratby) **6** 222
HOLYOAKS **4** xiii, 250
Holyoaks Lodge **4** 252
Holyoaks Wood **4** 252
Holywell Fm
(Ashby de la Zouch) **7** 8
(Ratby) **6** 222
Holywell Hall **7** 146
Holywell Ho., The **6** 123
Holywell Inn, The (P.H.) **6** 122
Holywell Rd **5** 19
Holywell Wood **7** 146
Home Barn **5** 205
Home Barn Fm **6** 227
Home Bridge Fm **6** 144
Home Cl. **4** 5
Home Covert **7** 195
Home Farm Lodge
(Cotesbach) **5** 76
(Old Dalby) **2** 51
Home Fm
(Ab Kettleby) **2** 158
(Ashby Parva) **5** 13
(Beeby) **3** 42
(Billesdon) **4** 5
(Blaston) **4** 14
(Bushby) **4** 282
(Castle Donington) **7** 48
(Chilcote) **7** 261
(Cotesbach) **5** 76

(Frolesworth) **5** 91
(Glooston) **4** 66
(Gumley) **4** 88
(Keythorpe) **3** 259
(Knighton) **5** 126
(Little Dalby) **2** 85
(Little Stretton) **4** 159
(Long Whatton) **7** 112
(Medbourne) **4** 188
(Normanton le Heath) **6** 197
(Osbaston) **6** 201
(Peatling Magna (×2)) **5** 174
(Prestwold) **3** 180
(Ravenstone) **7** 180
(Rolleston) **4** 221
(Sapcote) **6** 227
(Sheepy Parva) **6** 255
(Smeeton Westerby) **4** 246
(South Kilworth) **5** 194
(Staunton Harold) **7** 207
(Stoughton) **4** 259
(Stretton en le Field) **7** 289
(Thorpe Arnold) **2** 278
(Ulverscroft) **7** 238
(Upton) **6** 262
(Welham) **4** 290
(West Langton) **4** 293
Home Fm, The
(Asfordby) **3** 11
(Elmesthorpe) **6** 83
(Nanpantan) **7** 147
Home Lodge Hollow **2** 51
Home Plantation **4** 210
Home Spinney **5** 76
Homefield Lane **7** 185
Homefields Fm **7** 118
Homeleigh **3** 269
Homeleigh Fm **5** 76
Homeleys Fm **6** 10
Homestead Fm **3** 221
Homestead Spinney **3** 255
Homestead, The
(Frolesworth) **5** 91
(Kirby Muxloe) **6** 152
(Melton Mowbray) **2** 178
(Queniborough) **3** 183
(Rothley) **7** 185
(Walton on the Wolds) **3** 269
Honey Hill **7** 261
Honey Pot Lane **4** 120
Honey Pot Plantation **2** 149
Honeyhill Clump **7** 261
Hoo Ash Fm **7** 180
Hoo Hills **6** 266
Hooborough Brook
(Netherseal) **7** 207
(Oakthorpe) **7** 277
(Overseal) **7** 283
Hook Ho. **6** 194
Hook's Bridge **6** 166
Hookhill Cottage **7** 195
Hookhill Wood **7** 195
Hoothill Slang **3** 221
Hoothill Wood **3** 221
Hop Yard road **7** 10
Hope and Anchor (P.H.) **3** 229
Hoppage Spinney **6** 10
Hopyard Fm **6** 161
Hopyard Spinney **4** 204
Horngate **2** 171
HORNINGHOLD **4** 105
Horninghold Hall **4** 106
Horninghold Ho. **4** 106
Horninghold Lane **4** 14
Horninghold Rd **4** 95
Horninghold Wood **4** 106
Horse and Groom (P.H.)
(Queniborough) **3** 183
(Rearsby) **3** 198
Horse and Groom (P.H.)
(Evington) **4** 44
(Humberstone Gate) **1** 130
(Kegworth) **7** 97
(Staunton Harold) **7** 207
(Wymondham) **2** 288
Horse and Jockey (P.H.) **6** 241
Horse and Jockey (P.H.)
(Evington) **4** 44
(Hinckley) **6** 122
(Humberstone Gate) **1** 130
(Northgate St.) **1** 130
(Queniborough) **3** 183

Horse and Trumpet (P.H.) **5** 222
Horse and Trumpet (P.H.)
(Cranoe) **4** 31
(Earl Shilton) **6** 135
(Highcross St.) **1** 130
(Medbourne) **4** 188
(Sileby) **3** 216
Horse Brook **1** 225
Horse Close Plantation **6** 308
Horse Fair Close **1** 187
Horse Fair Cottage **7** 26
Horse Fair Garden **1** 177
Horse Fair Leys **1** 204
Horse Fair, The **1** 115
Horse Hill **4** 70
Horse Leys Fm **3** 55
Horse Malt Mill, The **1** 149
Horse Pool **1** 227
Horse Shoe Plantation **6** 10
Horse Shoes (P.H.) **6** 300
Horse Shoes, The (P.H.) **3** 11
Horseclose Spinney **4** 95
Horsefair St. **1** 43
Horseley Plantation **7** 261
Horsepool Grange **6** 272
Horsepool St. **1** 43
Horsepools Fm **3** 163
Horses Lane **7** 264
Horsewell Lane **5** 219
Horston Hill **4** 44
HOSE **2** xiii, 99
Hose Bridge **2** 99
Hose Gorse **2** 99
Hose Hill **2** 140
Hose Lodge **2** 95
Hose Villa **2** 90
Hospital Fm **2** 35
Hospital Lane
(Blaby) **5** 32
(Ravenstone) **7** 180
Hospital of St Edmund the Confessor and Archbishop **1** 93
Hospital of St John the Evangelist and St John the Baptist **1** 93
Hospital of St Lazarus **2** xiii, 63
Hospital of St Leonard **1** 94
Hospital of St Mary Magdalene and St Margaret **1** 94
Hospital of St Ursula **1** 95
Hospital of the Blessed Virgin Mary **1** 100
Hotel St.
(Coalville) **7** 62
(Leicester) **1** 43
Hotgate St. **1** xii, xiv, 43
HOTHORPE **4** xii, 273
Hothorpe Rd **4** 269
HOTON **3** 130
Hoton Hills **3** 130
Hoton Ho. **3** 131
Hoton Spinney **3** 180
Hough Hill **7** 211
Houghton Lodge **4** 109
HOUGHTON ON THE HILL **4** 109
Houghton Tollbar **4** 110
House Fm **7** 277
House of Correction **6** 120
Houston Kennels **6** 123
Hovel Buildings **4** 14
Hovel Hill **5** 209
Howe Arms (P.H.) **6** 308
Howe Lane **7** 185
Hubbard's Spinney **4** 58
Hubbards Fm **5** 10
Huckster's row **7** 130
Hudson St. **7** 128
Hudson's Bede House **2** 176
HUGGLESCOTE **7** 66
Hugglescote Grange **7** 66
Huit Lane **6** 134
Huit, The **6** 134
Hull St. **1** 44
Hull's Row **1** 44
Humber Stone **3** 134
HUMBERSTONE **3** xi, xiii, xv, 133
Humberstone: unindexed modern street-names **3** 135
Humberstone Fm **3** 134
Humberstone Gate **1** xii, 44
Humberstone Gate Bridge **1** 74
Humberstone Gate Dunghill **1** 108
Humberstone Gate Pavement **1** 79

Humberstone Grange **3** 134
Humberstone Ho. **3** 134
Humberstone Lane **3** 238
Humberstone Manor **3** 134
Humberstone Park **3** 134
Humberstone Rd **1** 44
Humberstone Tce **1** 44
Humble Fm **3** 60
Humble Lane **3** 60
Hume St. **7** 128
HUNCOTE **6** 139
Huncote Bridge **6** 139
Huncote Grange **6** 161
Huncote Lodge **6** 139
Huncote Lodge Fm **6** 139
Huncote Mill **6** 139
Huncote Rd
(Croft) **6** 67
(Narborough) **6** 187
(Stoney Stanton) **6** 283
HUNGARTON **3** xi, xiii, 144
Hungarton Lane **3** 42
Hungarton Rd **3** 173
Hungarton Spinneys **3** 144
Hunger Hill **7** 248
Hunger Wong **1** 188
Hungerford St. **1** 44
Hungerford's Clump **6** 318
Hungerton Ho. **5** 222
Hungry Hill **6** 110
Hunt's Hill **7** 157
Hunt's Lane
(Desford) **6** 73
(Hallaton) **4** 95
(Netherseal) **7** 207
Hunt's Lodge **5** 235
Hunters Arms, The (P.H.) **2** 288
Huntingdon Ho. **7** 12
Hunts Lane **6** 194
Hurst Fm
(Chilcote) **7** 261
(Nanpantan) **7** 147
HUSBANDS BOSWORTH **4** xiii, 118
Hut Spinney **6** 201
Hyam's Lane **7** 118
Hyde Lodge Rd **3** 244
Hye Crosse, the **2** 175
Hyssop's Lane **4** 44

IBSTOCK **6** xi, xii, 142
Ibstock: unindexed modern street-names **6** 144
Ibstock Grange **6** 143
Ibstock Lodge **6** 144
Ibstock Rd
(Nailstone) **6** 182
(Ravenstone) **7** 180
Ibstock Sidings **6** 144
Icehouse Plantation **3** 180
Idle Lane **1** 44
Iliffe Bridge **6** 63
Illston Grange **4** 129
Illston Lane **4** 129
Illston Lodge **4** 129
ILLSTON ON THE HILL **4** xi, xii, 128
Illston Rd **4** 210
Ilott Wharf **7** 264
Independent Chapel **1** 89
Independent Chapel **2** 175
Independent Meeting House **6** 121
Infirmary Sq. **1** 44
Infirmary St. **1** 44
Ingarsby Cottages **3** 153
Ingarsby Hollow **3** 153
Ingarsby Lane **3** 153
Ingarsby Lodge **3** 153
Ingarsby Old Hall **3** 153
Ingarsby Rd **3** 158
Ingle Bank **7** 8
Ingle's Hill **7** 8
Ingle's Hill Fm **7** 8
Ingleberry Cottage **7** 195
Ingleberry Ho. **7** 195
Ingleberry Lodge **7** 195
Ingleberry Rock **7** 195
Ingledene **7** 8
Inglenook **6** 127
Inkerman Lodge **3** 144
Inkersall Fm **5** 97
Inkersall Lodge **5** 97

Ireland Barn **7** 270
Ireland Ho. **5** 39
Irish Fm **6** 36
Iron Fm **7** 118
Iron Founders' Arms (P.H.) **1** 130
Ironmonger's Shop, The **1** 118
Ironmongers' Lane **1** xii, 44
Ironstone Fm **2** 163
Island Lane **6** 211
Island Lane Fm **6** 211
Islands, The **4** 298
Isley cum Langley **7** 91
ISLEY WALTON **7** x, 91
Isset's Lodge **3** 259
Ivanhoe Baths **7** 8
Ivanhoe Cottage **7** 12
Ivanhoe Fm **7** 9
Ivanhoe place **7** 10
Ivanhoe road **7** 10
Ivanhoe Terrace **7** 12
Ivanhoe Villa **6** 144
Iven's Fm, The **6** 127
Ives Head **7** 195
Iveshead Fm **7** 195
Iveshead Ho. **7** 195
Iveshead Lane **7** 195
Iveshead Rd **7** 195
Ivy Cottage
(Kirby Bellars) **3** 86
(Peatling Parva) **5** 178
(Wellsborough) **6** 266
(Wigston Magna) **5** 222
Ivy Cottages **7** 79
Ivy Fm **7** 280
Ivy Hall **6** 273
Ivy Ho.
(Measham) **7** 264
(Twyford) **3** 261
Ivy House Fm
(Ashby Parva) **5** 13
(Congerstone) **6** 241
(Holwell) **2** 163
(Odstone) **6** 244
(Sharnford) **6** 247
(Shenton) **6** 295
(Stoke Golding) **6** 276
Ivy Lodge Fm **4** 269
Ivydene **6** 134

Jackdaw Plantation **7** 157
Jackson St. **7** 62
Jackson's Bridge **6** 166
Jackson's Plantation **2** 55
Jailhall Lane **1** 45
James's St. **1** 45
Jamson's Plantation **7** 147
Jane Ball Covert **5** 123
Jarrom St. **1** xv, 45
Jasmine Cottages **7** 79
Jasmine Fm **2** 144
Jayes Barn **6** 161
Jeffcoats Lane **7** 211
Jelley's Closes **1** 188
Jenner's Lodge **3** 100
Jenny's Lane **7** 180
Jeremy's Ground Spinney **5** 76
Jericho **6** 123
Jericho Covert **2** 200
Jericho Lodge
(Barkestone) **2** 200
(Stapleford) **2** 140
(Thrussington) **3** 232
Jerviston **6** 152
Jewry Wall **1** 5
Jewry Wall St. **1** 45
Joe Moore's Lane **7** 249
John Ball Covert **5** 123
John Ball Fm **5** 188
John Ball Hill **5** 188
John o' Gaunt **3** 169
John o' Gaunt Fm **3** 261
John o' Gaunt Hotel **3** 261
John o' Gaunt Viaduct **3** 261
John St.
(Hinckley) **6** 117
(Loughborough) **7** 128
John's Lee Wood **7** 238
Johnson's St. **1** 45
Johnstone Spinney **6** 87
Joiner's Close **4** 210

Joiners' Arms (P.H.) **5** 50
Joiners' Arms (P.H.)
(Highcross St.) **1** 130
(Narborough) **6** 187
Jolly Anglers (P.H.) **1** 130
Jolly Bacchus (P.H.)
(Highcross St.) **1** 130
(Hinckley) **6** 122
Jolly Colliers (P.H.) **7** 74
Jolly Farmers (P.H.) **7** 198
Jolly Potters (P.H.) **7** 50
Jolly Topers (P.H.) **6** 39
Jones's Spinney **4** 259
Joseph (P.H.) **1** 130
Jubilee Cottages **7** 20
Jubilee Covert **5** 104
Jubilee Fm **5** 174
Jubilee Ho. **3** 261
Jubilee House Fm **6** 10
Jubilee Plantation **7** 180
Jubilee Rd **5** 38
Jubilee Spinney **6** 166
Jubilee Terrace **7** 280
Judge Meadow Spinney **4** 44
Junction Ho. **7** 164
Junior St. **1** 45

Kaffir Inn **5** 213
Kates Hill **4** 5
Kates Hill Fm **4** 5
Katharine Wheel Inn (P.H.) **4** 173
Katherine Wheel **4** 234
Kaye's Plantation **7** 170
Keats Lane **6** 134
Keck's Arms (P.H.) **1** 130
Keeper's Cottage **6** 291
Keeper's Lodge **7** 94
Keepers Cottage **7** 79
Keepers Fm **5** 32
Keepers house, the **5** 138
KEGWORTH **7** x, xi, xii, 96
Kegworth Bridge **7** 97
Kegworth Field **7** 97
Kegworth Mill **7** 97
Keithley Lodge Fm **7** 256
Kelham Bridge **7** 64
Kelham Bridge Fm **7** 64
Kellam's Fm **6** 36
Kelling's Croft **1** 188
Kelly's Factory **1** 146
Kendall's Barn **6** 201
Kennel Cottage **3** 221
Kennel Covert **6** 308
Kennel Lane **6** 322
Kennel Plantation **2** 104
Kennel Spinney **6** 166
Kennels Wood **2** 8
Kennels, The **6** 308
Kenney St. **1** 45
Kent St. **1** 46
Kent St. **1** xv, 46
Kenyon St. **1** 46
Kepeoven Lane **1** 46
Ketleby gate **2** 171
Kettering Rd **4** 185
Kettleby Bridge **2** 175
Kettlesborough
(Oadby) **5** 164
(Stoughton) **4** 259
KEYHAM **3** xi, xiii, xv, 157
Keyham Bridge **3** 158
Keyham High Leys **3** 158
Keyham Lane
(Beeby) **3** 42
(Humberstone) **3** 134
(Scraptoft) **4** 229
KEYTHORPE **3** 259
Keythorpe Court **3** 259
Keythorpe Grange **3** 178
Keythorpe Hall **3** 259
Keythorpe Hall Fm **3** 259
Keythorpe Ho. **3** 259
Keythorpe Lodge **3** 259
Keythorpe Lodge Fm **3** 259
Keythorpe Park **3** 259
Keythorpe Spinney **3** 259
Keythorpe Wood **4** 70
Kibbled Oaks **5** 28
KIBWORTH BEAUCHAMP **4** 132
Kibworth Beauchamp: unindexed modern street-names **4** 133
Kibworth Bridge **4** 138

Kibworth Cottage **4** 138
Kibworth Hall **4** 138
KIBWORTH HARCOURT **4** xi, 138
Kibworth Ho. **4** 138
Kibworth Rd
(Saddington) **4** 224
(Tur Langton) **4** 286
Kibworth Station **4** 133
Kicklewell Spinney **4** 154
KILBY **5** xix, 107
Kilby Bridge
(Kilby) **5** 107
(Wigston Magna) **5** 222
Kilby Bridge Fm **5** 224
Kilby Bridge Lock **5** 224
Kilby Canal Bridge **5** 223
Kilby Grange **5** 107
Kilby Lodge **5** 108
Kilby Rd **4** 51
Killock Ho. **4** 154
Kiln Close, The **2** 64
Kilnhouse Closes, The **1** 188
KILWARDBY **7** xi, 16
Kilwardby St. **7** 9
Kilworth Rd
(Husbands Bosworth) **4** 120
(Walton) **5** 114
Kimberley **7** 9
Kimberley Ho.
(Coleorton) **7** 79
(Leire) **5** 130
(Swannington) **7** 211
KIMCOTE **5** 112
Kimcote Rd **5** 114
Kinchley Hill **7** 185
Kinchley Ho. **7** 186
Kinchley Lane **7** 186
King (P.H.) **1** 131
King and Crown (P.H.) **1** 131
King Charles's Well **4** 286
King Dick's Hole **6** 257
King Lud's Entrenchments **2** 104
King Richard III (P.H.) **1** 131
King Richard's Well **6** 288
King St.
(Barkby Thorpe) **3** 29
(Barwell) **6** 127
(Coalville) **7** 62
(Leicester) **1** xiv, 46
(Loughborough) **7** 128
(Melton Mowbray) **2** 169
(Nether Broughton) **2** 46
(Scalford) **2** 210
(Seagrave) **3** 207
(Sileby) **3** 216
(Twyford) **3** 262
King Street **6** 118
King Street Lane **2** xii, 152
King Street Plantation **7** 97
King William (P.H.) **6** 135
King William III (P.H.) **1** 131
King William IV (P.H.) **6** 166
King William IV (P.H.)
(Enderby) **6** 87
(Loughborough) **7** 133
(Quorndon) **7** 170
(Wigston Magna) **5** 222
King William's Bridge **7** 3
King William's yard **7** 130
King's Arms (P.H.)
(Coleorton) **7** 79
(Hathern) **7** 84
(Scalford) **2** 210
(Whitwick) **7** 74
King's Arms (P.H.)
(Metcalf St.) **1** 131
(Ravenstone) **7** 180
(Sanvey Gate) **1** 131
(Silver St.) **1** 131
(Stathern) **2** 261
(Waltham on the Wolds) **2** 272
King's Bridge
(Hoton) **3** 131
(Market Bosworth) **6** 166
King's Brook **3** 131
King's Close **2** 210

King's Garden, The **1** 177
King's Head (P.H.)
(King St.) **1** 131
(Melton Mowbray) **2** 177
(Smeeton Westerby) **4** 246
King's Head (P.H.)
(Ashby de la Zouch) **7** 11
(Barrow upon Soar) **3** 36
(Castle Donington) **7** 50
(Great Easton) **4** 74
(Hinckley) **6** 122
(Isley cum Langley) **7** 94
(Market Harborough) **4** 173
(Swinesmarket) **1** 131
King's Head Hotel (P.H.) **7** 133
King's Hill Spinney **6** 295
King's Lane **1** 46
King's Lock **5** 19
King's Mills **7** 48
KING'S NORTON **4** 141
King's Prison, The **1** 109
King's Stand **6** 159
King's Water **1** 225
King's Wood **2** 15
King's yard **7** 10
Kings Lane **3** 73
Kingsfield Rd **5** 67
KIRBY BELLARS **3** xiv, xv, 10, 84
Kirby Bellars Priory **3** 86
Kirby Castle **6** 152
Kirby Cottage
(Kirby Bellars) **3** 86
(Kirby Muxloe) **6** 152
Kirby Fields **6** 152
Kirby Fm **6** 124
Kirby Gate **3** 86
Kirby Gate Fm **3** 86
Kirby Grange **6** 222
Kirby Hall **3** 86
Kirby Hall Fm **3** 86
Kirby Lane
(Eye Kettleby) **2** 189
(Kirby Muxloe) **6** 152
Kirby Lane Spinneys **6** 152
Kirby Lodge Fm **3** 86
KIRBY MUXLOE **6** xii, xiii, xiv, 150
Kirby Muxloe: unindexed modern street-names **6** 153
Kirby Muxloe Station **6** 152
Kirby Old Mill **3** 86
Kirby Park
(Kirby Bellars) **3** 86
(Kirby Muxloe) **6** 152
Kirby Rd
(Desford) **6** 73
(Glenfield) **6** 93
Kirby Way **1** 46
Kirk Gate **1** 46
Kirk Hill **7** 195
Kirk Lane
(Enderby) **6** 87
(Leicester) **1** 46
Kirkby Hall **6** 211
Kirkby Lane
Kirkby Lane
(Newbold Verdon) **6** 194
(Peckleton) **6** 207
Kirkby Lodge **6** 211
KIRKBY MALLORY **6** xiii, 210
Kirkby Moats **6** 211
Kirkby Old Parks **6** 211
Kirkby Park **6** 211
Kirkby Rd **6** 127
Kirkby Wood **6** 211
Kit's Pit **6** 308
Kitchener Rd **7** 3
Kite Hill **7** 57
Kitehill Plantation **7** 57
KNAPTOFT **5** 122
Knaptoft Church **5** 123
Knaptoft Cottage **5** 123
Knaptoft Grange **5** 123
Knaptoft Ho. **5** 123
Knaptoft Lodge **5** 123
Knave Hill **4** 255
Knight Thorpe **7** 143
Knight Thorpe Hall **7** 144
Knight Thorpe Lodge **7** 144
Knightcote's Wong **1** 188

KNIGHTON **5** 125
Knighton: unindexed
modern street-names **5** 126
Knighton Bridge **5** 126
Knighton Fields **5** 126
Knighton Grange **5** 165
Knighton Grange Rd **5** 165
Knighton Hall **5** 126
Knighton Hayes **5** 126
Knighton Hill Windmill **1** 150
Knighton Ho. **5** 126
Knighton Lane **5** 19
Knighton Piece **1** 188
Knighton Rd **1** 46
Knighton Spinney **5** 126
Knighton St. **1** 46
Knight's Bridge
(Glen Parva) **5** 104
(Wigston Magna) **5** 223
Knight's End **4** 178
KNIPTON **2** xi, xii, 14
Knipton Cottage **2** 15
Knipton Ho. **2** 15
Knipton Lodge **2** 15
Knipton Pasture **2** 15
Knipton Reservoir **2** 15
Knob Hill **4** 106
Knob Hill Fm **4** 106
Knoll Fm **6** 300
Knoll Spinney **6** 300
Knoll, The
(Frisby on the Wreake) **3** 81
(Kibworth Beauchamp) **4** 133
(Thurlaston) **6** 300
KNOSSINGTON **4** 146
Knossington Grange **4** 147
Knossington Lodge Fm **4** 147
Knossington Rd **4** 215
Knowle Hill **7** 79
Knowles Spinney
(Carlton) **6** 63
(Nailstone) **6** 182
Kylemore **7** 9
Kyte Hill **2** 241
Lady Acre **1** 199
Lady Gate **7** 118
Lady Hay Wood **6** 99
Lady Leys **5** 67
Lady Lodge **3** 11
Lady Wood
(Blackfordby) **7** 15
(Knossington) **4** 147
Lady's Bridge **1** 74
Lady's Close **7** 107
Lag Lane **2** 169
Lagos Fm **6** 308
Lake Spinney **2** 85
Lake, The
(Cold Overton) **4** 152
(Keythorpe) **3** 259
Lamb (P.H.) **7** 11
Lamb (P.H.)
(Belgrave Gate) **1** 131
(St Mary de Castro's) **1** 131
Lamb yard **7** 10
Lambert lane **2** 172
Lamlea **2** 166
Lammas Close **4** 120
Lancaster Arms (P.H.) **6** 73
Lancaster Pl. **1** 47
Land Society Lane **6** 134
Landfield Spinney **2** 85
Landyke Lane **2** 158
Landyke Lane Fm **2** 163
Lane's Spinney **4** 210
Langar Bridge **2** 95
Langham Bridge **6** 187
Langham Bridge Fm
(Cosby) **5** 67
(Narborough) **6** 187
Langham's Bridge **5** 223
LANGLEY **7** 92
Langley Lodge **7** 41
Langley Priory **7** xi, 92
Langley's School **7** 12
Langton Brook **4** xii, 38
Langton Brook Plantation **4** 55
Langton Caudle **4** 254

Langton Fm **6** 83
Langton Hall **4** 293
Langton Hall Fm **4** 293
Langton Rd
(Foxton) **4** 55
(Slawston) **4** 240
Lanktons mill **5** 223
Lant, The **7** 195
Lantern Cross **7** 227
Larch Plantation **4** 5
Larch Spinney
(Barton in the Beans) **6** 237
(King's Norton) **4** 142
Larches, The **6** 182
Larchwood Rise **4** 147
Large Meadow **1** 199
Lash Hill **6** 51
Lathams Cottages **7** 277
Lathkill St. **4** 172
Latimer's House **7** 230
Lattice Coppice **5** 104
LAUGHTON **4** 154
Laughton Hills **4** 154
Laughton Lane **4** 197
Laughton Rd **4** 164
LAUNDE **3** xiv, 160
Launde Abbey **3** xv, 160
Launde Big Wood **3** 161
Launde Cottage **3** 163
Launde Lodge **3** 161
Launde Park **3** 161
Launde Park Wood **3** 161
Launde Rd **3** 249
Launde Wood Fm **3** 161
Laurel Bank **5** 61
Laurel Fm **6** 99
Laurels Fm **6** 26
Laurels, The
(Frisby on the Wreake) **3** 81
(Peatling Parva) **5** 178
Lawn Barn **7** 9
Lawn Ho. **6** 288
Lawn Hollow Plantation **2** 104
Lawn Lane **2** 51
Lawn Lodge **7** 249
Lawn Plantation **7** 207
Lawn Wood **6** 99
Lawn, The
(Birstall) **7** 29
(Lubbesthorpe) **6** 161
Lawnfield **2** 51
Lawns, The **6** 124
Lawrence's Shop **1** 118
Laxton's Covert **2** 140
Lea Barn Fm **5** 147
Lea Cottage **7** 238
Lea Grange **6** 308
Lea Grange Fm **6** 308
Lea Lane **7** 238
Lea Wood **7** 238
Leachmore Ho. **6** 51
Leacroft Ho. **7** 180
Lead St. **1** 47
Leadenhall St. **1** xv, 47
Leaders Fm **5** 140
Leather Hall, The **1** 118
Lee St. **1** xv, 47
LEESTHORPE **2** 238
Leesthorpe Hill **2** 239
Leesthorpe Ho. **2** 239
Leesthorpe Lodge **2** 239
Legham **5** 129
Leicester **1** xi, 1
Leicester **6** xiv, xvii
Leicester Bridge **2** 174
Leicester County Lunatic Asylum **1** 97
Leicester East Aerodrome **4** 260
Leicester Forest **6** xii, xiii
LEICESTER FOREST EAST **6** xiii, 158, 159
LEICESTER FOREST WEST **6** 158, 159
Leicester Frith **1** xiii, 223
Leicester Gate **2** 176
Leicester Hill **7** 157
Leicester Hotel (P.H.) **7** 62
Leicester Infirmary **1** 97
Leicester Lane
(Desford) **6** 73
(Enderby) **6** 87
(Great Bowden) **4** 178

(Kirby Muxloe) **6** 152
(Swithland) **7** 228
Leicester Meadow **1** 199
Leicester Race Course **5** 165
Leicester Rd
(Ashby de la Zouch) **7** 9
(Billesdon) **4** 5
(Countesthorpe) **5** 79
(Fleckney) **4** 51
(Groby) **6** 99
(Hinckley) **6** 117
(Husbands Bosworth) **4** 120
(Kibworth Harcourt) **4** 138
(Loughborough) **7** 128
(Lutterworth) **5** 140
(Market Harborough) **4** 172
(Mowsley) **4** 197
(Narborough) **6** 187
(Oadby) **5** 165
(Ravenstone) **7** 180
(Sapcote) **6** 227
(Sharnford) **6** 247
(Shepshed) **7** 195
(Sutton in the Elms) **5** 40
(Syston) **3** 228
(Tilton) **3** 244
(Whitwick) **7** 73
(Wigston Magna) **5** 219
Leicester Road Fm **5** 67
Leicester St. **2** 169
Leicester Union Workhouse **1** 98
Leichpool **1** 228
Leichpool Crofts **1** 188
Leichpool Lane **1** 47
Leichpool Leys **1** 204
LEIRE **5** xiii, xv, 129
Leire Lane
(Ashby Parva) **5** 13
(Broughton Astley) **5** 38
(Dunton Bassett) **5** 83
Leire Mill **5** 130
Leire Rd **5** 91
Lenthill Fm **7** 157
Leopard's Head (P.H.) **3** 232
Lepers' Garden **1** 177
Leroe Close **1** 188
Leroes, The **1** 222
Lewin Bridge **3** 192
Lewin St. **1** 47
Lewin's Hook **4** 14
Lewin's Sq. **1** 47
Lewis's Almshouses **1** 97
Ley Fm **7** 9
Leys, The
(Anstey) **7** 3
(Barrow upon Soar) **3** 35
(Hathern) **7** 84
Leyslands, The **5** 32
Lichfield Tavern (P.H.) **6** 122
Life Guardsman (P.H.) **7** 198
Life Hill **4** 5
Lifehill Spinney **4** 5
Lilinge **5** xiii, 205
Lily Bank Cottage **7** 164
Lily Cottages **7** 79
Limby Hall **7** 211
Limby Hall Lane **7** 211
Lime Closes **1** 188
Lime Hole Plantation **3** 269
Lime Kiln (P.H.) **7** 37
Lime Kilns **1** 146
Lime Kilns Inn, The (P.H.) **6** 122
Lime Kilns, The **6** 124
Lime St. **2** 64
Lime Tree Cottage **5** 188
Limekiln Bridge **6** 124
Limekiln Spinney **3** 259
Limepit Fm **4** 129
Limes Fm **4** 63
Limes Fm, The **6** 227
Limes, The
(Blaby) **5** 32
(Ibstock) **6** 144
(Nailstone) **6** 182
(Ratcliffe Culey) **6** 330
(Syston) **3** 228
(Willoughby Waterleys) **5** 235
Linacre Grange **2** 278
Lincoln Gate **1** 47
Linden Ho. **5** 79
Linden Lane **6** 152
Linden Lodge **5** 39

LINDLEY **6** xii, 113
Lindley Grange **6** 110
Lindley Hall Fm **6** 110
Lindley Ho. **6** 110
Lindley Lodge **6** 110
Lindley Park **6** 110
Lindley Wood **6** 110
Lindridge **6** 77
Lindridge Fm **6** 26
Lindridge Hall Fm **6** 77
Lindridge Lane
  (Bagworth) **6** 26
  (Desford) **6** 77
Lindridge Wood **6** 77
Lineage Fm **6** 64
Ling Hill **7** 157
Lings Covert **2** 111
Lings Fm **2** 111
Lings Hill **2** 111
Linkfield Fm **7** 186
Links, The **6** 152
Linnage Ho. **6** 64
Lion (P.H.)
  (High Street) **1** 131
  (Market Harborough) **4** 173
  (St Peter's) **1** 131
Lion and Castle (P.H.) **4** 173
Lion and Dolphin (P.H.) **1** 131
Lion and Lamb (P.H.)
  (Gallowtree Gate) **1** 131
  (Lee St.) **1** 131
Lion Hotel (P.H.) **1** 131
Lion Yard **1** 172
Lionville **2** 210
Little Alton Fm **7** 180
Little Bagworth **6** 26
Little Beeby **3** 42
Little Belvoir **2** 166
Little Bones **5** 194
Little Bow Bridge **1** 74
LITTLE BOWDEN **4** 184
Little Bowden Fm **4** 185
Little Bowden Lodge Fm **4** 185
Little Burton **2** 64
Little Covert Fm **2** 42
Little Crown (P.H.) **1** 131
LITTLE DALBY **2** xii, 84
Little Dalby Lakes **2** 85
Little Dalby Lodge **2** 85
Little End **5** 50
Little Fields Fm **6** 127
Little Fox Covert **6** 26
Little Garendon **7** 195
Little Green Bridge **5** 104
Little Gunsel **3** 254
Little Haw **7** 195
Little Haw Lane **7** 196
Little Hill
  (Charley) **7** 57
  (Wigston Magna) **5** 224
Little Holme St. **1** 47
Little John **6** xiii, 177
Little Lane
  (Leire) **5** 130
  (Packington) **7** 286
Little Lane **1** 47
Little Ling Spinney **3** 181
Little London **2** 172
Little Low Woods Fm **7** 26
Little Lunnon **5** 84
Little Markfield **6** 177
Little Merrible Wood **4** 252
Little Mill Holme **1** 199
Little Moor **7** 128
Little Moor Lane **7** 128
Little North Bridge **1** 73
Little Orton **6** 318
Little Pitholme **1** 199
Little Rise Fm **7** 112
Little Shaw Lane **6** 177
Little Skeffington **3** 221
Little Snarestone **6** 268
Little Spinney **6** 305
LITTLE STRETTON **4** 159
Little Twycross **6** 308
Little Wigston **6** 12
LITTLETHORPE **5** xiv, 72
Littlethorpe Lodge **5** 73
LITTLEWORTH **7** x, 23
Lock Ho. **3** 61
Lock Ho., The **4** 133
Lockey Fm **6** 207

Lockhouse Spinney **4** 298
LOCKINGTON **7** xi, 103
Lockington Gorse **7** 103
Lockington Grange **7** 103
Lockington Grounds Fm **7** 103
Lockington Hall **7** 103
Lockington Park **7** 103
LOCKINGTON-HEMINGTON **7** 103
Lockwood Cottage **4** 147
LODDINGTON **3** 163
Loddington Hall **3** 163
Loddington Ho. **3** 163
Loddington Lane **3** 163
Loddington Lodge **3** 163
Loddington Mill **3** 163
Loddington Rd **3** 244
Loddington Reddish **3** 163
Lodge Cottage **5** 174
Lodge Farm Cottages **5** 91
Lodge Fm
(Allexton) **3** 4
(Atterton) **6** 326
(Billesdon) **4** 5
(Blaby) **5** 32
(Broughton Astley) **5** 39
(Cosby) **5** 67
(Dunton Bassett) **5** 84
(East Langton) **4** 38
(Fenny Drayton) **6** 329
(Frolesworth) **5** 91
(Husbands Bosworth) **4** 120
(Laughton) **4** 154
(Littlethorpe) **5** 73
(Mowsley) **4** 197
(Nailstone) **6** 182
(Nether Broughton) **2** 46
(Nevill Holt) **4** 204
(Rothley) **7** 186
(Scraptoft) **4** 229
(Sharnford) **6** 247
(Smeeton Westerby) **4** 246
(Stapleton) **6** 215
(Staunton Harold) **7** 208
(Stockerston) **4** 252
(Stoke Golding) **6** 276
(Sutton Cheney) **6** 288
(Sutton in the Elms) **5** 40
(Syston) **3** 228
(Theddingworth) **4** 269
(Thorpe Arnold) **2** 278
(Thurnby) **4** 278
(Walcote) **5** 149
(Wigston Magna) **5** 224
(Wigston Parva) **5** 232
(Willoughby Waterleys) **5** 235
Lodge Fm, The **6** 300
Lodge Mill Spinneys **5** 140
Lodge Plantations
(Cotesbach) **5** 76
(Twycross) **6** 308
Lodge Rd **7** 270
Lodge Spinney
(Husbands Bosworth) **4** 120
(Little Dalby) **2** 85
Lodge, The
(Barkestone) **2** 201
(Bitteswell (×3)) **5** 28
(Bottesford) **2** 24
(Burton Overy) **4** 21
(Earl Shilton) **6** 134
(Gilmorton) **5** 97
(Kibworth Harcourt) **4** 138
(King's Norton) **4** 142
(Laughton) **4** 154
(Little Stretton) **4** 159
(Long Clawson) **2** 90
(Lubenham) **4** 164
(Misterton) **5** 147
(Peckleton) **6** 207
(Rolleston) **4** 221
(Seagrave) **3** 207
(Thurnby) **4** 278
(Walcote) **5** 149
(Whetstone) **5** 213
(Wymondham) **2** 288
Lodge, The **3** 42
Logan St. **4** 172
Loggerheads (P.H.) **1** 132
London Lodge
(Twycross) **6** 308
(Walcote) **5** 149

London Rd
(Coalville) **7** 62
(Great Glen) **4** 80
(Kegworth) **7** 97
(Leicester) **1** 47
(Markfield) **6** 177
(Oadby) **5** 165
London Road **6** 118
London St. **3** 275
London Way **1** 47
Long Acre **4** 234
LONG CLAWSON **2** xii, 89
Long Clawson and Hose Station **2** 90
Long Clawson Bridge **2** 90
Longcliff Rd **7** 62
Long Covert **6** 241
Long Crofts **1** 188
Long Hedge Lane **7** 256
Long Holden **7** 118
Long Holme **1** 199
Long Lane
(Billesdon) **4** 5
(Great Easton) **4** 74
(Kegworth) **7** 97
(Leicester) **1** 48
(Owston) **4** 215
Long Mead **1** 199
Long Mere Fm **7** 118
Long Mere Lane **7** 118
Long Moor Fm **7** 181
Long Moor Spinney **7** 181
Long Plantation
(Illston) **4** 129
(Rolleston) **4** 222
Long Spinney
(Braunstone) **6** 45
(Burton Lazars) **2** 64
(Cotesbach) **5** 76
(Keythorpe) **3** 259
(Rothley) **7** 186
Long Spinneys **6** 207
Long St.
(Belton) **7** 26
(Stoney Stanton) **6** 283
(Wigston Magna) **5** 219
Long Walk
(Blaby) **5** 32
(Wistow) **4** 295
LONG WHATTON **7** xii, 111
Long Whatton Brook **7** 112
Long Whatton Mill **7** 112
Long Wood **7** 94
Longate Road **2** 172
Longcliff Cottage **7** 196
Longcliff Fm **7** 196
Longcliff Hill **2** 51
Longcliff Plantation **7** 196
Longcliffe Lodge Fm **7** 196
Longdale **7** 249
Longdale Cottage **7** 249
Longham Lodge **6** 226
Longhill Fm **7** 249
Longhill Plantation **7** 249
Longlands Fm **3** 192
Longore Bridge **2** 35
Longwood **7** 256
Lonsdale Hotel (P.H.) **7** 133
Looking Glass Pond **6** 166
Lord Aylesford's Covert **3** 111
Lord Bassett Arms (P.H.) **6** 227
Lord Durham (P.H.) **1** 132
Lord Lyon (P.H.) **3** 47
Lord Morton' s Covert **3** 173
Lord Nelson (P.H.) **6** 135
Lord Nelson (P.H.)
(Loughborough) **7** 133
(Melton Mowbray) **2** 177
(Tonge) **7** 41
Lord St. **1** 48
Lord Warden (P.H.) **2** 177
Lord Wilton's Gorse **3** 11
Lord's Fm **5** 140
Lord's Place, The **1** 154
Loseby Ho. **3** 86
Loseby Lane **1** xii, 48
Loudoun Arms (P.H.)
(Measham) **7** 264

(Wilson) **7** 43
LOUGHBOROUGH
7 x, xii, xiii, 125
Loughborough: unindexed modern street-names **7** 131
Loughborough lane **7** 130
Loughborough Meadows **7** 128
Loughborough Moors **7** 128
Loughborough Rd
(Birstall) **7** 29
(Quorndon) **7** 170
(Rothley) **7** 186
(Shepshed) **7** 196
(Swannington) **7** 211
(Thringstone) **7** 70
(Whitwick) **7** 73
Loundegat **2** 172
Lount **7** 206
Lount Fm **6** 201
Lount Rd **6** 201
Lount Wood **7** 208
Love Lane **6** 51
Lovers' Walk, The **6** 119
Loves Lane **5** 84
Lovett's Bridge **6** 255
Lovett's Bridge Cottages **6** 255
Low Pasture, The **1** 204
Low Spinney **5** 10
Low Woods **7** 26
Low Woods Fm **7** 26
Low Woods Lane **7** 26
Lowe's Spinney **7** 230
Lower Ambion Fm **6** 288
Lower Bawdon **7** 57
Lower Bond St. **6** 117
Lower Brookhill Fm **5** 174
Lower Broombriggs **7** 238
Lower Fields Fm **6** 288
Lower Grange **6** 177
Lower Grange Fm
(Hugglescote) **7** 67
(Old Dalby) **2** 51
Lower Hall Fm **2** 64
Lower King St. **1** 48
Lower Leesthorpe **2** 239
Lower Lodge **4** 164
Lower Mead **7** 17
Lower Pool **6** 305
Lower Rectory Fm **6** 11
LOWESBY **3** xii, xiii, xiv, 168
Lowesby Grange **3** 169
Lowesby Hall **3** 169
Lowesby Hall Fm **3** 169
Lowesby Park **3** 169
Lowesby Station **3** 169
Lowlands **7** 277
Lowlands Fm
(Cosby) **5** 67
(Oakthorpe) **7** 277
LUBBESTHORPE **6** xi, 160
Lubbesthorpe Brook
(Braunstone) **6** 45
(Lubbesthorpe) **6** 161
Lubcloud **7** 196
Lubcloud Fm **7** 196
LUBENHAM **4** xiii, 163
Lubenham Hill **4** 174
Lubenham Lodge **4** 164
Luke St. **1** 48
LUTTERWORTH
5 xi, xiii, xiv, xv, 137
Lutterworth: unindexed modern street-names **5** 141
Lutterworth Hall **5** 140
Lutterworth House **5** 140
Lutterworth Rd **1** 48
Lutterworth Rd
(Arnesby) **5** 5
(Aylestone) **5** 19
(Bitteswell) **5** 28
(Blaby) **5** 32
(Burbage) **6** 51
(Dunton Bassett) **5** 84
(Gilmorton) **5** 97
(Kimcote) **5** 113
(North Kilworth) **5** 156
(Shawell) **5** 183
(Swinford) **5** 201
(Ullesthorpe) **5** 206
(Walcote) **5** 149

Lutterworth Road **6** 119
Lychgate Lane
(Aston Flamville) **6** 22
(Burbage) **6** 51
Lynden Lea **6** 124
Lyndene Lodge **4** 120
Lyndon Lodge **4** 51
Lynwood **7** 15

Mabbs's Orchard **1** 177
Macauley Rd **7** 186
Madras School **1** 113
Magazine (P.H.) **1** 132
Magazine Gate **1** 99
Magpie and Crown (P.H.) **1** 132
Maida Ho. **3** 73
Maiden's Head (P.H.) **1** 132
Main Rd
(Ab Kettleby) **2** 158
(Cotesbach) **5** 76
(Dadlington) **6** 291
Main St.
(Albert Village) **7** 20
(Ashby Parva) **5** 13
(Barkby) **3** 21
(Barlestone) **6** 40
(Beeby) **3** 42
(Blackfordby) **7** 15
(Botcheston) **6** 79
(Bruntingthorpe) **5** 50
(Burton Overy) **4** 21
(Carlton) **6** 64
(Cold Newton) **3** 173
(Coleorton) **7** 79
(Congerstone) **6** 241
(Cosby) **5** 68
(Drayton) **4** 34
(Dunton Bassett) **5** 84
(Evington) **4** 44
(Fleckney) **4** 51
(Foxton) **4** 55
(Frolesworth) **5** 91
(Gilmorton) **5** 97
(Glenfield) **6** 93
(Great Glen) **4** 80
(Heather) **6** 104
(Higham on the Hill) **6** 110
(Houghton) **4** 110
(Humberstone) **3** 134
(Huncote) **6** 139
(Hungarton) **3** 144
(Illston) **4** 129
(Keyham) **3** 158
(Kibworth Harcourt) **4** 138
(Kilby) **5** 108
(Kimcote) **5** 113
(Kirby Bellars) **3** 86
(Kirby Muxloe) **6** 152
(Kirkby Mallory) **6** 211
(Laughton) **4** 154
(Leire) **5** 130
(Lubenham) **4** 164
(Market Bosworth) **6** 166
(Markfield) **6** 177
(Medbourne) **4** 188
(Mowsley) **4** 197
(Nailstone) **6** 182
(Netherseal) **7** 270
(Newbold Verdon) **6** 194
(Newton Burgoland) **7** 224
(Newtown Linford) **7** 157
(Normanton le Heath) **6** 198
(Oakthorpe) **7** 277
(Osgathorpe) **7** 164
(Owston) **4** 215
(Peatling Magna) **5** 174
(Peatling Parva) **5** 178
(Primethorpe) **5** 41
(Ratby) **6** 222
(Saxelby) **3** 108
(Scraptoft) **4** 229
(Shearsby) **5** 188
(Skeffington) **3** 221
(Snarestone) **6** 268
(Stanton under Bardon) **6** 273
(Stapleton) **6** 215
(Stoke Golding) **6** 276
(Sutton Cheney) **6** 288
(Swannington) **7** 211
(Swepstone) **7** 219
(Swithland) **7** 228
(Thornton) **6** 27

(Thringstone) **7** 70
(Thurlaston) **6** 300
(Thurnby) **4** 278
(Tilton) **3** 244
(Ullesthorpe) **5** 206
(Walton) **5** 114
(Willoughby Waterleys) **5** 235
(Worthington) **7** 256
Mains Lane **4** 21
Major's Close **1** 189
Major's Garden **1** 177
Mallory Park **6** 211
Malson's Close **1** 189
Malt Mill Bank **6** 127
Malt Mill, The **2** 180
Malt Shovel **5** 194
Malt Shovel (P.H.)
(Carlton) **6** 64
(Worthington) **7** 256
Malt Shovel (P.H.)
(Ashby de la Zouch) **7** 11
(Ashby Folville) **3** 100
(Church Gate) **1** 132
(Donisthorpe) **7** 280
(Frog Island) **1** 132
(Gaddesby) **3** 95
(Great Dalby) **2** 78
(Melton Mowbray) **2** 177
(South Croxton) **3** 73
Malt Shovel Inn, The **3** 21
Malthouse Cottages **7** 208
Mammoth St. **7** 62
Man within Compass (P.H.) **7** 74
Mancetter **6** xi
Manduessedum **6** *xi*
Manor Ash **7** 9
Manor Ash Fm **7** 9
Manor Cottage **5** 58
Manor Cottages **4** 234
Manor Farm Cottages
(Thurlaston) **6** 300
(Upton) **6** 262
Manor Fm
(Anstey) **7** 3
(Arnesby (×2)) **5** 5
(Asfordby) **3** 11
(Ashby Magna) **5** 10
(Ashby Parva) **5** 13
(Bagworth) **6** 26
(Barkby Thorpe) **3** 29
(Barkestone) **2** 201
(Barton in the Beans) **6** 237
(Barwell) **6** 128
(Beeby) **3** 42
(Belton) **7** 26
(Blaston) **4** 14
(Botcheston) **6** 79
(Braunstone) **6** 45
(Broughton Astley) **5** 39
(Burton on the Wolds) **3** 55
(Cadeby) **6** 59
(Chadwell) **2** 218
(Chilcote) **7** 261
(Claybrooke Magna) **5** 58
(Cold Overton) **4** 152
(Cosby) **5** 67
(Cotes) **3** 70
(Dadlington) **6** 291
(Desford) **6** 73
(Drayton) **4** 34
(Frolesworth) **5** 91
(Glenfield) **6** 93
(Goadby) **4** 70
(Holwell) **2** 163
(Humberstone) **3** 134
(Illston) **4** 129
(Kimcote) **5** 113
(Kirkby Mallory) **6** 211
(Knossington) **4** 147
(Laughton) **4** 154
(Loddington) **3** 164
(Marefield) **4** 170
(Mowsley) **4** 197
(Nailstone) **6** 182
(Newbold Verdon) **6** 194
(Newton Burgoland) **7** 224
(Normanton le Heath) **6** 198
(Oadby) **5** 165
(Owston) **4** 215
(Peatling Magna) **5** 174
(Peckleton) **6** 207
(Queniborough) **3** 183

(Ratcliffe Culey) **6** 330
(Saddington) **4** 224
(Shangton) **4** 234
(Sheepy Parva) **6** 255
(Sketchley) **6** 57
(Snarestone) **6** 268
(Stanton under Bardon) **6** 273
(Stapleton) **6** 215
(Stockerston) **4** 252
(Stoney Stanton) **6** 283
(Swannington) **7** 211
(Swepstone) **7** 219
(Thorpe Langton) **4** 276
(Thurcaston) **7** 230
(Thurlaston) **6** 300
(Tugby) **3** 255
(Upton) **6** 262
(Waltham on the Wolds) **2** 272
(Walton on the Wolds) **3** 269
(Wanlip) **7** 242
(Wellsborough) **6** 266
(Wigston Parva) **5** 224
(Willoughby Waterleys) **5** 235
(Worthington) **7** 256
(Wykin) **6** 137
Manor Ho.
(Ab Kettleby) **2** 158
(Appleby) **6** 10
(Ashby Folville) **3** 100
(Aston Flamville) **6** 22
(Aylestone) **5** 19
(Barkby) **3** 21
(Barlestone) **6** 40
(Beeby) **3** 42
(Bitteswell) **5** 28
(Blaston) **4** 14
(Bruntingthorpe) **5** 50
(Burrough on the Hill) **2** 232
(Cold Newton) **3** 173
(Cosby) **5** 68
(Coston) **2** 152
(Cotesbach) **5** 76
(Dadlington) **6** 291
(Dunton Bassett) **5** 84
(East Norton) **3** 178
(Easthorpe) **2** 33
(Edmondthorpe) **2** 298
(Foxton) **4** 55
(Gaddesby) **3** 95
(Galby) **4** 63
(Goadby) **4** 70
(Great Dalby) **2** 78
(Heather) **6** 104
(Illston) **4** 129
(Isley cum Langley) **7** 94
(Kegworth) **7** 97
(Kibworth Harcourt) **4** 138
(Knossington) **4** 147
(Lubenham) **4** 164
(Melton Mowbray) **2** 178
(Newton Harcourt) **4** 298
(Normanton le Heath) **6** 198
(Norton juxta Twycross) **6** 313
(Overseal) **7** 286
(Packington) **7** 286
(Peckleton) **6** 207
(Pickwell) **2** 241
(Plungar) **2** 205
(Rearsby) **3** 198
(Rotherby) **3** 122
(Saxby) **2** 135
(Saxelby) **3** 108
(Scalford) **2** 210
(Sheepy Parva) **6** 255
(South Kilworth) **5** 194
(Sproxton) **2** 246
(Stonesby) **2** 256
(Stonton Wyville) **4** 255
(Thurnby) **4** 278
(Tilton) **3** 244
(Tur Langton) **4** 286
(Twyford) **3** 262
(Ullesthorpe) **5** 206
(Welham) **4** 290
(Wellsborough) **6** 266
(Wigston Magna) **5** 222
(Wymeswold) **3** 275
(Wymondham) **2** 288
Manor Holt **7** 186
Manor House **6** 122

Manor House Fm
(Burton Overy) **4** 21
(Horninghold) **4** 106
(King's Norton) **4** 142
(Marefield) **4** 170
(Osgathorpe) **7** 164
Manor Lodge Fm
(Burton on the Wolds) **3** 55
(Dadlington) **6** 291
(Stapleton) **6** 215
Manor Rd
(Desford) **6** 73
(Donington le Heath) **7** 64
(Great Bowden) **4** 178
(Loughborough) **7** 132
(Medbourne) **4** 188
(Oadby) **5** 165
(Thurmaston) **3** 238
Manor, The
(Glen Parva) **5** 104
(Ibstock) **6** 144
(Little Stretton) **4** 159
(Long Clawson) **2** 90
(Norton juxta Twycross) **6** 312
(Thrussington) **3** 232
Manorhouse Fm **7** 64
Mansell Barn **2** 35
Mansfield St. **1** xv, 48
Mansfield Villa **6** 159
Mansfield's Head (P.H.) **1** 132
Mansion Street **6** 119
Mantle Lane **7** 61
Many Lees Fm **6** 139
Many Lees Lodge **6** 139
Maplewell
(Coalville) **7** 61
(Woodhouse) **7** 247
Maplewell Fm **7** 249
Maplewell Hall **7** 249
Marble Sq. **1** 48
Marble St. **1** 48
March Covert **7** 103
March Ho. **2** 78
Marclose, The **1** 189
MAREFIELD **4** 169
Marefield Lane
(Lowesby) **3** 169
(Tilton) **3** 244
(Twyford) **3** 262
Marefield Lodge **4** 219
Margaret St. **7** 62
MARKET BOSWORTH **6** xi, xii, xiii, 165
Market Bosworth Mill **6** 166
MARKET HARBOROUGH **4** xiii, xiv, 171
Market Harborough: unindexed modern street-names **4** 173
Market Harborough Station **4** 174
Market Place
(Kegworth) **7** 97
(Leicester) **1** 115
(Loughborough) **7** 128
(Market Bosworth) **6** 167
(Market Harborough) **4** 174
(Melton Mowbray) **2** 169
(Shepshed) **7** 196
Market place **7** 10
Market Place, The **6** 119
Market St.
(Ashby de la Zouch) **7** 9
(Bottesford) **2** 24
(Castle Donington) **7** 48
(Leicester) **1** 48
(Loughborough) **7** 128
(Lutterworth) **5** 140
MARKFIELD **6** xiii, 175
Markfield Hospital **6** 177
Markfield Kennels **6** 177
Markfield Knoll **6** 177
Markfield Lane
(Botcheston) **6** 79
(Newton Linford) **7** 157
(Ratby) **6** 222
(Thornton) **6** 27
Markfield Lodge **6** 177
Markfield Quarry **6** 177
Markfield Shaws **6** 177
Markham Ho. **3** 264
Marl Pit **1** 147

Marl Pit Fm **6** 134
Marlborough St. **1** 48
Marlborough's Head (P.H.) **1** 132
Marquis of Anglesey (P.H.) **7** 29
Marquis of Granby (P.H.) **7** 74
Marquis of Granby (P.H.)
(Aylestone) **5** 19
(Birstall) **7** 29
(Castle St.) **1** 132
(Great Easton) **4** 74
(Harby) **2** 95
(Hinckley) **6** 122
(London Rd) **1** 132
(Loughborough) **7** 133
(Melton Mowbray) **2** 177
Marquis of Hastings (P.H.) **1** 133
Marquis of Wellington (P.H.) **1** 133
Marquis St. **1** xiv, 49
Marriott's Bridge **2** 99
Marriott's Spinney **2** 51
Marriott's Wood **3** 108
Marsden Lane **5** 19
Marsh Drive **4** 138
Marsh Fm **7** 152
Marsh Hook Meadow **1** 200
Marsh Lane **1** xii, 49
Marsh, The **1** 204
Marshdale Fm **3** 61
Marston Close **6** 283
Marston Rd
(Croft) **6** 67
(Humberstone) **3** 134
(Lubenham) **4** 164
Marston's Closes **1** 189
Marston's Mill **1** 150
Marston's Tan Yard **1** 146
Martinshaw Wood **6** 222
Mary Holme **1** 200
Mary Lane **1** 49
Mary Lane **2** 250
Mary's Meadow **4** 80
Mason Fm **4** 133
Masons' Arms (P.H.)
(Donisthorpe) **7** 280
(South Croxton) **3** 73
(York Rd) **1** 133
Massingham **3** 228
Mausoleum, The **2** 8
Mawbrook Fm **2** 210
Mawbrook Lodge **2** 210
Mawby's Lane **6** 10
May's Fm **6** 283
Maycroft **3** 35
Mayfield **7** 9
Maynard Arms (P.H.) **6** 26
Mayor's Hall Lane **1** xiv, 49
Meadow Close **1** 189
Meadow Fm
(Coalville) **7** 61
(Thorpe Langton) **4** 276
Meadow Lane
(Birstall) **7** 29
(Coalville) **7** 61
(Loughborough) **7** 128
(Syston) **3** 228
Meadow Rd **7** 249
Meadow Row **6** 144
Meadow View Fm **3** 35
Meadowcroft **2** 210
Meadows Lane **2** 95
Meadows, The
(Fleckney) **4** 51
(Shepshed) **7** 196
Measham **6** xiii
MEASHAM **7** x, 263
Measham Colliery Siding **7** 264
Measham Fields Fm **7** 264
Measham Hall **7** 264
Measham Ho. **7** 264
Measham Lodge **7** 264
Measham Rd
(Donisthorpe) **7** 280
(Snarestone) **6** 268
(Willesley) **7** 18
MEDBOURNE **4** xi, xii, xiv, 187
Medbourne Brook **4** 188
Medbourne Grange **4** 188
Medbourne Manor **4** 188
Medbourne Rd
(Drayton) **4** 34
(Hallaton) **4** 96
(Slawston) **4** 240

Meer Bridge
(Measham) **7** 264
(Oakthorpe) **7** 277
Meer Lane **2** 172
Meeting House Lane **1** 49
Melbourne Lane **7** 37
Melbourne Lodge
(Staunton Harold) **7** 208
(Walcote) **5** 149
Melbourne Lodge Plantation **7** 208
Melbourne Rd **7** 64
Melbourne St. **7** 62
Melbourne street **2** 172
Melton Brook
(Belgrave) **3** 47
(Humberstone) **3** 134
Melton Hospital **2** 176
MELTON MOWBRAY **2** xi, xii, xiii, 168
Melton Mowbray: unindexed modern street-names **2** 173
Melton Rd
(Asfordby) **3** 11
(Barrow upon Soar) **3** 35
(East Langton) **4** 38
(Lowesby) **3** 169
(Scalford) **2** 210
(Skeffington) **3** 221
(Syston) **3** 228
(Tilton) **3** 244
(Tur Langton) **4** 286
Melton Spinney **2** 181
Melton Spinney Fm **2** 181
Mercers Arms (P.H.) **6** 122
Mercia **6** xii
Mere Barn **5** 13
Mere Cottages **7** 270
Mere Fm **4** 110
Mere Hill **3** 181
Mere Hill Cottages **3** 181
Mere Hill Spinney **3** 181
Mere Rd
(Evington) **4** 44
(Peatling Magna) **5** 174
(Stretton Magna) **4** 264
(Willoughby Waterleys) **5** 235
Mere, The **7** 270
Merevale Abbey **6** xiv
Merevale Close **1** 189
Mermaid (P.H.) **4** 173
Merrifield **6** 51
Merril Grange **7** 26
Merry Lees **6** 26
Merry Lees Rd **6** 26
Merrylees Rd **6** 194
Merrymans **7** 277
Merrymead **5** 224
Merton Fm **3** 21
Messenger's Barn
(Sapcote) **6** 227
(Sutton in the Elms) **5** 40
Messenger's Lodge **3** 95
Metcalf St. **1** 49
Methodist Chapel
(Belgrave) **3** 47
(Buckminster) **2** 55
(Cosby) **5** 68
(Donisthorpe) **7** 280
(Goadby Marwood) **2** 126
(Grimston) **3** 106
(Harby) **2** 95
(Holwell) **2** 163
(Muston) **2** 35
(Queniborough) **3** 183
(Rearsby) **3** 198
(Stathern) **2** 261
(Stonesby) **2** 256
(Thurmaston) **3** 238
(Tilton) **3** 244
(Wymeswold) **3** 275
(Wymondham) **2** 288
Methodist Chapel **2** 175
Methodist Church
(Burbage) **6** 51
(Ibstock) **6** 144
(Leire) **5** 130
(Netherseal) **7** 270
(Stapleton) **6** 215
(Stoney Stanton) **6** 283
(Thornton) **6** 27
(Willoughby Waterleys) **5** 235
(Worthington) **7** 256

Mettam's Spinney **6** 128
Meynell's Gorse **6** 45
Michael Spinney **5** 209
Mickle Croft **1** 189
Mickle Hill **6** 22
Mickle Hill Fm **6** 22
Mickle Hill Spinney **6** 22
Mickle Pitholme **1** 200
Micklin Fm **7** 26
Middle Field
(South Fields) **1** 212
(St Margaret's Fields) **1** 210
(West Fields) **1** 213
Middle Fm
(Misterton) **5** 147
(Shawell) **5** 183
(Walton on the Wolds) **3** 269
Middle Merril Grange **7** 26
Middle Park **3** 259
Middle Plantation **3** 269
Middle Poultney Fm **5** 149
Middle St. **1** 49
Middle St. **4** 55
Middlefield **6** 124
Middlefield Lane **6** 117
Middlefield Place **6** 124
Middlesdale **2** 8
Middlestile Bridge **2** 24
Midland Railway (P.H.) **3** 229
Midland St. **1** 49
Mile House Fm **6** 124
Miles Ford **6** 295
Milk Maid (P.H.) **1** 133
Milking Pens Spinney **4** 210
Mill Bank **6** 227
Mill Bank road **7** 10
Mill Close **7** 196
Mill Cottage **3** 275
Mill Covert **6** 167
Mill Dam Spinney **5** 178
Mill Field Farm **6** 45
Mill Fm
(Ashby Folville) **3** 100
(Broughton Astley) **5** 39
(Husbands Bosworth) **4** 120
(Lutterworth) **5** 140
(Markfield) **6** 177
(Medbourne) **4** 188
(Netherseal) **7** 270
(Odstone) **6** 244
(Ravenstone) **7** 181
(Slawston) **4** 240
(Stonton Wyville) **4** 255
Mill Hill
(Enderby) **6** 87
(Hinckley) **6** 124
(Laughton) **4** 154
(Lubenham) **4** 164
(Market Harborough) **4** 174
(Stoney Stanton) **6** 283
(Wyfordby) **2** 144
Mill Hill Fm
(Hinckley) **6** 123
(Ibstock) **6** 144
Mill Hill Lane **1** 49
Mill Hill Rd **5** 5
Mill Hill Spinney **2** 85
Mill Ho.
(Arnesby) **5** 5
(Asfordby) **3** 11
(Barkby) **3** 21
(Billesdon) **4** 5
(Gilmorton) **5** 97
(Huncote) **6** 139
(Quorndon) **7** 170
(Scalford) **2** 210
(Stathern) **2** 261
(Tilton) **3** 244
(Ullesthorpe) **5** 188
(Ulverscroft) **7** 238
Mill Holme **1** 200
Mill House Fm
(Thurcaston) **7** 230
(Worthington) **7** 256
Mill House, The **7** 152
Mill Lane
(Asfordby) **3** 11
(Barrow upon Soar) **3** 35
(Belton) **7** 26
(Blaby) **5** 33
(Bottesford) **2** 24
(Earl Shilton) **6** 134

(Enderby) **6** 87
(Gilmorton) **5** 97
(Heather) **6** 104
(Kegworth) **7** 97
(Kibworth Beauchamp) **4** 133
(Leicester) **1** 49
(Long Whatton) **7** 112
(Newbold Verdon) **6** 194
(Sharnford) **6** 247
(Shearsby) **5** 188
(Shenton) **6** 295
(Smeeton Westerby) **4** 246
(Thornton) **6** 27
(Thurmaston) **3** 238
Mill Lane
(Ab Kettleby) **2** 158
(Ashby de la Zouch) **7** 10
(Wigston Magna) **5** 220
Mill Lane Fm **5** 33
Mill Lane Road **2** 172
Mill Mound **4** 174
Mill Pond
(Easthorpe) **2** 33
(Market Bosworth) **6** 167
Mill Rd
(Thurcaston) **7** 230
(Ullesthorpe) **5** 206
(Woodhouse) **7** 249
Mill Spinney
(Quorndon) **7** 170
(Swithland) **7** 228
Mill St.
(Melton Mowbray) **2** 169
(Welford Rd) **1** 49
Mill St. **1** 49
Mill street **7** 130
Mill View **7** 196
Mill View **6** 122
Mill Walk **6** 119
Mill Way **1** 49
Mill, The
(Belton) **7** 26
(Broughton Astley) **5** 39
(Harby) **2** 95
(Thurmaston) **3** 238
Millerdale **4** 80
Millfield **6** 161
Millfield Clump **4** 210
Millfield Fm **6** 276
Mills' yard **7** 130
Millstone (P.H.) **1** 133
Millstone Lane
(Leicester) **1** xii, 50
(Syston) **3** 228
Milord's Fm **5** 140
Milton St. **1** 50
Minorca Fm **7** 219
Mires, The **7** 57
Miss Mason's Almshouses **1** 97
Mission Hall **5** 114
Miste, The **2** 210
MISTERTON **5** xiii, 147
Misterton Gorse **5** 147
Misterton Grange **5** 147
Misterton Hall **5** 147
Mitchell's Spring Fm **7** 112
Mitre (P.H.) **1** 133
Mitre and Keys (P.H.) **1** 133
Moat Fm **7** 128
Moat Hill **3** 70
Moat Hill Spinney **3** 70
Moat Ho.
(Appleby Parva) **6** 10
(Loughborough) **7** 128
Moat Orchard **1** 177
Moat Spinney **5** 109
Moat St. **5** 219
Moat Yard **1** 172
Moats, The
(South Kilworth) **5** 194
(Stoke Golding) **6** 276
Model Fm
(Catthorpe) **5** 54
(Kimcote) **5** 113
(Loughborough) **7** 128
(Oadby) **5** 165
(Tugby) **3** 255
Model School **1** 113
Moira **6** xiii
MOIRA **7** 23
Moira Arms (P.H.) **7** 23
Moira Arms Inn (P.H.) **7** 50

Moira Baths **7** 23
Moira Coal Wharf **6** 124
Moira Colliery **7** 23
Moira Rd
(Ashby de la Zouch) **7** 9
(Shellbrook) **7** 19
Moira St. **7** 128
Moira Station **7** 23
Mole Hill Fm **7** 97
Moll's Lane **6** 160
Money Hill
(Ashby de la Zouch) **7** 9
(Donisthorpe) **7** 280
Money Hill Fm **7** 9
Monk's Grave **3** 153
Montague Pl. **1** 50
Moor Barn Grange **6** 256
Moor Fm
(Coleorton) **7** 79
(Loughborough) **7** 128
Moor Hill
(East Norton) **3** 178
(Hallaton) **4** 96
Moor Hill Fm **4** 96
Moor Hill Spinneys **3** 259
Moor Holme **1** 200
Moor Lane
(Coleorton) **7** 79
(Loughborough) **7** 128
(Stathern) **2** 261
(Swannington) **7** 211
(Tonge) **7** 41
Moor Lane Bridge **7** 128
Moor Lane Fm **7** 128
Moor Leys Lane **2** 272
Moorbank Fm **4** 80
Moorbarns **5** 140
Moorbarns Fm **5** 140
Moorbarns Lane **5** 140
Moore Spinney **7** 228
Moore's Arms (P.H.)
(Appleby) **6** 10
(Norton juxta Twycross) **6** 313
Moore's Close **1** 189
Moore's Covert **6** 308
Moore's Lane **6** 87
Moorfield Place **7** 196
Moorfields Fm **7** 170
Moorgate Ave **7** 30
Moors, The
(Kegworth) **7** 97
(Medbourne) **4** 188
Morledge St. **1** 50
Morley Fm **7** 196
Morton's Close **1** 189
Moscow Lane **7** 196
Moseley's Plantation **7** 9
Moss Fm **4** 133
Mot, The **4** 88
Mother Head **1** 225
Moult Hill **7** 57
Mount Cottage, The **4** 174
Mount Ho. **7** 12
Mount Pleasant
(Barwell) **6** 128
(Burton Overy) **4** 21
(Castle Donington) **7** 48
(Claybrooke Magna) **5** 58
(Hose) **2** 100
(Leicester Forest West) **6** 159
(Leire) **5** 130
(Melton Mowbray) **2** 181
(Swannington) **7** 211
(Swepstone) **7** 219
(Wymondham) **2** 288
Mount Pleasant **1** 50
Mount Pleasant Barn **7** 270
Mount Pleasant Fm **3** 207
Mount Pleasant Lane **7** 270
Mount Pleasant Mill **1** 150
Mount Rd **5** 68
Mount St Bernard Abbey **7** xiii, 57
Mount, The
(Billesdon) **4** 5
(Fenny Drayton) **6** 329
(Great Glen) **4** 80
(Market Harborough) **4** 174
(Melton Mowbray) **2** 181
(Scraptoft) **4** 229
(Shawell) **5** 183
(Wistow) **4** 295
MOUNTSORREL **7** xii, 151

Mountsorrel: unindexed
modern street-names **7** 152
Mountsorrel Cottages **6** 283
Mountsorrel Lane
(Rothley) **7** 186
(Sileby) **3** 216
Mouse lane **5** 220
MOWSLEY **4** xi, 197
Mowsley End **5** 221
Mowsley Hills **4** 197
Mowsley Hills Fm **4** 197
Mowsley Lane **5** 114
Mowsley Lodge **4** 197
Mowsley Rd
(Husbands Bosworth) **4** 120
(Saddington) **4** 224
(Theddingworth) **4** 269
Moxon's Plantation **7** 289
Moyles Court Ho. **7** 26
Mr John Robinsons House **6** 122
Muckle Gate Lane **3** 207
Muckleborough Fm **4** 106
Muckleborough Lodge **4** 106
Muckleborough Lodge Fm **4** 106
Muckleborough Plantation **4** 106
Mucklin Lodge **7** 249
Mucklin Wood **7** 249
Mulberry Fd **6** 276
Munday Arms (P.H.) **7** 134
Munt, The **4** 138
Murfin's yard **7** 130
Mushill Fm **3** 275
Mushill Lane **3** 275
Mushroom Fm **4** 107
Mushroom Lane **7** 20
Musson Gap **2** 35
MUSTON **2** 35
Muston Gorse **2** 35
Muston Gorse Bridge **2** 35
Muston Gorse Covert **2** 35
Muston Gorse Fm **2** 35
Muston Gorse Wharf **2** 35
Mythe Cottage **6** 330
Mythe Lane **6** 330
Mythe, The **6** 258
Nag's Head (P.H.)
(Castle Donington) **7** 50
(Enderby) **6** 87
(Glenfield) **6** 93
(Market Harborough) **4** 173
(Stapleton) **6** 215
Nag's Head (P.H.)
(Granby St.) **1** 133
(Great Dalby) **2** 78
(Harby) **2** 95
(Highcross St.) **1** 133
(Loughborough) **7** 134
(Mountsorrel) **7** 152
(Northgate St.) **1** 133
(Overseal) **7** 283
(Saltby) **2** 251
Nag's Head and Star (P.H.) **1** 133
NAILSTONE **6** xi, 181
Nailstone Gorse **6** 182
Nailstone Grange **6** 182
Nailstone Wiggs **6** 182
Nailstone Wiggs Fm **6** 183
Nan Hill **7** 249
NANEBY **6** 58
Naneby Fm **6** 59
Naneby Hall Fm **6** 59
NANPANTAN **7** xiii, 145
Nanpantan Fm **7** 147
Nanpantan Hall **7** 147
Nanpantan Hill **7** 147
Nanpantan Ho. **7** 147
Napier Ho. **3** 95
NARBOROUGH **6** 186
Narborough: unindexed
modern street-names **6** 187
Narborough Bogs **6** 187
Narborough Hall **6** 187
Narborough Inn **6** 187
Narborough Park **6** 187
Narborough Rd
(Cosby) **5** 68
(Huncote) **6** 139
(Leicester) **1** 50
Narborough Wood **6** 161
Narrow Lane
(Aylestone) **5** 19

(Hathern) **7** 84
(Wymeswold) **3** 275
National School **1** 113
Navigation (P.H.) **5** 222
Navigation (P.H.)
(Belgrave Rd) **1** 133
(Kibworth Harcourt) **4** 139
Navigation Bridge **1** 74
Navigation Inn
(Barrow upon Soar) **3** 36
(Kegworth) **7** 97
(Moira) **7** 23
Navigation Inn (P.H.) **7** 11
Navigation St.
(Leicester) **1** xv, 50
(Measham) **7** 264
Neale St. **1** 50
Neale's Fm **6** 124
Near Coton **6** 165
Near Meadow **1** 200
Neate Drift, *the* **2** 172
Needle Gate **1** 51
Needless Inn (P.H.) **7** 134
Nelson (P.H.)
(Belgrave) **3** 47
(Humberstone Rd) **1** 133
Nelson Pl. **1** 51
Nelson St. **4** 172
Nelson St.
(Humberstone Gate) **1** xiv, 51
(London Rd) **1** xiv, 51
Nene House Fm **5** 235
Neptune (P.H.)
(Duns Lane) **1** 133
(Loughborough) **7** 134
NETHER BROUGHTON **2** xiii, 45
Nether Cottages **4** 210
Nether Court Fm **4** 5
Nether End **2** 78
Nether Field **1** 210
Nether Hall
(Keyham) **3** 158
(North Kilworth) **5** 156
(Scraptoft) **4** 229
Nether Hall Fm
(Scalford) **2** 210
(Scraptoft) **4** 229
Nethercote **7** 224
Nethercote Fm **7** 224
Netherfield **3** 35
Netherfield Barn **7** 97
Netherfield Lane **7** 107
NETHERSEAL **7** 268
Netherseal Hall **7** 270
Netherseal Old Hall **7** 270
Nettleham Fm **3** 255
Neugate **5** 220
Nevill Arms (P.H.) **4** 188
NEVILL HOLT **4** xii, xiii, 202
Nevill Holt Fm **4** 204
Nevill Holt Quarry **4** 204
Nevill Holt Rd **4** 34
New Barn **6** 288
New Bond St. **1** 51
New Bridge
(Belgrave) **3** 47
(Kirby Muxloe) **6** 152
New Bridge **1** 75
New Bridge Fm **6** 152
New Bridge St. **1** 51
New Cottages
(Foston) **5** 109
(Skeffington) **3** 221
New Covert
(Baggrave) **3** 151
(Chilcote) **7** 261
(Cotesbach) **5** 76
(Hoton) **3** 131
(Melton Mowbray) **2** 180
(South Croxton) **3** 73
(South Kilworth) **5** 194
New Crofts **1** 189
New Crown (P.H.) **4** 21
New Cut **1** 225
New Fm
(Burton on the Wolds) **3** 55
(Cadeby) **6** 59
(Stanton under Bardon) **6** 273

New Found Pool **1** 222
New Gravel Hill Spinney **5** 209
New Greyhound **4** 5
New Guadaloupe **2** 189
New Hall
(Leicester) **1** 143
(Queniborough) **3** 183
New Haven **6** 159
New Hays Ho. **6** 27
New Ho. **6** 161
New House Fm
(Dadlington) **6** 291
(Lubbesthorpe) **6** 161
(Nailstone) **6** 183
New Humberstone **3** 134
New Inn
(Enderby) **6** 88
(Oadby) **5** 165
New Inn
(Broughton Astley) **5** 39
(Coleorton) **7** 79
(Cosby) **5** 68
(Noseley) **4** 210
New Inn (P.H.)
(Belgrave Gate) **1** 133
(Belgrave) **3** 47
(Burbage) **6** 52
(Castle Donington) **7** 50
(Highcross St.) **1** 133
(Hinckley) **6** 122
(Loughborough) **7** 134
(Rolleston) **4** 222
(Sharnford) **6** 247
(Snibstone) **7** 182
(Whitwick) **7** 74
New Inn Fm **5** 188
New Inn Lane **4** 129
New Lane **3** 269
New Lane **1** 51
New Ingarsby **3** 153
New Lodge **4** 14
New Lodge Fm **3** 47
New Orchard **1** 178
New Park
(Melton Mowbray) **2** 181
(Noseley) **4** 210
New Park of Bird's Nest, The **1** xiii, 223
New Parks Fm **6** 211
New Parliament St. **1** 51
New Plantation
(Castle Donington) **7** 48
(Freeby) **2** 129
(Glenfield) **6** 93
(Markfield) **6** 177
(Quorndon) **7** 170
(Skeffington) **3** 221
(Staunton Harold) **7** 208
(Ulverscroft) **7** 238
New Plough Hotel (P.H.) **6** 122
New Queniborough **3** 183
New Quorndon **7** 170
New Rd
(Appleby) **6** 10
(Burbage) **6** 51
(Burton Lazars) **2** 64
(Coalville) **7** 62
(Coleorton) **7** 79
(Leicester) **1** 51
New Rolleston **4** 222
New Row **1** 51
New Row Cottages **2** 158
New Southfield Spinney **4** 210
New Spinney
(Enderby) **6** 88
(Thurlaston) **6** 305
New St.
(Leicester) **1** 51
(Measham) **7** 264
(Oadby) **5** 165
(Scalford) **2** 210
New Street
(Hinckley) **6** 119
(Melton Mowbray) **2** 172
New Swannington **7** 73
New Town **4** 133
New Town Arms (P.H.) **1** 133
New Walk **1** xiv, 143
New Wood **7** 118
New York **3** 22
New York Fm **3** 207
New York Spinney **4** 204

New Zealand Lane **3** 183
Newarke College **1** 100
Newarke Gate **1** 99
Newarke Grange, The **1** 180
Newarke Infants' School **1** 113
Newarke Lane **1** 51
Newarke Mills, The **1** 150
Newarke St. **1** 51
Newarke Tavern (P.H.) **1** 133
Newarke Tce **1** 51
Newarke, The **1** 99
Newberry's Orchard **1** 178
NEWBOLD **4** 218
Newbold **7** 254
Newbold Fm
(Newbold) **4** 219
(Worthington) **7** 256
NEWBOLD FOLVILLE **3** 99
Newbold Grange Fm **4** 219
Newbold Heath **6** 194
Newbold Lane
(Kirkby Mallory) **6** 211
(Worthington) **7** 256
Newbold Rd
(Barlestone) **6** 40
(Desford) **6** 73
(Owston) **4** 215
Newbold Spinney
(Newbold Verdon) **6** 194
(Worthington) **7** 256
NEWBOLD VERDON **6** xi, 193
Newcombe's Parlour **2** 90
Newfield Fm **7** 23
Newfields **7** 23
New Fm **5** 174
Newfoundland Lodge **3** 11
Newgate End **5** 221
Newhall Park **6** 299
Newholme **2** 205
Newhouse Grange **6** 257
Newlands **7** 15
Newlands, The **7** 9
Newpit Lane **6** 73
Newport Lodge **2** 178
Newport Pl. **1** 51
Newstead **4** 282
Newton Barn Fm **7** 224
Newton Bottom Lock **4** 298
Newton Bridge **4** 298
NEWTON BURGOLAND **7** 223
NEWTON HARCOURT **4** 297
Newton Lane
(Great Glen) **4** 80
(Wigston Magna) **5** 219
Newton Rd **7** 219
Newton Top Lock **4** 298
Newton Villas **3** 35
Newtown Grange **6** 80
NEWTOWN LINFORD **7** 155
Newtown Linford Lane **6** 99
Newtown Plantation **7** 157
Newtown St. **1** 51
NEWTOWN UNTHANK **6** 79
Nicholls Fm **5** 235
No Man's Heath **6** 10
Noah's Ark **6** 40
Nob, The **6** 308
Nock Verges
(Earl Shilton) **6** 134
(Stoney Stanton) **6** 283
Noel Arms (P.H.) **2** 177
Nook Fm
(Grimston) **3** 106
(Packington) **7** 286
(Ratby) **6** 222
Nook Lane
(Barrow upon Soar) **3** 35
(Bottesford) **2** 24
(Packington) **7** 286
Nook, The
(Anstey) **7** 3
(Barrow upon Soar) **3** 35
(Bitteswell) **5** 28
(Bottesford) **2** 24
(Cosby) **5** 68
(Great Glen) **4** 81
(Markfield) **6** 177
(West Langton) **4** 293
(Whetstone) **5** 213
Noon's Orchard **1** 178
Norman street **2** 172
Normandy **1** xi, 189

NORMANTON **2** 41
Normanton Cottages **6** 305
Normanton Hall **2** 42
Normanton House Fm
(Normanton Turville) **6** 305
(Ullesthorpe) **5** 206
Normanton Lane **6** 104
NORMANTON LE HEATH **6** 197
Normanton Little Fox Covert **2** 42
Normanton Lodge
(Normanton le Heath) **6** 198
(Normanton Turville) **6** 305
(Normanton) **2** 42
Normanton Lodge Fm **6** 198
Normanton Park **6** 305
Normanton Rd **7** 286
Normanton Thorns **2** 42
NORMANTON TURVILLE **6** xiii, 304
Normanton Wood **6** 198
Norris Hill **7** 21
Norrishill Cottages **7** 21
Norrishill Fm **7** 15
North Bridge **1** 75
North Close **1** 189
North Cottage **6** 207
North Crofts **1** 190
North End
(Hallaton) **4** 96
(Mountsorrel) **7** 152
North Fm
(Seagrave) **3** 207
(Sutton Cheney) **6** 288
North Gates **1** xiii, 8, 51
North Hill Fm **3** 207
NORTH KILWORTH **5** xiv, xv, 155
North Kilworth Ho. **5** 156
North Kilworth House Cottages **5** 156
North Kilworth Mill **5** 156
North Kilworth Mill Fm **5** 156
North Kilworth Rd **5** 194
North Kilworth Sticks **5** 156
North Kilworth Wharf **4** 120
North Lane **4** 55
North Lodge **2** 51
North Manor Ho. **3** 73
North Meadow **1** 200
North Mills Holme **1** 200
North Mills Lane **1** 52
North Mills, The **1** 152
North Park
(East Norton) **3** 178
(Normanton Turville) **6** 305
North Plantation **3** 269
North Quarter **1** xiii, 11
North St.
(Ashby de la Zouch) **7** 9
(Barrow upon Soar) **3** 35
(Rothley) **7** 186
(Syston) **3** 228
(Whitwick) **7** 73
North Suburb **1** 11
North Wood Gate **1** 52
North's Lodge **3** 192
Northampton Gate **2** 172
Northampton Rd **4** 172
Northampton St. **1** 52
Northamptonshire House (P.H.) **1** 133
Northfield **3** 35
Northfield Drive **7** 62
Northfield Fm **4** 152
Northfield Ho.
(Blaby) **5** 33
(Melton Mowbray) **2** 178
Northfield Rd **5** 33
Northfields
(Ashby de la Zouch) **7** 9
(Kibworth Harcourt) **4** 139
Northgate **7** 131
Northgate Shambles **1** 120
Northgate St. **1** 52
Northumberland House (P.H.) **1** 134
Northumberland Rd **1** 52
Northumberland St. **1** 52
Norton Barn Cottage **6** 313
Norton Coverts **6** 313
Norton Gorse **4** 142
Norton Ho. **6** 313
NORTON JUXTA TWYCROSS **6** xi, xii, xiii, 312

Norton Nook Spinney **6** 11
Norton St. **1** 52
Norwood Ho. **5** 222
NOSELEY **4** 209
Noseley Hall **4** 210
Noseley Home Fm **4** 210
Noseley Rd **4** 129
Noseley Wood **4** 210
Nottingham and Grantham Canal **2** 261
Nottingham Arms (P.H.) **1** 134
Nottingham Lane **2** 51
Nottingham Rd
(Ab Kettleby) **2** 158
(Ashby de la Zouch) **7** 9
(Bottesford) **2** 24
(Loughborough) **7** 128
(Melton Mowbray) **2** 169
Nottingham St. **2** 169
Nowell Spring Wood **7** 238
Nunckley Hill Spinney **7** 186
Nuneaton Lane **6** 110
Nurseries, The **7** 264
Nursery Barn **6** 167
Nursery Fm **7** 9
Nursery Lane **2** 163
Nursery place **2** 172
Nursery Plantation
(Branston) **2** 111
(Woodhouse) **7** 249
Nursery, The **3** 111
Nut Bush **4** 188
Nutt's Bridge **6** 124

OADBY **5** xiii, xiv, 163
Oadby: unindexed modern street-names **5** 166
Oadby Frith **5** 165
Oadby Grange **5** 165
Oadby Grange Fm **5** 165
Oadby Hill Ho. **5** 165
Oadby Lodge **5** 165
Oadby Lodge Fm **5** 165
Oadby Rd **5** 219
Oadby Way **1** 52
Oak Cottage **4** 81
Oak Field **7** 277
Oak Fm
(Ashby Magna) **5** 10
(Bagworth) **6** 26
(Blaby) **5** 33
(Burbage) **6** 51
(Gilmorton) **5** 97
Oak Ho. **3** 183
Oak Leigh **5** 194
Oak Lodge Fm **6** 283
Oak Plantation **3** 18
Oak Rd **6** 73
Oak Ring **6** 167
Oak Spinney
(Ashby Magna) **5** 10
(Gumley) **4** 88
Oak Villa **7** 277
Oakberry Fm **5** 140
Oakfield **6** 305
Oakham Rd
(Knossington) **4** 147
(Tilton) **3** 244
Oaklands
(Elmesthorpe) **6** 83
(Gaddesby) **3** 95
(Leicester Forest West) **6** 159
(Stoke Golding) **6** 276
Oaklands, The **6** 134
Oakleigh Ho. **7** 21
Oakley Grange **7** 84
Oakley Rd **7** 196
Oakley Wood **7** 111
Oakley Wood Cottages **7** 112
Oakmeadow Spinney **6** 93
Oaks Cottage **7** 57
Oaks Fm
(Charley) **7** 57
(Kirby Muxloe) **6** 152
Oaks Fm, The **5** 165
Oaks Nurseries **7** 196
Oaks Rd
(Charley) **7** 57
(Great Glen) **4** 81
(Whitwick) **7** 73
Oaks, The
(Anstey) **7** 3

(Barwell) **6** 128
(Charley) **7** 57
(Lutterworth) **5** 140
(Ratby) **6** 222
(Seagrave) **3** 207
(Swannington) **7** 211
OAKTHORPE **7** 276
OAKTHORPE AND DONISTHORPE **7** 276
Oback Fm **5** 147
Occupation Lane **7** 20
Occupation Rd
(Hinckley) **6** 119
(St Peter's Rd) **1** 53
(University Rd) **1** 52
Odd Barn
(Measham) **7** 264
(Nailstone) **6** 183
(Swepstone) **7** 219
Odd Fellows' Arms (P.H.)
(Ashby de la Zouch) **7** 11
(Kegworth) **7** 97
Odd Ho. **6** 128
Odd House Fm **7** 264
Oddfellows Arms (P.H.) **6** 110
ODSTONE **6** xii, 244
Odstone Barn **6** 244
Odstone Barn Fm **6** 244
Odstone Hall **6** 244
Odstone Hill Fm **6** 244
Odstone Lane **6** 244
Old Barn **3** 55
Old Blue Bell (P.H.) **6** 73
Old Bowling Green (P.H.) **1** 134
Old Brake **6** 159
Old Bridge **3** 47
Old Bull (P.H.) **5** 130
Old Bull's Head (P.H.) **6** 27
Old Canal
(Brentingby) **2** 133
(Edmondthorpe) **2** 298
Old Castle (P.H.) **7** 134
Old Cavalry Close **1** 190
Old Church St. **5** 19
Old Close Plantation **2** 149
Old Cock (P.H.) **5** 5
Old Cottage Fm **3** 221
Old Covert
(Market Bosworth) **6** 167
(South Kilworth) **5** 194
Old Crown (P.H.)
(Rothley) **7** 186
(Wigston Magna) **5** 222
Old Crown (P.H.)
(Burton Overy) **4** 21
(Market Harborough) **4** 173
(Shearsby) **5** 188
OLD DALBY **2** 50
Old Dalby Grange **2** 51
Old Dalby Hall **2** 51
Old Dalby Lodge **2** 51
Old Dalby Wood **2** 51
Old English Gentleman (P.H.) **7** 134
Old Fish Pond **6** 201
Old Ford **1** 227
Old Gate (P.H.) **7** 64
Old Gate Lane **3** 232
Old George (P.H.) **7** 11
Old George (P.H.) **4** 174
Old Grange **2** 46
Old Gravel Hill Spinney **5** 209
Old Greyhound (P.H.) **4** 5
Old Guadaloupe **2** 189
Old Guildhall Croft **1** 190
Old Hall
(Ashby Folville) **3** 100
(Bushby) **4** 282
(Cotes) **3** 70
(Croxton Kerrial) **2** 104
(Groby) **6** 99
(Keyham) **3** 158
(Little Bowden) **4** 185
(Lubenham) **4** 164
(North Kilworth) **5** 156
(Queniborough) **3** 183
(Welby) **3** 18
(Willoughby Waterleys) **5** 235
Old Hall Fm
(Bardon) **6** 36
(Braunstone) **6** 45
(Burton Lazars) **2** 64

Old Hall Lane **4** 164
Old Hall, The **3** 198
Old Hare (P.H.) **1** 134
Old Hays **6** 222
Old Hill **4** 5
Old Hill Fm **2** 195
Old Hills **2** 163
Old Hills Wood **2** 163
Old Ho. **6** 161
Old Holt Rd **4** 188
Old House **7** 289
OLD INGARSBY **3** xiii, xiv, 10, 152
Old John Spinney **7** 157
Old John Tower **7** 157
Old Keythorpe **3** 259
Old King's Head (P.H.) **1** 134
Old Leys **1** 205
Old Manor **3** 269
Old Manor Ho.
(Harby) **2** 95
(Long Clawson) **2** 90
Old Marefield **4** 219
Old Men's Hospital **3** 35
Old Mere
(Newton Harcourt) **4** 298
(Wigston Magna) **5** 224
Old Mill Barn **4** 154
Old Mill Ho. **2** 90
Old Mill Lane **1** 53
Old Mill Rd **5** 39
Old Mill, The **3** 114
Old Mitre (P.H.) **1** 134
Old Oakham Rd **4** 147
Old Orchard **4** 164
Old Park **4** 210
Old Park Fm, The **3** 55
Old Park Pale **7** 3
Old Park Spinney **6** 167
Old Park Wood **2** 8
Old Parks **7** 9
Old Parks Fm **7** 9
Old Parks Ho. **7** 9
Old Parsonage, The **3** 131
Old Peacock (P.H.) **1** 134
Old Plough (P.H.) **7** 144
Old Plough (P.H.) **1** 134
Old Pond Wood **4** 222
Old Quarry Ho. **7** 196
Old Rectory
(Osgathorpe) **7** 164
(Saddington) **4** 224
Old Rectory Close **5** 39
Old Rectory Ho. **4** 178
Old Rectory, The
(Appleby) **6** 11
(Cranoe) **4** 32
(Kirkby Mallory) **6** 211
(Leire) **5** 130
(Peatling Parva) **5** 178
(Shawell) **5** 183
(Welham) **4** 290
(Wyfordby) **2** 144
Old Red Lion (P.H.)
(Barlestone) **6** 40
(Cotes de Val) **5** 97
(Market Bosworth) **6** 167
(Welham) **4** 290
Old Red Lion (P.H.) **1** 134
Old Rise Rocks
(Bardon) **6** 36
(Markfield) **6** 177
Old Road Barn **5** 68
Old Royal Oak (P.H.) **5** 28
Old Shop, The **1** 106, 110
Old Soar **1** 226
Old Star (P.H.) **6** 247
Old Swan (P.H.) **4** 133
Old Swan (P.H.) **7** 256
Old Three Cranes (P.H.) **7** 97
Old Unicorn (P.H.) **1** 134
Old Warren Fm **6** 161
Old Wheel Inn **6** 73
Old White Horse (P.H.) **6** 73
Old White Horse (P.H.) **1** 134
Old White Swan (P.H.) **6** 195
Old White Swan (P.H.)
(Seagrave) **3** 207
(Desford) **6** 73
Old Windmill
(Broughton Astley) **5** 39
(Shepshed) **7** 194

(Wymeswold) **3** 275
Old Windmill, The **2** 104
Old Women's Hospital **3** 35
Old Wood
(Croxton Kerrial) **2** 104
(Groby) **6** 99
(Prestwold) **3** 181
Oldfield Fm **6** 273
Oldfields Lodge **2** 210
Oldlands **6** 291
Oldstone **7** 238
Olive Hill **1** 53
Olive St. **1** 53
Olveston Abbey **4** 215
One Ash **7** 170
One Barrow Lane **7** 196
One Barrow Lodge **7** 57
One Barrow Plantation **7** 196
One Barrow Viaduct **7** 57
Orange Hill Plantation **6** 233
Orange Tree (P.H.) **1** 134
Orchard Cottage **5** 178
Orchard Fm
(Burbage) **6** 51
(Cotesbach) **5** 76
(Sutton Cheney) **6** 288
(Walcote) **5** 149
Orchard Lane **4** 81
Orchard Row **1** 53
Orchard St.
(Croft) **6** 67
(Fleckney) **4** 51
(Leicester) **1** 53
(Loughborough) **7** 128
Orchard, The
(Breedon on the Hill) **7** 37
(Cadeby) **6** 59
(South Kilworth) **5** 194
Orchards, The **6** 93
Orchardways **6** 57
Orton Gorse **6** 318
Orton Hall **6** 318
Orton Hill **6** 318
Orton Ho. **6** 318
Orton House Fm **6** 318
Orton Lane
(Orton on the Hill) **6** 318
(Sheepy Parva) **6** 255
ORTON ON THE HILL **6** xiii, 317
Orton Park **6** 318
Orton St. **1** 53
Orton Wood **6** 308
Orton's Plantation **6** 308
OSBASTON **6** xii, xiii, 200
Osbaston Field **6** 201
Osbaston Gate **6** 201
Osbaston Hall **6** 201
Osbaston Ho. **6** 201
Osbaston Hollow **6** 201
Osbaston Lane **6** 201
Osbaston Lodge Fm **6** 201
Osbaston Lount **6** 202
Osborne St. **1** 53
Oseleshaw **1** 190
OSGATHORPE **7** 163
Osgathorpe Field **7** 164
Osgathorpe Field Fm **7** 164
Osgathorpe Hall Fm **7** 164
Osier Bed Plantation **7** 48
Osier Holt **2** 104
Osiers, The **6** 45
OTHORPE **4** xii, 239
Othorpe Ho. **4** 240
Oundle Fm **4** 215
Oundle Ho. **2** 241
Outer Yard Closes **1** 190
Outwoods
(Nanpantan) **7** 147
(Worthington) **7** 256
Outwoods Fm **7** 147
Outwoods, The **6** 124
Oval, The **6** 183
Over Meadow **1** 200
Over Street House Fm **6** 11
Overclose Spinney **4** 14
Overfield Fm **6** 255
OVERSEAL **7** 282
OVERTON **6** 142
Owen St. **7** 62
OWSTON **4** 214

Owston Abbey **4** xiii, 215
Owston Grange **4** 215
Owston Lodge
(Newbold) **4** 219
(Owston) **4** 215
Owston Rd **4** 147
Owston Woods **4** 215
Ox Brook **3** 232
Ox Hey **1** 200
Oxey Cross Roads **3** 164
Oxey Fm **3** 164
Oxford St.
(Barwell) **6** 128
(Coalville) **7** 62
(Leicester) **1** 53
(Lutterworth) **5** 140
Oxhay Ho. **6** 233
Oxley Grange **7** 196
Oxley Gutter **7** 196

Pack Horse (P.H.) **7** 134
Pack Horse (P.H.) **1** 134
Packe Arms Inn **3** 131
Packe St. **7** 128
Packhorse Lane **7** 128
PACKINGTON **7** xi, 285
Packington Hill **7** xi, 98
Packington Ho. **7** 286
Packington Nook Lane **7** 9
Packington Rd **7** 9
Paddock St. **5** 219
Paddock St. **1** 53
Paddock, The **7** 79
Paddocks, The **5** 113
Paddy's Lane **2** 51
Padge Hall
(Cossington) **3** 61
(Lutterworth) **5** 140
Padget's Fm **4** 188
Page Lane **7** 118
Paget Arms (P.H.) **7** 134
Paget Arms (P.H.) **4** 164
Paget Fm **6** 144
Paget's Spinney **2** 140
Paget's Wood **7** 57
Painters' Arms (P.H.) **3** 134
Palace Hill **4** 110
Pall Mall **2** 169
Palmer's Arms (P.H.) **4** 215
Palmer's Closes **1** 190
Palmer's Garden **1** 178
Palmer's Lane **4** 70
Pantiles, The **5** 165
Papillon Fm **4** 164
Papillon Hall **4** 164
Papillon Hall Fm **4** 164
Paradise **7** 196
Paradise Close **1** 190
Paradise Lane **2** 51
Paradise Pl. **1** 53
Paradise Row **1** 53
Paradise Spinney **6** 67
Parchment Lane **1** xii, 53
Pare's Bridge **6** 268
Pares St. **1** 54
Parish Workhouse **6** 120
Park Belt **5** 209
Park Cottages **4** 74
Park Fm
(Burton on the Wolds) **3** 55
(East Langton) **4** 38
(Great Easton) **4** 74
(Ibstock) **6** 144
(Loughborough) **7** 129
(Sapcote) **6** 227
(Stretton en le Field) **7** 289
(Whetstone) **5** 213
(Willesley) **7** 18
Park Grange **7** 128
Park Hill **3** 207
Park Hill Lane **3** 207
Park Ho.
(Birstall) **7** 30
(Croxton Kerrial) **2** 104
(Gaddesby) **3** 95
(Hinckley) **6** 124
(Moira) **7** 23
(Newtown Unthank) **6** 80
Park House Fm **6** 80
Park Lane **7** 49
Park Pale **7** 3
Park Plantation **3** 181

Park Rd
(Cosby) **5** 68
(Loughborough) **7** 128
(Lowesby) **3** 169
(Melton Mowbray) **2** 169
Park Side **7** 23
Park St.
(Fleckney) **4** 51
(Leicester) **1** 54
(Market Bosworth) **6** 167
Park terrace **2** 172
Park Villas **6** 22
Park Wood **4** 252
Park Wood Fm **3** 161
Park, The
(Burton Lazars) **2** 64
(Cadeby) **6** 59
(Coalville) **7** 61
(Cotesbach) **5** 76
(Enderby) **6** 88
(Quorndon) **7** 170
Parklands **6** 51
Parkleigh **3** 207
Parks Fm
(Cotes) **3** 70
(Nanpantan) **7** 147
Parliament St. **1** 54
Parrot (P.H.)
(Hallaton) **4** 97
(Market Pl.) **1** 134
Parsike Meadow **1** 201
Parson's Lane **6** 117
Parsons Barn **5** 97
Parsonwood Hill **7** 73
Partable Meadow **1** 201
Particular Baptist Chapel **2** 24
Paslewe's Wong **1** 190
Passion Lane **1** 54
Pasture Farm Cottage **4** 204
Pasture Fm
(Asfordby) **3** 11
(Ibstock) **6** 144
(Oakthorpe) **7** 277
Pasture Ho. **3** 11
Pasture Lane
(Hathern) **7** 84
(Hose) **2** 100
(Leicester) **1** 54
(Stathern) **2** 261
Pasture Wood **7** 37
Pastures Fm **7** 79
Pastures Lane **7** 277
Pastures Lodge **4** 14
Patrick St. **4** 172
Paudy Fm **3** 35
Paudy Lane **3**
Paudy Lodge **3** 35
Paudy Rise Fm **3** 35
Paul Pry (P.H.) **7** 208
Paundy Lane
(Barrow upon Soar) **3** 35
(Seagrave) **3** 207
Payne's Lane **4** 188
Peace Hill **4** 70
Peacock (P.H.)
(Belgrave Gate) **1** 135
(Loughborough) **7** 134
(Market Harborough) **4** 174
Peacock (P.H.)
(Croxton Kerrial) **2** 104
(Lutterworth) **5** 138
(Melton Mowbray) **2** 177
(Red Cross) **1** 135
(Southgate St.) **1** 135
(Syston) **3** 229
Peacock Fm **3** 86
Peacock Inn **2** 195
Peacock Lane **1** 55
Peacock, The **2** 8
Peak Hayes Fm **6** 177
Peake's Covert **2** 232
Pear Garden **1** 178
Pear Tree (P.H.) **7** 249
Pear Tree Fm **6** 57
Pear Tree, The **4** 269
Peas Hill Fm **3** 216
Peashill Fm **4** 197
Peashill Lodge **4** 197
Peaslands, The **3** 276
Peat's Barn **7** 152
Peatling Hall **5** 178
Peatling Ho. **5** 174

Peatling Lodge
(Peatling Magna (×2)) **5** 174
(Peatling Parva) **5** 178
Peatling Lodge Fm **5** 174
PEATLING MAGNA **5** xiii, 173
PEATLING PARVA **5** xiii, 178
Peatling Parva Lodge **5** 178
Peatling Rd **5** 79
Peatling Way **1** 55
Pebble Hall **4** 269
PECKLETON **6** xii, 205
Peckleton Common **6** 207
Peckleton Fields **6** 207
Peckleton Hall **6** 207
Peckleton Ho. **6** 207
Peckleton Lane
(Desford) **6** 73
(Kirkby Mallory) **6** 211
(Leicester Forest West) **6** 159
Peckleton Rise **6** 159
Peel St. **7** 128
Peel St. **1** xv, 55
Peep Row **4** 81
Pegg's Close **7** 264
Pegg's Close Bridge **7** 264
Pegg's Fm **7** 107
Peggs Fm **6** 318
Peggs Green **7** 79
Peldar Tor Quarry **7** 73
Pelham St. **1** 55
Pelican (P.H.) **1** 135
Pen Close **5** 19
Pen Crag **6** 88
Penarth **2** 178
Penhill **6** 88
Penistone St. **6** 144
Penn, The **2** 46
Penniless Bench **1** 95
Pennyhaven **3** 81
Pensioners (P.H.) **1** 135
Pentney Cottage **2** 33
Pentys lane **6** 119
Pepper's Fm **2** 64
Perchnell Mead **1** 201
Perkin's Lane **3** 106
Perkins' Arms (P.H.) **6** 318
Pesthouse Garden, The **1** 178
Pesthouse Yard **1** 172
Pesthouse, The **1** 96
Petersfield **6** 68
Pettifors Fm **6** 36
Pexsall Corner **1** 55
Pheasant Spinney **5** 156
Philip Spinney **4** 210
Phipps's Field **1** 190
Piazza, The **1** 107
Piccadilly **1** xv, 55
Pick St. **7** 196
Pick's Lodge **3** 86
Pickering Grange **6** 143
Pickering Grange Fm **6** 144
PICKWELL **2** 240
Pickwell Grange **2** 241
Pickwell Lodge Fm **2** 241
Pied Bull (P.H.) **7** 198
Pied Bull (P.H.) **1** 135
Pigeon Row **2** 172
Pike Head **1** 226
Pike St. **1** 55
Pile Bridge Fm **2** 135
Pilgrim's Cottage **6** 51
Pilling's Lock **7** 170
Pillory, The **1** 111
Pincet Lane **5** 156
Pincet Lodge **5** 156
Pinder's Close **1** 190
Pineapple (P.H.) **1** 135
Pines, The **3** 95
Pinfold
(Charley) **7** 57
(Normanton) **2** 42
(Orton on the Hill) **6** 318
(Redmile) **2** 195
Pinfold
(Ab Kettleby) **2** 158
(Leicester) **1** 116
(Sileby) **3** 216
Pinfold Gate **7** 128
Pinfold Ho. **4** 276
Pinfold Lane **2** 25
Pinfold Lane **2** 172
Pinfold Lees Hill **2** 133

Pinfold, The **7** 224
Pingle Fm **6** 187
Pingle Ho. **6** 187
Pingle Lane
(Earl Shilton) **6** 134
(Potters Marston) **6** 218
Pingle Plantation **7** 181
Pingle Spinney **6** 167
Pingle St. **1** 55
Pingle, The **2** 90
Pingle, The **1** 190
Pink's Park **5** 13
Pinslade **5** 122
PINWALL **6** 257
Pinwall Cottage **6** 257
Pinwall Grange **6** 257
Pinwall Hall **6** 257
Pinwall Lodge **6** 257
Pipe Lane **6** 318
Pipe Lane Spinney **6** 318
Piper Fm **7** 112
Piper Hole **2** 94
Piper Hole Fm **2** 121
Piper Lane **7** 181
Piper Wood **7** 112
Pipwell **7** 16
Pisea Lane **6** 104
Pit Hill **4** 246
Pit Wood **7** 49
Pitt Lane **7** 79
Plantation, The
(Orton on the Hill) **6** 318
(Peatling Magna) **5** 174
Plaster Pit Barn **3** 55
Platchetts **7** 37
Platchetts Ho. **7** 37
Platt Ho. **5** 41
Play Close **2** 181
Play Close Lane **2** 172
Playhouse, The **1** 143
Pleasant Row **1** 55
Plough (P.H.)
(Ashby de la Zouch) **7** 11
(Birstall) **7** 30
(Bruntingthorpe) **5** 50
(Diseworth) **7** 118
(Enderby) **6** 88
(Littlethorpe) **5** 73
(Wigston Magna) **5** 222
Plough (P.H.)
(Barsby) **3** 102
(Bitteswell) **5** 28
(Burbage) **6** 52
(Burton Lazars) **2** 64
(Drayton) **4** 34
(Hinckley) **6** 122
(Humberstone) **3** 134
(Mountsorrel) **7** 152
(Old Dalby) **2** 51
(Ravenstone) **7** 181
(Sileby) **3** 216
(Stanton under Bardon) **6** 273
(Stathern) **2** 261
(Thurmaston) **3** 238
(Twyford) **3** 262
Plough and Harrow (P.H.) **5** 91
Plough Inn
(Ratby) **6** 223
(Scalford) **2** 210
Plough Inn **6** 26
Plough Inn (P.H.)
(Earl Shilton) **6** 135
(Loughborough) **7** 134
Ploughman Lane **1** xiv, 55
PLUNGAR **2** 204
Plungar Bridge **2** 205
Plungar Grange **2** 205
Plungar Wood **2** 205
Plymouth Lodge **2** 191
Poachers Corner **7** 27
Pochin St. **6** 68
Pochin's Bridge **5** 223
Pocket Gate **7** 147
Pocket Gate Cottage **7** 147
Pocketgate Fm **7** 249
Pocklington's Walk **1** 143
Polebrook Wood **6** 27
Polly Bott's Lane **7** 238
Polton Hill **4** 260
Pond Bay **7** 49
Pond Spinney **6** 23
Pontylue Fm **3** 228

Pool Ho.
(Ashby Folville) **3** 100
(Groby) **6** 99
(Kirby Muxloe) **6** 152
(Newbold Verdon) **6** 195
Pool House Fm **6** 152
Pool, The **6** 45
Poole's Lodge Fm **2** 129
Poor Close Spinney **4** 264
Poor House **7** 12
Pope's Spinney **4** 222
Poplar Fm
(Kimcote) **5** 113
(Leire) **5** 130
Poplar Spinney **4** 210
Poplars Fm
(Barton in the Beans) **6** 237
(Croft) **6** 68
(Dadlington) **6** 291
(Kirby Bellars) **3** 86
(Walcote) **5** 149
Poplars, The
(Countesthorpe) **5** 79
(Dadlington) **6** 291
(Harby) **2** 95
(Plungar) **2** 205
(Sheepy Magna) **6** 252
(Worthington) **7** 256
(Wymondham) **2** 288
Port Bridge **4** 5
Port Hill
(Blaby) **5** 33
(Slawston) **4** 240
Port Hill Fm **6** 283
Portels Fm **3** 173
Porter's Barn **5** 209
Porter's Lodge (P.H.) **1** 135
Porter's Lodge **3** 169
Portgate **5** 221
Portland Ho. **6** 152
Portland House **5** 126
Portland St. **5** 68
Portland St. **1** 55
Portwey, The **3** 134
Post Office Lane **6** 322
Potter Hill **3** 18
Potter Hill Fm **3** 18
Potter's Wood **7** 270
POTTERS MARSTON **6** xiii, 218
Potters Marston Hall **6** 218
Potwells Fm **6** 198
POULTNEY **5** 148
Poultney Cottage **7** 238
Poultney Fm **7** 238
Poultney Grange **5** 149
Poultney Lane **5** 113
Poultney Wood **7** 238
Poultney's Close **1** 191
Poynton's Barn **7** 277
Prebend St. **1** 55
Prefabs, The **2** 158
Presbyterian Meeting House **6** 121
Presents Lane **7** 27
Prestgrave **4** xiii, 203
Preston Lodge **4** 147
Preston's Lane **7** 79
Preston's Lodge **4** 147
PRESTOP **7** 17
Prestop Park **7** 9
Prestop Park Fm **7** 9
PRESTWOLD **3** 180
Prestwold Hall **3** 181
Prestwold Park **3** 181
Priest Hill **3** 221
Priesthills Rd **6** 117
PRIMETHORPE **5** xiv, 40
Primitive Methodist Chapel
(Long Clawson) **2** 90
(Scalford) **2** 210
Primitive Methodist Chapel **2** 175
Primrose Hill Cottage **7** 211
Prince Blucher (P.H.) **1** 135
Prince of Wales (P.H.) **6** 122
Prince of Wales (P.H.)
(Loughborough) **7** 134
(Thringstone) **7** 71
(Whitwick) **7** 74
Prince of Wales Covert **3** 151
Prince of Wales Inn **2** 78
Prince Regent (P.H.) **1** 135
Prince's Feathers (P.H.) **6** 122
Prince's Hovel **2** 298

Princess Charlotte (P.H.) **1** 135
Princess St. **1** xiv, 56
Pringle **3** 86
Pringle St. **1** 56
Prior Park **7** 9
Priorfield **7** 9
Priory Church of St Mary Queen **6** 51
Priory Fm
(Knossington) **4** 147
(Nevill Holt) **4** 204
(Shoby) **3** 111
Priory Garden **6** 119
Priory House **6** 123
Priory, The
(Owston) **4** 216
(Ratcliffe on the Wreake) **3** 192
Privets, The **7** 147
Proprietary School **1** 113
Prospect Ho.
(Earl Shilton) **6** 134
(Worthington) **7** 256
Providence **7** 256
Providence Chapel **1** 89
Providence Cottage **2** 25
Providence Ho. **6** 144
Providence Pl.
(Navigation St.) **1** 56
(Wharf St.) **1** 56
Proving Ground **6** 110
Pump Lane **3** 11
Pumps, Various **1** 108
Punch Bowl Covert **2** 85
Pyeharps Rd **6** 51
Pywell's Lock **4** 139

Quadrant Ho., The **4** 5
Quaker Cottage **5** 40
Quaker's Plantation **7** 181
Quakers' Meeting House, The **6** 121
Quakesick Spinney **3** 134
Quarry Cottage **7** 61
Quarry Fm **6** 36
Quarry Hill Plantation **7** 49
Quarry Lane **6** 269
Quarry Lane Fm **6** 269
Quarry Plantation **6** 11
Quebec Ho. **3** 216
Queen (P.H.) **7** 62
Queen (P.H.) **4** 177
Queen and Rights of the People (P.H.) **1** 135
Queen St.
(Barkby Thorpe) **3** 29
(Barwell) **6** 128
(Bottesford) **2** 25
(Coalville) **7** 62
(Little Bowden) **4** 185
(Loughborough) **7** 129
(Rutland St.) **1** 56
(Shepshed) **7** 196
Queen St. **1** xiv, 56
Queen Street **2** 172
Queen Victoria (P.H.) **3** 229
Queen's Arms (P.H.) **5** 130
Queen's Head (P.H.)
(Ashby de la Zouch) **7** 11
(Barwell) **6** 128
(Belton) **7** 27
(Billesdon) **4** 5
(Coalville) **7** 62
(Heather) **6** 105
(Hinckley) **6** 122
(Markfield) **6** 177
(Nailstone) **6** 183
(Saddington) **4** 224
(Wigston Magna) **5** 222
Queen's Head (P.H.)
(Coleorton) **7** 79
(Friar Lane) **1** 135
(Gallowtree Gate) **1** 135
(Hallaton) **4** 97
(Lutterworth) **5** 138
(Measham) **7** 264
(Medbourne) **4** 188
(Shepshed) **7** 198
(Stapleton) **6** 215
(Thringstone) **7** 71
(Townhall Lane) **1** 135

Queen's Park
(Hinckley) **6** 124
(Loughborough) **7** 128
QUENBY **3** xiv, 10, 154, 183
Quenby Hall **3** 155
Quenby Lodge **3** 155
Quenby Park **3** 155
QUENIBOROUGH **3** xi, xiii, 2, 155, 182
Queniborough Brook **3** xiii, 183
Queniborough Cottage **3** 183
Queniborough Lodge **3** 183
Queniborough Rd **3** 22
Quorn and Woodhouse Station **7** 170
Quorn Court **7** 170
Quorn Cresc. **7** 62
Quorn Fields Fm **7** 171
Quorn Ho. **7** 171
Quorn House Park **7** 171
Quorn Hunt Kennels **3** 207
Quorn Lodge Fm **7** 171
QUORNDON (QUORN) **7** 169
Quorndon Mill **7** 170

Race Course **1** 143
Race Course Closes **1** 191
Race Ground Plantation **6** 11
Racecourse Fm **2** 64
Racecourse Spinney **7** 208
Radmoor Rd **7** 129
RAGDALE **3** 127
Ragdale Old Hall **3** 128
Ragdale Wolds Fm **3** 128
Ragdale Wood **3** 232
Ragdale Hall **3** 128
Railway (P.H.) **2** 177
Railway (P.H.)
(Countesthorpe) **5** 79
(Glenfield) **6** 93
(Mountsorrel) **7** 153
(Shepshed) **7** 198
Railway Arms **4** 133
Railway Cottage **7** 256
Railway Cottages **5** 222
Railway Hotel (P.H.) **6** 122
Railway Hotel (P.H.)
(Campbell St.) **1** 135
(Coalville) **7** 62
(Dunton Bassett) **5** 84
(Whitwick) **7** 74
(Wigston Magna) **5** 222
Railway Inn
(Ratby) **6** 223
(Sileby) **3** 216
Railway Inn
(Albert Village) **7** 20
(Kirby Muxloe) **6** 152
(Swannington) **7** 211
Railway Inn (P.H.)
(Barrow upon Soar) **3** 36
(Great Bowden) **4** 177
(West Bridge St.) **1** 136
Railway Tavern (P.H.)
(Ashby de la Zouch) **7** 11
(Loughborough) **7** 134
Railway Tavern **7** 256
Railways and Railway Stations **1** 80
Rainbow and Dove (P.H.) **1** 136
Ram (P.H.)
(Barrow upon Soar) **3** 36
(Loughborough) **7** 134
(Lutterworth) **5** 138
(Shepshed) **7** 198
(St Nicholas St.) **1** 136
Ram Inn (P.H.) **6** 145
Ram Inn (P.H.) **6** 122
Ram's Head (P.H.) **7** 198
Ram's Head Spinney **3** 178
Ramsley Brook **7** 44
Ramsley Lodge **2** 34
Rancliff Wood **3** 55
Randles Close **4** 282
Randolph's Meadow **1** 201
Range Rd **7** 9
Rangemoor **4** 282
Ranters' Chapel **1** 89
Raspberry Spinney **5** 149
Rat Catcher (P.H.) **6** 262
RATBY **6** xii, xiii, 221

Ratby Burroughs **6** 223
Ratby Lane
(Kirby Muxloe) **6** 153
(Markfield) **6** 177
Ratby Meadow Lane **6** 88
Ratby Rd **6** 99
Ratchet Hill **7** 73
Ratcliffe Barn **3** 192
Ratcliffe Bridge
(Kegworth) **7** 98
(Ratcliffe Culey) **6** 330
RATCLIFFE CULEY **6** xi, 329
Ratcliffe Cut **7** 98
Ratcliffe Hall **3** 192
Ratcliffe Ho. **6** 330
Ratcliffe Lane
(Kegworth) **7** 98
(Lockington) **7** 103
(Sheepy) **6** 252
Ratcliffe Mill **3** 192
RATCLIFFE ON THE WREAKE **3** 191
Ratcliffe Rd **3** 216
Ratcliffe Roman Catholic College **3** 61
Rathbone Pl. **1** 56
Ratis **1** 3, 4
Raunscliffe **6** 177
Ravenhead **3** 153
Ravens Rest **3** 259
Ravenslea **7** 181
RAVENSTONE **7** xi, 179
Ravenstone Hall **7** 181
Ravenstone Rd
(Coalville) **7** 62
(Heather) **6** 105
RAVENSTONE WITH SNIBSTONE **7** x, 179
Raw Dykes **1** 5
Raw Dykes Field **1** 212
Rawdon Arms (P.H.) **7** 23
Rawdon Hotel (P.H.) **7** 50
Rawdon Terrace **7** 24
Rawdon Villa **7** 24
Rawlett's Close **1** 191
Rawson St. **1** 56
Ray St. **1** 56
REARSBY **3** xiv, xv, 197
Rearsby Grange **3** 198
Rearsby Ho. **3** 198
Rearsby Lodge **3** 198
Rearsby Mill **3** 198
Rearsby Station **3** 198
Rearsby Wharf Lodge **3** 198
Recruiting Sergeant (P.H.)
(Newton Harcourt) **4** 298
(St Nicholas St.) **1** 136
Rectory Covert **2** 25
Rectory Fm
(Aston Flamville) **6** 23
(Barrow upon Soar) **3** 35
(Bottesford) **2** 25
(Hathern) **7** 84
(Rearsby) **3** 198
Rectory Ho. **4** 74
Rectory Lane
(Little Bowden) **4** 185
(Market Bosworth) **6** 167
(Medbourne) **4** 188
(Nailstone) **6** 183
(Thurcaston) **7** 230
Rectory Place **7** 129
Rectory Rd **7** 242
Rectory, The
(Allexton) **3** 4
(Anstey) **7** 3
(Asfordby) **3** 11
(Ashby Parva) **5** 13
(Aylestone) **5** 19
(Barwell) **6** 128
(Beeby) **3** 43
(Blaby) **5** 33
(Branston) **2** 111
(Broughton Astley) **5** 39
(Bruntingthorpe) **5** 50
(Burbage) **6** 51
(Burrough on the Hill) **2** 232
(Burton Overy) **4** 22
(Cadeby) **6** 59
(Carlton Curlieu) **4** 28
(Carlton) **6** 64
(Catthorpe) **5** 54

(Church Langton) **4** 37
(Cold Overton) **4** 152
(Coleorton) **7** 79
(Congerstone) **6** 241
(Cossington) **3** 61
(Coston) **2** 152
(Cotesbach) **5** 76
(Croft) **6** 68
(Desford) **6** 73
(Eastwell) **2** 121
(Edmondthorpe) **2** 298
(Fenny Drayton) **6** 329
(Foston) **5** 109
(Frolesworth) **5** 91
(Galby) **4** 63
(Gilmorton) **5** 97
(Glooston) **4** 66
(Goadby Marwood) **2** 126
(Gumley) **4** 88
(Hallaton) **4** 96
(Harby) **2** 95
(Harston) **2** 10
(Hathern) **7** 84
(Higham on the Hill) **6** 110
(Hoby) **3** 114
(Houghton) **4** 110
(Husbands Bosworth) **4** 120
(Ibstock) **6** 144
(Kegworth) **7** 98
(Kibworth Beauchamp) **4** 133
(Kimcote) **5** 113
(Knipton) **2** 15
(Knossington) **4** 147
(Laughton) **4** 154
(Leire) **5** 130
(Long Whatton) **7** 112
(Lutterworth) **5** 140
(Markfield) **6** 177
(Medbourne) **4** 188
(Misterton) **5** 148
(Mowsley) **4** 197
(Muston) **2** 35
(Narborough) **6** 187
(Nether Broughton) **2** 46
(Newbold Verdon) **6** 195
(Normanton le Heath) **6** 198
(North Kilworth) **5** 157
(Norton justa Twycross) **6** 313
(Peckleton) **6** 207
(Pickwell) **2** 241
(Rearsby) **3** 198
(Redmile) **2** 195
(Rotherby) **3** 122
(Sapcote) **6** 227
(Saxby) **2** 135
(Saxelby) **3** 108
(Seagrave) **3** 207
(Sharnford) **6** 247
(Sheepy Magna) **6** 252
(Sibson) **6** 258
(Skeffington) **3** 221
(Smeeton Westerby) **4** 246
(South Croxton) **3** 73
(South Kilworth) **5** 194
(Stathern) **2** 261
(Stoney Stanton) **6** 283
(Stonton Wyville) **4** 255
(Swepstone) **7** 219
(Swithland) **7** 228
(Thurcaston) **7** 230
(Waltham on the Wolds) **2** 272
(Walton on the Wolds) **3** 269
(Willoughby Waterleys) **5** 235
(Witherley) **6** 323
(Wymondham) **2** 288
Red Bank Fm **7** 264
Red Burrow Fm **7** 286
Red Burrow Lane **7** 286
Red Cow (P.H.) **4** 174
Red Cow (P.H.)
(Belgrave Gate) **1** 136
(Leicester Forest) **6** 159
(Loseby Lane) **1** 136
(Lubenham) **4** 165
Red Cross, The **1** 103
Red Gables Fm **6** 11
Red Hall **6** 128
Red Hill
(Birstall) **7** 30
(Narborough) **6** 187
(Swannington) **7** 211
Red Hill Barn **3** 55

Red Hill Fm
  (Narborough) **6** 187
  (Sapcote) **6** 227
Red Hill Lane **3** 238
Red Hill Quarry **6** 187
Red Ho. **7** 24
Red Holme Fm **7** 280
Red House (P.H.) **7** 62
Red House Fm **2** 210
Red House Fm **3** 47
Red House Meadows **1** 201
Red Hovel **4** 14
Red Lion (P.H.)
  (Barwell) **6** 128
  (Barwell) **6** 128
  (Bottesford) **2** 25
  (Burbage) **6** 52
  (Earl Shilton) **6** 135
  (Great Bowden) **4** 177
  (Highcross St.) **1** 136
  (Huncote) **6** 139
  (Markfield) **6** 177
  (Pinwall) **6** 257
  (Rothley) **7** 186
  (Sapcote) **6** 227
  (Shepshed) **7** 198
Red Lion (P.H.)
  (Appleby) **6** 11
  (Bringhurst) **4** 19
  (Coleorton) **7** 79
  (Hinckley) **6** 122
  (Husbands Bosworth) **4** 120
  (Kegworth) **7** 98
  (Little Stretton) **4** 159
  (Loughborough) **7** 134
  (Melton Mowbray) **2** 177
  (Mountsorrel) **7** 153
  (Sanvey Gate) **1** 136
  (Sileby) **3** 216
  (Southgate St.) **1** 136
  (Stathern) **2** 261
  (Tonge) **7** 41
  (Walcote) **5** 149
  (Walton) **5** 114
Red Lion Fm **6** 57
Red Lion Inn **6** 73
Red Lion Inn **2** 59
Red Lion yard **7** 131
Red Lodge **3** 86
Red Lodge Fm **3** 244
Red Lodge Rd **3** 244
Redbank Ho. **7** 264
Redbanks **4** 81
Redcross St. **1** xiii, 56
Rede's Close **1** 191
Redearth Fm **2** 210
Redhill Fm
  (Appleby Parva) **6** 11
  (Swannington) **7** 211
Redhill Lane **7** 211
Redholme Bungalow Fm **6** 144
Redlands **7** 64
REDMILE **2** 194
Redmile and Belvoir Station **2** 195
Redmile Windmill **2** 196
Redmoor **6** xv
Reed Pool **5** 109
Reed Pool Spinney **5** 109
Reedpool Spinney **3** 153
Reeds, The **5** 148
Reedy Sike **7** 238
Regent St.
  (Barwell) **6** 128
  (Hinckley) **6** 117
  (Loughborough) **7** 129
  (Lutterworth) **5** 140
  (Melton Mowbray) **2** 169
Regent St. (now Regent Rd) **1** xiv, 57
Regent St. **1** 57
Regent wharf **7** 131
Reindeer (P.H.) **1** 136
Rempstone Rd **7** 79
Renals Fm **7** 149
Repton and Gresley Hundred **7** 260
Reservoir Cottage
  (Branston) **2** 111
  (South Kilworth) **5** 194
Reservoir Covert **6** 233
Reservoir Inn **7** 234
Reservoir Rd **6** 27

Reservoir Wood **2** 15
Retreat Fm
(Thornton) **6** 27
(Willoughby Waterleys) **5** 235
Retreat, The **5** 10
Revell's Lane **1** 57
Rhododendron Hill **7** 148
Richmond Arms (P.H.) **7** 198
Richmond Park **6** 124
Rickett's Spinney **2** 135
Rickleburrow Hill **4** 147
Riddlesden Farm Cottages **5** 141
Riddlesden Fm **5** 141
Riddlestone Lodge **4** 260
Ridgemere Lane
(Barkby) **3** 2, 22
(Queniborough) **3** 183
(South Croxton) **3** 73
Ridgeway, The **7** 186
Ridings Spinney **7** 186
Ridings, The **7** 186
Rigget's Spinney **3** 131
Ring Fence **7** 196
Ringer's Spinney **5** 165
Ringing Hill **7** 196
Ringlethorpe **2** xiii, 208
Ringrose's Piece **1** 191
Rippon's Plantation **2** 144
Rise Hill Spinneys **2** 85
Rise Lane **7** 112
Rise Rocks Fm **6** 177
Rise, The **5** 84
Rising Sun (P.H.) **6** 233
Riverdale **3** 192
Riverside Cottages **6** 305
Riverside Fm **2** 191
Road Barn **5** 76
Road Barn Fm **5** 68
Roads yard **7** 131
Robie's Gorse **6** 241
Robin Hood (P.H.)
(Overseal) **7** 283
(Swannington) **7** 211
Robin Hood (P.H.)
(Abbey Gate) **1** 136
(Gallowtree Gate) **1** 136
(Wood Gate) **1** 136
Robin-a-Tiptoe Fm **3** 244
Robin-a-Tiptoe Hill **3** 245
Rock Cottage **7** 37
Rock Cottages **7** 256
Rock Fm **7** 57
Rock View Fm **7** 70
Rockside Cottage **6** 177
Rocky Plantation **7** 238
Roddyman's Lane **1** 57
Rodhill Fm **3** 245
Roe House Lane **6** 313
Roe's Plantation
(Charley) **7** 57
(Shepshed) **7** 197
Roebuck (P.H.)
(Burbage) **6** 52
(Countesthorpe) **5** 80
(Earl Shilton) **6** 135
(High St.) **1** 136
(Kirkby Mallory) **6** 211
Roebuck Inn **6** 73
Roecliffe Fm
(Newtown Linford) **7** 157
(Packington) **7** 286
Roecliffe Gorse **7** 157
Roecliffe Hill **7** 157
Roecliffe Manor **7** 157
Roecliffe Rd **7** 157
Roecliffe Spinney **7** 157
Roes Rest **6** 159
Rogue's Lane **6** 117
Rogue's Lane Nurseries **6** 124
ROLLESTON **4** xii, 221
Rolleston Hall **4** 222
Rolleston Lodge Fm **4** 222
Rolleston Rd **4** 5
Rolleston Wood
(Noseley) **4** 210
(Rolleston) **4** 222
Roman Catholic Chapel **2** 121
Roman Catholic Chapel
(Hinckley) **6** 121
(Melton Mowbray) **2** 175

Rookery Fm
(Fenny Drayton) **6** 329
(Overseal) **7** 283
Rookery Ho. **2** 288
Rookery Lane **6** 99
Rookery Plantation **3** 181
Rookery, The
(Barrow upon Soar) **3** 35
(Buckminster) **2** 55
(Coalville) **7** 61
(Isley cum Langley) **7** 94
(Osbaston) **6** 201
(Sapcote) **6** 227
(Walton on the Wolds) **3** 269
(Westrill and Starmore) **5** 209
Rope Walk **1** 146
Ropershill **7** 208
Rose (P.H.)
(Loughborough) **7** 134
(Stoney Stanton) **6** 283
(unlocated) **1** 136
Rose and Crown (P.H.)
(Hose) **2** 100
(Houghton) **4** 110
(Kibworth Harcourt) **4** 139
(Loughborough) **7** 134
(Thurnby) **4** 278
(Tilton) **3** 245
Rose and Crown (P.H.)
(Castle Donington) **7** 50
(Coleorton) **7** 79
(Crab St.) **1** 136
(Hathern) **7** 84
(Humberstone Rd) **1** 136
(Lutterworth) **5** 138
(Market Harborough) **4** 174
(Rearsby) **3** 198
(Shepshed) **7** 198
(Somerby) **2** 226
(Wymeswold) **3** 276
Rose Cottage
(Gaddesby) **3** 95
(Leicester Forest West) **6** 159
(Noseley) **4** 210
(Stapleton) **6** 215
Rose Cottage Fm
(Keythorpe) **3** 259
(Leicester Forest West) **6** 159
Rose Cottages **7** 108
Rose Fm **5** 80
Rose Mount **5** 68
Roseberry Rd **7** 3
Rosemary Lane **6** 118, 119
Ross Knob Plantation **7** 181
Ross Street **2** 172
Ross's Factory **1** 146
ROTHERBY **3** xi, xiv, xv, 121
Rotherby Lodge **3** 122
Rotherwood
(Ashby de la Zouch) **7** 9
(Desford) **6** 73
ROTHLEY **7** x, xii, 184
Rothley Brook **7** 186
Rothley Court Hotel **7** 186
Rothley Cross **7** 186
Rothley Grange **7** 186
Rothley Lodge **7** 186
Rothley Park **7** 186
Rothley Plain **7** 186
Rothley Temple **7** xii, 185
Rotten Row **7** 79
Rough Heath **7** 208
Rough Hill **7** 157
Rough Park **7** 79
Rough Spinney **4** 234
Rough, The
(Nanpantan) **7** 147
(Swithland) **7** 228
(Thurcaston) **7** 230
Round Close, The **1** 191
Round Covert **2** 90
Round Hill
(Shepshed) **7** 197
(Syston) **3** 228
Round Hill Spinney **3** 164
Round Hill, The **1** xii, 57
Round Ho. **6** 93
Round House **7** 256

Round House, The **5** 157
Round Spinney
(Keythorpe) **3** 259
(Noseley) **4** 210
Round Table (P.H.) **2** 177
Roundabout Spinney **6** 207
Roundheads Inn (P.H.) **1** 136
Rowan Ave. **7** 62
Rowden **6** 110
Rowden Gorse **6** 110
Rowden House Fm **6** 110
Rowhele Wood **7** 171
Rowlands, The **7** 211
Rowley Fields
(Braunstone) **6** 45
(Shearsby) **5** 188
Royal Arms (P.H.) **6** 288
Royal East St. **1** 57
Royal George (P.H.) **7** 134
Royal Horse Shoes (P.H.) **2** 272
Royal Hotel **5** 40
Royal Hotel (P.H.) **7** 11
Royal Kent St. **1** 57
Royal Mail (P.H.) **7** 134
Royal Oak (P.H.)
(Cossington) **3** 61
(Great Dalby) **2** 78
(Great Glen) **4** 81
(Ibstock) **6** 145
(Kirby Muxloe) **6** 153
(Long Whatton) **7** 112
(Loughborough) **7** 134
(Quorndon) **7** 171
(Rothley) **7** 186
(Wigston Magna) **5** 222
Royal Oak (P.H.)
(Ashby Folville) **3** 100
(Barrow upon Soar) **3** 36
(Bitteswell) **5** 28
(Claybrooke Magna) **5** 58
(Earl Shilton) **6** 135
(Frolesworth) **5** 91
(Great Bowden) **4** 177
(Hallaton) **4** 97
(Hinckley) **6** 122
(Kibworth Beauchamp) **4** 133
(Long Clawson) **2** 90
(Osgathorpe) **7** 164
(South Kilworth) **5** 194
(West Bridge St.) **1** 137
(Woodhouse) **7** 249
Royal Red Gate Inn **6** 329
Royce's Plantation **2** 152
Rubley's Close **1** 191
Ruding St. **1** 57
Ruding St. (now Ruding Rd) **1** 58
Ruding's Sheepcote **1** 181
Rugby Rd
(Cotesbach) **5** 76
(South Kilworth) **5** 194
(Westrill and Starmore) **5** 209
Rundle Beck **2** 205
Rupert St. **1** 58
Rupert's Ho. **4** 81
Rushall Field **7** 249
Rushall Field Fm **7** 249
Rushbrook Fm **5** 113
Rushes Lane **4** 165
Rushes, The **7** 129
Rushey Fields **3** 47
Rushey Fm **3** 47
Rushey Lane **7** 186
Rushy Field Fm **7** 249
Rushyfields **7** 249
Ruskington Lodge Fm **5** 224
Russell Sq. **1** xv, 58
Russell St. **7** 129
Russell St. **1** 58
Russell Tavern (P.H.) **1** 137
Rutland Arms (P.H.)
(Bottesford) **2** 25
(Hoby) **3** 114
(Melton Mowbray) **2** 178
Rutland Arms (P.H.)
(Horsefair St.) **1** 137
(Knipton) **2** 15
(Loughborough) **7** 134
Rutland Sq. **1** 58
Rutland St.
(Leicester) **1** 58
(Loughborough) **7** 129
(Melton Mowbray) **2** 170

Rutland terrace **2** 172
Rydal Manor **2** 189
Rye Close Spinney **5** 148
Rye Hill **5** 140
Rye Hills **6** 255
Rye Wong **1** 191
Ryeclose Spinney **7** 242
Ryecroft Fm **3** 35
Ryefield Lodge **3** 61

SADDINGTON **4** xi, 223
Saddington Hall **4** 224
Saddington Lodge **4** 224
Saddington Rd
(Mowsley) **4** 197
(Shearsby) **5** 188
(Smeeton Westerby) **4** 246
Saddington Reservoir **4** 224
Saddle (P.H.) **3** 262
Sadlers Wells **7** 27
Saffron Brook
(Knighton) **5** 126
(Leicester) **1** xi, 226
Saffron Hill **5** 19
Saffron Lane **5** 19
Saffron Rd **5** 220
Sage Cross Street **2** 172
Sage Crosse, the **2** 176
Sailor's Return (P.H.) **1** 137
St Andrew's Church
(Aylestone) **5** 19
(Burton Overy) **4** 22
(Carlton) **6** 64
(Coston) **2** 152
(Countesthorpe) **5** 80
(Foxton) **4** 55
(Great Easton) **4** 74
(Kegworth) **7** 98
(North Kilworth) **5** 157
(Owston) **4** 216
(Pearting Parva) **5** 178
(Prestwold) **3** 181
(Thringstone) **7** 70
(Tur Langton) **4** 286
(Twyford) **3** 262
(Welham) **4** 290
St Ann's Lane **7** 49
St Ann's Well **4** 37
St Anthony's Bridge **1** 75
St Augustine's Well **1** 229
St Bartholomew' s Church
(Foston) **5** 110
(Kirby Muxloe) **6** 153
(Quorndon) **7** 171
(Snarestone) **6** 269
(Sproxton) **2** 246
(Welby) **3** 18
St Bernard's Cottages **7** 57
St Botolph's Church
(Ratcliffe on the Wreake) **3** 192
(Shepshed) **7** 197
(Sibson) **6** 259
St Catherine's Church
(Burbage) **6** 51
(Houghton on the Hill) **4** 110
St Clement's Church **1** 83
St Clement's Lane **1** 58
St Cuthbert's Church **4** 81
St Denys' Church
(Eaton) **2** 119
(Goadby Marwood) **2** 126
St Denys's Church
(Evington) **4** 44
(Ibstock) **6** 144
(Stonton Wyville) **4** 255
St Edith's Church **6** 318
St Edward King and Martyr's
Church **7** 49
St Egelwin the Martyr's
Church **2** 210
St Francis' Garden **1** 178
St Francis' Lane **1** 58
St George St. **1** 58
St George's Charity School **1** 114
St George's Church
(Leicester) **1** 83
(Swannington) **7** 211
St George's Farm **6** 291
St George's Gate **1** 58
St George's Guildhall **1** 107

St George's Hill **7** 211
St Giles's Church
(Barlestone) **6** 40
(Blaston) **4** 14
(Medbourne) **4** 188
(Stretton Magna) **4** 264
St Guthlac's Church
(Branston) **2** 111
(Stathern) **2** 261
St Helen's Church
(Ashby de la Zouch) **7** 9
(Gumley) **4** 88
(Plungar) **2** 205
(Saddington) **4** 224
(Sharnford) **6** 247
St Helen's Cottage **7** 61
St Hilda's Church **7** 24
St James's Chapel Close **1** 191
St James's Chapel **1** 87
St James's Chapel **4** 34
St James's Church
(Ab Kettleby) **2** 158
(Birstall) **7** 30
(Burton Lazars) **2** 64
(Charley) **7** 58
(Coalville) **7** 61
(Dadlington) **6** 291
(Huncote) **6** 139
(Little Dalby) **2** 85
(Newbold Verdon) **6** 195
(Sutton Cheney) **6** 288
(Twycross) **6** 308
St James's Pl. **1** 59
St James's Sq. **1** 59
St James's St. **1** 59
St John St. **1** 59
St John the Baptist's Chapel **2** 175
St John the Baptist's Church
(Belton) **7** 27
(Billesdon) **4** 5
(Buckminster) **2** 55
(Croxton Kerrial) **2** 104
(Enderby) **6** 88
(Glooston) **4** 66
(Heather) **6** 105
(Hugglescote) **7** 67
(Hungarton) **3** 144
(King's Norton) **4** 142
(Little Stretton) **4** 159
(Muston) **2** 35
(Old Dalby) **2** 51
(South Croxton) **3** 73
(Whitwick) **7** 73
St John the Evangelist's Church **3** 238
St John's Church
(Cold Overton) **4** 152
(Donisthorpe) **7** 280
(Goadby) **4** 70
(Grimston) **3** 106
(Rolleston) **4** 222
(Shenton) **6** 295
St John's Close **1** 191
St John's Cross **1** 103
St John's Hospital **5** 141
St John's Hospital Garden **1** 178
St John's Lane **1** 59
St John's Orchard **1** 178
St John's, House called **1** 88
St Joseph's Cottage **7** 58
St Lawrence's Church **7** 264
St Leonard's Church
(Holwell) **2** 163
(Hoton) **3** 131
(Leicester) **1** 83
(Misterton) **5** 148
(Swithland) **7** 228
(Thorpe Langton) **4** 276
St Luke's Church
(Gaddesby) **3** 95
(Laughton) **4** 154
(Newton Harcourt) **4** 298
(Thurnby) **4** 278
St Margaret's Bed **1** 192
St Margaret's Charity School **1** 114
St Margaret's Church
(Blackfordby) **7** 15
(Leicester) **1** 83
(Stoke Golding) **6** 276
St Margaret's Church Lane **1** 59
St Margaret's Cowpasture **1** 205
St Margaret's Fields **1** xiii, 210

St Margaret's Guildhall **1** 107
St Margaret's Lane **1** xii, 59
St Margaret's National School **1** 114
St Margaret's St. **1** 59
St Margaret's Workhouse **1** 97
St Martin's Charity Schools **1** 114
St Martin's Church
(Desford) **6** 73
(Leicester) **1** 84
(Stapleton) **6** 215
St Martin's Convent **6** 276
St Martin's Lane **1** xii, 59
St Mary and All Saints' Church **6** 273
St Mary and St Hardulph's Church **7** 37
St Mary and St John the Baptist's Church **7** 186
St Mary and St Nicholas's Church **7** 242
St Mary in the Elms Church **7** 249
St Mary Magdalene's Church
(Kilby) **5** 108
(Knighton) **5** 126
(Shearsby) **5** 188
(Stapleford) **2** 140
(Waltham on the Wolds) **2** 272
St Mary's Bridge **4** 178
St Mary's Charity School **1** 114
St Mary's Church
(~ de Castro) **1** 85
(Anstey) **7** 3
(Ashby Folville) **3** 100
(Ashby Magna) **5** 10
(Barkby) **3** 22
(Barwell) **6** 128
(Bitteswell) **5** 28
(Bottesford) **2** 25
(Brentingby) **2** 133
(Broughton Astley) **5** 39
(Bruntingthorpe) **5** 50
(Burrough on the Hill) **2** 232
(Carlton Curlieu) **4** 28
(Chadwell) **2** 218
(Coleorton) **7** 79
(Congerstone) **6** 241
(Cotesbach) **5** 76
(Elmesthorpe) **6** 83
(Freeby) **2** 129
(Garthorpe) **2** 149
(Harby) **2** 95
(Hinckley) **6** 120
(Humberstone) **3** 134
(Lutterworth) **5** 141
(Melton Mowbray) **2** 175
(Nether Broughton) **2** 46
(Nevill Holt) **4** 204
(Noseley) **4** 210
(Osgathorpe) **7** 164
(Peckleton) **6** 207
(Potters Marston) **6** 218
(Queniborough) **3** 183
(Sileby) **3** 216
(Snibstone) **7** 182
(Stoughton) **4** 260
(Thorpe Arnold) **2** 278
(Walton on the Wolds) **3** 269
(Wigston Parva) **5** 224
(Willoughby Waterleys) **5** 235
(Wyfordby) **2** 144
(Wymeswold) **3** 276
St Mary's Close **1** 192
St Mary's Cottage **7** 58
St Mary's Cowpasture **1** 205
St Mary's Fields **1** xiii, 211
St Mary's Lane **7** 182
St Mary's Meadow **1** 200
St Mary's Mill **1** 152
St Mary's Mill Bridge **1** 76
St Mary's Mill Close **1** 192
St Mary's Mill Holmes **1** 201
St Mary's Priory **2** xiii, 6
St Mary's Rd **4** 172
St Mary's Workhouse **1** 97
St Matthew's Church
(Chilcote) **7** 261
(Overseal) **7** 283
(Worthington) **7** 256
St Michael and All Angels' Church **2** 10

St Michael's Church
(Appleby) **6** 11
(Blaston) **4** 14
(Brooksby) **3** 125
(Cosby) **5** 68
(Cranoe) **4** 32
(Croft) **6** 68
(Diseworth) **7** 118
(Eastwell) **2** 121
(Edmondthorpe) **2** 298
(Fenny Drayton) **6** 329
(Hallaton) **4** 96
(Hose) **2** 100
(Illston) **4** 129
(Loddington) **3** 164
(Markfield) **6** 177
(Ravenstone) **7** 181
(Rearsby) **3** 198
(Stoney Stanton) **6** 283
(Stretton en le Field) **7** 289
(Thorpe Satchville) **3** 264
(Thurmaston) **3** 238
(Wartnaby) **2** 166
St Michael's Church **1** 86
St Michael's Lane **1** 60
St Morrell's Chapel **4** 96
St Nicholas' Church **1** xiv, 86
St Nicholas' Shambles **1** 120
St Nicholas' Sq. **1** 60
St Nicholas' St. **1** 60
St Nicholas's Church
(Bringhurst) **4** 19
(Fleckney) **4** 51
(Frolesworth) **5** 91
(Little Bowden) **4** 185
(Lockington) **7** 103
(Mowsley) **4** 198
(Shangton) **4** 234
(South Kilworth) **5** 194
St Paul's Church **7** 249
St Peter's and St Paul's
Church **2** 201
St Peter's Bed **1** 192
St Peter's Church
(Allexton) **3** 4
(Arnesby) **5** 5
(Ashby Parva) **5** 13
(Aston Flamville) **6** 23
(Bardon) **6** 36
(Belgrave) **3** 47
(Braunstone) **6** 45
(Church Langton) **4** 38
(Claybrooke Parva) **5** 61
(Galby) **4** 63
(Glenfield) **6** 93
(Hathern) **7** 84
(Higham on the Hill) **6** 110
(Horninghold) **4** 107
(Kirby Bellars) **3** 86
(Knossington) **4** 147
(Leire) **5** 130
(Market Bosworth) **6** 167
(Markfield) **6** 177
(Mountsorrel) **7** 152
(Netherseal) **7** 270
(Oadby) **5** 165
(Redmile) **2** 196
(Saltby) **2** 251
(Saxby) **2** 135
(Saxelby) **3** 108
(Shackerstone) **6** 233
(Stockerston) **4** 252
(Stonesby) **2** 256
(Swepstone) **7** 219
(Syston) **3** 228
(Thornton) **6** 27
(Tilton) **3** 245
(Whetstone) **5** 213
(Witherley) **6** 323
(Wymondham) **2** 288
St Peter's Church **1** 87
St Peter's Ct. **1** 61
St Peter's Lane **1** 61
St Peter's St. **3** 228
St Philip and St James's
Church **6** 99

St Philip's Church **6** 223
St Remigius' Church **2** 90
St Sepulchre's Church **1** 87
St Sepulchre's Spring and Well **1** 229
St Simon and St Jude's Church **6** 134
St Sunday's Bridge **1** 75
St Swithin's Church **2** 78
St Thomas Becket's Church
(Skeffington) **3** 221
(Tugby) **3** 255
St Thomas of Canterbury's Church **3** 81
St Thomas's Church
(Catthorpe) **5** 54
(Glen Parva) **5** 104
(Willesley) **7** 18
St Wilfred's Church **4** 133
St Wistan's Church
(Wigston Magna) **5** 224
(Wistow) **4** 296
Salem Chapel **1** 89
Salem Rd **6** 51
Salisbury Arms (P.H.) **3** 249
Sallow Close **1** 192
Salmon street **7** 131
Salt Street **6** 11
Saltbeck **2** 7
SALTBY **2** xii, xiii, 250
Saltby Heath Fm **2** 251
Saltby Heath Lodge **2** 251
Saltby Lodge **2** 251
Saltby Pasture **2** 251
Saltegate **2** 172
Salter's Hill **2** 232
Saltersford Bridge **7** 277
Saltersford Brook **7** 277
Saltersford Cottages **7** 277
Saltersford Fm **7** 277
Saltersford Rd **3** 134
Sand Pit Close
(Aylestone Rd) **1** 192
(St Margaret's) **1** 192
Sand Pit Lane
(Belgrave Gate) **1** 61
(Russell Sq.) **1** 61
Sand Pit Meadow **1** 202
Sand Pits **1** 147
Sandacre St. **1** 61
Sandeford **6** xvii
Sander's Wood **6** 79
Sandfields Fm **7** 230
Sandford Rd **3** 228
Sandham Bridge **7** 230
Sandhills Lodge **7** 238
Sandhills Wood **7** 157
Sandhole Lane **7** 197
Sandhole Spinney **6** 211
Sandhurst **7** 270
Sandlen's Lodge **3** 11
Sandpit Cottages **6** 300
Sandpit Fm **2** 90
Sandpitt lane **5** 221
Sandtop Fm **7** 15
Sandtop Lane **7** 15
Sandy Lane
(Great Dalby) **2** 78
(Melton Mowbray) **2** 170
(Scalford) **2** 211
Sandy Walk **6** 124
Sanham Ho. **3** 86
Sanvey Cross **1** 103
Sanvey Gate **1** xi, xii, 61
Sanvey Lane **5** 19
Sapcoat's Lodge **2** 64
Sapcoat's Spinney **2** 64
SAPCOTE **6** 226
Sapcote Field Fm **6** 227
Sapcote Glebe Fm **6** 227
Sapcote Quarry **6** 227
Sapcote Rd
(Hinckley) **6** 117
(Stoney Stanton) **6** 283
Saracen's Head (P.H.)
(Hotel St.) **1** 137
(Staunton Harold) **7** 208
Saracen's Head (P.H.)
(Ashby de la Zouch) **7** 11
(Loughborough) **7** 134
Sarah St. **1** 62
Sash Row **1** 62

Saturday Market, The **1** 115
Saturday Shambles **1** 120
Saunt St. **1** 62
Sauvey Castle **2** xiii, 283
Sauvey Castle Fm **2** 284
Sawgate Lodge Fm **2** 140
Sawgate Rd
(Burton Lazars) **2** 65
(Stapleford) **2** 140
Sawgate Road Fm **2** 140
Sawley Cut **7** 104
SAXBY **2** xii, 135
Saxby Station **2** 136
SAXELBY **3** xiv, 108
Saxelby Barn **3** 108
Saxelby Lodge **3** 108
Saxelby Lodge Fm **3** 108
Saxelby New Wood **3** 108
Saxelby Pastures **3** 108
Saxelby Tunnel **3** 108
Saxelby Wood **3** 108
Saxelbye Park **3** 108
Saxelbye Road Fm **3** 11
Scaffacre Fm **7** 118
Scalacres **7** 207
SCALFORD **2** 208
Scalford Brook
(Melton Mowbray) **2** 181
(Scalford) **2** 211
Scalford Gorse **2** 163
Scalford Hall **2** 211
Scalford Hall Farm Cottage **2** 211
Scalford Lodge **2** 211
Scalford Rd **2** 170
Scalford Road Lodge **2** 178
Scalford Station **2** 211
Scam-Hazel Fm **7** 15
Scam-Hazel Wood **7** 15
Scamhazels Fm **7** 15
Schofield Fm **4** 55
Scholes Fm **3** 112
School Fm
(Loddington) **3** 164
(Orton on the Hill) **6** 318
(Staunton Harold) **7** 208
School House Lane **1** 62
School Houses **7** 24
School Lane
(Belton) **7** 27
(Birstall) **7** 30
(Coleorton) **7** 79
(Cranoe) **4** 32
(Husbands Bosworth) **4** 120
(Lubenham) **4** 165
(Market Harborough) **4** 172
(Newton Burgoland) **7** 224
(Peatling Magna) **5** 174
(Scalford) **2** 211
(Woodhouse) **7** 249
(Worthington) **7** 256
School St.
(Fleckney) **4** 51
(Loughborough) **7** 129
(Oakthorpe) **7** 277
(Syston) **3** 228
School, The **2** 129
Scoborough **4** 165
Scoborough Cottage **4** 165
Sconsborough Hill **4** 147
Scot's Lodge **3** 259
Scotland
(Burton Overy) **4** 22
(Houghton) **4** 110
(Staunton Harold) **7** 208
Scotland End **4** 185
Scotland Lane **4** 110
Scotlands Drive **7** 62
Scotlands Fm **7** 208
Scotlands Rd **7** 62
Scouthouse Hill **7** 197
SCRAPTOFT **4** xii, 229
Scraptoft: unindexed modern street-names **4** 230
Scraptoft Brook **4** 229
Scraptoft Gorse **4** 229
Scraptoft Hall **4** 229
Scraptoft Hill Fm **4** 229
Scraptoft Lane
(Beeby) **3** 43
(Humberstone) **3** 134
Scraptoft Lodge **4** 229
Scraptoft Long Spinney **4** 229

Scraptoft Rise **4** 230
Scrimshaw's Windmill **2** 25
SEAGRAVE **3** xii, 206
Seagrave Grange Fm **3** 207
Seagrave Rd **3** 216
Seagrave Wolds **3** 207
Seal Brook **7** 270
Seal Fields Fm **7** 270
Seal Ho. **7** 270
Seal Pasture **7** 270
Sealby **4** 282
Sealwood Fm **7** 270
Second Lock **4** 139
Seel's Yard **1** 172
Sefton Ho. **6** 40
Sefton House Fm **6** 40
Seine Lane **6** 88
Seinepool Cottages **6** 88
Selby's Lodge **4** 129
Seldom Seen Fm **4** 6
Sennel's Cottage **6** 318
Serpentine Garden **6** 119
Serpentine, The **5** 209
Severn Bridge **1** 76
Severn Leys **1** 205
Seward's row **7** 131
Sewers and Drains **1** 108
SEWSTERN **2** xiii, 58
Sewstern Grange **2** 59
Shackerdale Fm **5** 224
Shackerdale Rd **5** 220
SHACKERSTONE **6** xi, xiii, 232
Shackerstone Barn **6** 233
Shackerstone Fields **6** 233
Shackerstone Gorse **6** 233
Shackerstone Junction **6** 233
Shackerstone Park Coverts **6** 233
Shackerstone Station **6** 233
Shade Cottages **5** 224
Shade, The
(Sharnford) **6** 247
(Stapleton) **6** 215
Shadows Lane **6** 241
Shady Lane
(Evington) **4** 44
(Oadby) **5** 165
Shakespeare Park **6** 45
Shakespeare's Head (P.H.)
(Braunstone) **6** 45
(South Gates) **1** 137
Shambles Lane
(Leicester) **1** 62
(Lutterworth) **5** 139
Shamlys **2** 173
SHANGTON **4** xi, xii, 233
Shangton Grange **4** 234
Shangton Holt **4** 234
Shangton Lodge **4** 234
Shangton Manor **4** 234
SHARNFORD **6** xi, 246
Sharnford Cottage **6** 247
Sharnford Fields **6** 247
Sharnford Lodge **6** 247
Sharnford Lodge Fm **6** 247
Sharnford Rd
(Aston Flamville) **6** 23
(Sapcote) **6** 227
Sharp's Covert **6** 308
Sharpland **5** 19
Sharpley Ave. **7** 62
Sharpley Hill **7** 157
Sharrag Grounds **5** 149
Shaw Fm **6** 319
Shaw Lane **6** 177
Shaw's Bazaar **1** 119
Shaw's Fm **6** 218
Shaw's Green **7** 49
SHAWELL
5 xi, xii, xiii, xiv, xv, 182
Shawell Grange **5** 183
Shawell Hall **5** 183
Shawell Lodge **5** 183
Shawell Lodge Fm **5** 183
Shawell Manor **5** 183
Shawell Rd **5** 76
Shawell Wood **5** 148
SHEARSBY **5** xiii, xiv, 187
Shearsby Lodge **5** 188
Shearsby Spa **5** 188
Sheep Pen Lane **1** 62
Sheep Pens **1** 116
Sheep-Le Fm **3** 269

Sheepmarket, The **1** xiv, 117
Sheepthorns Fm **4** 286
Sheepthorns Spinney **4** 28
Sheepwash
(Allexton) **3** 4
(Sileby) **3** 216
(Waltham on the Wolds) **2** 272
(Withcote) **2** 284
(Wymeswold) **3** 276
Sheepwash Lane **7** 3
Sheepy Fields **6** 255
Sheepy Hall **6** 252
Sheepy Lodge **6** 252
Sheepy Lodge Fm **6** 252
SHEEPY MAGNA **6** 251
SHEEPY PARVA **6** 255
Sheepy Parva Fm **6** 155
Sheepy Rd **6** 252
Sheepy Wood
(Hinckley) **6** 124
(Twycross) **6** 309
Sheet Hedges Wood **7** 157
Shelbrook road **7** 11
Shelbrooke Ho. **6** 159
Shelford Lane **6** 313
SHELLBROOK **7** 17
Shellbrook Fm **7** 18
Shellbrook Ho.
(Anstey) **7** 3
(Shellbrook) **7** 18
SHELTHORPE **7** 147
Shelton Cottages **7** 256
SHENTON **6** xv, xvi, 295
Shenton Gorse **6** 295
Shenton Hall **6** 295
Shenton Lane
(Market Bosworth) **6** 167
(Sutton Cheney) **6** 288
(Upton) **6** 262
Shepe Cross **2** 176
Shepecote yard **6** 119
Shepherd and Shepherdess (P.H.) **7** 224
Shepherd's Hill **7** 141
Shepherd's Hill Plantation **6** 99
Shepherd's Ho. **6** 23
Shepherds Plantation **7** 94
SHEPSHED **7** xii, xiii, 193
Shepshed: unindexed modern street-names **7** 197
Shepshed Field **7** 112
Shepshed Fields **7** 112
Shepshed Mill **7** 197
Shepshed Nook **7** 197
Sherbrook Fox Covert **2** 90
Shericles Fm **6** 207
Sherrard St. **2** 170
Sherrier's School and Almshouses **5** 138
Sherwood Rd **6** 276
Sherwood Rise **4** 6
Shield, The **1** 202
Shieling, The **3** 11
Shilton Heath **6** 134
Shilton Rd
(Kirkby Mallory) **6** 211
(Thurlaston) **6** 305
Shipley Hill **3** 192
Shipley's Ct. **1** 62
Shipman's Barn Stud **2** 181
Shire Hall **1** 109
Shire Hall Close **1** 193
Shire Hall Orchard **1** 178
Shirtecoat **4** 176
Shittlewood's Barn **3** 269
SHOBY **3** xiv, 10, 11
Shoby Cottages **3** 112
Shoby House Fm **3** 112
Shoby Lodge **3** 112
Shoby Lodge Fm **3** 112
Shoby Scholes **3** 112
Shoemakers' Shops, The **1** 118
Shop in the Chequer **1** 118
Shops under the Gainsborough **1** 118
Shops under the Guildhall **1** 119
Shorn Hill **6** 39
Short Cliff **7** 197
Short Heath **7** 283
Short Lane **7** 49
Short St. **1** 63
Short St. **1** 63

Short Wood
(Isley cum Langley) **7** 94
(Netherseal) **7** 270
Shortcliffe Brook
(Garendon) **7** 141
(Shepshed) **7** 197
Shortcliffe Fm **7** 197
Shortesway **5** 139
Shortheath Fm **7** 283
Shortridge Lane **6** 88
Shoulder of Mutton (P.H.)
(Ashby de la Zouch) **7** 11
(Foxton) **4** 55
(Great Bowden) **4** 177
(Lubenham) **4** 165
(Oakthorpe) **7** 277
Shoulder of Mutton (P.H.)
(Arnesby) **5** 5
(Ashby Parva) **5** 13
(Barsby) **3** 102
(Dunton Bassett) **5** 84
(Great Easton) **4** 75
(High St.) **1** 137
(North Kilworth) **5** 157
(Shawell) **5** 183
(Stretton en le Field) **7** 290
(Wigston Magna) **5** 222
(Wymeswold) **3** 276
Shoulder of Mutton Hill **1** 222
Shrubberies, The **6** 269
Shrubbery Ho. **7** 12
Shrubbery Terrace **7** 12
Shrubbery, The
(Castle Donington) **7** 49
(Overseal) **7** 283
(Westrill and Starmore) **5** 209
Shuttleworth Lane **5** 68
Sibbertoft Rd **4** 120
SIBSON **6** 258
Sibson Grange **6** 258
Sibson Manor **6** 258
Sibson Mill **6** 258
Sibson Wolds **6** 266
Side Hollows **6** 11
Side Hollows Fm **6** 11
Sidney St. **1** 63
SILEBY **3** xiv, 215
Sileby Lodge **3** 216
Sileby Mill **3** 216
Sileby Rd **3** 35
Silk Mead **1** 202
Silver Birches **6** 124
Silver St.
(Leicester) **1** xiv, 63
(Oakthorpe) **7** 277
(Whitwick) **7** 73
Silverside **5** 141
Simon St. **1** 63
Simons' Hospital **1** 97
Simpkin's Bridge **5** 104
Simpson St. **1** 63
Sinope **7** 211
Sir Francis Burdett's Covert **2** 78
Sir Henry Hastings' Windmill **1** 153
Sir John Moore's School **6** 11
Sir John's Wood
(Belvoir) **2** 8
(Glen Parva) **5** 104
Sir Thomas White (P.H.) **1** 137
Six Acres **5** 39
Six Hills **3** 128
Six Hills Lane **2** 51
Six Hills Rd **3** 55
Six Leys **1** 205
SKEFFINGTON **3** xi, xv, 220
Skeffington Gap **3** 221
Skeffington Gap Fm **3** 221
Skeffington Glebe Rd **3** 221
Skeffington Hall **3** 221
Skeffington Lodge Fm **3** 221
Skeffington Vale **3** 221
Skeffington Wood **3** 221
Skeg Hill **3** 173
SKETCHLEY **6** 56
Sketchley Brook **6** 57
Sketchley Chapel **6** 57
Sketchley Fm **6** 57
Sketchley Grange **6** 57
Sketchley Hall **6** 57
Sketchley Hill **6** 57
Sketchley Hill Fm **6** 57
Sketchley Hill Ho. **6** 57

Sketchley Ho. **6** 57
Sketchley Lane **6** 57
Sketchley Manor **6** 57
Sketchley Rd **6** 57
Sketchley Road **6** 119
Skeyth, The **1** xi, 144
Slackey Lane **7** 24
Slade Fm **7** 98
Slade Hill **7** 197
Slade Ho. **7** 98
Slade Lane **7** 44
Slade Spinney **7** 98
Slades, The **7** 197
Slate Brook
(Groby) **6** 99
(Ratby) **6** 223
Slate Hills **6** 255
Slate Pit (P.H.) **7** 249
Slate St. **1** 63
Slater St. **1** 63
SLAWSTON **4** xii, xiv, 238
Slawston Hill **4** 240
Slawston Rd
(Medbourne) **4** 189
(Welham) **4** 290
Sledge Spinney **2** 85
Sliding Stone Enclosure **7** 158
Slip Inn Fm **5** 13
Sludge Hall
(Cold Newton) **3** 173
(Great Glen) **4** 81
Sludge Hall Fm **3** 173
Sludge Hall Hill **3** 173
Slyborough Hill **2** 90
Small Clump **3** 269
Smart's Close **1** 193
SMEETON **4** xii, 245
Smeeton Gorse **4** 246
Smeeton Hill **4** 246
Smeeton Ho. **4** 246
Smeeton Rd **4** 133
SMEETON WESTERBY **4** 246
Smisby Rd **7** 9
Smith's Fm **7** 64
Smith's Free School **2** 201
Smith's Lodge **2** 91
Smithy Fm **6** 283
Smithy Fm, The **6** 183
Smithy Lane **7** 112
SMOCKINGTON **6** 57
Smockington Ho. **6** 57
Smockington Hollow
(Smockington) **6** 57
(Wigston Parva) **5** 232
Smoile Cottage **7** 256
Smoile Farm Cottage **7** 256
Smoile Fm **7** 256
Smoile, The **7** 256
Smooth Coppice **7** 94
SNARESTONE **6** 268
Snarestone Ho. **6** 269
Snarestone Lodge **6** 269
Snarestone Rd **6** 11
Snarestone Station **6** 269
Snarrow's Fm **7** 164
Snarrow's Rd **7** 164
Snell's Nook **7** 147
Snell's Nook Lane **7** 147
Snell's Nook Lodge **7** 147
Snibston Barn **7** 181
Snibston Grange **7** 182
Snibston Lodge Fm **7** 182
SNIBSTONE **7** 182
Snow Hill **2** 170
Snow's Lodge **4** 230
Snowdon Lodge **5** 157
Snows Lane **3** 158
Soaper Lane **1** xii, 63
Soar Bank Fm **7** 187
Soar Brook
(Aston Flamville) **6** 23
(Sharnford) **6** 247
Soar Brook Spinney **6** 51
Soar Ho. **7** 171
Soar Lane **1** 64
Soar Lane **1** 64
Soar Mill **5** 40
Soars Lodge Fm **5** 110
Soho **2** 173
SOMERBY **2** 225
Somerby Grange **2** 227
Somerby Ho. **2** 227

Somerby Rd
(Cold Overton) **4** 152
(Knossington) **4** 148
Sopers Bridge **6** 283
Sopers Bridge Fm **6** 283
South Bridge **1** 76
South Close **1** 193
South Crofts **1** 193
SOUTH CROXTON **3** xi, xiii, 72
South Croxton Grange **3** 73
South End **7** 153
South End Terrace **3** 228
South Farthing **3** 221
South Field Close **1** 193
South Fields, The **1** xiii, xiv, 211
South Fields
(Barrow upon Soar) **3** 35
(Husbands Bosworth) **4** 120
(Tugby) **3** 255
South Fields Pl. **1** 64
South Gates **1** xiii, 8, 64
SOUTH KILWORTH **5** 193
South Kilworth Grange **5** 195
South Kilworth Lodge **5** 195
South Kilworth Rd **5** 157
South Knighton **5** 126
South Lodge
(Ab Kettleby) **2** 159
(Baggrave) **3** 151
(Cotesbach) **5** 76
(Lowesby) **3** 169
(Willesley) **7** 18
South Manor Ho. **3** 73
South parade **2** 173
South Park **6** 305
South Quarter **1** 11
South St.
(Ashby de la Zouch) **7** 9
(Barrow upon Soar) **3** 36
(Loughborough) **7** 129
(Scalford) **2** 211
(Whitwick) **7** 73
South View Fm **6** 227
South Wigston **5** 224
South Wood **7** 9
Southampton St. **1** 65
Southern Lane **2** 173
Southfield Fm **6** 23
Southfield Lodge
(Nevill Holt) **4** 204
(Syston) **3** 228
Southfield Spinney **4** 210
Southfields **2** 227
Southfields Fm **7** 187
Southfields Park **7** 129
Southfields Rd **7** 129
Southgate St. **1** 64
Southwood Fm **7** 9
Sowter's Lane **3** 55
Spa Gardens **1** 178
Spa Lane
(Hinckley) **6** 117
(Wigston Magna) **5** 220
Spa Pl. **1** 144
Spade Tree Inn **7** 224
Sparkenhoe **6** 262
Sparkenhoe Hundred **6** 1
Sparkenhoe St. **1** 65
Sparrow Hill **7** 129
Sparrow's Cottage **5** 157
Speechley's Close **1** 193
Spencefield Lane **4** 44
Spencer St. **1** xv, 65
Spinney Close **4** 139
Spinney Farm Cottage **2** 181
Spinney Fm
(Burton on the Wolds) **3** 55
(Melton Mowbray) **2** 181
(Orton on the Hill) **6** 319
(Ratcliffe on the Wreake) **3** 192
(Shawell) **5** 183
Spinney Hill **4** 88
Spinney Hills **1** 222
Spinney Ho.
(Barkby Thorpe) **3** 29
(Fleckney) **4** 51
Spinney Lodge **5** 68
Spinney Nook **3** 255
Spinney, The
(Breedon on the Hill) **7** 37
(Horninghold) **4** 107
(Melton Mowbray) **2** 181

(Norton Juxta Twycross) **6** 313
(Willesley) **7** 18
Spinneys, The
(Evington) **4** 44
(Peckleton) **6** 207
(Woodhouse) **7** 249
Spion Kop **5** 41
Spital Hill **7** 49
Spital Hill Fm **7** 49
Spital, The **7** 49
Spitelgate **2** 173
Spittle Bridge **1** 76
Spittle End **2** 173
Spittle House Close **1** 193
Spittle House Ford **1** 227
Spittle House Pool **1** 228
Spowtewell Strete **5** 221
Spread Eagle (P.H.)
(Church Gate) **1** 137
(Hinckley) **6** 122
Spring Burrow Lodge **7** 27
Spring Cottage
(Markfield) **6** 177
(Moira) **7** 24
(Swepstone) **7** 219
(Wigston Magna) **5** 222
Spring Cottage Bridge **7** 24
Spring farm **2** 180
Spring Fm
(Bagworth) **6** 26
(Coalville) **7** 61
Spring Gardens
(Hinckley) **6** 119
(Leicester) **1** 178
Spring Grange **3** 43
Spring Hill **7** 73
Spring Hill Fm
(Ashby Magna) **5** 10
(Wykin) **6** 137
Spring Hill Wood **7** 249
Spring Ho. **7** 98
Spring Lane
(Packington) **7** 286
(Shepshed) **7** 197
(Swannington) **7** 211
Spring Lodge **5** 222
Spring Plantation **7** 58
Spring Wood
(Cadeby) **6** 59
(Coleorton) **7** 79
(Ravenstone) **7** 181
(Staunton Harold) **7** 208
Springfield
(Ashby de la Zouch) **7** 10
(Bushby) **4** 282
(Twyford and Thorpe) **3** 262
Springfield Fm
(Chadwell) **2** 218
(Oakthorpe) **7** 277
(Ragdale) **3** 128
(Sapcote) **6** 227
(Smeeton Westerby) **4** 246
Springfield Hill **3** 173
Springfield Ho. **7** 211
Springfield House **5** 126
Springfield Lodge **4** 81
Springfield Rd
(Hinckley) **6** 117
(Shepshed) **7** 197
Springs Fm **4** 51
Springwell **5** 213
Springwell Lane **5** 213
Springwood Fm **7** 208
SPROXTON **2** xi, xii, 245
Sproxton Heath Gorse **2** 246
Sproxton Lodge **2** 246
Sproxton Thorns **2** 246
Spurr's Lodge **3** 95
Square and Compass (P.H.)
(Branston) **2** 111
(Snarestone) **6** 269
Square Covert
(Long Clawson) **2** 91
(Twycross) **6** 309
Square Spinney
(Great Glen) **4** 81
(Rothley) **7** 187
(Scraptoft) **4** 230
Square, The
(Bagworth) **6** 26
(Littlethorpe) **5** 73
(Long Whatton) **7** 112

(Oakthorpe) **7** 277
Squirrel Lane **7** 37
Stack House Fm **3** 134
Stackley Ho. **4** 81
Stackyard Spinney **5** 165
Staff of Life (P.H.) **4** 198
Stafford Leys **6** 153
Stafford Lodge **7** 171
Stag (P.H.) **6** 52
Stag and Castle (P.H.) **6** 27
Stag and Hounds (P.H.) **2** 232
Stag and Pheasant (P.H.) **7** 153
Stag and Pheasant (P.H.)
(Humberstone Gate) **1** 137
(Loughborough) **7** 134
(Lutterworth) **5** 138
Stag Inn **5** 174
Stag's Head (P.H.) **1** 137
Stallard Lodge **3** 100
Stamford and Warrington Arms (P.H.) **7** 62
Stamford and Warrington Arms (P.H.) **7** 37
Stamford Arms (P.H.) **6** 99
Stamford Arms (P.H.) **6** 223
Stamford St. **1** 65
Standard Hill **7** 182
Standing Dale **7** 256
Stanford Hall **5** 209
Stanford Park **5** 209
Stanford road **7** 131
Stanleigh Plantation **7** 280
Stanley St. **1** 65
Stanley's Close **1** 193
Stanley's Meadow **1** 202
Stanton Fields **6** 273
Stanton Ho. **6** 283
Stanton Lane
(Markfield) **6** 177
(Potters Marston) **6** 218
(Thornton) **6** 27
Stanton Lodge **6** 283
Stanton Plantation
(Halstead) **3** 249
(Welby) **3** 18
Stanton Rd
(Elmesthorpe) **6** 83
(Sapcote) **6** 228
STANTON UNDER BARDON **6** 272
STAPLEFORD **2** 139
Stapleford Barn **2** 140
Stapleford Hall **2** 140
Stapleford Lodge **2** 140
Stapleford Manor **2** 140
Stapleford Park **2** xii, 140
STAPLETON **6** xiii, 214
Stapleton Brockey **6** 215
Stapleton Fields **6** 215
Stapleton Lane
(Barwell) **6** 128
(Dadlington) **6** 292
(Kirkby Mallory) **6** 211
Stapleton Wood **6** 215
Star (P.H.)
(Thrussington) **3** 232
(Stoney Stanton) **6** 283
Star (P.H.)
(Belgrave Gate) **1** 137
(Hinckley) **6** 122
(Long Clawson) **2** 91
(Melton Mowbray) **2** 178
(Sapcote) **6** 228
(unlocated) **1** 137
Star and Ball (P.H.) **1** 137
Star and Garter (P.H.) **5** 222
Starkey Lane **7** 286
Starkey's Bridge **7** 49
Starkey's Hill **7** 49
STARMORE **5** xiii, xiv, 208
Starr Lane **1** 65
Start Barn **6** 51
Start Fm **6** 51
STATHERN **2** 260
Stathern Bridge **2** 261
Stathern Junction **2** 261
Stathern Lodge **2** 261
Stathern Wood **2** 261

Station **7** 129
Station Cottages
(East Norton) **3** 178
(Great Dalby) **2** 78
(Hallaton) **4** 96
(Lowesby) **3** 169
(Scalford) **2** 211
(West Langton) **4** 293
Station Fm
(Ashby Magna) **5** 10
(Bagworth) **6** 26
(Broughton Astley) **5** 39
(North Kilworth) **5** 157
(Saxelby) **3** 108
(Shenton) **6** 296
(Thurnby) **4** 279
Station Hill
(Swannington) **7** 211
(Twyford) **3** 262
Station Ho. **2** 211
Station Hotel **5** 39
Station Hotel (P.H.) **7** 134
Station Inn **7** 211
Station Lane
(Great Glen) **4** 81
(Kirby Bellars) **3** 86
(Leire) **5** 130
Station Rd
(Ashby de la Zouch) **7** 10
(Birstall) **7** 30
(Broughton Astley) **5** 39
(Castle Donington) **7** 49
(Countesthorpe) **5** 80
(Croft) **6** 68
(Desford) **6** 73
(Dunton Bassett) **5** 84
(Elmesthorpe) **6** 83
(Heather) **6** 105
(Hinckley) **6** 117
(Husbands Bosworth) **4** 120
(Littlethorpe) **5** 73
(Market Bosworth) **6** 167
(North Kilworth) **5** 157
(Old Dalby) **2** 51
(Ratby) **6** 223
(Stoke Golding) **6** 276
(Stoney Stanton) **6** 283
(Syston) **3** 228
(Ullesthorpe) **5** 206
(Wigston Magna) **5** 220
Station St.
(Kibworth Beauchamp) **4** 133
(Whetstone) **5** 213
Station Terrace **7** 12
Station Wharf **4** 279
STAUNTON HAROLD **7** 206
Staunton Harold Hall **7** 208
Staunton Lodge **7** 208
Staveley Lodge **2** 178
Steam Mill Bridge **7** 277
Steam Mill Inn **7** 277
Steeple Row **7** 129
Steins Lane **3** 134
Stemborough Lane **5** 130
Stemborough Lane Fm **5** 130
Stemborough Mill **5** 130
Stepping Stones Ford **3** 43
Stinking Wood **7** 158
Stints, The **7** 84
Stirling Castle (P.H.) **1** 137
Stock Leys Barn **2** 78
Stockdale Arms (P.H.) **1** 137
Stockdale Tce **1** 65
STOCKERSTON **4** xiii, 250
Stockerston Cross Roads **4** 14
Stockerston Hall **4** 252
Stockerston Lane **4** 75
Stockerston Rd **3** 4
Stocking Close **1** 193
Stocking Fm **7** 249
Stocking Head **6** 119
Stocking Lane **7** 37
Stocking Wood **1** 224
Stocking, The (P.H.) **1** 137, 222
Stockland Rd **5** 19
Stocks **1** 111
Stocks Ho. **6** 207
Stockwell **3** 276
Stockwell Head **6** 124
Stockwell Ho. **5** 97

Stockwell Lane **6** 119
Stoke Fields Fm
(Hinckley) **6** 123
(Stoke Golding) **6** 276
STOKE GOLDING
6 xi, xii, xiv, xv, xvi, xvii, 275
Stoke Golding Wharf **6** 276
Stoke Grange **6** 110
Stoke Lane
(Hinckley) **6** 117
(Stoke Golding) **6** 276
Stoke Lodge **6** 276
Stoke Rd
(Hinckley) **6** 117
(Upton) **6** 262
Stokes Croft **5** 84
Stone Bridge **2** 175
Stone Bridge Cottage **6** 283
Stone Close **1** 193
Stone Cottage **4** 204
Stone Ho.
(Cold Overton) **4** 152
(Market Harborough) **4** 174
Stone Houses **7** 94
Stone Lodge
(Groby) **6** 99
(Halstead) **3** 249
Stone Pit Close **1** 193
Stone Pit Lodge **3** 173
Stone Quarries **1** 147
Stone Row **7** 61
Stone Rows **7** 24
Stone St. **7** 84
Stonebridge **5** 223
Stonefield Ho. **2** 241
Stoneham Ho. **3** 238
Stonehill Ave **7** 30
Stonehouse Fm
(Carlton) **6** 64
(Packington) **7** 286
Stoneleigh **3** 238
Stonemasons' Arms (P.H.) **1** 138
Stonepit Houses **2** 166
Stonepit Plantation **7** 197
Stonepit Spinney **2** 166
Stonepit Terrace **2** 241
STONESBY **2** xii, 255
Stonesby Gorse **2** 256
Stonesby House Fm **3** 18
Stonesby Lodge **2** 256
Stonesby Spinney **2** 256
Stoney Bridge **5** 39
Stoney Cove **6** 283
Stoney Lane
(Appleby) **6** 11
(Coleorton) **7** 79
(Markfield) **6** 177
STONEY STANTON **6** 282
Stoney Stanton Fm **6** 283
Stoney Stanton Sidings **6** 283
Stoney Way Plantation **6** 11
Stoneygate **5** 126
Stoneywell Cottage **7** 238
Stoneywell Wood **7** 238
Stonton Rd **4** 38
Stonton Wood **4** 255
STONTON WYVILLE **4** 254
Stony Bridge **6** 218
Stony Cottage **7** 79
Stonycroft Cottage **7** 164
Stonygate **6** 118
Stordon Grange **7** 164
Stordon Lane **7** 164
Storehouses **1** 107
Storer's Almshouse **2** 176
Storkit Lane **3** 276
Stormsworth **5** xiv, 208
Story Arms (P.H.) **7** 164
STOUGHTON **4** 259
Stoughton Grange **4** 260
Stoughton Grange Fm **5** 165
Stoughton Hall **4** 260
Stoughton Lodge **4** 260
Stoughton Rd **5** 166
Stoughton waye **5** 221
Strancliffe **3** 36
Strancliffe Ho. **3** 36
Strancliffe Lane **3** 36
Stratho Coppice **6** 153
Straw Hall
(Peatling Magna) **5** 174
(Stanton under Bardon) **6** 273

Straw Hall Fm **6** 273
Strawberry Cottage **6** 228
Strawberry Garden Fm **6** 88
Strawberry Hill Plantation **7** 58
Strawberry Lane **7** 15
Strawfield Ho. **5** 150
Streethill Fm **3** 169
Stretchnook Fm **6** 300
Stretton Bridge **7** 290
STRETTON EN LE FIELD **7** x, 289
Stretton Firs **6** 57
Stretton Hall **4** 265
Stretton Hall Fm **4** 81
Stretton Hill **7** 290
Stretton Lane **4** 110
Stretton Lodge **4** 265
STRETTON MAGNA **4** 264
Stretton Mill **7** 290
Stretton Pines **6** 57
Stretton Rd **4** 81
Strifts Plantation **2** 150
Stubble Hills **6** 296
Stud Brook **7** 49
Stud Fm
(Desford) **6** 73
(Peckleton) **6** 207
(Shenton) **6** 296
(Stanton under Bardon) **6** 273
Stud Fm, The **4** 120
Studbrook Hollow **7** 49
Stult Bridge **5** 33
Stump Cross **3** 81
Sturgess' Sq. **1** 65
Sturrad Spinney **4** 14
Stye Hills **7** 249
Sugar Loaf (P.H.) **2** 159
Sulby Rd **4** 120
Sullington (P.H.) **7** 198
Sullington Rd **7** 197
Summer Lees Plantation **3** 108
Summerpool Brook **7** 129
Summerpool Rd **7** 129
Sun (P.H.) **4** 75
Sun (P.H.)
(Barkestone) **2** 201
(Church Gate) **1** 138
(Market Harborough) **4** 174
(Northgate St.) **1** 138
Sun Inn **6** 252
Sunday School, The **2** 100
Sunny Leys **4** 110
Sunnydale **6** 124
Sunnyhill **6** 51
Sunnyside Fm
(Eye Kettleby) **2** 189
(Hinckley) **6** 124
Sunnyside Terrace **6** 144
SUTTON CHENEY **6** xiii, xv, 287
Sutton Cheney Wharf **6** 288
Sutton Fields Fm **5** 40
Sutton Fm **5** 40
Sutton Hill Bridge **5** 40
Sutton Hill Bridge Fm **5** 40
SUTTON IN THE ELMS **5** 39
Sutton Lane **6** 167
Sutton Lodge **5** 39
Sutton Wharf Bridge **6** 289
Sutton's Close **1** 193
Swains Lodge **4** 44
Swainspark **7** 20
Swallow Hole **2** 104
Swallowhole Covert **2** 251
Swan (P.H.)
(North Kilworth) **5** 157
(Stoke Golding) **6** 276
Swan (P.H.)
(Hallaton) **4** 97
(Measham) **7** 265
(Melton Mowbray) **2** 178
(Mountsorrel) **7** 153
(Shawell) **5** 183
(South Gates) **1** 138
(Wigston Magna) **5** 222
Swan and Fish (P.H.) **1** 138
Swan and Rushes (P.H.) **1** 138
Swan and Salmon (P.H.) **2** 178
Swan Fm **6** 124

Swan Inn **5** 206
Swan Inn (P.H.) **6** 145
Swan Lane **1** 65
Swan St.
(Leicester) **1** 65
(Loughborough) **7** 129
(Seagrave) **3** 208
Swan with Two Necks (P.H.) **1** 138
Swan with Two Necks (P.H.) **3** 208
Swan's Close **1** 193
Swan's Nest **2** 181
SWANNINGTON **7** xi, 210
Swannington Common **7** 211
Swannington Rd **7** 181
Swannymoat Fm **7** 27
Swannymote Rd **7** 73
Swannymote Rock **7** 58
Swedish Houses **6** 207
Sweet Hills **7** 58
Sweethill **7** 21
Sweethill Cottage **7** 18
Sweethill Lodge **7** 21
Sweethill Oak **7** 18
SWEPSTONE **7** x, 218
Swepstone Fields **7** 225
Swepstone Ho. **7** 219
Swepstone Rd
(Heather) **6** 105
(Measham) **7** 265
(Snarestone) **6** 269
Swine Lane **1** 66
Swinesmarket, *The* **1** xiii, 117
SWINFORD **5** xiii, xiv, 200
Swinford Corner **5** 201
Swinford Covert **5** 201
Swinford Lodge **5** 201
Swinford Rd **5** 148
Swingbridge Fm **7** 129
Swingbridge Rd **7** 129
Swingbridge St. **4** 55
SWITHLAND **7** xiii, 227
Swithland Hall **7** 228
Swithland Rd
(Coalville) **7** 62
(Thurcaston) **7** 230
Swithland Reservoir **7** 228
Swithland Wood **7** 158
Swynlane **2** 173
Sycamore Cottage **6** 283
Sycamore Fm **6** 237
Sycamore Lane **1** 66
Sydney street **2** 173
Sykes Spinney **3** 245
SYSONBY **2** xii, xiii, 190
Sysonby Church **2** 191
Sysonby Cottage **2** 191
Sysonby Fm **2** 191
Sysonby Grange **2** 191
Sysonby Grange Fm **2** 191
Sysonby Grange Lane **2** 191
Sysonby Hall **2** 191
Sysonby Knoll **2** 191
Sysonby Lodge **2** 191
Sysonby Lodge Fm **2** 191
Sysonby Upper Lodge **2** 191
SYSTON **3** xi, 2, 227
Syston Grange **3** 22
Syston Lodge **3** 228
Syston Mills **3** 228

Tabbermear's Fm **5** 114
Tailor's Yard **1** 172
Tailors' Arms (P.H.)
(Chatham St.) **1** 138
(Northgate St.) **1** 138
Talbot (P.H.)
(Cotes de Val) **5** 97
(Market Harborough) **4** 174
Talbot (P.H.)
(Belgrave Gate) **1** 138
(Denman St.) **1** 138
(Loughborough) **7** 134
(Mountsorrel) **7** 153
(South Kilworth) **5** 195
(Talbot Lane) **1** 138
(Walton) **5** 114
Talbot Arms (P.H.) **7** 74
Talbot House Fm **7** 211
Talbot Inn (P.H.) **3** 47
Talbot Inn **7** 211

Talbot Lane
(Leicester) **1** 66
(Swannington) **7** 211
(Thringstone) **7** 70
Talbot Place **7** 280
Talbot Sq. **1** 66
Tamborough Fm **4** 63
Tampion's Coppice **4** 147, 148
Tamworth Rd
(Appleby Parva) **6** 11
(Ashby de la Zouch) **7** 10
(Willesley) **7** 18
Tangle-Trees Wood **7** 158
Taske's Holme **1** 202
Tatborough Spinney **6** 313
Tavern, The (P.H.) **6** 122
Taylor's Bridge **5** 223
Taylor's Close **1** 194
Taylor's Rock **7** 249
Taylor's Turnover Lock **4** 139
Taylors' Farm **1** 181
Tealby's Fm **5** 97
Tebbutt's Sq. **1** 66
Tempe **7** 219
Temperance Ho. **2** 104
Temperance Hotel **2** 34
Temperance terrace **2** 173
Temple Fm
(Stanton under Bardon) **6** 273
(Wellsborough) **6** 266
Temple Hall
(Rothley) **7** 185
(Wellsborough) **6** 266
Temple Hill **7** 73
Temple Mill **6** xiii, 266
Temple of Venus **7** 141
Temple Row **1** 66
Temple Walk **1** 205
Temple, The **6** 265
Ten Acre Plantation **3** 108
Ten Bells (P.H.) **1** 138
Tennis Wood **3** 249
Tent, The **2** 251
Tenter Croft **1** 146, 194
Tentercroft Ave **3** 228
Terrace Bridge **6** 241
Terrace Hill Fm **2** 111
Terrace Hills **2** 111
Terrace, The
(Charley) **7** 58
(Upton) **6** 262
Thames St. **1** 66
Theatre, The **1** 144
THEDDINGWORTH **4** xiii, 268
Theddingworth Hollow Spinney **4** 269
Theddingworth Lodge **4** 269
Theddingworth Rd
(Husbands Bosworth) **4** 120
(Lubenham) **4** 165
(Mowsley) **4** 198
Theddingworth Station **4** 269
Thimble Hall Rd **3** 262
Thirteen Acre Plantation **7** 49
Thistle Hall **5** 235
Thistley Close Cottages **4** 129
Thompson's Sq. **1** 66
Thorn Hills **6** 187
Thorn Spinney **7** 158
Thornborough **7** 73
Thornborough Fm **5** 148
Thornborough Rd **7** 62
Thornborough Spinney **5** 148
Thorne Lodge **4** 230
Thorney Crofts **6** 124
Thorney Fields Fm **6** 83
Thorney Hollow **2** 51
Thorney Plantation **3** 19
Thorneyfields Fm **6** 153
Thornfield Ho. **6** 276
THORNTON **6** 26
Thornton Lane **1** xiv, 66
Thornton Lane
(Bagworth) **6** 26
(Stanton under Bardon) **6** 273
Thornton Mill **6** 27
Thornton Reservoir **6** 27
Thorntop **7** 15
Thorntree Cottage **3** 36
Thorntree Fm **7** 249
Thornyfields **6** 153
THORPE ACRE **7** 143

THORPE ARNOLD **2** 277
Thorpe Ashes **2** 278
Thorpe Bridge **2** 174
Thorpe End **2** 181
Thorpe End Villa **2** 78
Thorpe Hill **7** 144
Thorpe Hindles **2** 278
THORPE LANGTON **4** xii, 276
Thorpe Langton Rd
(East Langton) **4** 38
(Welham) **4** 290
Thorpe Lodge **2** 278
Thorpe Rd **2** 170
THORPE SATCHVILLE **3** xv, 263
Thorpe Side **2** 211
Thorpe Trussels **3** 264
Three Ashes **6** 59
Three Boundary Fm **5** 40
Three Cranes (P.H.)
(Gallowtree Gate) **1** 138
(Humberstone Rd) **1** 138
Three Crowns (P.H.)
(Barwell) **6** 128
(Hathern) **7** 84
(Loughborough) **7** 134
(Whitwick) **7** 74
(Wymeswold) **3** 276
Three Crowns (P.H.)
(Gallowtree Gate) **1** 138
(Market Harborough) **4** 174
(Melton Mowbray) **2** 178
(Somerby) **2** 227
Three Crowns Inn (P.H.) **3** 36
Three Gate Rd **4** 210
Three Gates **4** 129
Three Gates Fm **4** 129
Three Horse Shoes (P.H.)
(Hemington) **7** 108
(Stoke Golding) **6** 276
Three Horse Shoes (P.H.)
(Breedon on the Hill) **7** 37
(Great Bowden) **4** 177
(Hugglescote) **7** 67
(Loughborough) **7** 134
(Twyford) **3** 262
Three Horseshoes (P.H.)
(Kibworth Harcourt) **4** 139
(Whitwick) **7** 74
Three Horseshoes (P.H.)
(Sproxton) **2** 246
(Wymondham) **2** 288
Three Owls (P.H.) **5** 33
Three Pots (P.H.) **6** 52
Three Pots Fm **6** 57
Three Shire Bush **2** 42
Three Shire Oak **2** 42
Three Swans (P.H.) **4** 174
Three Tuns (P.H.) **6** 40
Three Tuns (P.H.)
(Earl Shilton) **6** 135
(Hinckley) **6** 122
(Kegworth) **7** 98
(Loughborough) **7** 134
(Melton Mowbray) **2** 178
Threeways Fm **6** 51
THRINGSTONE **7** xi, xiii, 69
Throne's Barn **5** 28
THRUSSINGTON **3** xiii, 231
Thrussington Grange **3** 232
Thrussington Lodge **3** 232
Thrussington Mill **3** 232
Thrussington Wolds Gorse **3** 232
THURCASTON **7** x, xi, 229
Thurcaston Glebe Lodge **7** 230
Thurcaston Grange **7** 230
Thurcaston Lane **7** 230
THURLASTON **6** 299
Thurlaston Brook
(Croft) **6** 68
(Thurlaston) **6** 300
Thurlaston Fields **6** 300
Thurlaston Lane
(Croft) **6** 68
(Earl Shilton) **6** 134
(Huncote) **6** 140
Thurlaston Lodge **6** 300
THURMASTON
3 xi, xii, xiii, xiv, xv, 237
Thurmaston: unindexed
modern street-names **3** 238

Thurmaston Hall **3** 238
Thurmaston Lodge **3** 238
THURNBY **4** xii, 278
Thurnby: unindexed modern street-names **4** 279
Thurnby and Scraptoft Station **4** 279
Thurnby Brook **4** 279
Thurnby Gate **1** 66
Thurnby Grange **4** 279
Thurnby Hill **4** 279
Thurnby Lane **4** 260
Thurnby Lodge **4** 279
Thurnby Nurseries **4** 279
Tickhill Lane **7** 197
Tickow Lane **7** 197
Tie Barn **6** 198
TILTON **3** xi, 244
Tilton Grange **3** 245
Tilton Lane **4** 6
Tilton Station **3** 249
Tilton Wood **3** 245
Timber Hill **2** 173
Timberwood Hill **7** 58
Timberwood Hill Plantation **7** 58
Timm's Bridge **6** 233
Tin House Fm **4** 178
Tinker's Barn **7** 270
Tinker's Gate Cottage **7** 270
Tinker's Gate Fm **7** 270
Tiny Cottage **7** 104
Tip Cottages **2** 51
Tippets, The **1** 194
Tipping's Gorse **2** 104
Tithe Abbey Meadows **1** 202
Tithe Barn Lodge **5** 174
Tithe Fm **3** 36
Tithebarn Fm **3** 100
Tivey's Fm **6** 233
Toft's Hill **2** 261
Toft's Lane **2** 261
Tolbooth, The **1** 107, 110
Tolbothe, le **7** 131
Toll Gate Fm **5** 97
Toll gate Ho. **3** 47
Toll Gate Ho. **5** 141
Tollgate Cottage **7** 18
Tollgate Cottages **7** 10
Tomley Hall **5** xv, 54
TONGE **7** 41
Tonge and Breedon Station **7** 41
Tonge Fm **7** 41
Tonge Gorse **7** 41
Tonge Hall Fm **7** 41
Tonge Lane **7** 37
Tooley Cottage **6** 207
Tooley Fm **6** 207
Tooley Park **6** 206
Tooley Park Cottages **6** 207
Tooley Spinneys **6** 207
Toot Hill **6** 228
Toothill Rd **7** 129
Top Bridge **7** 171
Top Coppice **6** 88
Top Fm
(Burton on the Wolds) **3** 55
(Little Stretton) **4** 159
Top Ho. **6** 244
Top Lock **4** 133
Top Lodge **4** 210
Top Merril Cottage **7** 26
Top Merril Grange **7** 26
Top Park **2** 65
Top Rectory Fm **6** 11
Top Spinney **6** 289
Top St. **6** 12
Top Town Plantation **3** 269
Top Yard Fm **4** 178
Tophouse Fm
(Knaptoft) **5** 123
(Shenton) **6** 296
Torchmere **1** xi, 228
Toston Hill **2** 33
Tower Fm **5** 150
Tower Hayes **6** 144
Tower Hayes Fm **6** 273
Tower Mill **1** 153
Tower St. **1** 66
Towers Hospital, The **3** 134
Towers, The **6** 153
Town Arms (P.H.) **1** 139
Town Bridge **6** 233

Town Close **4** 22
Town Ditch **1** 7
Town End **7** 118
Town End Cottage **4** 107
Town End Fm **5** 76
Town End Plantation **3** 55
Town Gaol **1** 110
Town Gaol, The **6** 120
Town Green **7** 187
Town Hall **1** 105
Town Hall **6** 120
Town Hall Garden **1** 178
Town Hall Tavern (P.H.) **6** 122
Town Hall Yard **1** 172
Town Library **1** 144
Town Walls **1** 7
Town Wards **1** 11, 251
Townend Rd
(Barwell) **6** 128
(Enderby) **6** 88
Townhall Lane **1** 67
Townsend Bridge **5** 223
Townsend Close Spinney **4** 222
Townsend Fm **6** 289
Townsend Lane **7** 64
Townsend's Mill **1** 153
Trent Fm **7** 49
Trent Lane **7** 49
Tressal Rd **7** 62
Triangle Spinney **6** 266
Trinity Hospital **1** 100
Trinity Lane **6** 118
Trinity Rd **5** 213
Tripontium **5** xii, 54, 76, 182, 185
Triumphal Arch **7** 141
Tryon Spinney **3** 245
Tucker's Holt **7** 225
Tucker's Holt Fm **7** 225
Tuckett Rd **7** 249
TUGBY **3** xi, xiii, xiv, 254
Tugby Bushes **3** 255
Tugby Rd **4** 71
TugbyWood **3** 255
Tugwell Lane **4** 96
Tumblin Fds **6** 73
Tunnel Fm **3** 106
Tunnel Ho. **7** 12
Tunnel Lodge **2** 51
Tunnel Plantation **3** 106
Tunnel Wood **7** 10
TUR LANGTON **4** xii, 285
Tur Langton Lodge **4** 286
Tur Langton Rd **4** 139
Turk's Head (P.H.) **7** 50
Turk's Head (P.H.) **1** 139
Turn Bridge **6** 233
Turn Inn **7** 84
Turn St. **3** 229
Turner's Barn Fm **4** 129
Turnover Bridge
(Newton Harcourt) **4** 298
(Snarestone) **6** 269
(Wigston Magna) **5** 223
Turnpike Fm **6** 313
Turnpost Fm **3** 276
Turry Log **7** 71
Turry Log Cottage **7** 71
Turry Tor **7** 71
Turvey **7** 112
Turvey Ho. **7** 249
Turvey Lane **7** 112
Twenty Acre **3** 55
Twentysteps **7** 71
Two Acre Spinney **5** 19
TWYCROSS **6** 307
Twycross Hill **6** 309
Twycross Lane **6** 239
Twycross Park **6** 309
TWYFORD **3** xiii, 261
Twyford Rd
(Burrough on the Hill) **2** 232
(Lowesby) **3** 169
Tyburn **7** 158
Tylecoat Ho. **6** 12
Tyler Bridge **7** 197
Tylers Rd **7** 27
Tysoe Hill **6** xii, 93
Tythe Fm **6** 273
Tythorn Bridge **5** 223
Tythorn Hill
(Newton Harcourt) **4** 298
(Wigston Magna) **5** 224

Tythorn Hill Fm **5** 224
Tythorn Lodge **5** 222

ULLESTHORPE
5 xi, xii, xiii, xiv, xv, 204
Ullesthorpe Court **5** 206
Ullesthorpe Grange **5** 206
Ullesthorpe Lodge **5** 206
Ullesthorpe Rd
(Ashby Parva) **5** 13
(Bitteswell) **5** 28
(Gilmorton) **5** 97
Ullesthorpe Station **5** 206
ULVERSCROFT **7** x, 236
Ulverscroft Cottage **7** 239
Ulverscroft Grange **7** 239
Ulverscroft Lane **7** 158
Ulverscroft Lodge **7** 239
Ulverscroft Mill **7** 239
Ulverscroft Priory **7** xi, 236
Ulverscroft Wood **7** 239
Underwood's Lodge **3** 95
Unicorn (P.H.) **7** 134
Unicorn (P.H.)
(Belgrave Gate) **1** 139
(Lutterworth) **5** 138
Unicorn Orchard **1** 178
Unicorn St. **3** 238
Unicorn, The (P.H.) **6** 319
Union (P.H.) **5** 19
Union (P.H.)
(Glen Parva) **5** 104
(Great Bowden) **4** 177
(Hinckley) **6** 122
(Measham) **7** 265
Union Anchor (P.H.) **4** 120
Union Arms (P.H.) **1** 139
Union Chapel **5** 157
Union Lodge **7** 20
Union mill **5** 223
Union passage **7** 11
Union Row **4** 174
Union St. **7** 129
Union St.
(Freeschool Lane) **1** xiv, 67
(Marlborough St.) **1** xiv, 67
Union street **2** 173
Union Wharf **4** 174
Union Workhouse **7** 12
Union Workhouse
(Billesdon) **4** 6
(Blaby) **5** 33
(Hinckley) **6** 120
(Lutterworth) **5** 138
(Melton Mowbray) **2** 176
Unitarian Chapel **1** 89
University Fm **3** 229
Uplands **6** 153
Upper Bond St. **6** 117
Upper Broombriggs **7** 250
Upper End **2** 78
Upper Fields **7** 219
Upper Grange **6** 177
Upper Grange Fm
(Hugglescote) **7** 67
(Old Dalby) **2** 51
Upper Green Place **4** 178
Upper King St. **1** 67
Upper Mill **3** 55
Upper Pool **6** 305
Upper Rectory Fm **6** 11
Uppingham Rd
(Blaston) **4** 14
(Houghton) **4** 110
(Humberstone) **3** 134
(Medbourne) **4** 189
(Skeffington) **3** 221
(Stockerston) **4** 252
UPTON **6** xii, xvi, 261
Upton Lodge **6** 262
Upton Park **6** 262
Usher Fm **5** 97

Vale Cottage **3** 221
Vale Fm **6** 110
Vale Ho. **2** 205
Vale of Belvoir **2** xi, xii, xiii, 3
Valley Farm **6** 110
Valley Farm Cottages **6** 269
Valley Fm
(Bitteswell) **5** 28
(Ibstock) **6** 144

(North Kilworth) **5** 157
(Othorpe) **4** 240
(Snarestone) **6** 269
(Wellsborough) **6** 266
(Willesley) **7** 19
Valley Lane **5** 28
Valley View Fm **5** 131
Valley, The **3** 11
Van and Horses (P.H.) **1** 139
Vane Fm **3** 255
Various Pumps **1** 108
Vaughan St. **7** 62
Vauxhall Ct. **1** 67
Vauxhall Gardens **1** 144, 178
Vauxhall St. **1** 67
Vauxhall Wharf (P.H.) **1** 139
Venonis
5 xii, xiii, 65, 66, 205, 231, 232
Verney Spinney **5** 209
Vero's Lane **6** 183
Vicarage Closes **1** 194
Vicarage Drive **4** 55
Vicarage Fm
(Billesdon) **4** 6
(Scalford) **2** 211
Vicarage Forest Fm **7** 73
Vicarage Ho. **4** 230
Vicarage Lane
(Belgrave) **3** 47
(Humberstone) **3** 135
(Packington) **7** 286
Vicarage, The
(Ab Kettleby) **2** 159
(Arnesby) **5** 5
(Ashby de la Zouch) **7** 12
(Ashby Folville) **3** 100
(Ashby Magna) **5** 10
(Barkby) **3** 22
(Barkestone) **2** 201
(Barlestone) **6** 40
(Barrow upon Soar) **3** 36
(Belgrave) **3** 47
(Belton) **7** 37
(Billesdon) **4** 6
(Bitteswell) **5** 28
(Blackfordby) **7** 15
(Breedon on the Hill) **7** 37
(Buckminster) **2** 55
(Castle Donington) **7** 49
(Claybrooke Parva) **5** 61
(Countesthorpe) **5** 80
(Croxton Kerrial) **2** 104
(Diseworth) **7** 118
(Donisthorpe) **7** 280
(Dunton Bassett) **5** 84
(Earl Shilton) **6** 134
(Eaton) **2** 119
(Enderby) **6** 88
(Evington) **4** 44
(Fleckney) **4** 51
(Frisby on the Wreake) **3** 81
(Garthorpe) **2** 150
(Great Dalby) **2** 78
(Great Easton) **4** 75
(Great Glen) **4** 81
(Horninghold) **4** 107
(Hose) **2** 100
(Humberstone) **3** 134
(Hungarton) **3** 145
(Kilby) **5** 108
(Little Dalby) **2** 85
(Lockington) **7** 104
(Loddington) **3** 164
(Long Clawson) **2** 91
(Lowesby) **3** 169
(Lubenham) **4** 165
(Melton Mowbray) **2** 178
(Mountsorrel) **7** 153
(Newton Linford) **7** 158
(Old Dalby) **2** 51
(Orton on the Hill) **6** 319
(Packington) **7** 286
(Plungar) **2** 205
(Queniborough) **3** 183
(Quorndon) **7** 171
(Ratby) **6** 223
(Ratcliffe on the Wreake) **3** 192
(Rothley) **7** 187
(Saltby) **2** 252
(Scalford) **2** 211
(Shackerstone) **6** 233
(Sileby) **3** 216

(Slawston) **4** 240
(Somerby) **2** 227
(Sproxton) **2** 246
(Stoke Golding) **6** 276
(Stonesby) **2** 256
(Sutton Cheney) **6** 289
(Swannington) **7** 212
(Swinford) **5** 201
(Syston) **3** 229
(Theddingworth) **4** 269
(Thornton) **6** 27
(Thorpe Arnold) **2** 278
(Thringstone) **7** 71
(Thrussington) **3** 232
(Thurmaston) **3** 238
(Thurnby) **4** 279
(Tilton) **3** 245
(Tugby) **3** 255
(Twycross) **6** 309
(Wartnaby) **2** 166
(Whetstone) **5** 213
(Whitwick) **7** 73
(Wigston Magna) **5** 222
(Worthington) **7** 256
(Wymeswold) **3** 276
Vicarage, The **6** 123
Vicarage Yard **1** 172
Vicars Road **7** 11
Vicary Fm **7** 250
Vicary Lane **7** 250
Vice's Bridge **5** 223
Victoria (P.H.) **7** 74
Victoria (P.H.)
(Church Gate) **1** 139
(Great Bowden) **4** 177
(Lutterworth) **5** 138
Victoria Arms (P.H.) **7** 198
Victoria Cottage **2** 36
Victoria Cottages **6** 99
Victoria Fm
(Claybrooke Magna) **5** 58
(Lutterworth) **5** 141
Victoria Gardens **6** 51
Victoria Pl. **1** 67
Victoria Rd
(Burbage) **6** 51
(Coalville) **7** 62
(Ibstock) **6** 144
(Whetstone) **5** 213
(Woodhouse) **7** 250
Victoria St.
(Fleckney) **4** 51
(Loughborough) **7** 129
(Melton Mowbray) **2** 170
(Wigston Magna) **5** 220
Victoria St.
(Lee St.) **1** 67
(New Bridge St.) **1** 68
Victory Park **5** 68
Vine (P.H.)
(Highcross St.) **1** 139
(Market Harborough) **4** 174
(Shepshed) **7** 198
(Vine St.) **1** 139
Vine Cottage
(Bottesford) **2** 25
(Markfield) **6** 177
Vine House Fm **7** 230
Vine St. **1** 68
Vine Terrace **3** 131
Vine Yard **1** 172
Vinegar Hill **7** 256
Vineries, The **5** 68
Volunteer (P.H.)
(Ashby de la Zouch) **7** 11
(Loughborough) **7** 134
Vowe's Gorse **4** 96
Vyne Ho. **6** 262

Wade Lodge **4** 129
Wadlands Fm **7** 283
Wagon and Horses (P.H.) **6** 145
Waggon and Horses (P.H.)
(Ashby de la Zouch) **7** 11
(Belgrave Gate) **1** 139
(Coalville) **7** 62
(Granby St.) **1** 139
(Hinckley) **6** 122

(Markfield) **6** 177
(Sewstern) **2** 59
(Swannington) **7** 212
(Whitwick) **7** 74
(Worthington) **7** 256
Wain Bridge **4** 298
Wainhouse, The **1** 181
Wakeley Fm **5** 150
Walberton **6** 153
WALCOTE **5** xiii, 149
Walcote Ho. **5** 150
Walcote Lodge **5** 150
Walcote Rd **5** 195
Walcotefield **5** 149
Walker Crofts **1** 146
Walker Holme **1** 202
Walker Lane **1** xii, 68
Walker's Fm **6** 244
Walker's Ho. **6** 283
Walks, The **6** 119
Wall's Windmill **1** 153
Wallend Plantation **7** 250
Walnut Fm
(Cosby) **5** 68
(East Norton) **3** 178
Walsh Gate **1** 68
Walsh Hall **1** 154
Walsh Hall Close **1** 194
Walsh Meadow **1** 202
Waltham Ho. **2** 272
Waltham Lodge **2** 272
Waltham New Covert **2** 272
WALTHAM ON THE WOLDS **2** xii, 271
Waltham Pasture Fm **2** 272
Waltham Thorns **2** 272
WALTON **5** xiii, 113
Walton Brook **3** 269
Walton Fields **3** 107
Walton Grange
(Walton on the Wolds) **3** 269
(Walton) **5** 114
Walton Hill **7** 94
Walton Holme **3** 269
Walton Holt **5** 114
Walton Holt Gorse **5** 114
Walton Lane **3** 36
Walton Lodge
(Kirby Muxloe) **6** 153
(Walton on the Wolds) **3** 269
(Walton) **5** 114
Walton Lodge Fm **5** 40
WALTON ON THE WOLDS **3** xii, 268
Walton Thorns **3** 269
Walton Top Fm **3** 269
Walton Way **7** 277
Walton Way Cottages **7** 277
WANLIP **7** 242
Wanlip Hall **7** 243
Wanlip Hill **7** 243
Wanlip Lane **7** 30
Wanlip Rd **3** 229
Ward's Cottage **6** 326
Ward's End **7** 129
Ward's lane **7** 131
Ward's Plantation **7** 290
Warden Ho. **6** 110
Warner St. **3** 36
Warner's Garden **1** 179
Warner's lane **7** 131
Warner's Nurseries **1** 179
Warren Fm
(Enderby) **6** 88
(Knaptoft) **5** 123
(Lockington) **7** 104
(Misterton) **5** 148
(Tur Langton) **4** 286
Warren Hill **7** 158
Warren Hills **7** 58
Warren Ho. **7** 24
Warren House Fm **7** 24
Warren Lane
(Belton) **7** 27
(Lockington) **7** 104
Warren Lodge **7** 27
Warren Pond **7** 208
Warren, The
(Kibworth Beauchamp) **4** 133
(Tur Langton) **4** 286
Warrington St. **1** 68
WARTNABY **2** xii, 165

Wartnaby Hall **2** 166
Wartoft Grange **7** 92
Warwellmill **2** 180
Warwick Lane **6** 167
Warwick Rd
(Kibworth Harcourt) **4** 139
(Whetstone) **5** 213
Wash Brook **5** 166
Wash Dyke **2** 95
Wash Dyke Bridge **4** 110
Wash Lane **7** 181
Wash Pit Lane **6** 40
Washbrook Lane **4** 22
Washdike Bridge **2** 34
Washdyke Rd **4** 216
Washpit Lane **4** 165
Washpit Spinney **4** 129
Washstones Bridge **3** 81
Washstones Lodge **3** 114
Water Close **1** 194
Water Field **1** 213
Water Laggs, The **1** 194
Water Lane
(Frisby on the Wreake) **3** 81
(Long Clawson) **2** 91
Water lane **2** 173
Water Mill Ho. **4** 255
Water Works **7** 234
Watergate Lane **6** 45
Waterlock, The **1** 194
Waterloo Lodge **3** 151
Waterloo St. **1** xiv, 68
Waterman's Spinney **4** 296
Watermill, (The) **5** 223
Waterworks Cottage
(North Kilworth) **5** 157
(Oakthorpe) **7** 277
Watery Gate Ford
(Earl Shilton) **6** 134
(Normanton Turville) **6** 305
Watery Gate Lane **6** 305
Watery Lane **1** 68
Watling Sq. **1** 68
Watling St. **1** xv, 68
Watling Street **6** xi, xv
Watling Street Fm **6** 57
Watson's Gorse **4** 34
Watson's Spinney **3** 151
Wavendon Grange **2** 51
Wayside Fm **6** 247
Weaver's Arms (P.H.) **6** 122
Wednesday Market **1** 118
Weekday Shambles **1** 120
Weir Fm **4** 133
Weir Ho. **4** 133
Weir Lane **4** 110
Weir Rd
(Kibworth Beauchamp) **4** 133
(Saddington) **4** 224
WELBY **3** xiv, xv, 18
Welby Grange **3** 19
Welby Ho. **3** 19
Welby House Fm **3** 19
Welby Lane
(Ab Kettleby) **2** 159
(Melton Mowbray) **2** 170
(Welby) **3** 19
Welby Lodge **3** 19
Welby Osier Beds **3** 19
Welcomb **5** 131
Welford Pl. **1** 69
Welford Rd
(Arnesby) **5** 5
(Blaby) **5** 33
(Husbands Bosworth) **4** 120
(Kilby) **5** 108
(Knaptoft) **5** 123
(Leicester) **1** 69
(Shearsby) **5** 188
(South Kilworth) **5** 195
(Wigston Magna) **5** 220
Welford Wharf **4** 120
WELHAM **4** 290
Welham Lane **4** 32
Welham Lodge **4** 290
Welham Rd
(Great Bowden) **4** 178
(Slawston) **4** 240
(Thorpe Langton) **4** 277
Well **2** 65
Well Ho. **7** 250
Well Lane **2** 159

Well Lane **6** 119
Well Wong **1** 195
Welland Park **4** 174
Wellehaw **1** 195
Wellhead **3** 221
Wellington and Castle (P.H.) **1** 139
Wellington St.
(Leicester) **1** xiv, 69
(Loughborough) **7** 129
(Syston) **3** 229
WELLSBOROUGH **6** xiii, 264
Wellsic Lane **7** 187
Welsboro Bridge **6** 167
Welsh Myers **3** 221
Wembley Ho. **3** 107
Wentworth Arms (P.H.) **6** 83
Wentworth Arms (P.H.) **6** 211
Wentworth Rd **7** 62
Wesley's Methodist Meeting House **6** 121
Wesleyan Chapel **3** 178
Wesleyan Methodist Chapel
(Leicester) **1** 89
(Long Clawson) **2** 91
(Nether Broughton) **2** 46
(Scalford) **2** 211
West Bank **3** 276
West Beacon Fm **7** 250
West Bridge **1** 77
West Bridge Dunghill **1** 108
West Bridge Pavement **1** 79
West Cote **5** 84
West Cotes **1** 218
West Cotes Grange **1** 181
West Cottage **3** 276
West Cottages **5** 76
West Ellistown Terrace **6** 144
West End
(Barrow upon Soar) **3** 36
(Long Clawson) **2** 91
West End Fm
(Bitteswell) **5** 28
(Brentingby) **2** 133
(Keyham) **3** 158
(Willoughby Waterleys) **5** 235
West Field Fm
(Earl Shilton) **6** 134
(Hinckley) **6** 124
West Fields
(Carlton) **6** 64
(Rothley) **7** 187
West Fields, The **1** xiii, 213
West Fm **7** 79
West Gate **1** 69
West Gates **4** 240
West Gates **1** xiii, 8
West Goscote Hundred **7** 1
West Green **6** 128
West Lane
(Billesdon) **4** 6
(Ravenstone) **7** 181
WEST LANGTON **4** xi, xii, 293
West Langton Lodge **4** 38
West Lodge **2** 85
West Mains **3** 255
West Meadow Fm **7** 49
West Meadow Lane **7** 112
West Park **3** 259
West Quarter **1** xiii, 11
West St. **3** 229
West St. **1** 69
West street **7** 131
West View **2** 278
West View Fm
(Netherseal) **7** 270
(Walcote) **5** 150
West Walk **6** 144
West Wong **2** 8
Westbrooke Ho. **4** 185
Westbury **6** 128
Westdale Fm **5** 174
Westdale Ho. **5** 174
WESTERBY **4** xii, 245
Westerby Fm **4** 246
Westerby Ho. **4** 246
Western Ave. **7** 62
Western Cottages **5** 157
Western Fm **5** 174

Western Lodge Fm **6** 140
Westfield
(Kibworth Harcourt) **4** 139
(Sileby) **3** 216
Westfield Cottage **5** 5
Westfield Fm **7** 171
Westfield Ho. **5** 5
Westfield Lane **7** 187
Westfield Rd **6** 118
Westfields **6** 40
Westgate Ho. **5** 213
Westgate Lane **4** 165
Westhill Fm **6** 12
Westlands
(Blackfordby) **7** 15
(Ratcliffe Culey) **6** 330
Westmeadow Brook
(Belton) **7** 27
(Long Whatton) **7** 112
Westminster **2** 8
Westminster Yard **6** 119
Westmoreland **6** 124
Weston **6** 321
Westover **5** 141
WESTRILL **5** xiii, 208, 209
Westrill Spinney **5** 209
Westthorpe **2** 23
Wetherby Ho. **3** 183
Wetherley Ho. **3** 183
Whalebones **4** 148
Wharf Fm **6** 234
Wharf House Hotel **4** 120
Wharf Inn (P.H.) **6** 122
Wharf Lane **6** 289
Wharf road **5** 221
Wharf St. **1** xv, 69
Wharf, The **2** 173
Whartop Grange **7** 92
WHATBOROUGH **3** 272
Whatborough Fm **3** 273
Whatborough Hill **3** 273
Whatborough Rd
(Owston) **4** 216
(Whatborough) **3** 273
Whatoffs Fm **7** 171
Whatton Fields **7** 112
Whatton Hall **7** 112
Whatton Ho. **7** 112
Whatton Mere Barn **7** 98
Whatton Rise **7** 112
Wheat Hill Spinney **2** 85
Wheat Sheaf (P.H.)
(Loughborough) **7** 134
(Market Bosworth) **6** 167
Wheat Sheaf (P.H.)
(Aylestone) **5** 19
(Husbands Bosworth) **4** 121
(Lutterworth) **5** 138
Wheat St. **1** 69
Wheathill Fm **5** 188
Wheatsheaf (P.H.)
(Melton Mowbray) **2** 178
(Muston) **2** 36
(Thurcaston) **7** 230
(Whetstone) **5** 213
(Woodhouse) **7** 250
Wheatsheaf (P.H.)
(Gallowtree Gate) **1** 139
(Market Harborough) **4** 174
(Rotherby) **3** 122
(Wheat St.) **1** 139
Wheel (P.H.) **3** 198
Wheel (P.H.) **2** 272
Wheel Inn **2** 111
Wheelwright's Shop
(Cossington) **3** 61
(Gaddesby) **3** 95
Wheler Lodge **4** 121
Wheler Lodge Fm **4** 121
WHETSTONE **5** xv, 212
Whetstone Brook **5** 213
Whetstone Gorse **5** 213
Whetstone Gorse Cottages **5** 213
Whetstone Gorse East **5** 213
Whetstone Gorse Lane **5** 213
Whetstone Gorse West **5** 213
Whetstone Grange **5** 213
Whetstone Ho. **5** 213
Whetstone Lodge **5** 213
Whetstone Pastures **5** 213
Whetstone's Mill **1** 153
Whiles Wood **6** 27

Whinney Pit Spinney **4** 222
Whitborough Fm **7** 21
Whitcroft's Lane **7** 239
White Barn Cottage **5** 68
White Barn Drive **5** 68
White Barn Fm **5** 68
White Bear (P.H.)
(Redcross St.) **1** 139
(Thornton Lane) **1** 139
White Bear Inn (P.H.) **6** 122
White Bull (P.H.) **3** 178
White Cottage **3** 22
White Gables Fm **6** 329
White Gate Fm **6** 330
White Hall **4** 6
White Hart (P.H.)
(Ashby de la Zouch) **7** 11
(Billesdon) **4** 6
(Harby) **2** 95
(Loughborough) **7** 134
(Melton Mowbray) **2** 178
(Quorndon) **7** 171
(South Kilworth) **5** 195
(Thurmaston) **3** 238
(Whitwick) **7** 74
White Hart (P.H.)
(Haymarket) **1** 139
(Hinckley) **6** 122
(Lutterworth) **5** 138
(Measham) **7** 265
(Wharf St.) **1** 140
White Hill **6** 177
White Ho.
(Appleby) **6** 12
(Barlestone) **6** 40
(Burbage) **6** 52
(Coleorton) **7** 79
(Hinckley) **6** 124
(Kirby Muxloe) **6** 153
(Saddington) **4** 224
(Stathern) **2** 261
(Whitwick) **7** 73
(Worthington) **7** 256
White Ho., The
(Arnesby) **5** 5
(Burton Lazars) **2** 65
(Huncote) **6** 140
White Ho., The **4** 14
White Horse (P.H.)
(Birstall) **7** 30
(Broughton Astley) **5** 39
(Leire) **5** 131
(Quorndon) **7** 171
(Seagrave) **3** 208
(Shepshed) **7** 198
(Whitwick) **7** 74
White Horse (P.H.)
(Ashby de la Zouch) **7** 11
(Belgrave Gate) **1** 140
(Duke St.) **1** 140
(Gallowtree Gate) **1** 140
(Loughborough) **7** 134
(Oadby) **5** 166
(Pickwell) **2** 241
(Wymeswold) **3** 276
White Horse Inn **6** 153
White Horse Wood **7** 197
White House Fields Fm **7** 256
White House Fm
(Barwell) **6** 128
(Beeby) **3** 43
(Bruntingthorpe) **5** 50
(Burbage) **6** 52
(Dadlington) **6** 292
(Eye Kettleby) **2** 189
(Fleckney) **4** 51
(Holwell) **2** 163
(Netherseal) **7** 270
(Newbold) **4** 219
(Owston) **4** 216
(Shellbrook) **7** 18
(Stapleton) **6** 215
(Wellsborough) **6** 266
(Worthington) **7** 256
White House Fm, The **3** 153
White House, The
(Isley cum Langley) **7** 94
(Swithland) **7** 228
White Lees **3** 36
White Lion (P.H.) **5** 157
White Lion (P.H.)
(Gumley) **4** 88

(Hinckley) **6** 122
(Loughborough) **7** 134
(Market Pl.) **1** 140
(Mountsorrel) **7** 153
White Lion Hotel (P.H.) **2** 178
White Lodge
(Ab Kettleby) **2** 159
(Cossington) **3** 61
(Dunton Bassett) **5** 84
(Goadby Marwood) **2** 126
(Great Bowden) **4** 178
(Halstead) **3** 249
(Kirby Muxloe) **6** 153
(KirbyBellars) **3** 86
(Little Dalby) **2** 85
(Shepshed) **7** 197
(Skeffington) **3** 221
(Thorpe Satchville) **3** 264
White Lodge Fm
(Ab Kettleby) **2** 159
(Walton on the Wolds) **3** 269
White St. **1** 69
White Stacks Fm **4** 133
White Swan (P.H.)
(Coston) **2** 152
(Melton Mowbray) **2** 178
(Mountsorrel) **7** 153
White Swan (P.H.)
(Belgrave Gate) **1** 140
(Loughborough) **7** 134
(Lubenham) **4** 165
(Market Place) **1** 140
(Syston) **3** 229
White's Barn **3** 173
Whitehill **7** 67
Whiteholm **7** 98
Whitehouse Fm **5** 174
Whitemoor **6** xv, xvi, xvii
Whitemoor Covert **6** 296
Whitemoors **6** xv, 296
Whitemore Fm **6** 296
Whittington and His Cat (P.H.) **6** 309
Whittington Edge **6** 223
Whittington Grange **6** xii, 221
Whittington Rough **6** 223
Whittle Hill **7** 58
WHITWICK **7** x, xii, 71
Whitwick Colliery (P.H.) **6** 153
Whitwick Park **7** 73
Whitwick Rd
(Coalville) **7** 62
(Markfield) **6** 177
Whitwick Waste **7** 73
Whitworth Tce **1** 69
Whytemorefeld **6** xv
Wicket Nook **7** 10
Wickliffe terrace **5** 139
Wicklow Lodge **2** 178
Wide Bridge **4** 39
Wide Lane **3** 276
Wigg Fm **6** 26
Wightman's Farm **1** 181
Wigley Rd **3** 135
Wigley's Arms (P.H.) **4** 230
Wignell Hill **4** 204
Wigston **6** 12
Wigston Cemetery **5** 225
Wigston Central Junction **5** 225
Wigston Fields **5** 225
Wigston Grange **5** 222
Wigston Hall
(Wigston Magna) **5** 222
(Wigston Parva) **5** 224
Wigston Junction **5** 225
Wigston Lane **5** 19
Wigston Lodge **5** 224
WIGSTON MAGNA **5** xiii, xiv, xv, 218
Wigston Magna: unindexed modern street-names **5** 221
WIGSTON PARVA **5** xi, xii, 231
Wigston Rd
(Blaby) **5** 33
(Oadby) **5** 166
Wigston Sidings **5** 225
Wigston South Junction **5** 225
Wigston St. **1** 69
Wigston's Hospital **1** 95
Wild's Lodge **2** 65

Wilderness, The
(Cadeby) **6** 59
(Market Bosworth) **6** 167
(Staunton Harold) **7** 208
(Stretton Magna) **4** 265
Wilford Ho. **7** 79
Wilfred Place **7** 10
Wilkins Lane **7** 67
Wilkins's Close **1** 195
WILLESLEY **7** 18
Willesley Basin **7** 280
Willesley Hall **7** 19
Willesley Lane **7** 19
Willesley Park **7** 19
Willesley Road **7** 11
Willesley Wood **7** 19
Willesley Wood Side **7** 19
Willey Crossing **5** 25
Willey Gates **5** 25
William IV (P.H.)
(Countesthorpe) **5** 80
(Thurcaston) **7** 230
William IV (P.H.)
(Barsby) **3** 102
(Colton St.) **1** 140
(Cosby) **5** 68
(Holwell) **2** 163
(Market Harborough) **4** 174
(Measham) **7** 265
(Mountsorrel) **7** 153
(Queniborough) **3** 183
Willn Close **7** 62
Willoughby Gorse **3** 276
Willoughby Lane **1** xii, 70
Willoughby Lodge Fm **5** 235
Willoughby Rd
(Ashby Magna) **5** 10
(Whetstone) **5** 213
WILLOUGHBY WATERLEYS,
~ WATERLESS **5** xiv, 234
WILLOUGHES **3** 127
Willow Brook **1** 226
Willow Brook Fm **5** 114
Willow Cottage **7** 79
Willow Fm
(Ashby Magna) **5** 10
(Blaby) **5** 33
(Normanton) **2** 42
(Stoke Golding) **6** 276
Willow Holt **1** 224
Willowbank **5** 39
Willowbrook Nurseries **6** 241
Willows, The
(Barrow upon Soar) **3** 36
(Castle Donington) **7** 49
(Fleckney) **4** 51
(Holwell) **2** 163
(Knossington) **4** 148
WILSON **7** x, 43
Wilson Arms (P.H.) **3** 5
Wilson House Fm **7** 44
Wilson Nurseries **7** 44
Wilton Rd **2** 170
Winchester Rd **5** 33
Windesers **7** 124
Windmill (P.H.)
(Loughborough) **7** 135
(Wymeswold) **3** 276
Windmill (P.H.)
(Church Gate) **1** 140
(Eaton) **2** 119
(Humberstone) **3** 135
(Walton) **5** 114
Windmill Ave **7** 30
Windmill Close **1** 195
Windmill Cottage **7** 197
Windmill Fm
(Kibworth Harcourt) **4** 139
(Walton) **5** 114
Windmill Hill
(Ashby de la Zouch) **7** 10
(Belton) **7** 27
(Croxton Kerrial) **2** 104
(Woodhouse) **7** 250
Windmill Inn **2** 196
Windmill Lodge **4** 148
Windmill Rd **7** 129
Windmill Rise **7** 250

Windmill, The
(Arnesby) **5** 5
(Barkestone) **2** 201
(Long Clawson) **2** 91
(Waltham on the Wolds) **2** 273
Windmill, The
(Melton Mowbray) **2** 180
(Twyford) **3** 262
Windrush **6** 153
Windsor Hill **2** 15
Windsor St. **6** 52
Windy Haw **7** 147
Windyridge
(Ashby de la Zouch) **7** 10
(Isley cum Langley) **7** 94
(Kirby Muxloe) **6** 153
Windyridge Fm **3** 86
Wine Vaults (P.H.) **6** 122
Winfield's Lane **3** 276
Winfrey Fm **6** 215
Winger Place **1** 155
Wingfield Spinney **4** 204
Winkadale **4** 282
Winkadale Hill **4** 282
Winning Post, The (P.H.) **5** 138
Winterbeck **2** 23
Winterbeck Bridge **2** 25
Winterfield Spinney **5** 150
Winton Fm **5** 150
Wishing Stone **7** 158
WISTOW **4** 295
Wistow Grange **4** 296
Wistow Hall **4** 296
Wistow Home Fm **4** 296
Wistow Lodge **4** 296
Wistow Rd
(Kibworth Harcourt) **4** 139
(Kilby) **5** 108
Witham Villa **5** 41
WITHCOTE **2** xi, 282
Withcote Hall **2** 284
Withcote Lodge **2** 284
WITHERLEY **6** xii, 322
Witherley Bridge **6** 323
Witherley Fields Fm **6** 323
Witherley Glebe Fm **6** 322
Witherley Hall **6** 323
Witherley Mill **6** 323
Withers' Farm **1** 181
Wodegate, le **5** 221
Wold Ho. **2** 278
Wolds Fm
(Scalford) **2** 211
(Wymeswold) **3** 276
Wolds, The **2** xi, xii, xiii, 3
Wolsey Lane **4** 51
Wolsey Rd **7** 62
Wolvey Road **6** 119
Women's Market, The **1** 116
Womens Market Cross, the **2** 176
Wood Bridge **5** 141
Wood Bridge Fm **5** 141
Wood Bridge Hill **5** 141
Wood Brook **7** 147
Wood Close Plantation **6** 161
Wood End Fm **5** 28
Wood Farm Cottages
(Misterton) **5** 148
(Willesley) **7** 19
Wood Field **1** 213
Wood Fm
(Freeby) **2** 129
(Misterton) **5** 148
(Netherseal) **7** 270
(Skeffington) **3** 221
(Stanton under Bardon) **6** 273
(Tilton) **3** 245
(Willesley) **7** 19
Wood Gate
(Leicester) **1** 70
(Loughborough) **7** 129
Wood House Fm **6** 124
Wood Lane
(Higham on the Hill) **6** 110
(Loddington) **3** 164
(Norton juxta Twycross) **6** 313
(Tugby) **3** 255
Wood Rd **6** 183
Wood St.
(Ashby de la Zouch) **7** 10
(Hinckley) **6** 118
(Leicester) **1** 70

Wood View Fm **6** 215
Wood's Fm **5** 150
Wood's Hill **2** 51
Woodbine Cottage
(Fleckney) **4** 51
(Gaddesby) **3** 95
Woodbine Fm **2** 144
Woodboy (P.H.) **1** 140
Woodboy St. **1** 70
Woodbrook Fm **7** 147
Woodby Lane **5** 28
Woodcock Fm **7** 187
Woodcock Lane **7** 11
Woodcock Well **6** 93
Woodcock's Charity School **3** 158
WOODCOTE **7** 19
Wooden Bungalow, The **5** 141
Wooden Nook **7** 118
Woodfield Rd **7** 187
Woodgate
(Barkby) **3** 22
(Rothley) **7** 187
Woodgate Hill **2** 78
Woodgate Ho. **3** 276
WOODHOUSE **7** xi, 246
Woodhouse Eaves **7** 247
Woodhouse Fields **7** 250
Woodhouse Fm
(Elmesthorpe) **6** 84
(Langley) **7** 94
(Market Bosworth) **6** 167
Woodhouse Lane **7** 147
Woodhouse Rd
(Coalville) **7** 62
(Quorndon) **7** 171
Woodland Ave. **6** 52
Woodland Cottage **3** 276
Woodlands
(Eye Kettleby) **2** 189
(Houghton on the Hill) **4** 110
(Long Whatton) **7** 113
Woodlands, The
(Botcheston) **6** 79
(Great Glen) **4** 81
(Kirkby Mallory) **6** 211
(Moira) **7** 24
(Narborough) **6** 187
Woodman's Arms (P.H.) **1** 140
Woodmarket **5** 141
Woods Fm **6** 26
Woodside
(Quorndon) **7** 171
(Walcote) **5** 150
Woodside Cottage
(Netherseal) **7** 270
(Quorndon) **7** 171
(Worthington) **7** 256
Woodside Fm
(Husbands Bosworth) **4** 121
(Netherseal) **7** 270
(Oadby) **5** 166
(Osgathorpe) **7** 164
(Shellbrook) **7** 18
(Twycross) **6** 309
WOODTHORPE **7** xii, 149
Woodthorpe Bridge **7** 171
Woodway Cottage **5** 61
Woodway Lane **5** 61
Woodway Rd **5** 141
Woodwell Head **2** 298
Woodyard Plantation **7** 112
Woodyton Fm **7** 27
Wool Hall, The **1** 118
Woolcombers' Arms (P.H.)
(Church Gate) **1** 140
(Royal East St.) **1** 140
Woolpack (P.H.)
(Melton Mowbray) **2** 178
(New Bond St.) **1** 140
Woolpits Planting **4** 210
Woolrooms **7** 256
Woolstaplers' Arms (P.H.) **1** 140
Woolstich Fm **7** 270
Workhouse Cottages **6** 228
Workhouse Garden **1** 179
Workhouse Lane
(Burbage) **6** 52
(Coleorton) **7** 79
Workhouse Piece **1** 195
World's End (P.H.) **1** 141
Worrall's Close **1** 195
Worship street **5** 139

WORTHINGTON **7** xi, 254
Worthington Field **7** 256
Worthington Lane **7** 257
Worthington Station **7** 257
Wortley Cottages **6** 84
Wrask Fm **6** 195
Wreake House Fm **3** 192
Wrenbury Fm **4** 246
Wright's Close **1** 195
Wulfrun Lane **1** 70
Wycliffe Fm **5** 141
Wycliffe Ho. **2** 178
Wycliffe St. **1** 71
WYCOMB **2** xii, 218
Wye Close **1** 195
WYFORDBY **2** xii, 142
Wyfordby Grange **2** 144
Wyfordby Grange Cottage **2** 144
WYKIN **6** 136
Wykin Fields **6** 137
Wykin Fm **6** 137
Wykin Hall **6** 137
Wykin Hollow **6** 137
Wykin House Fm **6** 137
Wykin Lane
  (Stoke Golding) **6** 276
  (Wykin) **6** 137
Wykin Lodge **6** 137
Wykin Rd **6** 118
Wykin Spinney **6** 110
Wylde's Leys **1** 205
Wymeshead, The **7** 98
WYMESWOLD **3** xi, xii, xiii, xv, 2, 3, 46, 274
Wymeswold Hall **3** 276
Wymeswold Lodge **3** 276
WYMONDHAM **2** xii, xiii, 286
Wymondham: unindexed dwellings **2** 288
Wymondham Banks **2** 288
Wymondham Grammar School **2** 288
Wymondham Grammar School Fm **2** 180
Wymondham Ho. **2** 288
Wymondham Lodge **2** 288
Wymondham Rough **2** 288
Wymondham Windmill **2** 288
Wyndham Lodge **2** 179
Wyndmill gate **5** 221
Wyndmill, The **5** 223
Yaxley Ho. **3** 19
Yennards Cottages **6** 300
Yennards Fm **6** 300
Yennards Lodge **6** 134
Yennards, The **6** 134
Yenwoods, The **6** 161
Yeoman Lane **1** 71
Yeoman Sq. **1** 71
Yeoman St. **1** 71
Yew Barn Cottages **7** 261
Yew Tree Fm
  (Barton in the Beans) **6** 237
  (Great Dalby) **2** 78
  (Holwell) **2** 163
  (Kirby Bellars) **3** 86
  (Nailstone) **6** 183
Yew Tree Ho. **2** 211
Yews Fm **7** 182
York Castle (P.H.) **1** 141
York Fm **3** 81
York Sq. **1** 71
York St. (York Rd) **1** xiv, 71
York St. **1** xiv, 71
Zion Chapel **6** 276
Zion Hill **7** 79
Zoar Chapel **1** 89
Zoar Chapel **6** 121
Zouch Bridge **7** 84
Zouch Mill **7** 84